U0930139

2015
青岛统计年鉴

QINGDAO STATISTICAL YEARBOOK

(总 第36期 VOL.36)

青 岛 市 统 计 局
国家统计局青岛调查队 编
QINGDAO MUNICIPAL STATISTICS BUREAU
NBS SURVEY OFFICE IN QINGDAO

中国统计出版社
China Statistics Press

图书在版编目(CIP)数据

青岛统计年鉴. 2015 / 青岛市统计局, 国家统计局青岛调查队编. -- 北京 : 中国统计出版社, 2015.8
ISBN 978-7-5037-7494-2

Ⅰ. ①青… Ⅱ. ①青… ②国… Ⅲ. ①统计资料－青岛市－2015－年鉴 Ⅳ. ①C832.523-54

中国版本图书馆CIP数据核字(2015)第166545号

青岛统计年鉴-2015

作　　者/ 青岛市统计局 国家统计局青岛调查队
责任编辑/ 陈越月
装帧设计/ 青岛天之韵广告文化传播有限公司
出版发行/ 中国统计出版社
地　　址/ 北京市丰台区西三环南路甲6号　邮政编码/ 100073
电　　话/ 邮购（010）63376909　书店（010）68783171
网　　址/ http://csp.stats.gov.cn
印　　刷/ 青岛国彩印刷有限公司
经　　销/ 新华书店
开　　本/ 890x1240毫米 1/16
字　　数/ 1100千字
印　　张/ 25.25
版　　别/ 2015年8月第 1 版
版　　次/ 2015年8月第 1 次印刷
定　　价/ 280.00元

如有印装差错，由本社发行部调换。

全市生产总值构成（%）

Composition Of Gross Domestic Product（%）

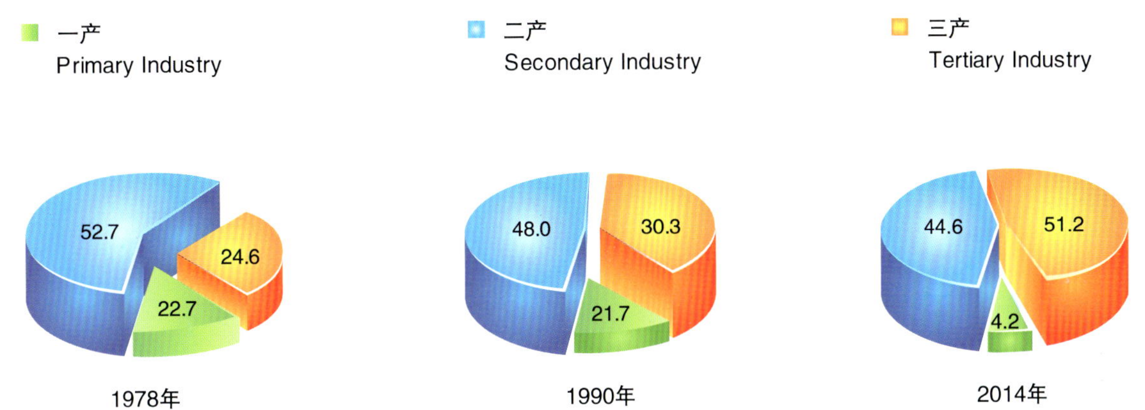

全市生产总值（亿元）

Gross Domestic Product (100 million yuan)

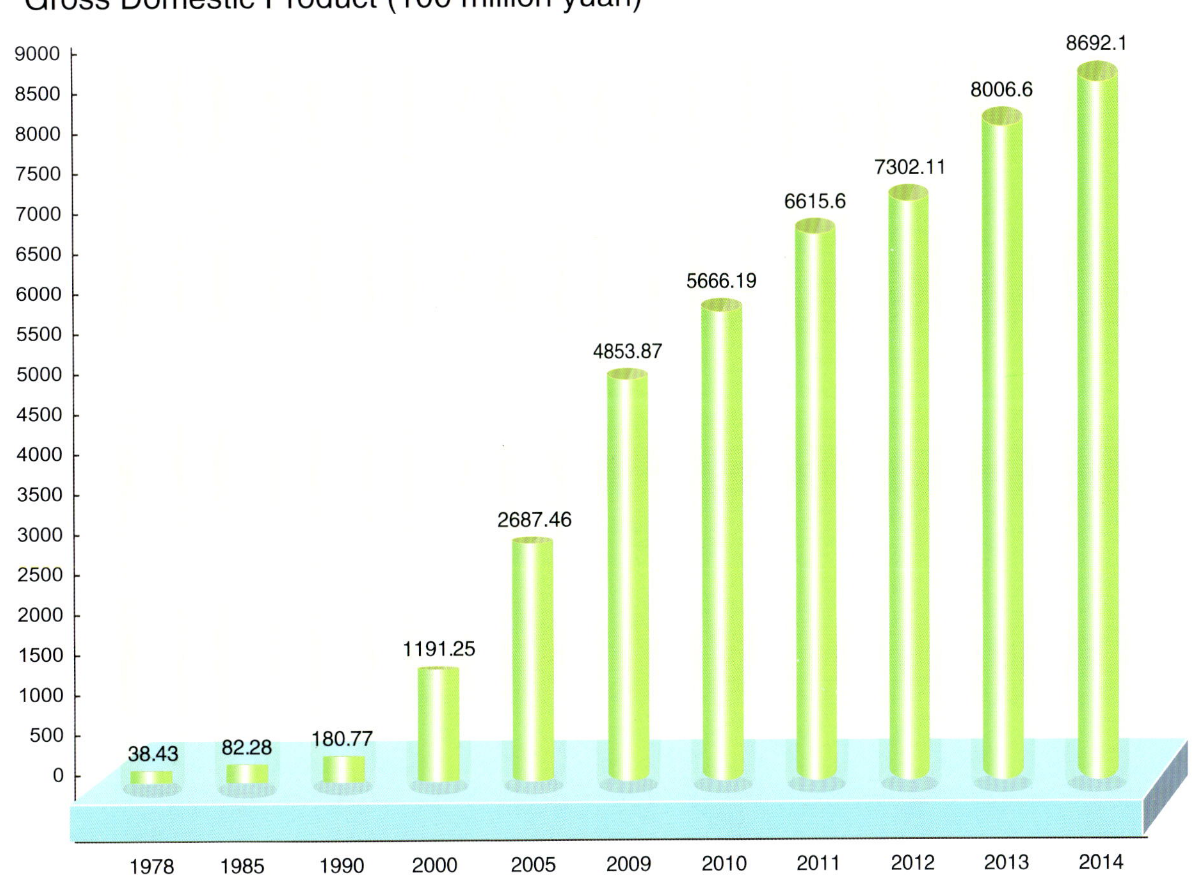

农林牧渔业总产值（亿元）
Gross Output Value Of Agriculture (100 million yuan)

主要农产品产量（万吨）
Output Of Farm Products (10000 tons)

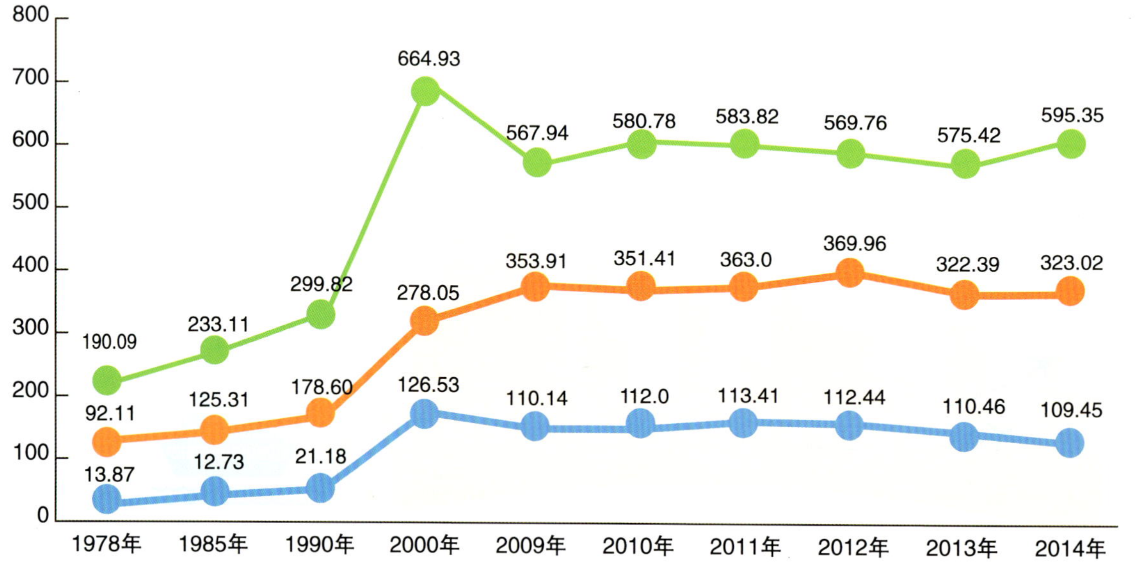

工业总产值（亿元）

Gross Industrial Output Value (100 million yuan)

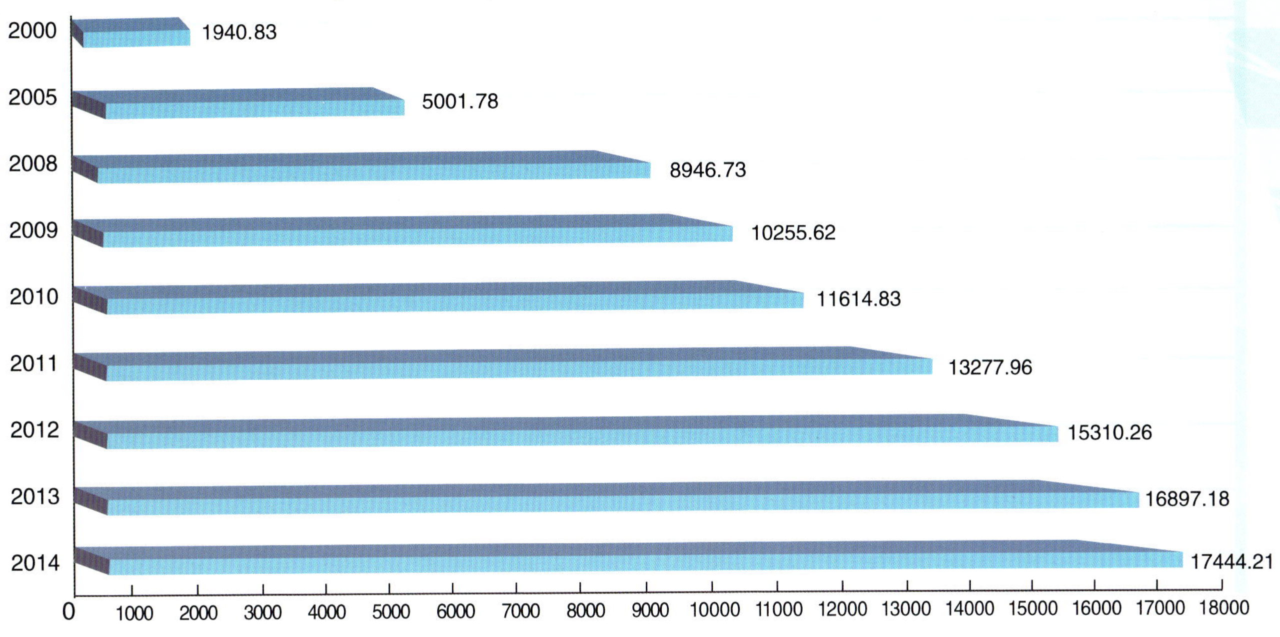

规模以上工业实现利税总额（亿元）

Total Profits And Taxes Of Industry Above Designated Size (100 million yuan)

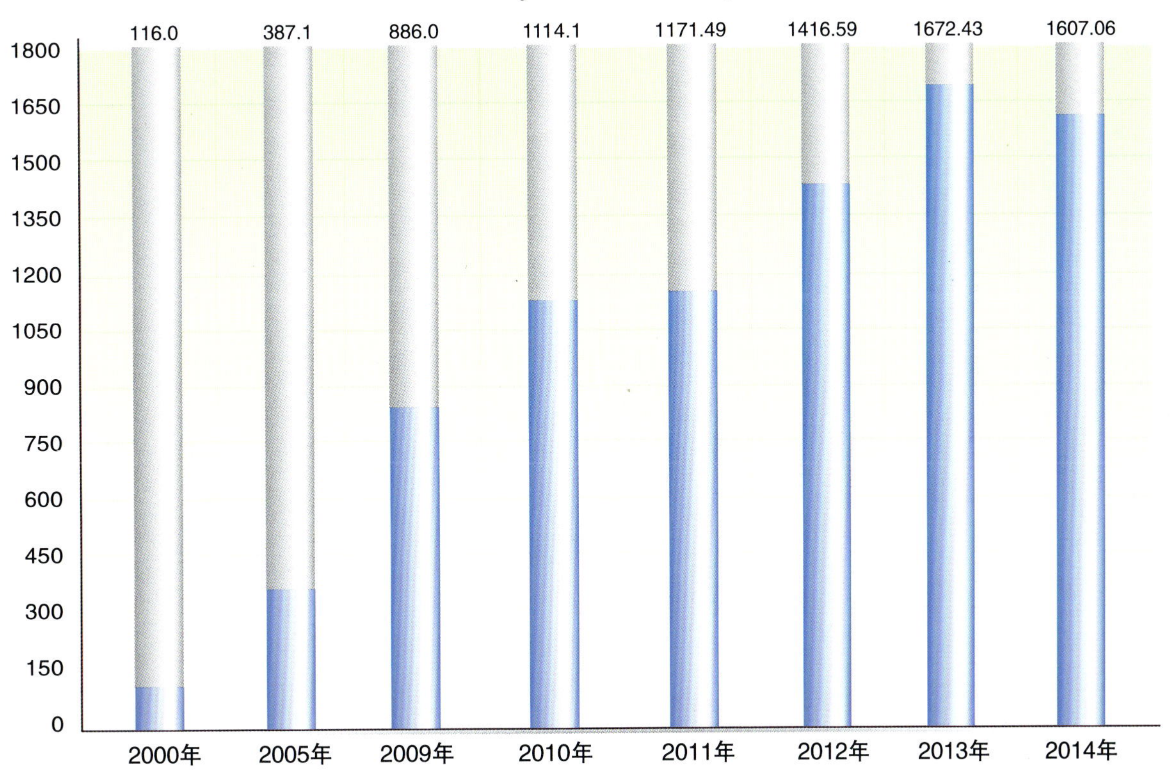

固定资产投资（亿元）
Investment In Fixed Assets (100 million yuan)

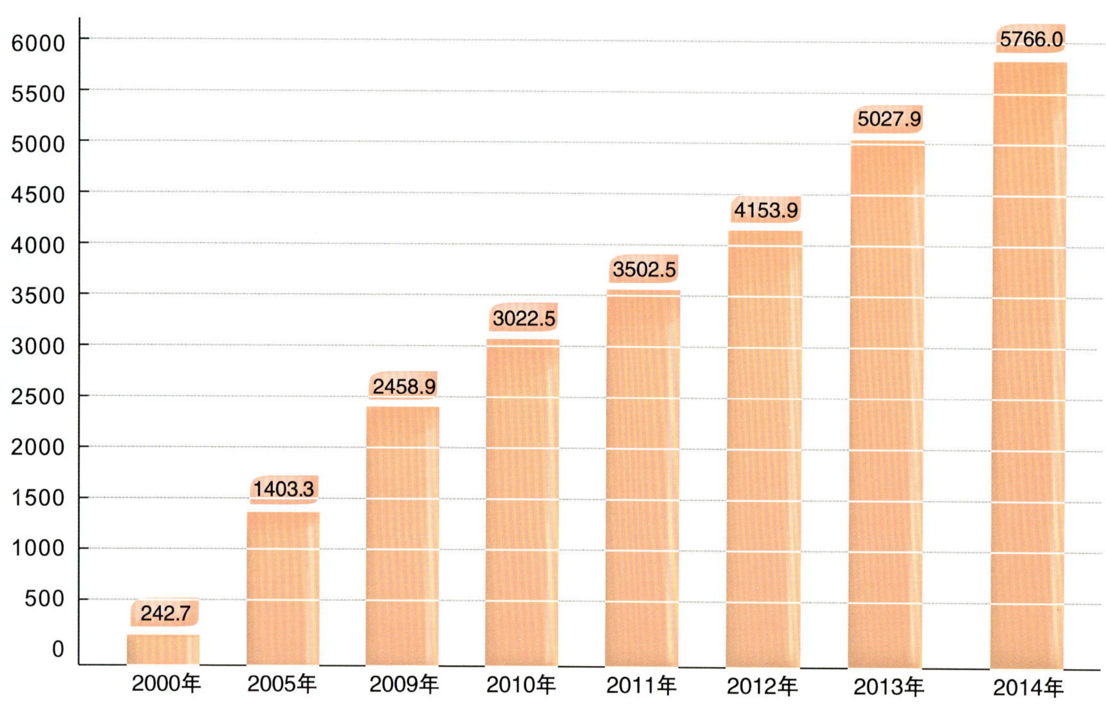

房地产开发投资（亿元）、房屋销售面积（万平方米）
Investment In Real Estate Development (100 million yuan)，Floor Space Of Commercial Buildings Sold (10000 sq.m)

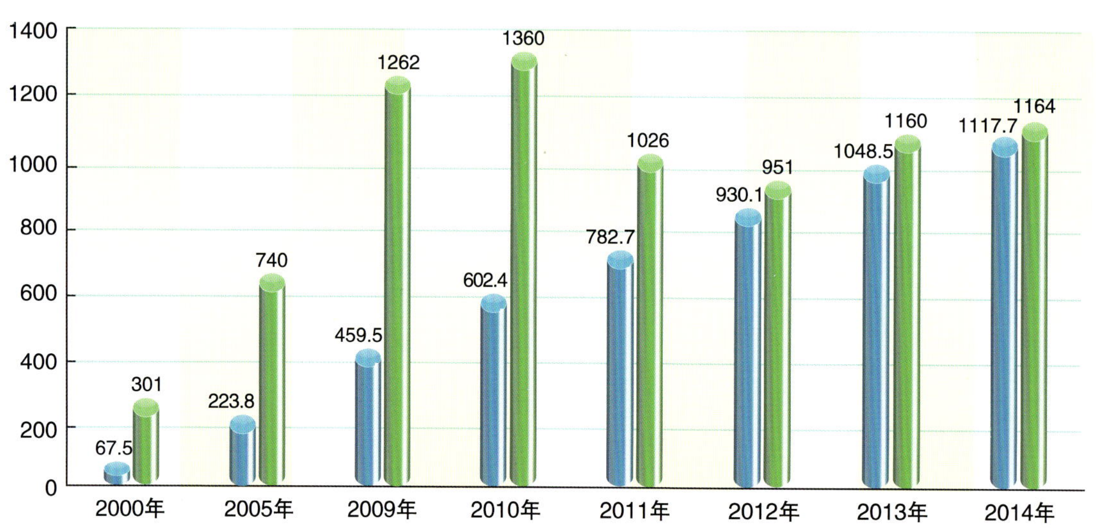

消费构成（%）(2014年)

2014 Composition Of Consumption (%)

社会消费品零售总额（亿元）

Total Retail Sales Of Consumer Goods(100 million yuan)

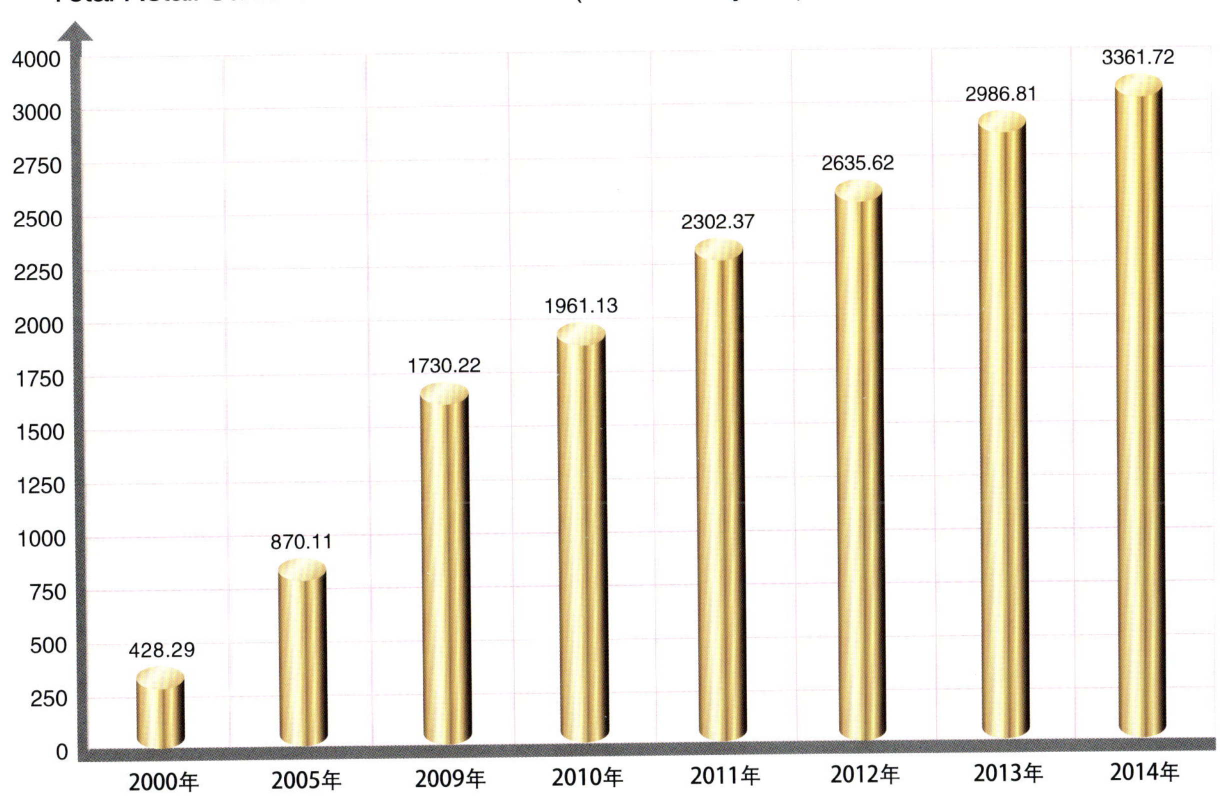

进出口总额（亿美元）
Total Imports And Exports (100 million USD)

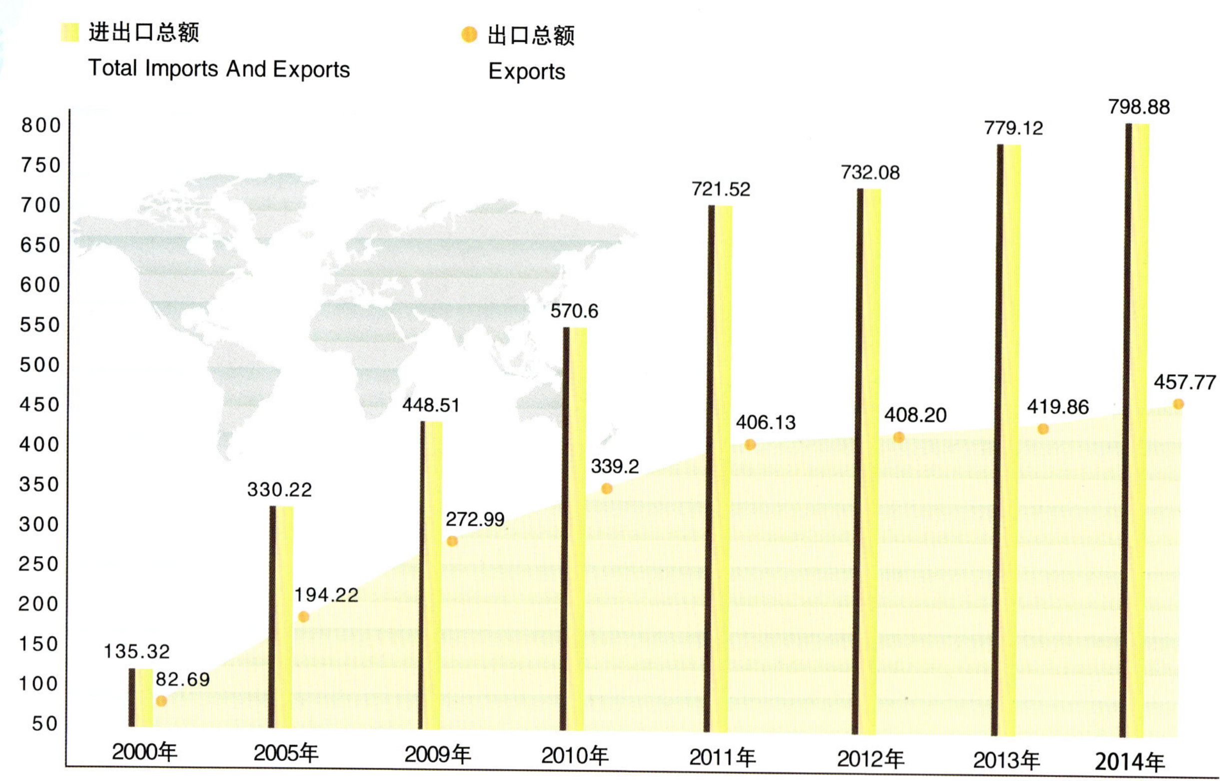

旅游总人数（万人次）
Number Of Tourists (10000 person-times)

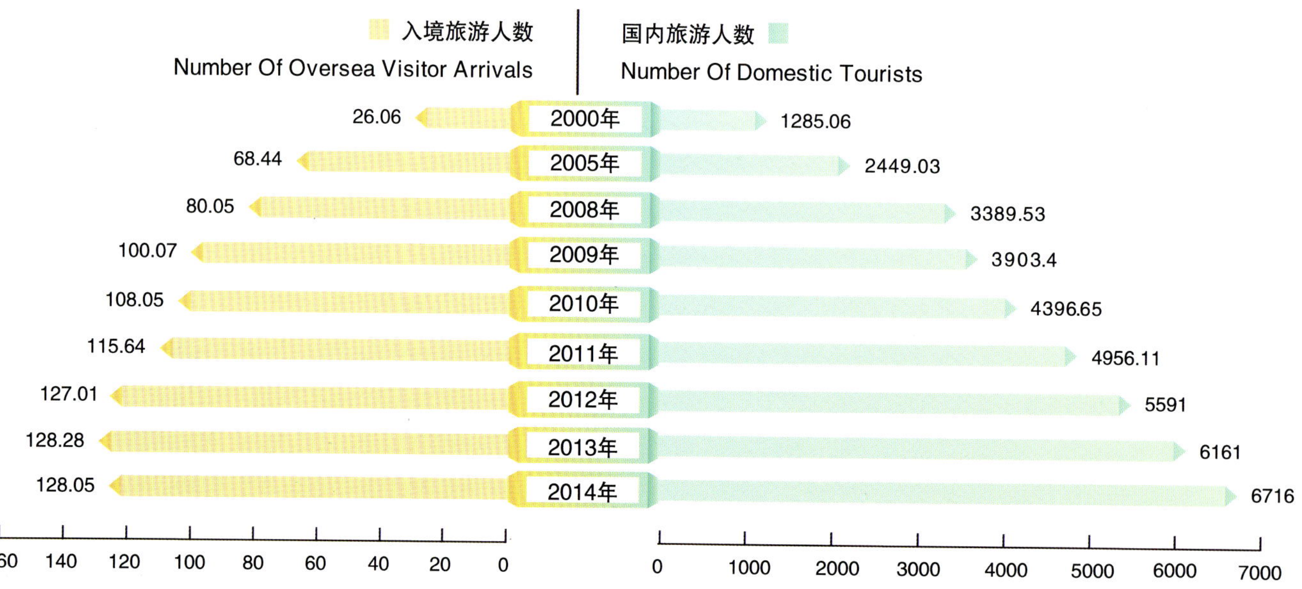

地方财政收入（亿元）
Revenue Of Local Government Finance (100 million yuan)

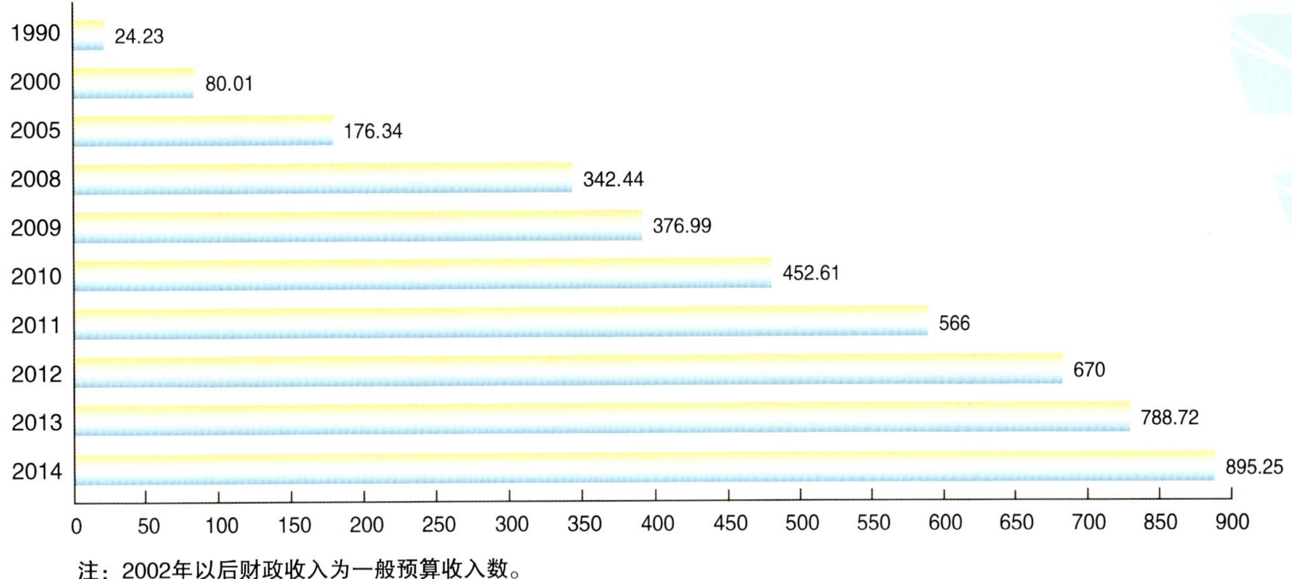

注：2002年以后财政收入为一般预算收入数。
Note:Since 2002,revenue of government finance refers to general budgetary revenue.

金融机构年末人民币存贷款余额（亿元）
Year-end Savings Deposits And Loans Of Financial Institution(RMB) (100 million yuan)

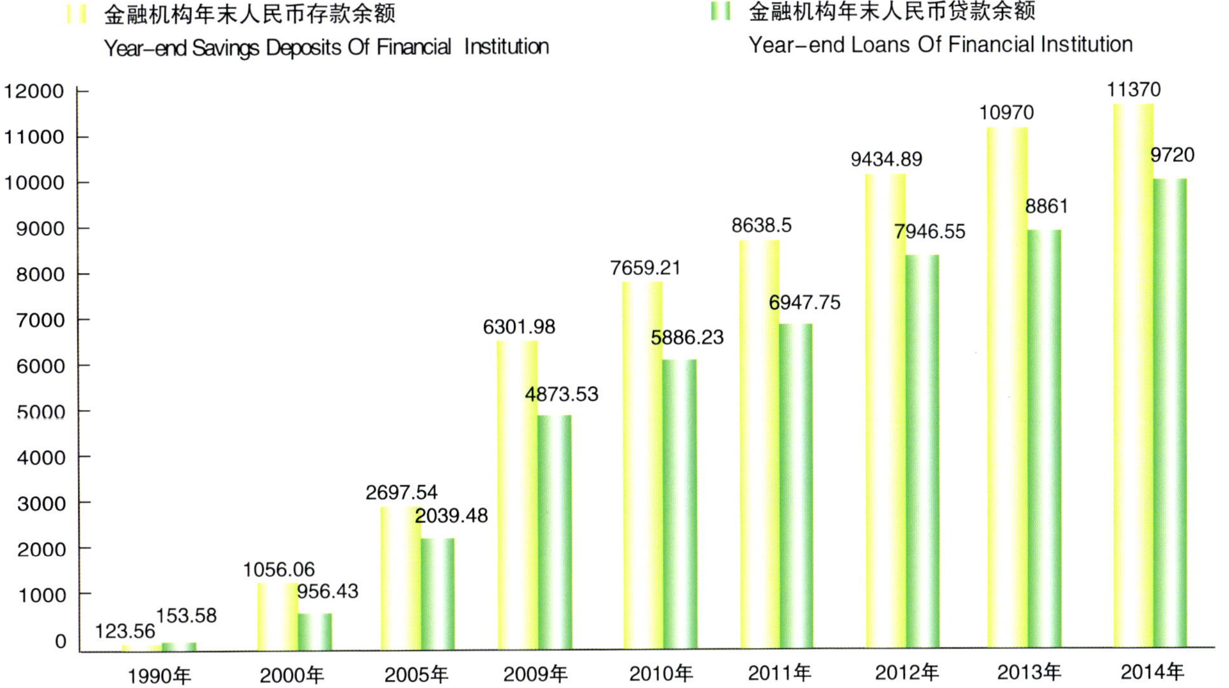

社会从业人数(万人)
Social Employment(100 million persons)

在岗职工平均工资(元)
Average Wage Of Employed Staff And Workers(yuan)

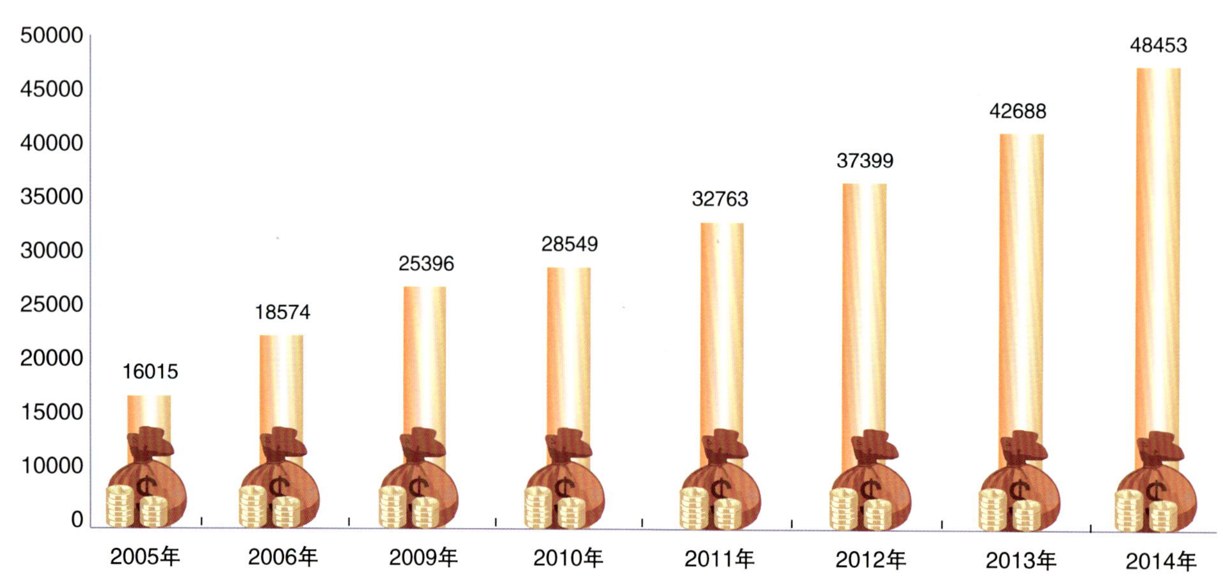

城乡居民收入（元）

Income Of Urban And Rural Households (yuan)

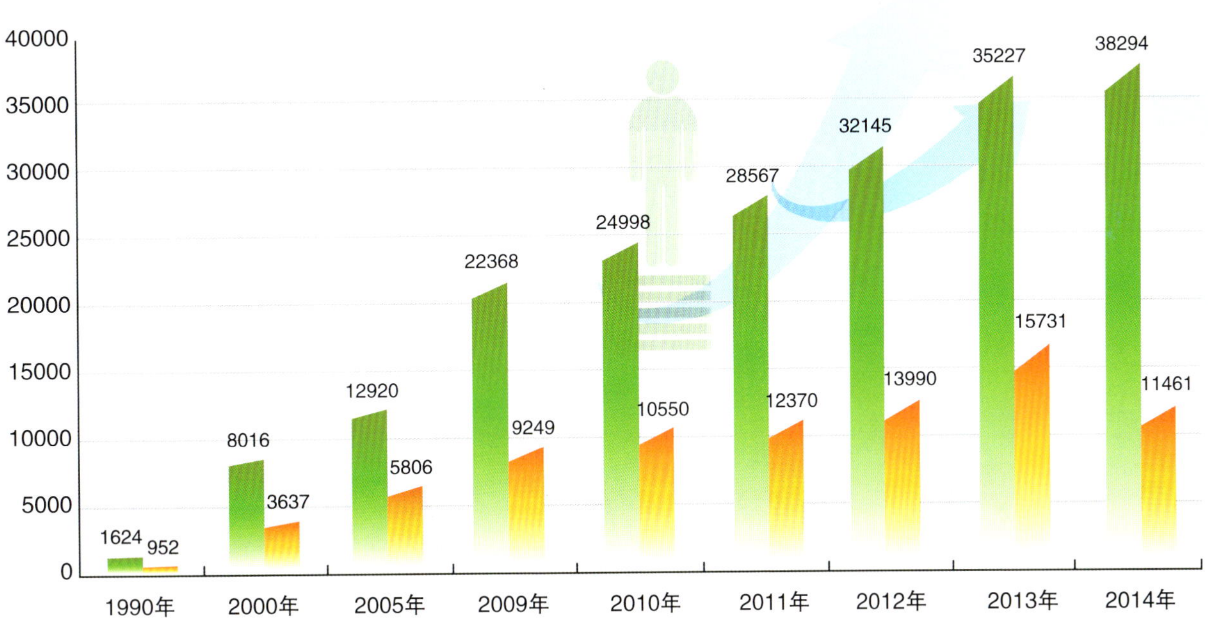

城乡居民人民币储蓄存款余额（亿元）

Savings Deposit Of Urban And Rural Households (RMB)(100 million yuan)

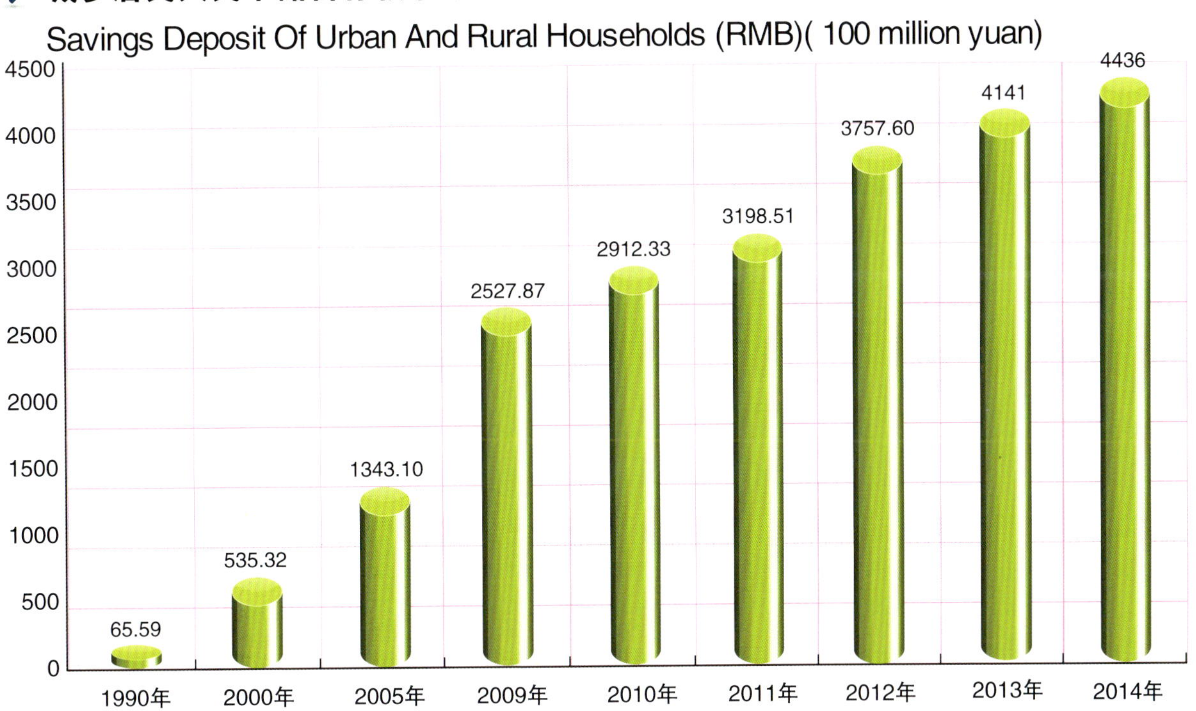

居民消费价格指数(上年=100)
Consumer Price Indices(preceding year=100)

商品零售价格指数(上年=100)
Retail Price Indices(preceding year=100)

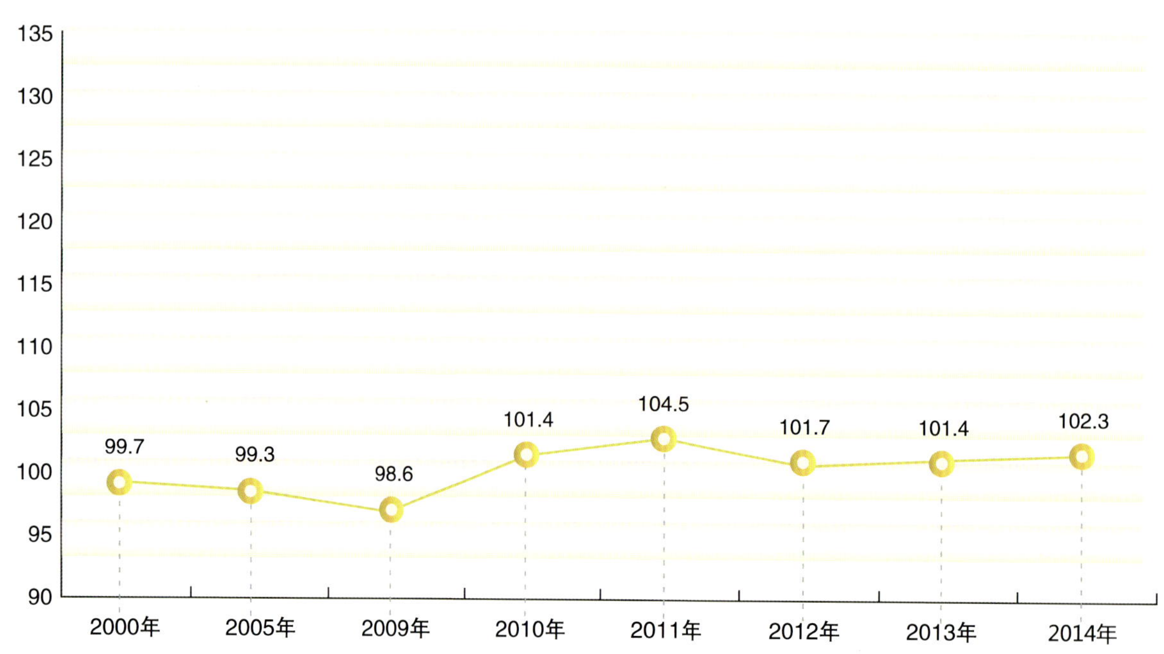

城市建成区面积、铺装道路面积

Developed Area Of the City And Area Of Roads

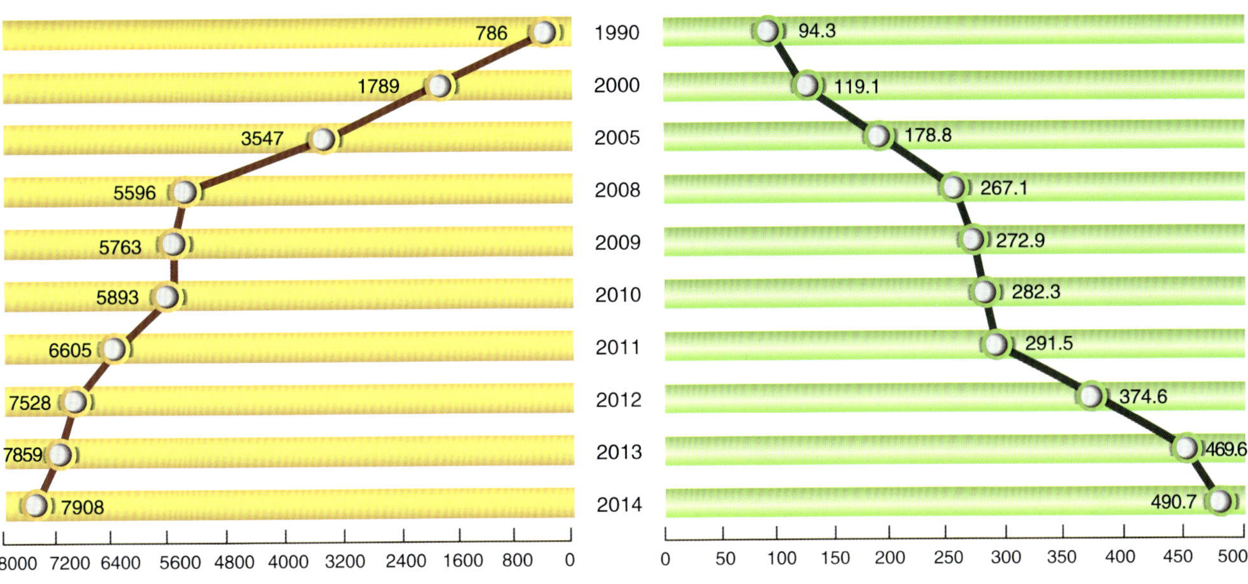

建成区绿化覆盖率（%）

Green Coverage Rate Of Developed Area(%)

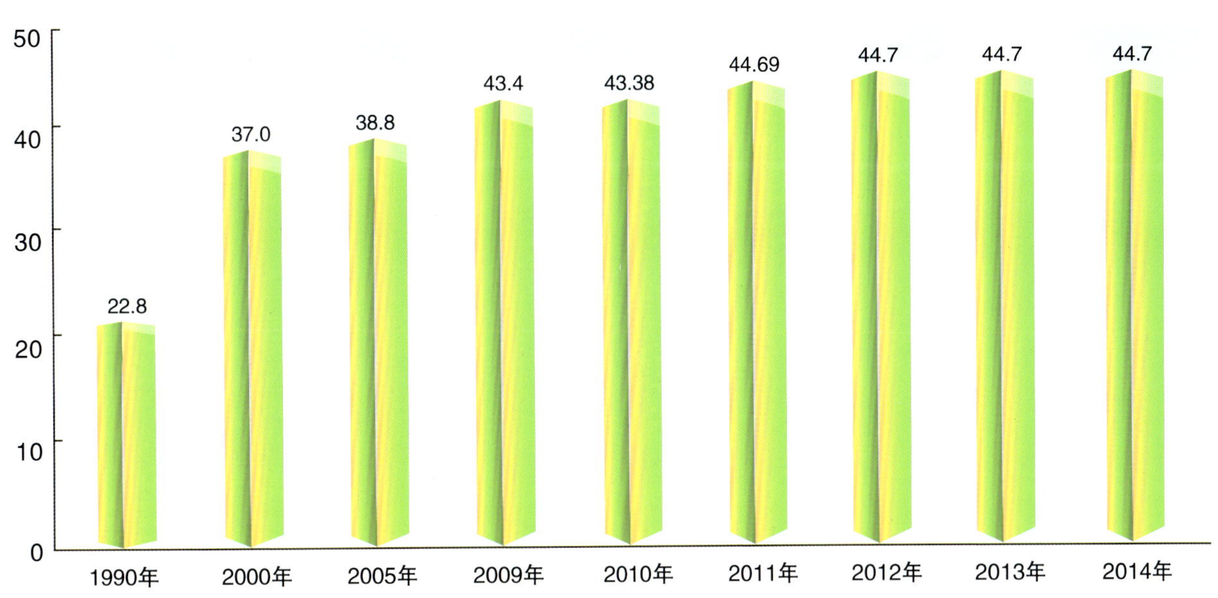

医疗卫生机构（个）Health Care Institutions(unit)

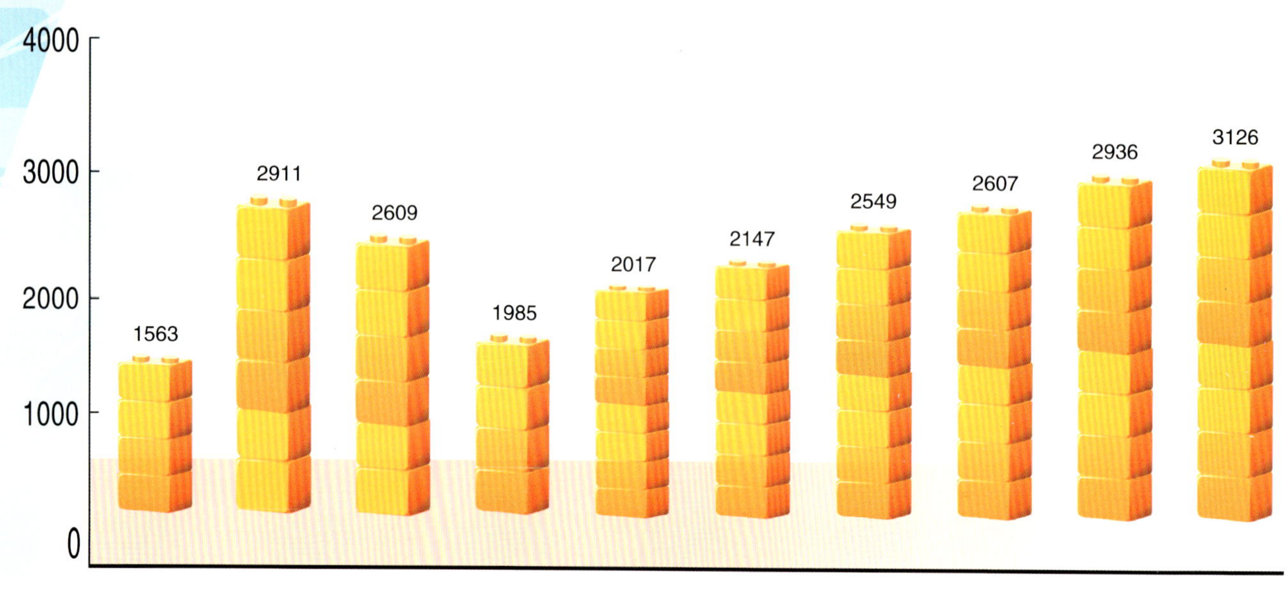

普通高校在校人数（万人）
Students Enrollment Of Regular Institutions Of Higher Education(10000 persons)

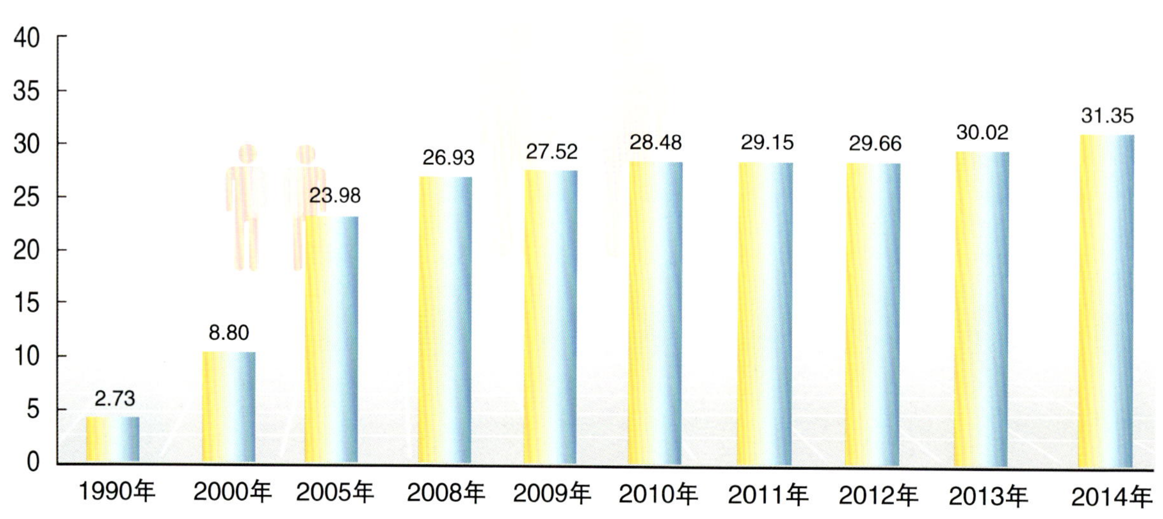

编辑委员会

EDITORIAL BOARD

编者说明

一、《青岛统计年鉴 -2015》是一部全面反映青岛市国民经济和社会发展情况、信息高度密集的资料工具书。

二、《青岛统计年鉴 -2015》共包括发展成果图、统计公报、统计表、附录四大部分。

统计表部分收录了 2014 年青岛市经济和社会等各方面的统计数据，以及建国以来重要年份和改革开放以来的主要统计数据，包括: 综合，人口，从业人员及职工工资，固定资产投资，对外经济贸易，城市建设、环境保护，能源消耗，财政金融和保险业，价格指数，人民生活，农业，工业，建筑业，运输、邮电，批发和零售业，住宿、餐饮业和旅游，教育、科技和文化，体育、卫生和民政、司法。

为方便读者正确地使用年鉴资料，各篇章前设有《简要说明》，概括介绍各篇主要内容和资料来源；篇末还附有《主要统计指标解释》。

三、本《年鉴》部分历史数据已根据经济普查数据进行了调整，在此之前公布的数据凡与本年鉴数字不符的一律以本年鉴为准。

四、本年鉴中的符号说明：年鉴各表中的“空格”表示该项统计指标数据不足本表最小单位数、数据不详或无该项数据；"#" 表示其中的主要项。

五、《青岛统计年鉴》自公开出版以来，受到社会各界的关心和支持，对于年鉴的内容和编辑工作提出了许多宝贵的意见，对此我们深表谢意。限于我们的水平，欢迎读者继续对年鉴的不足之处给予批评和指正，帮助我们进一步改进年鉴编辑工作，以期更好地为广大读者服务。

《青岛统计年鉴》编委会

2015年7月

Editor's Note

Ⅰ. *Qingdao Statistical Yearbook 2015* is a very important reference book, which reflects various aspects of Qingdao's social and economic development and contains High-density information.

Ⅱ. The yearbook contains the following four parts: achievement graphs, statistic gazette, statistics and appendixes.

Statistics contains all kinds of data on Qingdao's social and economic development in 2014, and data in significant year or data since the beginning of reform and opening up, including: General Survey; Population; Employment and Wages; Investment in Fixed Assets; Foreign Trade; City Construction and Environment Protection; Consumption of Energy; Government Finance ,Financial Intermediation and Insurance; Price; People's Living Conditions; Agriculture; Industry; Construction; Transport, Postal and Telecommunication Services; Wholesale and Retail Trades; Hotels, Catering Services and Tourism; Education, Science and Culture; Sports, Public Health and Civil Affairs, Judicial Affairs; Enterprises Survey.

In brief introduction at the beginning of each chapter, main coverage, data sources and statistical coverage are concerned. Meanwhile explanatory notes on major statistical indicators have been attached for readers to use the data correctly.

Ⅲ. All of the data in the book are in accordance with new administrative division.

Some of the data have been adjusted on the basis of statistics of economic census. In any case the data of this book shall be deemed as the authentic ones.

Ⅳ. Marks in this book:

"(blank)" indicates that the figure is not large enough to be measured with the smallest unit in the table, the data is not available, or the data is not available;

"#" indicates the major items of the total.

Ⅴ. Previous editions of *Qingdao Statistical Yearbook* have won wide acclaim among the readers. In order to excel, we welcome all candid comments and criticism from our readers.

Editorial Board

July, 2015

目　录
CONTENTS

一、综　合
Chapter 1. GENERAL SURVEY

二、人　口

Chapter 2. POPULATION

三、从业人员及职工工资

Chapter 3. EMPLOYMENT AND WAGES

四、固定资产投资

Chapter 4. INVESTMENT IN FIXED ASSETS

五、对外经济贸易

Chapter 5. FOREIGN TRADE

六、城市建设、环境保护

Chapter 6. CITY CONSTRUCTION AND ENVIRONMENT PROTECTION

七、能源消耗

Chapter 7. CONSUMPTION OF ENERGY

八、财政、金融和保险业

Chapter 8. GOVERNMENT FINANCE, FINANCIAL INTERMEDIATION AND INSURANCE

九、价格指数

Chapter 9. PRICE INDEXES

十、人民生活

Chapter 10. PEOPLE'S LIVING CONDITIONS

十一、农　业
Chapter 11. AGRICULTURE

十二、工　业

Chapter 12. INDUSTRY

十三、建 筑 业

Chapter 13. CONSTRUCTION

十四、运输、邮电

Chapter 14. TRANSPORT, POSTAL AND TELECOMMUNICATION SERVICES

十五、批发和零售业

Chapter 15. WHOLESALE AND RETAIL TRADES

十六、住宿、餐饮业和旅游

Chapter 16. HOTELS, CATERING SERVICES AND TOURISM

十七、教育、科技和文化

Chapter 17. EDUCATION, SCIENCE & TECHNOLOGY AND CULTURE

十八、体育、卫生和民政、司法

Chapter 18. SPORTS,PUBLIC HEALTH AND CIVIL AFFAIRS,JUDICIAL AFFAIRS

附　录
APPENDIX

2014年
青岛市国民经济和社会发展
统 计 公 报

青岛市统计局

国家统计局青岛调查队

（2015年3月30日）

2014 年，面对复杂严峻的外部环境和艰巨繁重的发展任务，在市委市政府的领导下，全市坚持稳中求进工作总基调，积极作为，真抓实干，统筹推进稳增长、促改革、调结构、惠民生，新常态下全市呈现经济平稳发展、民生持续改善、社会和谐稳定的良好局面。

一、综 合

年末全市常住总人口为 904.62 万人，增长 0.92%；其中，市区常住人口 487.59 万人，增长 1.29%。

表 1：全市常住人口分布情况

区 市	数量(万人)
总 计	904.62
市南区	56.74
市北区	106.90
李沧区	54.14
崂山区	42.75
黄岛区	146.52
城阳区	68.80
即墨市	119.42
胶州市	87.10
平度市	135.44
莱西市	75.07
高新区	9.84
保税区	1.90

初步核算，2014 年全市生产总值 8692.1 亿元，按可比价格计算，增长 8.0%。其中，第一产业增加值 362.6 亿元，增长 3.9%；第二产业增加值 3882.4 亿元，增长 8.4%；第三产业增加值 4447.1 亿元，增长 7.9%。三次产业比例为 4.2:44.6:51.2。人均 GDP 达到 96524 元。民营经济增加值 3323.4 亿元，增长 8.3%。

图 1：2014 年季度 GDP 及增速

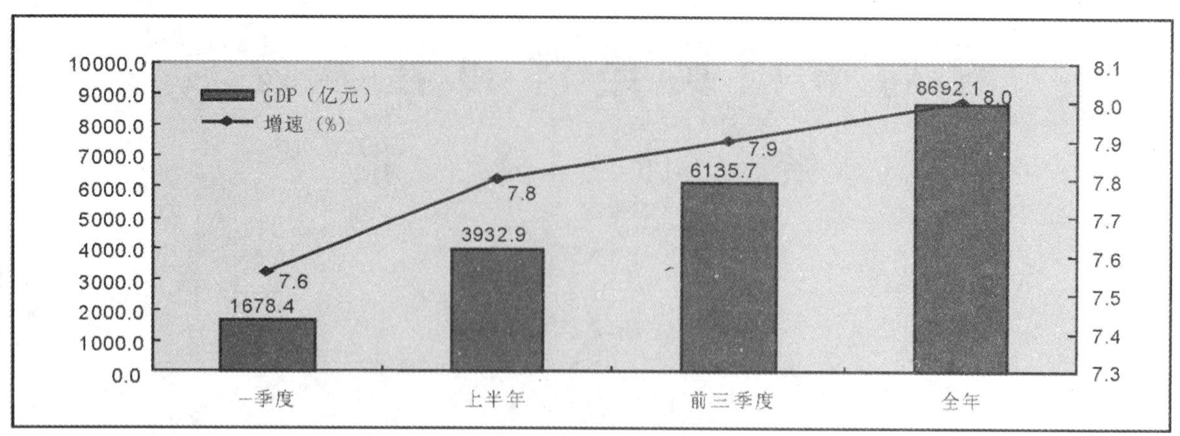

图 2：2013、2014 年 GDP 三次产业增加值构成

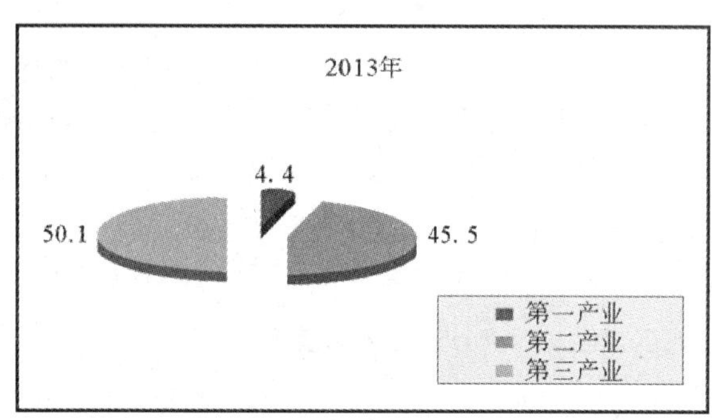

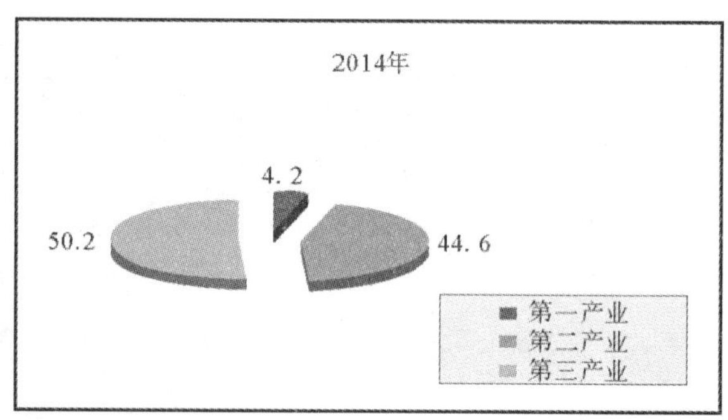

全年财政总收入实现 2800.4 亿元，增长 8.5%；一般公共预算收入 895.2 亿元，增长 13.5%；一般公共预算支出 1074.7 亿元，增长 6.0%。全年国税系统组织税收收入(含海关代征)1340.1 亿元，增长 0.6%；其中，国内税收 691.4 亿元，增长 8.3%。地税税收收入 599.0 亿元，增长 12.7%。

全年居民消费价格比上年上涨2.6%,其中，食品价格上涨4.4%。全年工业生产者出厂价格下降0.8%，工业生产者购进价格下降2.6%。12月份市区新建住宅价格同比下降6.2%；二手住宅价格同比下降5.2%。

表 2：居民消费价格比上年涨跌幅度

指标名称	比上年涨跌（±%）
居民消费价格	2.6
非食品价格	1.9
服务项目价格	1.9
消费品价格	2.9
1. 食品	4.4
#粮食	6.5
猪肉	-3.1
蛋	17.2
鲜菜	-7.6
2. 烟酒及用品	0.1
3. 衣着	3.2
4. 家庭设备用品及维修服务	2.0
5. 医疗保健和个人用品	2.0
6. 交通和通信	0.3
7. 娱乐教育文化用品及服务	1.4
8. 居住	2.2

图 3：居民消费价格月度同比涨幅（%）

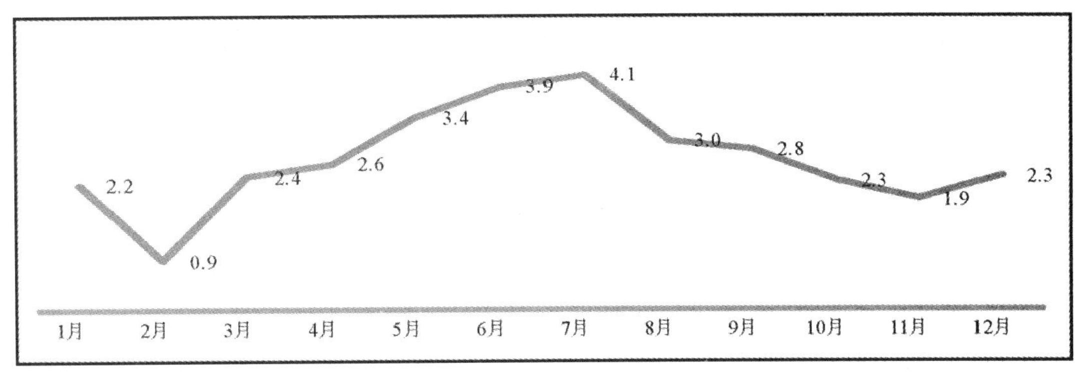

二、农 业

全市粮食播种面积49.55万公顷，下降0.99%，粮食总产量达到323万吨，增长0.2%；其中，小麦152.1万吨，玉米166.8万吨。

表3：主要畜产品产量及增速

产品名称	产量(万吨)	比上年增长(%)
肉类	59.55	-3.1
其中：猪肉	27.36	-2.0
禽肉	30.36	-5.3
牛、羊奶	37.54	1.1
禽蛋	19.11	0.5

全年完成造林面积1.04万公顷，增长4.0%；森林覆盖率39.5%，提高0.1个百分点。

水产品总产量109.45万吨，下降0.9%。其中，捕捞产量26.78万吨，增长0.5%；养殖产量82.67万吨，下降1.4%。海、淡水养殖面积5.01万公顷，下降2.1%。

年末全市拥有农业机械总动力826.93万千瓦，增长2.2%。农用拖拉机20.51万台。农田有效灌溉面积32.17万公顷，其中，节水灌溉面积12.52万公顷。

三、工业与建筑业

全年全部工业完成增加值3419.8亿元，增长8.3%。全年规模以上工业4603家，实现增加值增长9.4%。按轻重工业分，重工业增长11.3%，轻工业增长6.6%；按类型分，国有控股企业增长5.1%，集体企业增长10.7%，股份制企业增长9.6%，外商及港澳台商投资企业增长9.3%。

全年规模以上工业企业完成工业总产值16761亿元，增长9.6%。其中,高新技术产业产值增长16.7%，占比为40.7%，较年初提高 0.8个百分点；十条工业千亿级产业链产值增长10.2%，占比为75.3%；规模以上工业战略性新兴产业产值增长20.2%。

表4：规模以上工业战略性新兴产业发展情况

产业名称	企业户数(户)	总产值(亿元)	增速(%)	主营业务收入(亿元)	增速(%)
战略性新兴产业	603	3019.2	20.2	2894.4	22.9
新材料产业	180	557.7	22.3	547.1	27.9
生物产业	51	170.2	19.0	168.2	20.2
高端装备制造产业	198	1151.1	22.6	1097.8	35.1
新能源产业	26	78.8	40.1	77.7	35.6
节能环保产业	45	92.8	22.6	90.0	24.3
新一代信息技术产业	99	944.2	16.0	1046.0	8.6
新能源汽车产业	4	24.5	-7.0	24.9	-6.2

表5：规模以上工业主要产品产量及增速

产品名称	单位	产量	比上年增长(%)
彩色电视机	万台	1714.9	7.7
家用电冰箱	万台	610.1	16.4
家用洗衣机	万台	591.0	-2.6
房间空气调节器	万台	685.9	7.6
卷烟	亿支	560.3	3.4
啤酒	万千升	162.6	-7.3
碳酸钠（纯碱）	万吨	67.8	10.0
橡胶轮胎外胎	万条	5199.1	8.0
平板玻璃	万重量箱	612.4	0.4
粗钢	万吨	214.4	-9.0
汽车	万辆	77.0	8.6
动车组	辆	684	3.0
金属集装箱	万立方米	1853.9	15.2
原油加工量	万吨	1544.6	-2.0
发电量	亿千瓦时	178.3	-3.5

规模以上工业实现利税总额1564.8亿元，增长9.3%；利润835.5亿元，增长5.6%；主营业务收入16143.9亿元，增长10.7%。资本保值增值率128.2%，产品销售率98.5%。

表6：规模以上工业分经济类型利润情况

指标名称	利润总额（亿元）	增速（%）
总计	835.5	5.6
其中，国有控股经济	105.1	-4.7
集体经济	77.0	24.1
股份制经济	500.0	3.5
外商及港澳台投资经济	229.0	3.8

全年建筑业实现增加值462.6亿元，增长8.9%。实现利税总额82.3亿元，增长9.2%；其中，国有及国有控股企业实现利税22.4亿元，增长9.8%。

四、固定资产投资

全市固定资产投资(包括城镇、农村500万元以上投资项目)5766亿元，增长16.1%。其中，第一产业投资104.7亿元，增长11.4%；第二产业投资2817.9亿元，增长16%；第三产业投资2843.4亿元，增长16.4%。

表7：分行业固定资产投资（不含农户）及其增速

行　　业	投资额（亿元）	比上年增长(%)
总　计	5766.0	16.1
农、林、牧、渔业	104.7	11.4
采矿业	13.6	11.9
制造业	2666.3	15.3
电力、热力、燃气及水的生产和供应业	48.3	-27.6
建筑业	89.7	140.0
批发和零售业	239.4	57.3
交通运输、仓储和邮政业	314.0	13.3

住宿和餐饮业	54.8	-1.9
信息传输、软件和信息技术服务业	33.5	37.6
金融业	9.3	5.5
房地产业	1346.8	0.9
租赁和商务服务业	179.7	120.0
科学研究和技术服务业	64.7	71.9
水利、环境和公共设施管理业	254.6	-10.9
居民服务和其他服务业	14.7	53.3
教育	73.5	18.5
卫生和社会工作	12.5	-35.4
文化、体育和娱乐业	193.9	293.5
公共管理和社会组织	52.2	15.2

全年固定资产投资施工项目4580个，新开工项目3568个，竣工项目3623个；在建项目计划总投资规模14426.2亿元，增长12.9%。全年新增固定资产3813.2亿元，项目建成投产率79.1%，固定资产交付使用率66.1%。

全年房地产开发完成投资1117.7亿元，增长6.6%。商品房竣工1135.7万平方米，增长18.6%。

表8：房地产开发主要指标完成情况及其增速

指　　标	单位	绝对数	比上年增长%
投资额	亿 元	1117.7	6.6
其中：住宅	亿 元	731.1	9.4
其中：90平方米及以下	亿 元	280	1.2
房屋施工面积	万平方米	8170.7	15.5
其中：住宅	万平方米	5333.5	13.7
房屋新开工面积	万平方米	2044.2	10.5
其中：住宅	万平方米	1333.7	13.7
房屋竣工面积	万平方米	1135.7	18.6
其中：住宅	万平方米	809.8	20
本年到位资金	亿 元	1465.5	-12.4
其中：国内贷款	亿 元	363.2	-18.4

五、国内贸易

全年实现社会消费品零售额3268.8亿元，增长12.6%。分地域看，城市市场实现零售额2731.6亿元，增长12.8%；农村市场实现零售额537.2亿元，增长11.3%。分行业看，批发和零售业实现零售额2862.2亿元，增长12.6%；住宿和餐饮业实现零售额406.6亿元，增长12.2%。

全年限额以上法人企业实现消费品零售额1231.6亿元，增长12.4%。限额以上法人企业汽车类零售额366.1亿元，增长10.4%；石油及制品类零售额175.7亿元，增长8.2%；粮油、食品、饮料、烟酒类零售额145.1亿元，增长13.1%；日用品类零售额34.9亿元，增长14.3%；化妆品类零售额21.1亿元，增长7.6%。

六、对外经济

全市实现外贸进出口总额798.9亿美元，增长2.5%。其中，出口额457.8亿美元，增长9.1%，进口额341.1亿美元，下降5.2%。按可比价格口径，进出口实际增长5.3%。

表9：全市主要商品进出口情况

单位：亿美元、%

项　目	进出口		出　口		进　口	
	金额	增长	金额	增长	金额	增长
纺织服装	85.0	0.8	77.1	1.9	7.9	-8.4
农产品	109.8	7.8	52.0	3.5	57.8	12.0
机电产品	255.3	17.8	179.3	17.6	76.1	18.3
高新技术产品	77.3	31.9	38.1	42.1	39.2	23.3

表10：对主要国家和地区货物进出口额及其增速

单位：亿美元、%

国别（地区）	出口额	比上年增长	进口额	比上年增长
合　计	457.7	9.0	337.2	-5.6
亚洲	201.4	8.1	164.1	-1.7
香港	14.4	25.7	1.2	-11.8
台湾	5.2	9.7	14.0	12.1
日本	59.9	-5.0	21.3	5.1
韩国	47.7	17.7	42.4	-5.9
东盟	37.1	8.8	42.3	-23.2
南亚	13.2	25.7	7.9	-10.7
中东	22.1	10.0	28.3	61.5
非洲	24.5	14.1	24.8	-7.9
南非	3.6	0.3	5.6	-40.4
欧洲	93.9	9.2	39.1	-10.7
欧盟	82.3	8.7	24.8	2.2
英国	14.3	-0.7	1.4	13.2
德国	16.2	13.2	9.0	23.1
法国	9.0	10.1	2.3	12.6
意大利	6.5	7.0	3.2	16.4
独联体及东欧	9.1	5.5	11.3	-34.2
俄罗斯	6.8	8.9	9.3	-37.7
南美洲	31.8	7.2	41.9	-5.2
巴西	6.0	-13.3	25.0	-7.6
北美洲	93.2	14.2	30.0	-6.1
美国	83.4	14.9	24.2	-4.3
加拿大	8.7	13.8	5.6	-12.9
大洋洲	13.0	-11.8	37.3	-14.5
澳大利亚	11.2	-15.3	34.2	-16.9

注：本表非全口径。

据青岛海关统计，青岛口岸对外贸易进出口总额1651.3亿美元，增长5.4%。其中，出口额874.4亿美元，增长13.6%；进口额776.9亿美元，下降2.5%。

实际到账外资金额60.8亿美元，增长10.1%。引进青岛市以外国内资金1380.8亿元，增长13.5%。

全年对外承包工程业务新签合同金额22.8亿美元，下降27.1%；完成营业额35.9亿美元，增长2.4%；对外劳务合作派出各类劳务人员13107人次，增长18.5%。

七、交通运输、邮电和旅游业

全市港口吞吐量4.8亿吨，增长4.2%；外贸吞吐量3.2亿吨，增长0.8%；集装箱吞吐量1658万标准箱，增长6.8%。

表11：铁路、公路及水上运输完成的运输量及增速

运输方式	运输量(单位)	比上年增长(%)
客运周转量	145.5亿人公里	6.7
铁路	70.2亿人公里	12.0
公路	75.0亿人公里	2.6
水运	0.3亿人公里	-36.0
货运周转量	1037.9亿吨公里	9.8
铁路	169.2亿吨公里	-11.2
公路	441.7亿吨公里	5.5
水运	427亿吨公里	27.1

年末拥有国内航线111条，国际航线17条，港澳台地区航线5条，全年航空旅客吞吐量达到1641.2万人次，增长13.1%；航空行货邮吞吐量20.4万吨，增长9.8%。

全年完成邮电业务总量261.5亿元，增长7.2%。其中，邮政业务总量30.9亿元，增长29.8%；电信业务总量230.6亿元，增长4.8%。信函0.7亿件，下降27.3%。互联网用户累计达697.4万户，增长3.8%，使用时长达3787.7亿分钟，增长53.2%。年末固定电话用户达到206.6万户；全市移动电话发展到1301.1万户，其中，年内新增325.3万户。

全年全市旅游总收入1061.1亿元，增长15.0%。其中国内旅游收入1010.7亿元，增长15.7%；入境旅游（外汇）收入8.2亿美元，增长3.7%。全年共接待国内外游客6843.9万人次，增长8.8%；其中国内游客6715.9万人次，增长8.9%；入境游客128.1万人次，增长3.6%。年末A级旅游景区91处，其中，5A级旅游景区1处，4A级旅游景区22处。

八、金融业

年末金融机构本外币存款余额11908.0亿元，比年初增加480.5亿元；人民币存款余额11370.3亿元，比年初增加400.7亿元。其中，个人存款4680.5亿元，比年初增加312.1亿元。本外币贷款余额10530.6亿元，比年初增加868.9亿元；人民币贷款余额9720.1亿元，比年初增加840.1亿元。

全年全市承保金额61163.3亿元，增长24.3%，实现保费收入203.1亿元，增长13.5%。其中：财产险保费收入88.1亿元，增长17.3%；人身险保费收入115.0亿元，增长10.8%。赔款支出金额76.7亿元，增长22.4%；其中财产险赔付金额44.7亿元，人身险赔付金额32.0亿元。

全年辖区证券经营机构累计代理交易额22382.8亿元，增长36.1%。

九、科学技术和教育

初步统计，全年全市共取得重要科技成果415项。获得国家级科技奖励7项，其中，自然科学奖2项，技术发明奖1项，科技进步奖4项；获得省级科技奖励57项，其中，省科学技术最高奖1项，自然科学奖9项，技术发明奖6项，科技进步奖41项。

全年共成交技术合同项目3743项，成交额60.53亿元。全年发明专利申请39995件，发明专利授权2863件。

年末全市共有各类大专院校(含民办高校)23所，其中普通高校22所，在校学生31.3万人，增长4.4%。普通中学295所，在校学生36.3万人，下降0.7%；中等专业学校和技工学校83所，在校学生12.72万人，下降5.4%。接受中等职业教育的学生占高中阶段在校生的51.4%。共有小学794所，在校学生51.65万人，增长4.1%。小学学龄人口入学率100%，初中学龄人口入学率100%。

十、文化、卫生和体育

全市共有各类文化机构488处。其中，影剧院43处，文化馆(站)156处，博物馆41处，公共图书馆13处，艺术表演团体8个，广播电台8座、13套节目，电视台8座、15套节目，全市有线电视用户达到225.32万户，数字电视用户达到225.29万户。全市共有档案馆12处。

年末全市共有卫生机构(含诊所) 3126处，其中，医院、卫生院297处，疾病预防控制中心27处，妇幼保健机构13处，门诊部(所)、卫生保健所、医务室2338处。年末各类卫生技术人员6.3万人，其中，医生2.5万人。全市拥有医疗床位4.5万张，其中，医院、卫生院床位4.2万张。

全市运动员在各项比赛中共获得金牌271.5枚，银牌147.5枚，铜牌157.5枚。全市共有体育专业队1个，队员38人。重点体校2所，学员1021人，业余体校10所，学员1667人。

十一、城市建设

年末全市城镇化率达到68.41%，全市建成区面积490.7平方公里，增长4.5%。城市平均每天供水量116万吨，下降1.8%。城市全年实际用水量3.6亿吨，下降2.2%，其中生产用水和生活用水分别为1.3亿吨和2.3亿吨。

城市使用液化气、煤制气、天然气的总户数达到151.2万户，全年供应液化气总量3.9亿吨，供应天然气总量7.5亿立方米。城市气化率达到100%。

全年新增供热面积551万平方米，年末供热面积达到1.2亿平方米，增长4.9%。

年末市区公共汽、电车线路388条，增长35.7%；共有营运的公交汽、电车6515辆；共有出租汽车9720辆。

年末城市道路总长度4518.5公里，城市下水道总长度6898公里。

据抽样调查，年末城市居民人均现住房建筑面积29.8平方米，农民人均拥有住房面积34.2平方米。

十二、能源、环境和安全生产

初步统计，全年全市规模以上工业综合能源消费量1489.6万吨标准煤，下降6%。其中，原煤消费量1403.8万吨，下降8.1%，原油消费量1549.2万吨，增长2.3%，天然气消费量4.8亿立方米，增长1.3%。全社会用电量337.8亿千瓦时，下降0.4%。其中，工业用电205.8亿千瓦时，城乡居民生活用电60亿千瓦时，分别增长2%和4.2%。

全年全市能源生产总量2701.4万吨标准煤，下降2.9%。其中，原油加工量1544.6万吨，下降2%，汽油生产量447.5万吨，增长11.3%，柴油生产量465.7万吨，下降10.9%，火力发电量168.9亿千瓦时，下降5.6%，风力发电量9.4亿千瓦时，增长60.5%。

全市年平均气温13.7℃，平均年降水量为631.2毫米，年平均日照总时数为2312小时。市区空气质量优良天数达到262天，优良率71.8%。主要污染物可吸入颗粒物（PM2.5）、二氧化硫、二氧化氮年均值分别为0.059、0.037、0.043毫克/立方米，与上年相比,PM2.5下降10.6%,二氧化硫下降31.5%，二氧化氮升高7.5%。全市近岸海域水质达到或好于二类海水水质标准的点位数占78.1%,近岸海域功能区水质达标率为84.4%。全市重点监控河流主要污染物化学需氧量和氨氮浓度同比分别下降10.2%和6.5%。市区区域环境噪声平均值58.2分贝，市区交通干线噪声平均值67.8分贝。建成区绿化覆盖率达到44.7%。市区园林绿地面积达3万公顷，增长7.7%；人均公园绿地面积14.6平方米。全市现有公园、动物园89个。

全市七个行业（领域）发生各类生产安全事故392起，死亡210人，事故起数比上年上升7.1%，死亡人数比上年下降10.6%。道路交通事故万车死亡1.58人，下降9.7%。

十三、海洋经济、重大项目建设和现代服务业

据初步测算，全年实现海洋生产总值1751.1亿元，增长13.1%（现价），占GDP比重为20.2%。

全年全市计划总投资亿元及以上的新开工项目（含房地产项目）717个，下降4.6%。从区域分布看，市区新开工项目94个，四市新开工项目333个，红岛经济区新开工项目30个。重点基础设施项目：世园会建设项目计划总投资143亿元，本年完成投资76.2亿元；青岛—龙口高速公路青岛段计划总投资71亿元，本年完成投资32.9亿元；地铁2号线计划总投资185.3亿元，本年完成投资19.2亿元；地铁3号线计划总投资175.4亿元，本年完成投资26.7亿元。重点区域建设：2014年西海岸经济新区完成投资1444.1亿元，增长17.8%；蓝色硅谷区域共有在建产业类项目（房地产开发类除外）198个，比上年增加57个，完成投资299亿元，增长72.6%。

据初步测算，全年现代服务业实现增加值2262.0亿元，增长12.0%（现价），占GDP比重为26.0%，占服务业比重为50.9%。

十四、人民生活和社会保障

城市居民人均可支配收入38294元，增长8.7%；城市居民人均消费性支出24016元，增长8.9%。城市居民家庭食品消费支出占家庭消费性支出的35.7%。

---

[1] 见注释7。

表12：城市居民每百户家庭主要耐用消费品拥有量

消费品名称	单 位	数 量
钢琴	架	10
微波炉	台	80
电冰箱	台	105
淋浴热水器	台	98
洗衣机	台	99
彩色电视机	台	109
计算机	台	105
摄像机	架	21
照相机	架	79
空调器	台	104
固定电话	部	64
移动电话	部	235
健身器材	套	9
家用汽车	辆	34
摩托车	辆	12
助力车	辆	7

农民人均纯收入17461元，增长11.0%；农民人均生活消费支出10808元，增长10.4%。农村居民家庭食品消费支出占家庭生活消费支出的33.8%。

表13：农村居民每百户家庭主要耐用消费品拥有量

消费品名称	单 位	数 量
微波炉	台	32
电冰箱	台	102
淋浴热水器	台	85
洗衣机	台	93
彩色电视机	台	106
家用电脑	台	61
摄像机	架	7
照相机	架	24
空调器	台	49
固定电话	部	59
移动电话	部	225
家用汽车	辆	26
摩托车	辆	74

年末全市城镇登记失业率为2.97%，较上年同期下降0.01个百分点。

年末全市城镇职工基本养老保险参保缴费人数为237.55万人，参加失业保险人数为178.17万人，全年累计领取失业保险金的人数为6.66万人。

全市各类社会福利院床位达4.7万张，收养25047人。

注：

1、公报中统计数据均为初步统计数。

2、全市GDP及各产业增加值绝对数按现价计算，增长速度按可比价计算。

3、规模以上工业企业为年主营业务收入2000万元及以上企业；限额以上贸易企业为批发业年主营业务收入在2000万元及以上、零售业500万元及以上、住宿和餐饮业200万元及以上的单位；固定资产投资项目统计的起点标准为计划总投资额500万元。

4、战略性新兴产业根据国家规划，现阶段主要包括节能环保、新一代信息技术、生物、高端装备制造、新能源、新材料、新能源汽车等七个产业领域。

5、常住人口包括：①住本户、户口在本乡镇街道的人（含户口在本户，外出不满半年的人）；②住本户半年以上，户口在外乡镇街道的人；③住本户不满半年，户口在外乡镇街道，离开户口登记地半年以上的人；④住本户，户口待定的人。

6、建成区面积、供水、供热、供气、植树、绿化、道路、公园、动物园等数据系市城乡建设委提供，为初步统计数，统计范围为区划调整后的六区。

7、各类生产安全事故起数、死亡人数统计范围包括生产经营性道路交通、水上交通、铁路交通、民航飞行、农业机械、渔业船舶和工矿商贸七个行业（领域）发生的事故，不再包括森林火灾、火灾事故和非生产经营性道路交通。

8、由于2014年城乡一体化住户调查采用新的统计制度及数据处理方式，新老制度的数据在口径范围上有较大差别，目前暂不公布城乡居民收入中位数和五等份数据。

STATISTICS COMMUNIQUÉ QINGDAO'S ECONOMIC AND SOCIAL DEVELOPMENT DURING 2014

Qingdao Statistics Bureau

NBS Qingdao Survey Office

March 30, 2015

The economic characteristics of 2014 were marked by complex and severe external environmental issues and difficult development tasks. During this period, under the leadership of the municipal government, Qingdao adhered to the guidelines of making progress while maintaining stability. The city took positive actions and made serious efforts to develop comprehensive plans, promote steady growth, reform and restructure the economic system, and improve the livelihood of its citizens. It has created favorable conditions under the "new normal," including steady economic growth, continued improvement in living standards, social harmony and stability.

I. General

The total number of permanent residents of Qingdao was 9,046,200 by the end of 2014, increasing by 0.92%; of which 4,875,900 were registered permanent residents in urban areas, up 1.29%.

Table 1: Distribution of permanent resident population in Qingdao city

Region	Amount (10000 persons)
Total	904.62
Shinan District	56.74
Shibei District	106.90
Licang District	54.14
Laoshan District	42.75
Huangdao District	146.52
Chengyang District	68.80
Jimo	119.42
Jiaozhou	87.10
Pingdu	135.44
Laixi	75.07
High-tech Zone	9.84
Qingdao Free Trade Port Area of China	1.90

Preliminary statistics showed a gross domestic product (GDP) of RMB 869.21 billion, up 8.0% over the previous year. Of the total, primary industries contributed RMB 36.26 billion in added value, up 3.9%, secondary industries contributed RMB 388.24 billion, up 8.4%, and tertiary industries contributed RMB 444.71 billion, up 7.9%. The ratio of primary, secondary and tertiary industries was 4.2, 44.6 and 51.2, and the per capital GDP reached RMB 96,524. The private sector finished RMB 332.34 billon in added value, up 8.3%。

Graph 1: Quarterly GDP of Qingdao and Growth Rate

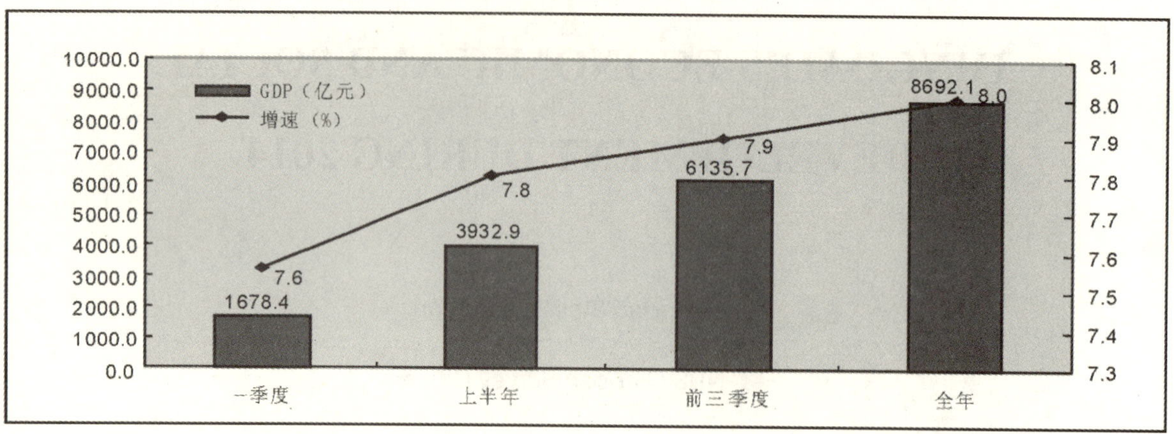

Graph 2: Composition of Values Added to GDP by the Three Industries in 2013 and 2014

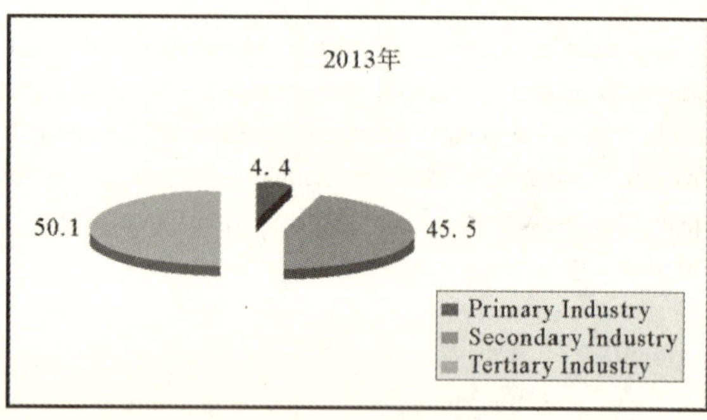

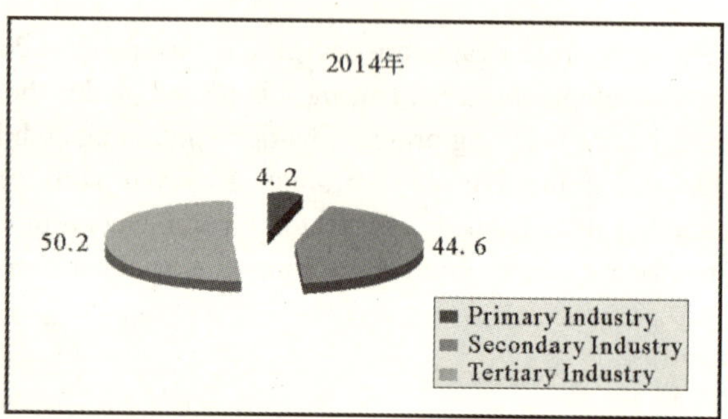

Qingdao realized RMB 280.04 billion in the local government's general revenue, up 8.5%, RMB 89.52 billion in the public budget revenue, up 13.5% and RMB 107.47 billion in the public budget expenditure, up 6.0%. The national tax revenue (including those collected by customs) rose by 0.6% to RMB 134.01 billion. Internal revenue increased by 8.3% to RMB 69.14 billion and local tax revenue increased by 12.7% to RMB 59.9 billion.

The total consumer price index increased by 2.6% over the previous year. Food prices rose 4.4%. The factory price index for main industrial products decreased 0.8%. The purchase price index decreased 2.6%. In December, urban newly-built residential housing prices decreased by 6.2% while second-hand residential housing prices decreased by 5.2% year-on-year.

Table 2: Movements of Consumer Price Index in 2014 over the previous year

Description	+/-% over the previous year
Consumer Price Index	2.6
Non-food	1.9
Services	1.9
Consumption goods	2.9
1. Food	4.4
Grain	6.5
Pork	-3.1
Eggs	17.2
Fresh vegetables	-7.6
2. Tobacco and wine	0.1
3. Clothes	3.2
4. Household appliances and repair services	2.0
5. Medical care and personal articles	2.0
6. Transportation and communications	0.3
7. Entertainment, educational and cultural products and services	1.4
8. Housing	2.2

Graph 3: Increase/decrease in consumer price index (CPI) compared to the same month of the previous year (%)

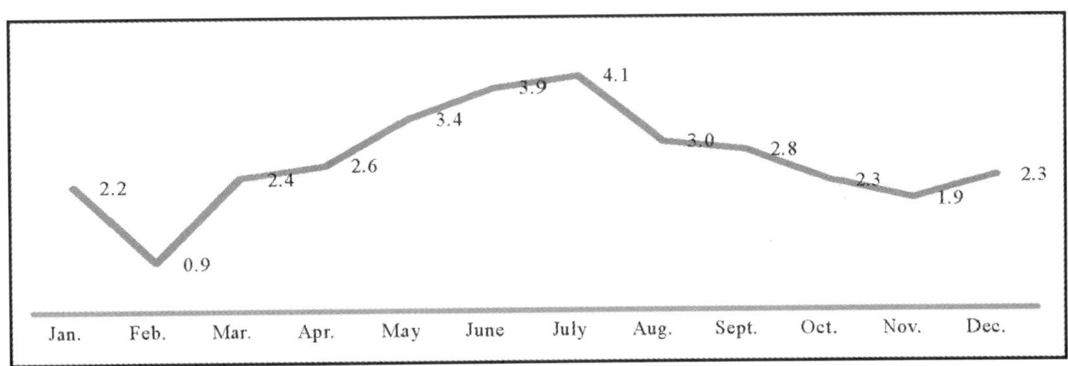

II. Agriculture

The sown area for crops totaled 495,500 hectares, down 0.99%. The total grain output reached 3,230,000 tons, up 0.2%. Of the total, 1,521,000 tons were wheat and 1,668,000 tons were corn.

Table 3: Output of major livestock products and growth rate

Description	Output (ton)	+/-% over the previous year
Meets	595,500	-3.1
Pork	273,600	-2.0
Poultry meet	303,600	-5.3
Cow and goat's milk	375,400	1.1
Fowl eggs	191,100	0.5

10,400 hectares of trees were planted in the year, up 4.0%. Forest coverage reached 39.5%, up 0.1 percent.

The total output of aquatic products reached 1,094,500 tons, down 0.9%. Of the total, 267,800 tons were from fishing, up 0.5% and 826,700 tons were from farmed fish, a decrease of 1.4%. The combined seawater and freshwater farming area was 50,100 hectares, down 2.1%.

By the end of 2014, power from farming machines totaled 8,269,300 KW, up 2.2%. Farming tractors totaled 205,100 units. Effective irrigation area was 321,700 hectares, including 125,200 hectares of water-saving irrigation area.

III. Industry and Construction

In 2014, the industrial sector generated RMB 341.98 billion in added value, up 8.3%. The Industrial Enterprises above Designated Size (Industrial Corporate Enterprises with an annual operating income of RMB 20,000,000 or more) number 4,603. Their industrial added value grew by 9.4%. By industry, heavy industry increased by 11.3% while light industry rose 6.6%. The state-owned and controlled enterprises grew by 5.1%; collective enterprises increased by 10.7%; shareholder enterprises rose 9.6%; enterprises invested by foreign companies and by compatriots from Hong Kong, Macao and Taiwan, increased by 9.3%.

The Industrial Enterprises above Designated Size finished a total output of RMB 1,676.1 billion, up 9.6%. Hi-tech Industries increased by 16.7%, or 40.7% of the total, an increase of 0.8 percentage point from the beginning of the year. The production value of ten 100-billion-level industry chains rose 10.2%, accounting for 75.3% of the total. The production value of strategic emerging industries above the designated size grew by 20.2%.

Table 4: Developments of strategic emerging industries above the designated size

Description	Number of Enterprises	Total Production Value (billion RMB)	Growth Rate (%)	Operating Revenue (billion RMB)	Growth Rate (%)
Strategic emerging industries	603	301.92	20.2	289.44	22.9
New material industry	180	55.77	22.3	54.71	27.9
Biological industry	51	17.02	19.0	16.82	20.2
High-end equipment manufacturing industry	198	115.11	22.6	109.78	35.1
New energy industry	26	7.88	40.1	7.77	35.6
Energy-saving and environmental protection industry	45	9.28	22.6	9.00	24.3
New generation information technology industry	99	94.42	16.0	104.60	8.6
New energy vehicles	4	2.45	-7.0	2.49	-6.2

Table 5: The output and growth rate of the main products of industries above designated size

Description	Output	+/-% over the previous year
Color TV sets	17,149,000 sets	7.7
Household refrigerators	6,101,000 sets	16.4
Household washing machine	5,910,000 sets	-2.6
Room air conditioners	6,859,000 sets	7.6
Cigarettes	56,030,000,000 pieces	3.4
Beer	1,626,000 kilolitres	-7.3
Sodium carbonate(soda ash)	678,000 tons	10.0
Tire casings	51,991,000 pieces	8.0
Sheet glass	6,124,000 weight cases	0.4
Raw steel	2,144,000 tons	-9.0
Motor vehicles	770,000 units	8.6
Motor train units or electric Multiple Unit (EMU)	684 units	3.0
Metal shipping containers	18,539,000 M^3	15.2
Crude oil processed	15,446,000 tons	-2.0
Power output	17,830,000,000 KWh	-3.5

Industrial enterprises above the designated size realized the total pre-tax profits of RMB 156.48 billion, up 9.3%, with after-tax profits of RMB 83.55 billion, up 5.6%. Operating incomes totaled RMB 1,614.39 billion, up 10.7%. The capital maintenance and appreciation ratio was 128.2 %. The sales ratio was 98.5%.

Table 6: Profits of industrial enterprises above the designated size by business type

Description of indicators	Total profits (billion RMB)	Growth rate (%)
Total	83.55	5.6
State-owned and state-controlled businesses	10.51	-4.7
Collective businesses	7.70	24.1
Shareholder businesses	50.00	3.5
Businesses invested by foreign business people and by compatriots from Hong Kong, Macao and Taiwan	22.90	3.8

The construction industries generated RMB 46.26 billion in added value, up 8.9% and RMB 8.23 billion in pre-tax profit, up 9.2%, of which RMB 2.24 billion was finished by the state-owned and controlled enterprises, up 9.8 %.

IV. Fixed Assets Investment

The fixed asset investment (including the projects with investment over RMB 5,000,000 in townships and rural areas) totaled RMB 576.6 billion, up 16.1%. Of that figure, RMB 10.47 billion was invested in primary industries, up 11.4%, RMB 281.79 billion in secondary industries, up 16% and RMB 284.34 billion in tertiary industries, up 16.4%.

Table 7: Investment in fixed assets by industry (excluding farmers) and growth rate

Sector	Amount of investment (Billion RMB)	+/-% over the previous year
Total	5766.0	16.1
Agriculture Forestry Animal Husbandry and Fishery	104.7	11.4
Mining	13.6	11.9
Manufacturing	2666.3	15.3
Production and Supply of Electricity Heat Gas and Water	48.3	-27.6
Construction	89.7	140.0
Wholesale and Retail Trades	239.4	57.3
Transport Storage and Post	314.0	13.3
Hotels and Catering Services	54.8	-1.9
Information Transmission Computer Services and Software	33.5	37.6
Financial Intermediation	9.3	5.5
Real Eatate	1346.8	0.9
Leasing and Business Services	179.7	120.0
Scientific Research Technical Services	64.7	71.9
Management of Water Conservancy Environment and Public Facilities	254.6	-10.9
Services to Households Repair and Other Services	14.7	53.3
Education	73.5	18.5
Health and Social Work	12.5	-35.4
Culture Sports and Entertainment	193.9	293.5
Public Management Social Security and Social Organizations	52.2	15.2

The fixed assets investment construction projects number 4,580. New start-up projects number 3,568 and completed projects number 3,623. The amount of investment in projects in progress was RMB 1,442.62 billion, up 12.9%. Another RMB 381.32 billion was invested in fixed assets for the whole year. The project completion ratio was 79.1% and the fixed asset delivery ratio was 66.1%.

Finished investment in real estate development for the whole year reached RMB 111.77 billion, up 6.6%. Completed commercial housing totaled 11,357,000 square meters, up 18.6%.

Table 8: The main indicators of real estate development and sales accomplished and growth rates

Index	Unit	Absolute numbers	+/-% over the previous year
Amount of Investment	Billion RMB	1117.7	6.6
Including Homes	Billion RMB	731.1	9.4
Including 90 Square Meters and Less	Billion RMB	280	1.2
Housing Construction Area	Square Meter	8170.7	15.5

Including Homes	Square Meter	5333.5	13.7
Construction Area of New Housing	Square Meter	2044.2	10.5
Including Homes	Square Meter	1333.7	13.7
FLoor Space of Buildings Completed	Square Meter	1135.7	18.6
Including Homes	Square Meter	809.8	20
The Funds Available for This Year	Billion RMB	1465.5	-12.4
Including Domestic Loans	Billion RMB	363.2	-18.4

V. Domestic Trade

In 2014, total retail sales of consumer goods increased by 12.6% to RMB 326.88 billion. Geographically, RMB 273.16 billion was generated by the urban market, up 12.8% and RMB 53.72 billion by the rural market, up 11.3%. By industry, wholesale and retail industries realized sales of RMB 286.22 billion, up 12.6%, while the lodging and catering industries generated RMB 40.66 billion, up 12.2%.

In 2014, the retail sales of consumer goods of enterprises (units) above the designated size amounted to RMB 123.16 billion, up 12.4%. The retail sales of motor vehicles above the limited value reached RMB 36.61 billion, up 10.4%; that of petroleum and petroleum products totaled RMB 17.57 billion, up 8.2%; that of grain and oil, food, beverages, cigarettes and alcohols amounted to RMB 14.51 billion, up 13.1%; that of daily necessities added up to RMB 3.49 billion, up 14.3%; and that of cosmetics totaled RMB 2.11 billion, up 7.6%.

VI. Foreign Trade

Qingdao's import and export volume was USD 79.89 billion, up 2.5%, with exports amounting to USD 45.78 billion, up 9.1% and imports amounting to USD 34.11 billion, down 5.2%. Exports and imports grew 5.3% based on comparable prices.

Table 9: The import & exports of main commodities from Qingdao

Category	Import & Export		Export		Import	
	Amount (USD)	Growth Rate%	Amount (USD)	Growth Rate%	Amount (USD)	Growth Rate%
Textiles and garments	8,500,000,000	0.8	7,710,000,000	1.9	790,000,000	-8.4
Agricultural products	10,980,000,000	7.8	5,200,000,000	3.5	5,780,000,000	12.0
Electrical and mechanical products	25,530,000,000	17.8	17,930,000,000	17.6	7,610,000,000	18.3
High-tech products	7,730,000,000	31.9	3,810,000,000	42.1	3,920,000,000	23.3

Table 10: The import from & export to major countries and regions and growth rates

Country/Region	Export Amount (billion USD)	+/-% over the previous year	Import Amount (billion USD)	+/-% over the previous year
Total	457.7	9.0	337.2	-5.6
Asia	201.4	8.1	164.1	-1.7
Hong Kong	14.4	25.7	1.2	-11.8
Taiwan	5.2	9.7	14.0	12.1
Japan	59.9	-5.0	21.3	5.1
Korea	47.7	17.7	42.4	-5.9
ASEAN	37.1	8.8	42.3	-23.2
South Asia	13.2	25.7	7.9	-10.7
Middle East	22.1	10.0	28.3	61.5

Africa	24.5	14.1	24.8	-7.9
South Africa	3.6	0.3	5.6	-40.4
Europe	93.9	9.2	39.1	-10.7
EU	82.3	8.7	24.8	2.2
U.K.	14.3	-0.7	1.4	13.2
Germany	16.2	13.2	9.0	23.1
France	9.0	10.1	2.3	12.6
Italy	6.5	7.0	3.2	16.4
CIS and Eastern Europe	9.1	5.5	11.3	-34.2
Russia	6.8	8.9	9.3	-37.7
South America	31.8	7.2	41.9	-5.2
Brazil	6.0	-13.3	25.0	-7.6
North America	93.2	14.2	30.0	-6.1
U.S.A.	83.4	14.9	24.2	-4.3
Canada	8.7	13.8	5.6	-12.9
Oceania	13.0	-11.8	37.3	-14.5
Australia	11.2	-15.3	34.2	-16.9

Note: This table is not full measurement.

According to Qingdao Customs' statistics, imports and exports registered at Qingdao ports totaled USD 165.13 billion, up 5.4%. Of the total, USD 87.44 billion were exports, up 13.6% and USD 77.69 billion were imports, down 2.5%.

In 2014, direct foreign investment reached USD 6.08 billion, up 10.1% while domestic investment from outside investors totaled RMB138.08 billion, up 13.5%.

Total contracted value of overseas contractor projects and services was USD 2.28 billion, down 27.1%. Turnover amounted to USD 3.59 billion, up 2.4%; the number of personnel sent overseas reached 13,107, up 18.5%.

VII. Transportation, Post, Telecommunications and Tourism

Port throughput totaled 0.48 billion tons for the whole year, up 4.2%, with 0.32 billion tons handled for foreign trade, up 0.8%. Container throughput reached 16,580,000 TEUs, up 6.8%.

Table 11: Volume completed by various transportation means and increase/decrease

Transportation means	Volume	+/-% over the previous year
Passenger volume	14.55 billion person-km	6.7
Railways	7.02 billion person-km	12.0
Highways	7.50 billion person-km	2.6
Waterways	0.03billion person-km	-36.0
Cargo volumes	103.79 billion ton-km	9.8
Railways	16.92 billion ton-km	-11.2
Highways	44.17 billion ton-km	5.5
Waterways	42.7 billion ton-km	27.1

By the end of the year, there were 111 domestic airlines, 17 international airlines and 5 airlines to/from Hong Kong, Macao and Taiwan. The airport passenger throughput for the whole year reached 16,412,000 person-times, up 13.1% and air cargo and mail throughput was 204,000 tons, up 9.8%.

Postal and telecommunication service business transactions in 2014 totaled RMB 26.15 billion, up 7.2%. Of the total, RMB 3.09 billion was from the postal service, up 29.8%, and RMB 23.06 billion from the telecommunication service, up 4.8%. The total number of letters handled was 70 million, down 27.3%. Internet users number 6,974,000 in 2014, up 3.8% and time online reached 378.77 billion minutes, up 53.2%. At the end of the year, fixed-line telephone users number 2,066,000. Mobile phone users number 13,011,000, of which 3,253,000 were new users.

Tourism income for the year totaled RMB 106.11 billion, up 15.0%. Of the total, RMB 101.07 billion was from domestic tourism, up 15.7% and USD 0.82 billion from international tourism, up 3.7%. Tourists to Qingdao during the year totaled 68,439,000 person-times, up 8.8%. Of the total, 67,159,000 were domestic tourists, up 8.9% and 1,281,000 overseas tourists, up 3.6%. By the end of the year, there were 91 A-rated tourist attractions, of which one is 5A-rated and 22 are 4A rated.

VIII. Finance

At year-end, the balance of local and foreign currencies on the deposit accounts with financial institutions in Qingdao stood at RMB 1,190.80 billion, an increase of RMB 48.05 billion from the beginning of this year. The balance of deposits in local currency (RMB) was RMB 1,137.03 billion, an increase of RMB 40.07 billion from the beginning of the year. Of the total, the balance of savings was RMB 468.05 billion, an increase of RMB31.21 billion from the beginning of the year. The loan balance in local and foreign currencies reached RMB 1,053.06 billion, an increase of RMB 86.89 billion from the beginning of this year. The loan balance in local currency (RMB) was RMB 972.01 billion, an increase of RMB 84.01 billion from the beginning of the year.

The insured amount was RMB 6,116.33 billion, up 24.3%. The insurance premium totaled RMB 20.31 billion, up 13.5%. Of the total, RMB 8.81 billion was for property insurance, up 17.3%; and RMB 11.50 billion for personal insurance, up 10.8%. Expenses for claims amounted to RMB 7.67 billion, up 22.4%. Of this figure, RMB 4.47 billion was for property claims and RMB 3.20 billion for personal claims.

The trading amount of the securities companies for the whole year reached RMB 2,238.28 billion, up 36.1%.

IX. Science, Technology and Education

Preliminary statistics show that Qingdao achieved 415 key scientific and technological results in 2014 and received 7 national scientific and technological prizes. Of the total, 2 were for natural science, 1 were for technological inventions, and 4 were for scientific and technological progress; it also received 57 provincial-level scientific and technological prizes. Of them, one was the highest provincial-level scientific and technological prize, 9 were for natural science, 6 were for technological inventions, and 41 were for scientific and technological progress.

In 2014, there were a total of 3,743 technology transfer contracts completed with a value of RMB 6.053 billion; 39,995 patents were pending and 2,863 were granted with patent certificates.

By the end of 2014, there were 23 higher education schools (including private schools) including 22 ordinary colleges and universities. There were 313,000 students enrolled, up 4.4%. 295 were ordinary middle schools, enrolling 363,000 students, down 0.7%; technical secondary schools and vocational schools number 83, enrolling 127,200, down 5.4%. The number of students in vocational secondary schools accounted for 51.4% of the number of senior middle school students. There were 794 primary schools enrolling 516,500 pupils, up 4.1% and 100% of pre-school aged children were schooled. The schooling of youngsters for junior middle school was 100%.

X. Culture, Public Health Services and Sports

There were a total of 488 cultural institutions in Qingdao, including 43 cinemas and theaters, 156 cultural centers (stations), 41 museums, 13 public libraries, 8 performing arts troupes, 8 radio and broadcasting stations with 13 programs and 8 TV stations with 15 programs. Cable TV users number 2,253,200. Digitalization TV users number 2,252,900. There were 12 archives in Qingdao.

At the end of the year, there were 3,126 public health institutions (including clinics). Of the total, there were 297 hospitals, 27 epidemic prevention institutions, 13 children and women's health care centers and 2,338 clinical and medical health locations. There were 63,000 medical professionals, including 25,000 doctors. Medical beds number 45,000, with 42,000 beds in hospitals and clinics.

Qingdao athletes won 271.5 gold medals, 147.5 silver medals and157.5 bronze medals in various games. There was

1 professional sport team totaling 38 members. Key sports schools number 2, enrolling 1,021 students. Part-time sports schools number 10, enrolling 1,667 students.

XI. Urban Construction

At the end of the year, the urbanization rate accounts for 68.41% of the city. Built-up area reached 490.7 square kilometers, up 4.5%. Urban water supply averaged 1,160,000 tons per day, down 1.8%. The actual urban water consumption for the year totaled 0.36 billion tons, down 2.2%, including 0.13 billion tons for production use and 0.23 billion tons for residential use.

Liquefied petroleum fuel, coal gas and natural gas users number 1,512,000. The total supply for liquefied petroleum fuel for the year was 0.39 billion tons, and for natural gas was 0.75 billion cubic meters. The urban gas coverage was 100%.

Total heating space increased by 5,510,000 square meters to 0.12 billion square meters by the end of the year, up 4.9%.

At the end of the year, there were 388 public bus and trolley lines operating in urban areas, up 35.7%. 6,515 public buses and trolleys were in operation. Taxicabs number 9,720.

Distance covered by roads in urban areas totaled 4,518.5 km. The total length of underground sewers was 6,898 km.

A survey showed that the per capita average floor space in urban areas was 29.8 square meters at the end of the year, and the per capita average floor space for rural residents was 34.2 square meters.

XII. Energy, Environment and Work Safety

Preliminary statistics showed that the total energy consumption of industrial enterprises above the designated size in Qingdao in 2014 was 14,896,000 tons of standard coal, down 6% from the previous year. Consumption of raw coal totaled 14,038,000 tons, down 8.1%; consumption of crude oil was 15,492,000 tons, up 2.3%; and consumption of natural gas was 0.48 billion cubic meters, up 1.3%. The total power consumption was 33.78 billion kilowatt-hours, down 0.4%. Industrial power consumption was 20.58 billion kilowatt-hours; rural and urban residents' power consumption was 6 billion kilowatt-hours, up 2% and 4.2% respectively.

The total power output in Qingdao in 2014 was 27,014,000 tons of standard coal, down 2.9% from the previous year. Of the total, the amount of crude oil processed was 15,446,000 tons, down 2%, the output of gasoline was 4,475,000 tons, up 11.3%, and the output of diesel oil was 4,657,000 tons, down 10.9%. The total thermal power output was 16.89 billion kilowatt-hour, down 5.6%; while the amount of wind power generation was 0.94 billion kilowatt-hour, up 60.5%.

The average temperature was 13.7℃ for the whole year, the average amount of precipitation was 631.2 millimeters and annual average sunshine time reached 2,312 hours. Acceptable air quality percentages in urban areas reached 262 days, accounting for 71.8% of the whole year. Major pollutants inhalable particulate matter (PM2.5), sulfur dioxide and nitrogen dioxide averaged 0.059, 0.037 and 0.043 milligram/cubic meter respectively. Compared to the previous year, the amount of PM2.5 decreased by 10.6%, sulfur dioxide dropped 31.5%, and nitrogen dioxide increased by 7.5%. The area of the city's coastal water up to or better than the second class of sea water quality standard was 78.1% of the total. The compliance rate of water in the inshore functional areas was 84.4%. COD (Chemical Oxygen Demand) and ammonia nitrogen concentration of major pollutants in key rivers being monitored by the city government fell 10.2% and 6.5% respectively. Environmental noise pollution in urban areas averaged 58.2 dB. Noise pollution at traffic trunk lines in urban areas averaged 67.8 dB. "Green area" coverage in built-up areas reached 44.7%. The "green area" of parks and gardens in urban areas totaled 30,000 hectares, up 7.7%. Per capita "green area" was 14.6 square meters. There are 89 parks and zoos in Qingdao.

There were 392 accidents happened at work of 7 industries (sectors), up 7.1%, with 210 people died, down 10.6%. The road traffic death toll per 10 thousand vehicles was 1.58 persons, a decrease of 9.7%.

XIII. The Blue Economy, the construction of major projects and modern service industry

Preliminary statistics showed that the Blue Economy created RMB 175.11 billion in added value for the whole year, up 13.1% (based on current prices), accounting for 20.2% of GDP.

The new projects including real estate projects whose construction was started in 2014, each with a planned investment of RMB 0.1 billion or more, number 717, down 4.6%. By geography, 94 projects were in urban areas, 333 in four outskirts, and 30 in Hongdao Economic Zone. Key infrastructure projects include Qingdao International Horticultural Exposition Construction Project with total planned investment of RMB 14.3 billion, of which RMB 7.62 billion was invested in 2014; the Qingdao section of Qingdao-Longkou Highway project with total planned investment of RMB 7.1 billion, of which RMB 3.29 billion was invested in 2014; the subway line No.2 with total planned investment of RMB 18.53 billion, of which RMB 1.92 billion was invested in 2014; the subway line No.3 with total planned investment of RMB 17.54 billion, of which RMB 2.67 billion was invested in 2014. For major regional constructions in 2014, RMB 144.41 billion has been invested in Qingdao West-coast Economic New District, up 17.8%; there were 198 industrial projects (excluding real estate development) under construction in the Blue Silicon Valley, 57 more than the previous year, which have used RMB 29.9 billion of investment, up 72.6%.

Preliminary statistics showed that modern service industry generated a total of RMB 226.20 billion in added value, up 12.0% (based on current prices), accounting for 26.0% of GDP or 50.9% of the total of service industry.

XIV. Living Conditions and Social Security

The per capita disposable income of urban residents was RMB 38,294, up 8.7%. The per capita consumption expense of urban residents was RMB 24,016, up 8.9%. The food consumption expense of urban residents accounted for 35.7% of household consumption expenditure.

Table 12: Amount of major durable consumer goods owned by every 100 urban households

Item	Unit	Quantity
Pianos	set	10
Microwave ovens	set	80
Refrigerators	set	105
Water heaters	set	98
Washing machines	set	99
Color TV sets	set	109
Computers	set	105
Video cameras	set	21
Cameras	set	79
Air-conditioners	set	104
Fixed-line telephones	set	64
Mobile telephones	set	235
Body building equipments	set	9
Household automobiles	unit	34
Motorcycles	unit	12
Motorbikes	unit	7

The average net income among farmers was RMB 17,461, up 11.0%; per capita consumption expense was RMB 10,808, up 10.4%. The food consumption expense of rural residents accounted for 33.8% of household consumption expenditure.

Table 13: Amount of major durable consumer goods owned by every 100 rural households

Item	Unit	Quantity
Microwave ovens	set	32
Refrigerators	set	102
Water heaters	set	85

Washing machines	set	93
Color TV sets	set	106
Computers	set	61
Video cameras	set	7
Cameras	set	24
Air-conditioners	set	49
Fixed-line telephones	set	59
Mobile telephones	set	225
Household automobiles	unit	26
Motorcycles	unit	74

At year-end, the registered urban unemployment rate was 2.97%, down 0.01 percentage point year-on-year.

At the end of 2014, the number of people covered under the basic pension program was 2,375,500, people who participated in the unemployment insurance program number 1,781,700, and people who received payment from the unemployment insurance program number 66,600.

Nursing homes registered 47,000 beds with 25,047 residents.

Note:

1. Figures reported herein are preliminary statistics.
2. The total production value and the absolute added value of the industries in Qingdao were calculated at current prices and growth rates were calculated at comparable prices.
3. According to the national planning, the strategic emerging industries refer to the seven industries or sectors including energy conservation and environmental protection, the new generation of information technology, biology, high-end equipment manufacturing, new energy, new materials and new energy vehicles.
4. The data of the built-up area, water supply, heating, gas supply, tree planting, greening, road, park, zoo, etc. are preliminary statistics provided by Qingdao Rural and Urban Construction Commission. The statistics include the data of the newly-divided six districts of Qingdao City.
5. The statistics of various accidents happened at workplace and death toll cover that happened in 7 industries or sectors, including productive or operative road traffic, waterway, railway, civil aviation flight, agricultural machinery, fishing boats, and industrial and mining business and trade, excluding forest fire, fire accident and non-productive or operative road traffic.
6. As a new statistics system and data processing method were used in the household survey in urban and rural area in 2014, there was a significant statistic difference between the new and old systems. Therefore, the statistics of the median income and the five equal income groups of urban residents are not included herein.

1 综　合

GENERAL SUREY

简要说明

一、本篇资料的主要内容

本篇资料是对我市行政区划、气象情况、分行业法人单位数、各部门机构数和国民经济、社会发展的综合反映，主要包括行政区划、气象情况、分行业法人单位数、各部门机构数、国民经济主要比例关系、国民经济和社会发展主要指标占全国全省比重、国民经济和社会发展主要指标及其增长速度等资料。

二、本篇资料的来源

1、“行政区划”主要包括2014年底各区(市)街道办事处(乡镇)、社区居委会(村民委员会)区划资料，数据来源于市民政局。

2、“气象情况”包括分区市、市区分月气象资料，数据来源于市气象局。

3、“全市生产总值”来源于国民经济核算统计报表，由市统计局国民经济核算处整理提供。

4、国民经济和社会发展综合部分来源于本年鉴各篇章中的资料，由市统计局国民经济综合统计处加工整理。

Brief Introduction

I. Main Content

Data in this chapter cover the main indicators on divisions of administrative areas, meteorology, corporate units, number of grass-roots units and national economy and social development, including divisions of administrative areas, meteorology, number of corporate units, number of grass-roots units, average daily social and economic activities, ratio, and percentage of main indicators of Qingdao to the whole nation and the whole province and growth rate of main indicators.

II. Source of Data

(1) Data on divisions of administrative areas are mainly including the information on sub-district offices (villages and towns) and community neighborhood committees (villagers residents' committees) at the end of 2014.The data are provided by Qingdao Municipal Bureau of Civil Affairs.

(2)Data on meteorology are provided by Qingdao Municipal Meteorological Bureau.

(3)Data on gross national product are prepared according to the data of national accounts and compiled by the Division of National Accounts of Qingdao Municipal Bureau of Statistics.

(4)Data on general survey of economy and society are based on those of different chapters and compiled by the Division of Comprehensive Statistics of Qingdao Municipal Bureau of Statistics.

1-1 行政区划(2014 年底)
ADMINISTRATIVE DIVISION(END OF 2014)

单位:个(unit)

市、区名称	Region	街道办事处 Subdistrict Offices 小计 Sub-total	社区居委会 Community Residents' Committees	镇 Town 小计 Sub-total	村民委员会 Villagers' Committees
全 市	**Whole Municipality**	**102**	**1 196**	**43**	**5 445**
市南区	Shinan District	14	65		
市北区	Shibei District	31	173		
李沧区	Licang District	11	121		
崂山区	Laoshan District	4	157		
黄岛区	Huangdao District	12	259	10	962
城阳区	Chengyang District	8	245		1
即墨市	Jimo	8	54	7	1 028
胶州市	Jiaozhou	6	51	6	811
平度市	Pingdu	5	42	12	1 782
莱西市	Laixi	3	29	8	861

1 –2 气象情况(2014 年)
METEOROLOGY(2014)

市、区名称	Region	平均气温(摄氏度) Average Temperature (℃)	极端气温 Extreme Temperature(centigrade)		降水量(毫米/年) Precipitation (millimeter/year)	日照时数(小时/年) Sunshine Hours (hour/year)	平均气压(百帕) Average Atmospheric Pressure(100 pa)
			最高(摄氏度) Maximum(℃)	最低(摄氏度) Minimum(℃)			
市　区	Urban Area	13.8	35.1	-6.9	666.9	2 184.6	1 008.2
崂山区	Laoshan District	14.7	36.1	-7.1	611.2	2 302.7	1 012.2
黄岛区	Huangdao District	13.9	37.5	-8.4	735.9	2 287.1	1 016.2
即墨市	Jimo	14.0	36.6	-9.6	530.1	2 390.6	1 013.9
胶州市	Jiaozhou	13.6	37.0	-8.9	727.6	2 245.6	1 007.4
平度市	Pingdu	13.5	38.0	-10.7	506.0	2 392.6	1 009.8
莱西市	Laixi	12.8	37.6	-11.1	640.5	2 379.9	1 008.1

注:以上为7个国家基准站或基本站。
Note:These are 7 national reference or base stations.

1 –3 市区分月气象情况(2014 年)
MONTHLY METEOROLOGY OF URBAN AREA(2014)

月　份	Month	平均气温(摄氏度) Average Temperature (℃)	降水量(毫米) Precipitation (millimeter)	日照时数(小时) Sunshine Hours (hour)
一月	Jan.	2.6	2.7	159.9
二月	Feb.	1.5	17.4	148.5
三月	Mar.	8.1	3.6	229.8
四月	Apr.	12.5	41.3	201.3
五月	May	18.4	87.3	274.8
六月	June	21.3	40.9	143.4
七月	July	24.3	235.8	164.3
八月	Aug.	25.3	80.1	202.7
九月	Sept.	21.6	82.3	150.5
十月	Oct.	16.8	41.7	209.1
十一月	Nov.	10.5	32.3	126.9
十二月	Dec.	2.2	1.5	173.4
全年	Annual Total	13.8	666.9	2 184.6

1－4 各部门机构数(2014 年底)
GRASS-ROOTS UNITS IN VARIOUS SECTORS(END OF 2014)

项　目	Item	单位	Unit	机构数 Grass-roots Units
农村基层单位	**Rural Grass-roots Units**			
镇政府	Town Governments	个	unit	43
乡村户数	Number of Rural Households	万户	10 000 households	156.99
工业企业单位	**Industrial Enterprises**	**个**	**unit**	**25 104**
规模以上工业	Above Designated Size	个	unit	4 790
#国有企业	State-owned Enterprises	个	unit	132
集体企业	Collective-owned Enterprises	个	unit	19
外商及港澳台商投资企业	Enterprises with Funds from Hong Kong, Macao, Taiwan and Foreign Countries	个	unit	1 445
规模以下工业	Under Designated Size	个	unit	20 314
交通运输业	**Transportation**			
铁路	Railway	个	unit	
公路	Highway	个	unit	91
水运	Waterway	个	unit	25
邮电业	**Postal and Telecommunication Services**			
邮电局所	Post Offices	处	unit	645
建筑业企业	**Construction Enterprises**	**个**	**unit**	**556**
国有企业	State-owned Enterprises	个	unit	22
集体企业	Collective-owned Enterprises	个	unit	22
其他	Others	个	unit	512
批发和零售业、住宿和餐饮业	**Wholesale & Retail Trades, Hotels and Catering Services**			
限额以上批发业	Wholesale Trade above Designated Size	个	unit	1 040
限额以上零售业	Retail Trade above Designated Size	个	unit	639
限额以上住宿业	Hotel above Designated Size	个	unit	155
限额以上餐饮业	Catering Service above Designated Size	个	unit	174

1 -4 续表
continued

项 目	Item	单位	Unit	机构数 Grass-roots Units
教育事业	**Education**			
普通高等学校	Regular Institutions of Higher Education	所	unit	22
中等专业学校	Specialized Secondary Schools	所	unit	6
普通中学	Regular Secondary Schools	所	unit	295
普通小学	Regular Primary Schools	所	unit	794
幼儿园	Kindergartens	所	unit	2 340
科研机构	**Science and Technology Institutions**	**个**	**unit**	**50**
中央属	Central Level	个	unit	18
地方属	Local	个	unit	32
文化及相关产业	**Culture and Related Industry**			
文化事业机构	Cultural Institutions	个	unit	262
公共图书馆	Public Libraries	个	unit	13
影剧院	Cinemas	个	unit	43
广播、电视台	**Radio and Television Broadcasting Stations**			
广播电台	Radio Stations	个	unit	8
电视台	Television Stations	个	unit	9
卫生事业	**Public Health**	**个**	**unit**	**3 126**
#医院	Hospitals	个	unit	297
民政行政单位	**Civil Affairs Departments**			
#社会福利事业机构	Institutions of Social Welfare	个	unit	267

1 -5 按行业分法人单位数
NUMBER OF CORPORATE UNITS BY SECTOR

单位:个(unit)

行　业	Sector	2014
总　计	**Total**	**188 314**
农、林、牧、渔业	Agriculture Forestry Animal Husbandry and Fishery	3 176
采矿业	Mining	140
制造业	Manufacturing	38 104
电力、燃气及水的生产和供应业	Production and Supply of Electricity Gas and Water	288
建筑业	Construction	10 166
批发和零售业	Wholesale and Retail Trades	68 638
交通运输、仓储和邮政业	Transport Storage and Post	7 366
住宿和餐饮业	Hotels and Catering Services	2 099
信息传输、软件和信息技术服务业	Information Transmission Computer Services and Software	4 346
金融业	Financial Intermediation	1 093
房地产业	Real Estate	4 572
租赁和商务服务业	Leasing and Business Services	18 784
科学研究和技术服务业	Scientific Research and Technical Services	6 520
水利、环境和公共设施管理业	Management of Water Conservancy Environment and Public Facilities	1 130
居民服务、修理和其他服务业	Services to Households and Other Services	4 046
教　育	Education	3 546
卫生和社会工作	Health Social Security and Social Welfare	1 497
文化、体育和娱乐业	Culture Sports and Entertainment	2 315
公共管理、社会保障和社会组织	Public Management and Social Organizations	10 488
国际组织	International Organization	

1 –6 国民经济主要平均指标
AVERAGE INDICATORS ON NATIONAL ECONOMY

指　标	Indicator	单 位	Unit	2000	2005
人口密度	Density of Population	人/平方公里	person/sq. km	664	695
每户年平均人口	Average Household Size	人	person	3.14	3.12
非私营单位在岗职工年平均工资	The Average Wage of Workers in the Posts in Non-Private Units	元	yuan	10 072	19 086
城市居民人均年可支配收入	Annual Per Capita Disposable Income of Urban Households	元	yuan	8 016	12 920
农民人均年纯收入	Annual Per Capita Net Income of Rural Households	元	yuan	3 637	5 806
每一播亩平均粮食产量	Output of Grain Per Mu of Sowing Area	千克	kg	411	421
每亩蔬菜平均产量	Average Output of Vegetables Per Mu	千克	kg	2 735	2 985
每亩茶叶平均产量	Average Output of Tea Per Mu	千克	kg	8.1	16.5
每亩花生平均产量	Average Output of Peanut Per Mu	千克	kg	298	327
每亩棉花平均产量	Average Output of Cotton Per Mu	千克	kg	83	74
每台拖拉机负担耕地面积	Cultivated Area Ploughed by Per Tractor	亩/台	mu/unit	56	39
每亩耕地施用化肥量（折纯）	Chemical Fertilizer Consumption Per Mu(convert to pure amount)	千克	kg	45	52
每人平均消费品零售额	Per Capita Retail Sales of Consumer Goods	元	yuan	6 077	11 822
城市每天平均生活用水量	Daily Residential Consumption of Water	万吨	10 000 tons	33.33	34.35
城市每人平均公园绿地面积	Per Capita Public Green Areas	平方米	sq. m	8.50	11.82
每万人拥有医疗床位	Number of Hospital Beds per 10000 Population	张	bed	34.5	41.3
每万人拥有医生数	Number of Doctors per 10000 Population	人	person	21.0	20.3
每万人中高等学校学生数	Students Enrollment of Institutions of Higher Education per 10 000 Population	人	person	65	324
每万人中中等学校学生数	Students Enrollment of Secondary Schools per 10 000 Population	人	person	704	768
每万人中小学学生数	Students Enrollment of Primary Schools per 10000 Population	人	person	757	648

2006	2007	2008	2009	2010	2011	2012	2013	2014
703	711	715	676	677	679	682		
3.13	3.14	3.13	3.12	3.1	3.09	3.09		
22 575	26 201	29 404	32 507	37 501	43 077	49 052	55 363	62 104
15 328	17 856	20 464	22 368	24 998	28 567	32 145	35 227	38 294
6 546	7 477	8 509	9 249	10 550	12 370	13 990	15 731	17 461
407	422	436	446	437	444	456	430	435
3 078	3 166	3 511	3 562	3 606	3 759	3 756	3 802	3 786
18.0	21.0	28.0	28	30	30	33	29	30
309	312	315	312	303	313	321	309	299
76	75	78	79	78	87	105	100	111
36	36	36	35	32	31			38
52	55	50	48	47	47			37
13 640	16 137	19 640	22 699	25 694	30 043	34 248	38 606	43 064
29.27	31.25	30.96	33.56	34.31	27.53	33.21	32.50	40.60
11.80	13.30	14.53	14.50	14.58	14.58	14.60	14.60	14.60
38.3	39.7	42.5	43.0	47.2	52.2	61.4	58.0	60.3
20.6	19.8	21.4	21.9	23.2	23.9	28.1	31.2	32.0
347	349	354	361	373	380	386	388	402
740	737	765	740	701	659	635	626	614
646	640	627	610	606	626	630	642	662

1-7 主要年份社会经济主要指标
MAJOR YEAR'S INDICATORS ON SOCIETY AND ECONOMY

指　　标	Indicator	单　位	Unit	2000	2005
人口	**Population**				
总人口(年末)	Population at Year-end	万人	10 000 persons	706.65	740.91
男性人口	Male	万人	10 000 persons	357.74	374.03
女性人口	Female	万人	10 000 persons	348.91	366.87
市区人口	Urban Area	万人	10 000 persons	234.60	265.43
就业	**Employment**				
社会从业人员	Employment	万人	10 000 persons	397.6	471.0
#单位从业人员	Employed Persons in Units	万人	10 000 persons	118.3	224.3
经济总量	**Gross Economic Amount**				
全市生产总值(当年价)	GDP(at current price)	亿元	100 million yuan	1 191.25	2 687.46
第一产业增加值	Primary Industry	亿元	100 million yuan	140.85	178.33
第二产业增加值	Secondary Industry	亿元	100 million yuan	555.21	1 392.02
第三产业增加值	Tertiary Industry	亿元	100 million yuan	495.19	1 117.10
人均生产总值	Per Capita GDP	元	yuan	16 009	33 085
农林牧渔业总产值(当年价)	Gross Output Value of Farming, Forestry, Animal Husbandry and Fishery (at current price)	亿元	100 million yuan	248.33	320.51
工业总产值(当年价)	Gross Industrial Output Value (at current price)	亿元	100 million yuan	1 940.83	5 001.78

注:1. 单位从业人员2004年以前为职工人数(不含私营企业)。
2. 规模以上固定资产投资数据2003年以前为城镇以上统计范围。
3. 2002年以前地方财政一般公共预算收支数据为地方财政收支口径。

Note: 1. Before 2004, the data of employed persons in units refers to the number of staff and workers(excluding private enterprises).
2. Before 2003, the data of investment in fixed assets above designated size refers to urban investment.
3. Before 2002, the data of general budgetaty revenue and expenditure of local government finance refers to revenue and expenditure of local government finance.

2006	2007	2008	2009	2010	2011	2012	2013	2014
749.38	757.99	761.56	762.92	763.64	766.36	769.56		
377.99	381.66	382.46	382.35	381.92	382.69	383.82		
371.39	376.33	379.10	380.56	381.72	383.67	385.74		
270.99	275.55	276.25	275.47	275.50	277.09	279.57		
490.1	505.8	513.8	525.7	540.3	551.2	559.9	571.5	589.0
243.2	249.8	254.1	260.5	269.4	275.9	283.2	293.7	303.0
3 183.18	3 750.16	4 401.56	4 853.87	5 666.19	6 615.60	7 302.11	8 006.56	8 692.10
183.95	203.59	223.40	230.25	276.99	306.38	324.41	340.50	349.62
1 666.96	1 934.52	2 234.83	2 420.14	2 758.62	3 150.72	3 402.23	3 651.39	3 890.41
1 332.28	1 612.05	1 943.33	2 203.48	2 630.58	3 158.50	3 575.47	4 014.67	4 452.07
38 608	44 964	52 266	57 251	65 827	75 563	82 680	89 797	96 524
339.61	342.99	400.85	408.61	483.18	535.93	566.52	611.86	630.04
5 918.81	7 430.64	8 946.73	10 255.62	11 614.83	13 277.96	15 306.32	16 897.18	17 444.21

1 -7 续表 1
continued

指　　标	Indicator	单 位	Unit	2000	2005
财政	**Government Finance**				
一般公共预算收入	General Public Budget Revenue	亿元	100 million yuan	80.01	176.34
一般公共预算支出	General Public Budget Expenditure	亿元	100 million yuan	87.87	203.06
规模以上固定资产投资额	**Investment in Fixed Assets above Designated Size**	**亿元**	**100 million yuan**	**242.68**	**1 403.30**
社会消费品零售额	**Total Retail Sales of Consumer Goods**	**亿元**	**100 million yuan**	**428.29**	**870.11**
港口吞吐量	**Volume of Freight Handled in Ports**	**万吨**	**10 000 tons**	**8 661**	**18 727**
集装箱吞吐量	**Volume of Containers Handled**	**万标箱**	**Ten Thousand TEUs**	**212.0**	**630.7**
民航货邮吞吐量	**Volume of Freight and Mail Handled in Civil Aviation**	**万吨**	**10 000 tons**	**4.84**	**8.91**
对外贸易	**Foreign Trade**				
外贸进出口总额	Imports and Exports (excluding central and provincial companies)	亿美元	100 million USD	108.31	304.55
#出口总额	Exports	亿美元	100 million USD	61.14	175.88
教育、卫生、文化	**Education Public Health, Culture**				
小学在校学生数	Students Enrollment in Primary Schools	万人	10 000 persons	53.49	47.98
普通中学在校学生	Students Enrollment in Regular Secorndary Schools	万人	10 000 persons	39.85	39.11

2006	2007	2008	2009	2010	2011	2012	2013	2014
225.77	292.58	342.44	376.99	452.61	566.14	670.18	788.93	895.25
236.79	321.18	369.41	433.58	532.39	658.06	765.98	1 014.23	1 074.71
1 485.69	**1 635.36**	**2 019.01**	**2 458.89**	**3 022.48**	**3 502.54**	**4 153.91**	**5 027.86**	**5 766.03**
1 016.35	**1 216.22**	**1 492.22**	**1 730.22**	**1 961.13**	**2 302.37**	**2 635.62**	**2 986.81**	**3 361.72**
22 438	**26 507**	**30 029**	**31 668**	**35 012**	**37 971**	**41 465**	**45 782**	**47 701**
770.0	**946.6**	**1 037.7**	**1 027.7**	**1 201**	**1 302**	**1 450**	**1 552**	**1 658**
10.10	**11.57**	**13.05**	**13.54**	**16.37**	**16.65**	**17.19**	**18.62**	**20.44**
365.57	436.05	521.59	439.86	561.49	712.63	732.08	779.12	798.88
216.45	267.76	314.62	269.22	333.51	400.56	408.20	419.86	457.77
48.39	48.48	47.72	46.50	46.27	47.95	49.50	49.63	51.65
36.52	36.04	37.39	37.74	38.00	37.32	36.96	36.51	36.26

1-7 续表2
continued

指　标	Indicator	单位	Unit	2000	2005
高等学校在校学生	Students Enrollment in Institutions of Higher Education	万人	10 000 persons	4.61	23.98
小学专任教师	Full-time Teachers in Primary Schools	万人	10 000 persons	3.17	3.17
普通中学专任教师	Full-time Teachers in Regular Secorndary Schools	万人	10 000 persons	2.63	2.97
影剧院	Cinemas	个	unit	45	39
医生总数	Doctors	万人	10 000 persons	1.49	1.50
医院床位数	Hospital Beds	万张	10 000 beds	2.01	2.86
人民生活	**People's Living Conditions**				
在岗职工工资总额	Total Wage Bill of Employed Staff and Workers	亿元	100 million yuan	120.40	367.84
城市居民人均可支配收入	Per Capita Disposable Income of Urban Households	元	yuan	8 016	12 920
农民人均纯收入	Per Capita Net Income of Rural Households	元	yuan	3 637	5 806
城乡人民币储蓄存款余额	Savings Deposit of Urban and Rural Households	亿元	100 million yuan	535.32	1 343.10
物价指数	**Price Indexes**				
商品零售价格指数(以1950年价格为100)	Retail Price Index(1950 = 100)	%	%	520.5	495.0
居民消费价格指数(以1950年价格为100)	Consumer Price Index(1950 = 100)	%	%	711.9	753.1
#食品价格指数(以1950年价格为100)	Food Price Index(1950 = 100)	%	%	800.1	871.8

注:在岗职工工资总额2005年前统计范围为全部职工不含私营企业。

Note: Before 2005, the statistics range of total wage bill of employed staff and workers is all the staff and workers except those in private enterprises.

2006	2007	2008	2009	2010	2011	2012	2013	2014
26.03	26.49	26.93	27.52	28.49	29.15	29.66	30.02	31.35
3.22	3.26	3.24	3.22	3.2	3.16	3.17	3.28	3.22
2.92	2.96	2.99	3.06	3.08	3.14	3.20	3.18	3.2
40	40	40	40	40	40	36	40	43
1.55	1.50	1.63	1.67	1.77	1.83	2.16	2.41	2.5
2.67	2.81	2.99	3.05	3.34	3.56	4.12	3.97	4.3
454.12	526.74	587.62	646.29	746.2	877.5	1 044.3	1 251.7	1 456.0
15 328	17 856	20 464	22 368	24 998	28 567	32 145	35 227	38 294
6 546	7 477	8 509	9 249	10 550	12 370	13 990	15 731	17 461
1 567.62	1 702.04	2 123.36	2 527.88	2 912.33	3 198.51	3 757.60	4 141	4 436
493.5	506.8	526.6	519.2	526.5	550.2	559.6	567.4	580.5
759.9	794.1	831.4	835.6	854.0	896.7	920.9	943.9	968.4
886.6	989.5	1 105.3	1 123.0	1 194.9	1 327.5	1 384.6	1 458.0	1 522.2

1-8 国民经济主要结构指标
COMPOSITION INDICATORS ON NATIONAL ECONOMY

指　标	Indicator	2000	2005	2006
社会从业人员	**Employment**			
产业结构	Industrial Composition			
第一产业	Primary Industry	36.4	22.2	21.0
第二产业	Secondary Industry	33.9	41.8	42.8
第三产业	Tertiary Industry	29.7	36.0	36.2
全市生产总值	**GDP**			
产业结构	Industrial Composition			
第一产业	Primary Industry	11.8	6.6	5.8
第二产业	Secondary Industry	46.6	51.8	52.4
第三产业	Tertiary Industry	41.6	41.6	41.8
农业	**Agriculture**			
农林牧渔业产值结构	Composition of Farming, Forestry, Animal Husbandry and Fishery			
#农业	Farming	45.0	39.5	40.1
林业	Forestry	0.8	0.8	0.7
牧业	Animal Husbandry	27.9	33.4	31.7
渔业	Fishery	26.4	26.3	25.2
工业	**Industy**			
轻重工业产值结构	Composition of Output Value of Light and Heavy Industry			
轻工业	Light Industry	64.1	49.4	48.5
重工业	Heavy Industry	35.9	50.6	51.5
固定资产投资	**Investment in Fixed Assets**			
投资结构	Composition of Investment			
生产性	Productive	54.0	65.4	62.0
非生产性	Non-productive	46.0	34.6	38.0

单位:%

2007	2008	2009	2010	2011	2012	2013	2014
20.2	19.9	20.1	19.5	19.2	18.8	18.8	18.4
43.1	43.0	41.9	41.4	41.2	41.0	40.6	39.0
36.7	37.1	38.0	39.1	39.6	40.2	40.6	42.6
5.4	5.1	4.7	4.9	4.6	4.4	4.3	4.0
51.6	50.8	49.9	48.7	47.6	46.6	45.6	44.8
43.0	44.1	45.4	46.4	47.8	49.0	50.1	51.2
43.3	44.4	45.4	48.4	44.1	44.0	46.4	47.6
0.6	0.6	0.5	0.4	0.4	0.4	0.4	0.4
28.4	30.3	28.4	26.2	29.1	27.9	26.8	26.3
24.2	21.4	22.0	21.8	23.0	24.2	22.8	21.8
45.0	42.3	41.7	38.7	38.3	39.5	39.5	38.8
55.0	57.7	58.3	61.3	61.7	60.5	60.5	61.2
62.6	61.6	56.3	53.6	53.2	58.4	61.65	57.08
37.4	38.4	43.7	46.4	46.8	41.6	38.35	42.92

1 –9 平均每天主要社会经济活动
SELECTED INDICATORS ON AVERAGE DAILY SOCIAL AND ECONOMIC ACTIVITIES

指　　标	Indicator	单位	Unit	2000	2005
全市生产总值	GDP	万元	10 000 yuan	32 637	73 629
工业总产值	Gross Industrial Output Value	万元	10 000 yuan	53 174	137 035
农林牧渔业总产值	Gross Output Value of Farming, Forestry, Animal Husbandry and Fishery	万元	10 000 yuan	6 803	8 781
主要工业产品产量	Output of Major Industrial Products				
发电量	Electricity	万千瓦时	10 000 kW · h	2 489	2 701
钢材	Rolled-steel	吨	ton	2 558	9 049
纱	Yarn	吨	ton	191	198
布	Cloth	万米	10 000 m	114	141
家用电冰箱	Refrigerator	台	unit	8 523	24 899
彩色电视机	Color TV set	台	unit	10 395	36 282
社会消费品零售总额	Total Retail Sales of Consumer Goods	万元	10 000 yuan	11 734	23 839
固定资产投资	Investment in Fixed Assets above Designated Size	万元	10 000 yuan	6 649	38 446
外贸进出口总额	Imports and Exports	万美元	10 000 USD	3 707	9 047
港口吞吐量	Volume of Freight Handled in Ports	万吨	10 000 tons	23.73	51.31

注:固定资产投资包括城镇、农村500万元以上投资项目。

Note: Investment in fixed assets includes construction projects involving an urban or rural investment of 5,000,000 yuan and over.

2006	2007	2008	2009	2010	2011	2012	2013	2014
87 210	102 744	120 591	132 983	155 238	181 249	200 058	219 359	238 140
162 159	203 579	245 116	280 976	318 215	363 780	419 351	462 936	477 924
9 304	9 397	10 982	11 195	13 238	14 683	15 521	16 763	17 261
3 412	4 255	4 509	4 730	4 984	4 759	4 787	4 935	4 885
10 288	10 015	9 593	9 579	9 136	9 101	7 525	6 312	5 830
154	131	118	106	97	53	53	92	89
151	121	133	85	48	120	134	141	122
35 342	22 173	19 813	22 663	21 951	19 686	15 754	14 366	16 714
33 030	23 989	22 922	29 170	30 444	31 622	39 452	41 426	46 984
27 845	33 321	40 883	47 403	52 130	63 079	72 209	81 831	92 102
40 704	44 804	55 315	67 367	82 808	95 960	113 806	137 751	157 973
12 527	12 527	14 695	12 288	15 633	19 768	20 057	21 346	21 887
61.47	72.62	82.27	86.76	96	104	114	125	131

1－10 主要指标占全国全省比重(2014 年)
PERCENTAGE OF MAIN INDICATORS TO CHINA AND SHANDONG(2014)

指 标	Indicator	单位	Unit
一、生产总值	GDP	亿元	100 million yuan
第一产业	Primary Industry	亿元	100 million yuan
第二产业	Secondary Industry	亿元	100 million yuan
第三产业	Tertiary Industry	亿元	100 million yuan
二、年末总人口(常住人口)	The Total Population (Resident Population) at the End of the Year		
三、主要工业产品产量	Output of Major Industrial Products		
纱	Yarn	万吨	10 000 tons
布	Cloth	亿米	100 million m
家用电冰箱	Refrigerator	万台	10 000 units
彩色电视机	Color TV Set	万部	10 000 units
发电量	Electricity	亿千瓦时	100 million kW · h
钢材	Rolled-steel	万吨	10 000 tons
水泥	Cement	万吨	10 000 tons
四、主要农产品产量	Output of Major Farm Products		
粮食	Grain	万吨	10 000 tons
油料	Oil Plants	万吨	10 000 tons
棉花	Cotton	万吨	10 000 tons
肉类产量	Meat	万吨	10 000 tons
水产品	Aquatic Products	万吨	10 000 tons
五、固定资产投资额	Investment in Fixed Assets	亿元	100 million yuan
六、社会消费品零售总额	Total Retail Sales of Consumer Goods	亿元	100 million yuan
七、高等学校在校学生	Students Enrollment of Institutions of Higher Education	万人	10 000 persons

注:1. 本表全国、全省均为公报数。
2. 青岛市主要工业产品产量数据为本地口径。

Note:1. The number of the country and the province in the table are obtained from the statistical report.
2. The output of main industrial products of qingdao are at local calibre.

全国 China	全省 Shandong	青岛市 Qingdao	青岛市占全国比重(%) Qingdao/China	青岛市占全省比重(%) Qingdao/Shandong
636 463	59 426.6	8 692.1	1.37	14.63
58 332	4 798.4	362.56	0.62	7.56
271 392	28 788.1	3 882.41	1.43	13.49
306 739	25 840.1	4 447.13	1.45	17.21
136 782	9 789.43	904.62	0.66	9.24
3 379.2	855.5	3.23	0.10	0.38
893.7	115.4	4.46	0.50	3.86
8 796.1	620.1	610.07	6.94	98.38
14 128.9	1 784.2	1 714.93	12.14	96.12
56 495.8	3 676.9	178.29	0.32	4.85
112 557.2	8 939.4	212.79	0.19	2.38
248 000	16 406	597.35	0.24	3.64
60 710	4 597	323.02	0.53	7.03
3 517	336	39.80	1.13	11.85
616	67	0.25	0.04	0.37
8 707	758	59.60	0.68	7.86
6 450	867	109.45	1.70	12.62
502 005	41 599.1	5 766.03	1.15	13.86
262 394	24 492	3 361.72	1.28	13.73
2 547.7	179.7	31.35	1.23	17.45

1－11 主要年份全市生产总值(按当年价格计算)

MAJOR YEAR'S GROSS DOMESTIC PRODUCT(AT CURRENT PRICE)

单位:亿元 (100 million yuan)

年 份 Year	全市生产总值 GDP	第一产业 Primary Industry	第二产业 Secondary Industry	#工　业 Industry	第三产业 Tertiary Industry	人均生产总值(元) Per Capita GDP (yuan)
1949	2.87	1.19	1.10	-	0.58	71
1952	6.74	1.76	3.25	2.95	1.73	163
1957	10.82	2.00	5.76	5.39	3.06	239
1962	9.69	1.11	4.68	4.27	3.90	205
1965	15.50	1.80	9.36	8.48	4.74	325
1970	23.23	3.15	14.46	13.86	5.62	451
1975	29.07	6.93	15.39	14.67	6.75	522
1978	38.43	8.73	20.25	19.15	9.45	663
1980	48.65	10.19	26.27	24.28	12.19	819
1985	82.28	21.29	37.55	34.03	23.44	1 311
1988	142.87	32.72	70.32	63.42	39.83	2 199
1989	159.68	30.79	82.03	74.33	46.86	2 426
1990	180.77	39.26	86.76	79.34	54.75	2 714
1991	205.65	43.04	98.94	89.64	63.67	3 053
1992	261.35	43.92	130.27	117.61	87.16	3 856
1993	371.90	62.20	183.35	164.35	126.35	5 455
1994	510.81	85.12	244.30	218.87	181.39	7 436
1995	631.45	112.53	294.43	263.98	224.49	9 089
1996	713.60	133.27	322.33	289.87	258.00	10 130
1997	802.59	117.47	378.25	342.80	306.87	11 235
1998	901.19	140.66	409.60	369.89	350.93	12 443

1-11 续表
continued

年份 Year	全市生产总值 GDP	第一产业 Primary Industry	第二产业 Secondary Industry	#工业 Industry	第三产业 Tertiary Industry	人均生产总值(元) Per Capita GDP (yuan)
1999	1 018.97	138.19	468.67	424.15	412.11	13 884
2000	1 191.25	140.85	555.21	504.44	495.19	16 009
2001	1 368.55	144.35	643.44	582.99	580.76	18 128
2002	1 583.51	147.21	758.33	686.55	677.97	20 655
2003	1 869.44	148.92	923.76	832.31	796.76	23 986
2004	2 270.16	163.49	1 149.94	1 032.50	956.73	28 540
2005	2 687.46	178.33	1 392.02	1 259.06	1 117.10	33 085
2006	3 183.18	183.95	1 666.96	1 517.28	1 332.28	38 608
2007	3 750.16	203.59	1 934.52	1 766.28	1 612.05	44 964
2008	4 401.56	223.40	2 234.83	2 034.25	1 943.33	52 266
2009	4 853.87	230.25	2 420.14	2 174.43	2 203.48	57 251
2010	5 666.19	276.99	2 758.62	2 454.19	2 630.58	65 827
2011	6 615.60	306.38	3 150.72	2 794.56	3 158.50	75 563
2012	7 302.11	324.41	3 402.23	3 041.31	3 575.47	82 680
2013	8 006.56	340.50	3 651.39	3 234.56	4 014.67	89 797
2014	8 692.10	349.62	3 890.41	3 434.97	4 452.07	96 524

注:1. 人均生产总值按常住人口计算。

2. 自2005年起三次产业分类采用《国民经济行业分类》(GB/T4754-2002)标准,自2013年起,根据《国民经济行业分类》(GB/T4754-2011)和《三次产业划分规定》(国统字[2012]108号),将农林牧渔业中的农林牧渔服务业以及工业中的开采辅助活动和金属制品、机械和设备修理业归入第三产业。

Note:1. Per capita GDP are calculated at permanent population.

2. Three Industries are grouped by "Classification and Code of the Sectors of the National Economy" (GB / T4754-2002) since 2005, from 2013 on, According to the Industrial Classification for National Economic Activities (GB/T4754-2011) and the Rules for Classification of Three Industries (NBS No. [2012]108), the service industries of Agriculture, Forestry, Animal Husbandry and Fishery and mining auxiliary activities and metal products, machinery and equipment repair industries in the Industry are classified into the tertiary industry.

1-12 主要年份全市生产总值构成(以全市生产总值为100)

COMPOSITION OF MAJOR YEAR'S GROSS DOMESTIC PRODUCT(GROSS DOMESTIC PRODUCT = 100)

单位:%

年 份 Year	全市生产总值 GDP	第一产业 Primary Industry	第二产业 Secondary Industry	#工 业 Industry	第三产业 Tertiary Industry
1952	100	26.1	48.2	43.8	25.7
1957	100	18.5	53.3	49.8	28.2
1962	100	11.4	48.3	44.1	40.3
1965	100	11.6	57.8	54.7	30.6
1970	100	13.6	62.2	59.7	24.2
1975	100	23.9	52.9	50.5	23.2
1978	100	22.7	52.7	49.8	24.6
1980	100	21.0	54.0	49.9	25.1
1985	100	25.9	45.6	41.4	28.5
1988	100	22.9	49.2	44.4	27.9
1989	100	19.3	51.4	46.6	29.3
1990	100	21.7	48.0	43.7	30.3
1991	100	20.9	48.1	43.6	31.0
1992	100	16.8	49.8	45.0	33.4
1993	100	16.7	49.3	44.2	34.0
1994	100	16.7	47.8	42.8	35.5
1995	100	17.8	46.6	41.8	35.6
1996	100	18.7	45.2	40.6	36.2
1997	100	14.6	47.1	42.7	38.2
1998	100	15.6	45.5	41.0	38.9
1999	100	13.6	46.0	41.6	40.4
2000	100	11.8	46.6	42.3	41.6
2001	100	10.5	47.0	42.6	42.4
2002	100	9.3	47.9	43.4	42.8
2003	100	8.0	49.4	44.5	42.6
2004	100	7.2	50.7	45.5	42.1
2005	100	6.6	51.8	46.8	41.6
2006	100	5.8	52.4	47.7	41.8
2007	100	5.4	51.6	47.1	43.0
2008	100	5.1	50.8	46.2	44.1
2009	100	4.7	49.9	44.8	45.4
2010	100	4.9	48.7	43.3	46.4
2011	100	4.6	47.6	41.5	47.8
2012	100	4.4	46.6	41.6	49.0
2013	100	4.3	45.6	40.4	50.1
2014	100	4.0	44.8	39.5	51.2

1-13 主要年份全市生产总值增长速度(以上年为100)

GROWTH RATE OF MAJOR YEAR'S GROSS DOMESTIC PRODUCT(PRECEDING YEAR=100)

单位:%

年份 Year	全市生产总值 GDP	第一产业 Primary Industry	第二产业 Secondary Industry	第三产业 Tertiary Industry	人均生产总值 Per Capita GDP
1979	12.0	10.6	12.9	11.4	10.4
1980	10.4	4.3	13.1	10.3	9.4
1981	-2.0	-9.1	-2.4	4.7	-3.2
1982	4.1	5.5	-0.2	11.9	2.6
1983	16.9	42.8	9.3	12.7	15.3
1984	13.0	18.9	11.5	10.3	12.0
1985	9.9	5.4	5.8	21.3	9.3
1986	9.2	2.6	12.1	10.0	8.3
1987	12.0	3.6	16.0	12.0	10.6
1988	13.8	-0.3	21.5	11.2	12.1
1989	5.1	-0.8	4.6	9.9	3.8
1990	9.3	9.8	7.3	12.2	8.0
1991	10.6	9.9	11.0	10.5	9.4
1992	18.1	2.7	23.5	20.7	17.4
1993	22.4	20.5	21.1	25.6	21.7
1994	14.4	3.6	14.7	20.2	13.5
1995	12.0	10.9	12.1	12.4	10.8
1996	7.2	7.7	7.6	6.4	5.7
1997	11.5	-10.6	16.8	14.6	9.9
1998	12.9	17.6	11.3	13.4	11.3
1999	13.9	4.1	15.5	15.3	12.4
2000	15.2	6.5	16.4	16.4	13.6

1－13 续表
continued

单位:%

年份 Year	全市生产总值 GDP	第一产业 Primary Industry	第二产业 Secondary Industry	第三产业 Tertiary Industry	人均生产总值 Per Capita GDP
2001	13.7	2.3	16.3	14.2	12.1
2002	14.5	3.2	16.9	14.6	12.7
2003	16.3	2.5	20.1	14.9	14.4
2004	16.7	2.7	20.3	15.2	14.3
2005	16.6	0.4	19.6	15.7	14.1
2006	15.3	0.9	16.8	15.8	13.6
2007	15.5	-2.6	15.3	18.3	14.2
2008	13.2	1.4	11.1	17.1	12.1
2009	12.2	3.0	12.8	12.5	11.4
2010	12.9	1.4	12.6	14.4	11.2
2011	11.7	5.0	11.6	12.4	9.8
2012	10.6	3.2	11.5	10.5	9.7
2013	10.0	2.0	10.1	10.6	9.0
2014	8.0	3.8	8.5	7.9	6.9
1978－2010 平均每年增长 1978－2010 Average Increase Rate	12.4	5.3	13.1	13.9	11.0
1991－2010 平均每年增长 1991－2010 Average Increase Rate	14.2	4.2	15.5	15.3	12.8
1996－2010 平均每年增长 1996－2010 Average Increase Rate	13.8	2.5	15.2	14.5	13.0
2001－2010 平均每年增长 2001－2010 Average Increase Rate	14.7	1.5	16.1	15.2	13.0
2006－2010 平均每年增长 2006－2010 Average Increase Rate	13.8	0.8	13.7	15.6	12.5

1-14 分市、区生产总值(2014 年)
GROSS DOMESTIC PRODUCT BY REGION(2014)

单位:亿元(100 million yuan)

市、区名称	Region	地区生产总值 GDP	第一产业 Primary Industry	第二产业 Secondary Industry	第三产业 Tertiary Industry
市南区	Shinan District	873.72		77.73	795.99
市北区	Shibei District	598.05		122.40	475.65
李沧区	Licang District	302.71		112.25	190.46
崂山区	Laoshan District	478.99	5.53	242.80	230.66
黄岛区	Huangdao District	2 272.20	60.24	1 165.68	1 046.28
保税港区	Qingdao Free Trade Port Area of China	91.29		21.84	69.45
城阳区	Chengyang District	834.66	3.46	461.25	369.95
即墨市	Jimo	1 025.98	59.53	573.46	392.99
胶州市	Jiaozhou	916.17	49.47	494.88	371.82
平度市	Pingdu	733.45	100.66	386.10	246.69
莱西市	Laixi	492.99	59.03	244.32	189.64
红岛经济区	Qingdao National High-tech Industrial Development Zone	76.03	12.92	37.75	25.36

1－15 按支出法计算的全市生产总值(2014 年)
GROSS DOMESTIC PRODUCT BY EXPENDITURE APPROACH(2014)

单位:亿元(100 million yuan)

项　目	Item	2014	2013	2014 年为 2013 年% 2014/2013(%)
支出法计算的全市生产总值	**Gross Domestic Product by Expenditure Approach**	**8 692.10**	**8 006.56**	**108.0**
(一)最终消费	Final Consumption Expenditures	3 009.94	2 740.82	111.1
1.居民消费	Household Consumption Expenditures	2 221.66	2 032.05	111.6
农村居民	Rural Household	386.77	346.72	115.3
城镇居民	Urban Household	1 834.89	1 685.33	110.9
2.政府消费	Government Consumption Expenditures	788.28	708.77	109.6
(二)资本形成总额	Gross Capital Formation	5 323.52	4 842.58	109.5
1.固定资本形成总额	Gross Fixed Capital Formation	5 196.23	4 642.92	111.5
2.存货增加	Change in Inventories	127.30	199.66	64.8
(三)货物和服务净流出	Net Exports of Goods and Services	358.64	423.20	87.8

注:绝对额按当年价格计算,速度按可比价格计算。

Note:The absolute numbers are calculated at current price, their growth are calculated at constant price.

1-16 全市生产总值构成(2014 年)

COMPOSITION OF GROSS DOMESTIC PRODUCT(2014)

指　　标	Indicator	增加值(亿元) Added Value (100 million yuan)	2014 年为 2013 年% 2014/2013(%)
地区生产总值	**GDP**	**8 692.10**	**108.0**
农、林、牧、渔业	Farming, Forestry, A nimal Husbandry and Fishery	362.56	103.9
农、林、牧、渔服务业	Agriculture, Forestry, Animal Husbandry and Fishery Service Industry	12.94	106.0
工业	Industry	3 434.97	108.4
#开采辅助活动	# Mining Auxiliary Activities	0.08	508.3
#金属制品、机械和设备修理业	#Metal Products, Machinery and Equipment Repair Industries	7.06	100.5
建筑业	Construction	462.59	108.9
批发和零售业	Wholesale and Retail Trade	1 068.49	106.2
交通运输、仓储和邮政业	Transport, Storage and Post	620.95	108.6
住宿和餐饮业	Hotels and Catering Services	183.43	107.3
信息传输、软件和信息技术服务业	Information Transmission Computer Services and Soft-war	159.30	110.0
金融业	Financial Intermediation	521.30	109.9
房地产业	Real Estate	441.84	101.9
租赁和商务服务业	Leasing and Business Services	285.82	103.6
科学研究和技术服务业	Scientific Research and Technical Services	142.63	117.1
水利、环境和公共设施管理业	Management of Water Conservancy Environment and Public Facilities	59.53	117.2
居民服务、修理和其他服务业	Services to Households and Other Services	162.82	123.7
教育	Education	262.07	102.7
卫生和社会工作	Health Social Security and Social Welfare	148.59	109.6
文化、体育和娱乐业	Culture Sports and Entertainment	68.78	125.4
公共管理、社会保障和社会组织	Public Management and Social Organizations	306.44	109.3
第一产业	Primary Industry	349.62	103.8
第二产业	Secondary Industry	3 890.41	108.5
第三产业	Tertiary Industry	4 452.07	107.9

主要统计指标解释

国内生产总值(GDP)　指按市场价格计算的一个国家(或地区)所有常住单位在一定时期内生产活动的最终成果。国内生产总值有三种表现形态,即价值形态、收入形态和产品形态。从价值形态看,它是所有常住单位在一定时期内生产的全部货物和服务价值超过同期中间投入的全部非固定资产货物和服务价值的差额,即所有常住单位的增加值之和;从收入形态看,它是所有常住单位在一定时期内创造并分配给常住单位和非常住单位的初次收入分配之和;从产品形态看,它是所有常住单位在一定时期内最终使用的货物和服务价值与货物和服务净出口价值之和。在实际核算中,国内生产总值有三种计算方法,即生产法、收入法和支出法。三种方法分别从不同的方面反映国内生产总值及其构成。对于一个地区来说,称为地区生产总值或地区 GDP。

人均 GDP　人均 GDP 是一定时期内 GDP 与同期人口平均数的比值。按照国际标准,人口平均数应该是同期平均常住人口。我国在核算制度中也规定,无论是国家还是地区,人口数都采用常住人口。国家统计局规定从 2004 年开始,过去采用户籍人口计算人均 GDP 的地区,作为过渡性措施,可在两年内同时计算两种口径的人均 GDP(数据后面必须注明是什么口径),两年后取消按户籍人口计算的人均 GDP。我市采用常住人口计算人均 GDP。

三次产业　是根据社会生产活动历史发展的顺序对产业结构的划分,产品直接取自自然界的部门称为第一产业,对初级产品进行再加工的部门称为第二产业,为生产和消费提供各种服务的部门称为第三产业。它是世界上通用的产业结构分类,但各国的划分不尽一致。我国的三次产业划分是:

第一产业:是指农业、林业、畜牧业、渔业和农林牧渔服务业。

第二产业:是指采矿业,制造业,电力、燃气及水的生产和供应业;建筑业。

第三产业:除第一、第二产业以外的其他行业。

支出法国内生产总值　是从最终使用角度反映一个国家(或地区)一定时期内生产活动最终成果的一种方法,包括最终消费支出,资本形成总额及货物和服务净出口三部分。对于地区,名称为“支出法地区生产总值”。

最终消费　指常住单位为满足物质、文化和精神生活的需要,从本国经济领土和国外购买的货物和服务的支出;不包括非常住单位在本国经济领土内的消费支出。最终消费分为居民消费和政府消费。

居民消费　指常住住户在一定时期内对货物和服务的全部最终消费支出。居民消费支出除了直接以货币形式购买货物和服务的消费之外,还包括以其他方式获得的货物和服务的消费支出,即所谓的虚拟消费支出。居民虚拟消费支出包括以下几种类型:单位以实物报酬及实物转移的形式提供给劳动者的货物和服务;住户生产并由本住户消费了的货物和服务,其中的服务仅指住户的自有住房服务和付酬的家庭雇员提供的家庭和个人服务;金融机构提供的金融媒介服务。

政府消费　指政府部门为全社会提供公共服务的消费支出和免费或以较低价格向居民住户提供的货物和服务的净支出。前者等于政府服务的产出价值减去政府单位所获得的经营收入的价值;后者等于政府部门免费或以较低价格向居民住户提供的货物和服务的市场价值减去向住户收取的价值。

资本形成总额　指常住单位在一定时期内获得的减去处置的固定资产和存货的净额,包括固定资本形成总额和存货增加。

固定资本形成总额　指常住单位在一定时期内获得的固定资产减处置的固定资产的价值总额。固定资产是通过生产活动生产出来的,且使用年限在一年以上、单位价值在规定标准以上的资产,不包括自然资产。分有形固定资产形成总额和无形固定资产形成总额。有形固定资产形成总额包括一定时期内完成的建筑工程、安装工程和设备工器具购置(减处置)价值,以及土地改良、新增役、种、奶、毛、娱乐用牲畜和新增经济林木价值。无形固定资产形成总额包括矿藏的勘探、计算机软件等获得减处置。

存货增加　指常住单位在一定时期内存货实物量变动的市场价值,即期末价值减期初价值的差额,再扣除当期由于价格变动而产生的持有收益。存货增加可以是正值,也可以是负值;正值表示存货上升,负值表示存货下降。它包括生产单位购进的原材料、燃料和储备物资等存货,以及生产单位生产的产成品、在制品和半成品等存货。

货物和服务净出口　指货物和服务出口减货物和服务进口的差额。出口包括常住单位向非常住单位出售或无偿转让的各种货物和服务的价值;进口包括常住单位从非常住单位购买或无偿得到的各种货物和服务的价值。由于服务活动的提供与使用同时发生,一般把常住单位从国外得到的服务作为进口,非常住单位从本国得到的服务作为出口。货物的出口和进口都按离岸价格计算。

气候　指地球与大气之间长期能量交换与质量交换所形成的一种自然环境状态,它是多种因素综合作用的结果。气候既是人类生活和生产的环境要素之一,又是供给人类生活和生产的重要资源。气温、降水、湿度等气象要素的多年平均值是用来描述一个地区气候状况的主要参数,而各种气象要素某年、某月的平均值(或总量)则可以反映出该时期天气气候状况的重要特征。

气温　指空气的温度,我国一般以摄氏度(℃)为单位表示。气象观测的温度表是放在离地面约1.5米处通风良好的百叶箱里测量的,因此,通常说的气温指的是离地面1.5米处百叶箱中的温度。其统计计算方法为:月平均气温是将全月各日的平均气温相加,除以该月的天数而得。

年平均气温　是将12个月的月平均气温累加后除以12而得。

降水量　指从天空降落到地面的液态或固态(经融化后)水,未经蒸发、渗透、流失而在地面上积聚的深度。其统计计算方法为:月降水量是将全月各日的降水量累加而得。年降水量是将12个月的月降水量累加而得。

Explanatory Notes on Main Statistical Indicators

Gross Domestic Product(GDP)　refers to the final products at market prices producted by all resident units in a country(or a region) during a certain period of time. Gross domestic product is expressed in three different persperctives, namely value, income, and products respectively. GDP in its value perspective refers to the total value of all goods and services produced by all resident units during a certain period of time, minus the total value of input of goods and services of the nature of non-fixed assets; in other words, it is the sum of the value-added of all resident units. GDP from the perspective of products refers to the value of all goods and services for final consumption by all resident units minus the net exports of goods and services during a given period of time. In the practice of national accounting, gross domestic product is calculated from three approaches, namely production approach, income approach and expenditure approach, which reflect gross domestic product and its composition from different angles. For a certain region, it refers region gross product or region GDP.

Per Capita GDP　refers to the ratio of GDP in a certain term and average population in the same term. According to the international standard, average population should be average permanent population in the same term. In the account regulation, population of both the country and the region should be permanent population. In the after two yers since 2004, per capita GDP can be calculated at two coverage. i. e. at permanent population and household registered population(the note of coverage should follow the data.) The per capita GDP calculated with household registered population will be abolished after two years. Per capita GDP of Qingdao is calculated at permanent population.

Three Strata of Industries　has been classfied according to the historical sequence of development. Primary industry refers to extraction of natural resources; secondary industry involves processing of primary products; and tertiary industry provides services of various kinds for production and consumption. The above classification is universal although it varies to some extent form country to country. In China economic activities are categorized into the following three strata of industry:

Primary industry refers to farming, forestry, animal husbandryand fishery and services in support of these industries.

Secondary industry refers to mining and quarrying, manufacturing, production and supply of electricity, water and gas, and construction.

Tertiary industry refers to all other economic activities not included in primary or secondary industries.

GDP by Expenditure Approach　refers to the method of measuring the final results of production activities of a country (region) during a given period from the perspective of final use. It includes final consumption, total capital formation and net export of goods and services. It reflects use and composition of gross domestic product. For a certain region, it refers region gross product by expenditure approach.

Final Consumption refers to the total expenditure of resident units for purchases of goods and services from both the domestic economic territory and abroad to meet the needs of material, cultural and spiritual life. It does not include the expenditure of non-resident units on consumption in the economic territory of the country. The final consumption is broken down into household consumption and government consumption.

Household Consumption refers to the total expenditure of resident households on the final consumption of goods and services. In addition to the consumption of goods and services bought by the households directly with money, the household consumption also includes expenditure on goods and services obtained by the households in other ways, i. e. the so-called imputed consumption, which includes the following: (a) the goods and services provided to households by employers in the form of payment in kind and transfer in kind; (b) goods and services produced and consumed by the households themselves, in which the services refer to the owner-occupied housing and services offered by payed family employees; (c) financial intermediate services provided by financial institution.

Government Consumption refers to the consumption expenditure spent for the provision of public services provided by the government to the whole country and the net expenditure on the goods and services provided by the government to households free of charge or at reduced prices. The former equals to the output value of the government services minus the value of operating income obtained by the government departments. The latter equals to the market value of the goods and services provided by the government free of charge or at reduced prices to the households minus the value received by the government from the households.

Gross Capital Formation refers to the fixed assets acquired less disposal and the net value of inventory, thus including the gross fixed capital formation and charges in inventories.

Gross Fixed Capital Formation refers to the value of acquisitions less those disposals of fixed assets during a given period. Fixed assets are the assets produced through production activities with unit value above a specified amount and which could be used for over one year. Natural assets are not included. Gross fixed capital formation can be categorized into total tangible fixed capital formation and total intangible fixed capital formation. Total tangible fixed capital formation includes the value of the construction projects and installation projects completed and the equipment, apparatus and instruments purchased (less those disposed) as well as the value of land improved, the value of draught animals, breeding stock and animals for milk, for wool and for recreational purposes and the newly increased forest with economic value. Total intangible fixed capital formation includes the prospecting of minerals and the acquisition of computer software minus the disposal of them.

Charges in Inventories refers to the market value of the change in the physical volume of inventory of resident units during a given period, i. e. the difference between the values at the beginning and at the end of the period minus the gains due to the change in prices. The changes in inventories can have a positive or a negative value. A positive value indicates an increase in inventory while a negative value indicates a decrease in inventory. The inventory includes raw materials, fuels and reserve materials purchased by the production units as well as the inventory of finished products, semi-finished products and work-in-progress.

Net Export of Goods and Services refers to the exports of goods and services subtracting the imports of goods and services. Exports include the value of various goods and services sold or gratuitously transferred by resident units to non-resident units. Imports include the value of various goods and services purchased or gratuitously acquired resident units from non-resident units. Because the provision of services and the use of them happen simultaneously, the acquisition of services by resident units from abroad is usually treated as import while the acquisition of services by non-resident units in this country is usually treated as export. The exports and imports of goods are calculated at FOB.

Climate refers to the natural environmental status formed by the long-term exchange of energy and mass between the earth and the air, and is the results of interaction of many factors. Climate is both one of the environment factors and the important resources for the living and production activities of the human being. The average values across several years of meteorological factors such as temperature, rainfall and humidity are used as important parameters to describe the climate of a region, while the average values (or total values) of a given year or month of meteorological factors reflect the key characteristics of climate for that period of time.

Temperature refers to the air temperature. China uses centigrade as the unit. The thermometry used for weather observation is put in a breezy shutter, which is 1.5 meters high from the ground. Therefore, the commonly used temperature refers to the temperature in the breezy shutter 1.5 meters away from the ground. The calculation method is as follows:

Monthly average temperature is the summation of average daily temperature of one month divided by the actual days of that particular month.

Annual average temperature is the summation of monthly average of a year divided by 12 months.

Volume of Precipitation refers to the deepness of liquid state or solid state (thawed) water falling from the sky to the ground that has not been evaporated, infiltrated or run off. The calculation method is as follows:

Monthly precipitation is the summation of daily precipitation of a month.

Annual precipitation is the summation of 12 months precipitation of a year.

人　口 2

POPULATION

简要说明

一、本篇资料的主要内容

本篇资料主要反映了全市人口方面的基本情况，包括全市主要年份和区（市）的户数、人口数、人口密度、土地面积数据、人口出生率、死亡率、自然增长率、计划生育等数据。另外还对建国以来开展的六次人口普查主要数据进行了比较。

二、本篇资料的来源

本篇资料分别来源于国家开展的人口普查、人口抽样调查和市公安局的户籍登记资料，由市统计局人口和社会科技统计处整理提供。

Brief Introduction

I. Main Content

Data in this chapter show the basic condition of population, such as the basic condition of districts and county-level cities, household, population, density of population, birth rate, death rate, natural growth rate and family planning situation. Furthermore, relevant figures obtained from the six national population censuses have been compared.

II. Source of Data

Data in this chapter are from national population censuses, national sample survey. Some are derived from household registration provided by Qingdao Municipal Bureau of Public Security. The data are compiled by the Division of Population and Science & Technology of Qingdao Municipal Bureau of Statistics.

2-1 主要年份全市户籍人口数
MAJOR YEAR'S TOTAL REGISTERED POPULATION

单位：人(person)

年　份 Year	总人口 Total Population	按性别分 Grouped by Sex 男 Male	 女 Female	平均人口 Average Population
1949	4 056 550	1 997 293	2 059 257	4 054 431
1952	4 233 586	2 125 392	2 108 194	4 203 428
1957	4 822 756	2 424 729	2 398 027	4 773 862
1962	4 627 432	2 319 658	2 307 774	4 578 313
1965	4 901 670	2 461 629	2 440 041	4 859 712
1970	5 391 852	2 720 633	2 671 219	5 337 282
1975	5 742 206	2 904 347	2 837 859	5 717 456
1978	5 853 321	2 959 800	2 893 521	5 841 638
1980	5 961 129	3 015 357	2 945 772	5 937 187
1985	6 267 223	3 185 409	3 081 814	6 253 157
1988	6 516 920	3 319 534	3 197 386	6 474 541
1989	6 571 597	3 348 454	3 223 143	6 544 259
1990	6 666 482	3 392 253	3 274 229	6 619 040
1991	6 709 277	3 411 776	3 297 501	6 687 880
1992	6 731 072	3 420 886	3 310 186	6 720 175
1993	6 753 497	3 431 149	3 322 348	6 742 285
1994	6 785 291	3 446 019	3 339 272	6 769 394
1995	6 846 346	3 476 300	3 370 046	6 815 819
1996	6 902 677	3 502 600	3 400 077	6 874 512
1997	6 954 391	3 527 588	3 426 803	6 928 534
1998	6 995 666	3 545 403	3 450 263	6 975 029
1999	7 029 707	3 561 061	3 468 646	7 012 687
2000	7 066 481	3 577 367	3 489 114	7 048 094
2001	7 104 875	3 595 652	3 509 223	7 085 678
2002	7 156 537	3 619 778	3 536 759	7 130 706
2003	7 206 806	3 644 032	3 562 774	7 181 672
2004	7 311 228	3 692 991	3 618 237	7 259 017
2005	7 409 052	3 740 309	3 668 743	7 360 140
2006	7 493 812	3 779 891	3 713 921	7 451 432
2007	7 579 910	3 816 620	3 763 290	7 536 861
2008	7 615 647	3 824 665	3 790 982	7 597 779
2009	7 629 161	3 823 534	3 805 627	7 622 404
2010	7 636 392	3 819 240	3 817 152	7 632 777
2011	7 663 612	3 826 931	3 836 681	7 650 002
2012	7 695 585	3 838 205	3 857 380	7 679 599

注：截止出书前，未获得公安部门青岛市 2013 年和 2014 年户籍人口信息。

Note: Data come from the Qingdao Nunicipal Public Security Bureau, and the Data of 2013 and 2014 are absent.

2-2 主要年份全市户数、人口数、人口密度(户籍)

MAJOR YEAR'S HOUSEHOLDS, POPULATION AND DENSITY OF POPULATION(WITH PERMANENT RESIDENCE)

年 份 Year	总户数(万户) Total Households (10000 households)		总人口(万人) Total Population (10000 persons)		平均每户人口(人) Average Persons Per Household(person)		人口密度(人/平方公里) Density of Population (person/sq. km)	
	全市 Whole Municipality	市区 Urban Area	全市 Whole Municipality	市区 Urban Area	全市 Whole Municipality	市区 Urban Area	全市 Whole Municipality	市区 Urban Area
1949	90.64	21.68	405.66	103.69	4.48	4.78	381	941
1952	93.96	22.70	423.36	107.62	4.51	4.74	397	977
1957	102.56	27.41	482.28	134.76	4.70	4.92	453	1 223
1962	106.11	29.29	462.74	137.86	4.36	4.71	434	1 251
1965	105.31	29.64	490.17	146.74	4.65	4.95	460	1 332
1970	113.07	32.14	539.19	150.81	4.77	4.69	506	1 369
1975	123.18	36.56	574.22	161.13	4.66	4.41	539	1 462
1978	131.27	40.08	585.33	168.00	4.46	4.19	549	1 525
1980	138.44	43.03	596.11	175.27	4.31	4.07	560	1 591
1985	157.06	53.43	626.72	190.87	3.99	3.57	588	1 732
1988	169.72	58.95	651.69	201.38	3.84	3.42	612	1 827
1989	177.47	61.57	657.16	203.63	3.70	3.31	617	1 848
1990	186.79	63.94	666.65	205.78	3.57	3.22	626	1 867
1991	192.46	67.15	670.93	207.22	3.49	3.09	630	1 880
1992	199.08	68.94	673.11	209.28	3.38	3.04	632	1 899
1993	201.36	70.13	675.35	212.06	3.35	3.02	634	1 924
1994	204.05	71.24	678.53	214.97	3.33	3.02	637	1 951
1995	208.13	72.53	684.63	218.38	3.29	3.01	643	1 982
1996	212.40	75.11	690.27	223.86	3.25	2.98	648	2 032
1997	215.12	76.39	695.44	227.22	3.23	2.97	653	2 062
1998	218.59	77.90	699.57	229.58	3.20	2.95	657	2 084
1999	222.61	79.27	702.97	231.94	3.16	2.93	660	2 105
2000	224.73	80.46	706.65	234.60	3.14	2.92	664	2 129
2001	227.43	81.41	710.49	237.60	3.12	2.92	667	2 156
2002	229.67	82.85	715.65	241.74	3.12	2.92	672	2 194
2003	232.26	84.15	720.68	246.77	3.10	2.93	677	2 240
2004	235.29	86.93	731.12	258.40	3.11	2.97	686	2 229
2005	237.35	87.99	740.91	265.43	3.12	3.02	695	2 290
2006	239.33	89.12	749.38	271.00	3.13	3.04	703	2 338
2007	241.55	90.21	757.99	275.55	3.14	3.05	711	2 377
2008	243.18	91.22	761.56	276.25	3.13	3.03	715	2 384
2009	244.74	92.15	762.92	275.47	3.12	2.99	676	1 873
2010	246.11	93.30	763.64	275.50	3.10	2.95	677	1 873
2011	247.94	94.69	766.36	277.09	3.09	2.93	679	1 884
2012	249.27	95.87	769.56	279.57	3.09	2.92	682	1 901

2-3 主要年份全市常住人口数
MAJOR YEAR'S TOTAL RESIDENT POPULATION

单位:万人(10000 persons)

年份 Year	总人口 Total Population
2005	819.55
2006	829.42
2007	838.67
2008	845.61
2009	850.03
2010	871.51
2011	879.51
2012	886.85
2013	896.41
2014	904.62

2-4 青岛市常住人口(2014年底)
TOTAL RESIDENT POPULATION(END OF 2014)

市、区名称	Region	2014	2013	2014年比2013年±% 2014/2013(±%)
全市	**Whole Municipality**	**904.62**	**896.41**	**0.92**
市南区	Shinan District	56.74	56.05	1.23
市北区	Shibei District	106.9	105.92	0.93
李沧区	Licang District	54.14	53.56	1.08
崂山区	Laoshan District	42.75	41.89	2.05
黄岛区	Huangdao District	148.42	146.37	1.40
城阳区	Chengyang District	68.8	67.83	1.43
即墨市	Jimo	119.42	118.73	0.58
胶州市	Jiaozhou	87.1	86.37	0.85
平度市	Pingdu	135.44	135.09	0.26
莱西市	Laixi	75.07	74.83	0.32
红岛经济区	Qingdao National High-tech Industrial Development Zone	9.84	9.77	0.72

2－5 分市、区土地面积(2012年底)
LAND AREA(END OF 2012)

市、区名称	Region	土地面积 Land Area	
		面积(平方公里) Area(sq. km)	比重(%) Percentage(%)
总　计	**Total**	**11 282**	**100.00**
市　区	Urban Area	1 471	13.03
即墨市	Jimo	1 921	17.03
胶州市	Jiaozhou	1 324	11.74
原胶南市	Original Jiaonan	1 822	16.15
平度市	Pingdu	3 176	28.15
莱西市	Laixi	1 568	13.90

注:土地面积为第二次全国土地调查数据。
Note:Data on land area are based on the data of the Second China Land Census.

2-6 第一、二、三、四、五、六次人口普查主要数据

MAIN DATA FROM THE SIX NATIONAL POPULATION CENSUSES

项　目	Item	第一次人口普查 1st National Population Census	第二次人口普查 2nd National Population Census	第三次人口普查 3rd National Population Census	第四次人口普查 4th National Population Census	第五次人口普查 5th National Population Census	第六次人口普查 6th National Population Census
一、总人口（万人）	**Total Population (10000 persons)**	**91.68**	**138.34**	**422.76**	**666.40**	**749.42**	**871.51**
按性别分	By Sex						
男（万人）	Male(10000 persons)	48.44	69.64	214.09	338.86	375.74	439.18
女（万人）	Female(10000 persons)	43.24	68.71	208.67	327.54	373.68	432.33
二、总户数（万户）	**Total Household (10000 households)**	**19.27**	**28.01**	**101.41**	**186.61**	**241.62**	**296.64**
家庭户（万户）	Family Household (10000 households)			101.09	185.56	232.70	282.43
平均家庭户规模（人）	Average Family Household Size(person)			4.07	3.49	2.97	2.79
三、民　族	**Ethnicity**						
民族个数（个）	Number of Ethnic Groups (unit)	14	16	25	41	51	53
汉族人口（万人）	Population of Han (10000 persons)	91.33	137.76	422.09	665.58	746.12	863.84
少数民族人口（万人）	Populaiton of Ethnic Minorities(10000 persons)	0.36	0.58	0.67	0.82	3.3	7.67
四、各种文化程度人口	**Popution with Various Education Attainments**						
大学（万人）	College(10000 persons)		1.51	3.62	12.39	41.64	129.54
高中（万人）	Senior Secondary School (10000 persons)		4.86	34.82	68.42	111.40	150.82
初中（万人）	Junior Secondary School (10000 persons)		13.72	102.28	195.10	281.91	334.22
小学（万人）	Primary School (10000 persons)		51.25	144.52	236.34	206.91	170.77

2-7 计划生育情况(1978-2014年)
FAMILY PLANNING SITUATION(1978-2014)

年 份 Year	已婚有生育能力的人数(人) Married and Fertile Persons(person)	节育人数(人) Persons under Birth Control(person)	节育率(%) Contraceptive Prevalence Rate(%)	四项手术人数(人) Persons Performed Four-operation(person)	#放环人数 Persons Set Rings
1978	694 292	571 077	82.25	125 913	68 475
1980	763 226	673 069	88.19	180 979	70 927
1985	1 017 649	929 284	91.32	146 742	67 234
1990	1 258 232	1 165 216	92.61	149 327	70 964
1991	1 319 722	1 219 795	92.43	153 970	77 406
1992	1 348 503	1 256 271	93.16	90 107	56 226
1993	1 380 717	1 271 884	92.12	76 783	45 492
1994	1 400 425	1 268 378	90.57	73 169	41 482
1995	1 427 442	1 285 264	90.04	84 099	52 716
1996	1 459 465	1 316 516	90.21	84 370	57 648
1997	1 482 204	1 340 399	90.43	76 579	55 285
1998	1 505 499	1 367 648	90.84	74 199	50 526
1999	1 523 471	1 378 131	90.46	73 663	44 976
2000	1 521 331	1 371 447	90.15	74 285	45 999
2001	1 514 274	1 360 543	89.85	70 205	43 601
2002	1 541 855	1 400 145	90.81	50 575	45 453
2003	1 518 448	1 354 917	89.23	57 458	47 953
2004	1 540 706	1 357 703	88.04	52 934	42 859
2005	1 590 476	1 417 755	89.14	58 097	49 716
2006	1 604 665	1 427 785	88.98	51 864	42 457
2007	1 595 390	1 426 787	89.43	50 074	41 198
2008	1 587 344	1 410 426	88.85	120 539	93 291
2009	1 623 969	1 418 178	87.33	111 084	100 193
2010	1 591 103	1 377 726	86.59	78 721	51 794
2011	1 581 231	1 355 808	85.74	70 823	48 210
2012	1 575 996	1 349 572	85.63	62 880	43 021
2013	1 527 731	1 293 810	84.69	53 252	30 851
2014	1 506 274	1 275 142	84.66	34 008	12 827

2 -8 分市、区计划生育情况(2014 年)
FAMILY PLANNING SITUATION BY REGION(2014)

市、区名称	Region	计划生育率(%) Fertility Rate(%)	计划内出生(人) Birth within the Plan(person)		计划外出生(人) Birth without the Plan(person)		多胎(人) Third Birth and Above (person)
			一胎 First Birth	二胎 Second Birth	一胎 First Birth	二胎 Second Birth	
全市	**Whole Municipality**	**97.08**	**63 947**	**29 069**	**214**	**2081**	**504**
市南区	Shinan District	98.50	6 181	1 043	11	89	10
市北区	Shibei District	97.67	8 303	1 287	18	196	15
李沧区	Licang District	96.72	3 210	532	5	112	10
崂山区	Laoshan District	98.55	2 435	821	0	42	6
黄岛区	Huangdao District	95.66	10 230	4 599	37	543	93
城阳区	Chengyang District	98.32	4 677	2 068	5	91	19
即墨市	Jimo	97.40	7 961	5 343	26	243	86
胶州市	Jiaozhou	97.29	5 790	4 021	26	190	57
平度市	Pingdu	96.04	9 778	5 944	62	421	166
莱西市	Laixi	97.56	5 382	3 411	24	154	42
红岛经济区	Qingdao National High-tech Industrial Development Zone						

主要统计指标解释

人口数　指一定时点、一定地区范围内有生命的个人总和。

出生率(又称粗出生率)　指在一定时期内(通常为一年)一定地区的出生人数与同期内平均人数(或期中人数)之比,用千分率表示。本资料中的出生率指年出生率,其计算公式为:

$$出生率=\frac{年出生人数}{年平均人数}\times 1000‰$$

式中:出生人数指活产婴儿,即胎儿脱离母体时(不管怀孕月数),有过呼吸或其他生命现象。

死亡率(又称粗死亡率)　指在一定时期内(通常为一年)一定地区的死亡人数与同期内平均人数(或期中人数)之比,用千分率表示。本资料中的死亡率指年死亡率,其计算公式为:

$$死亡率=\frac{年死亡人数}{年平均人数}\times 1000‰$$

人口自然增长率　指在一定时期内(通常为一年)人口自然增加数(出生人数减死亡人数)与该时期内平均人数(或期中人数)之比,用千分率表示。计算公式为:

$$人口自然增长率=\frac{本年出生人数-本年死亡人数}{年平均人数}\times 1000‰$$
$$=人口出生率-人口死亡率$$

Explanatory Notes on Main Statistical Indicators

Total Population　refers to the total number of people alive at a certain point of time within a given area.

Birth Rate (or Crude Birth Rate)　refers to the ratio of the number of births to the average population (or mid-period population) during a certain period of time (usually a year), expressed in ‰. Birth rate in the chapter refers to annual birth rate. The following formula is used:

Birth Rate = (Number of Births/Average Number of Population) × 1000‰

Number of births in the formula refers to live births, i. e. when a baby has breathed or showed any vital phenomena regardless of the length of pregnancy.

Annual average number of population is the average of the number of population at the beginning of the year and that at the end of the year. Sometimes it is substituted by the mid-year population.

Death Rate (or Crude Death Rate)　refers to the ratio of the number of deaths to the average population (or mid-period population) during a certain period of time (usually a year), expressed in ‰. Death rate in the chapter refers to annual death rate. The following formula is used:

Death Rate = (Number of Deaths/Annual Average Number of Population) × 1000‰

Natural Growth Rate of Population　refers to the ratio of natural increase in population (number of births minus number of deaths) in a certain period of time (usually a year) to the average population (or mid-period population) of the same period, expressed in ‰. The following formula is applied:

Natural Growth Rate of Population = [(Number of Births-Number of Deaths)/Average Number of Population] × 1000‰

Natural Growth Rate of Population = Birth Rate-Death Rate

3 从业人员及职工工资

EMPLOYMENT AND WAGES

简要说明

一、本篇资料的主要内容

本篇资料主要反映了全市从业人员和职工工资方面的基本情况，主要包括全市社会从业人数及各区（市）单位从业人数、在岗职工工资总额和平均工资等方面的资料。

二、本篇资料的来源

单位从业人员和职工工资来源于劳动统计年报，全市从业人员根据劳动统计年报、农村年报和市工商行政管理局、市人力资源和社会保障局、市交通委相关资料测算。由市统计局人口和社会科技统计处整理提供。

Brief Introduction

I. Main Content

Data in this chapter show the basic conditions of Qingdao's employment and wages, including the main data on labor statistics of employment, number of employment of the whole city and 10 district and county-level cities, total wage bill and average wage of staff and workers, etc.

II. Source of Data

Data on employment and wages are prepared according to the annual reports of labor statistics.Data on social employment are measured according to the annual reports of labor statistics,countryside statistics and related information from Industry & Commerce Administration Bureau,Human Resources & Social Security Bureau and Transportation Commision.

Data in this chapter are compiled by the Division of Population and Science & Technology of Qingdao Municipal Bureau of Statistics.

3 -1 社会从业人数(1978 -2014 年)
SOCIAL EMPLOYMENT(1978 -2014)

单位:万人(10 000 persons)

年 份 Year	合 计 Total	第一产业 Primary Industry	第二产业 Secondary Industry	第三产业 Tertiary Industry
1978	256.70	157.40	65.60	33.70
1979	265.60	156.10	72.20	37.30
1980	270.10	153.60	82.10	43.20
1981	278.90	153.60	82.10	43.20
1982	282.70	151.10	86.20	45.40
1983	289.60	156.40	85.00	48.10
1984	304.20	149.20	97.70	57.40
1985	315.30	149.20	104.50	61.70
1986	326.40	149.90	112.10	64.60
1987	334.80	149.90	120.20	64.70
1988	336.50	147.60	123.20	65.70
1989	344.20	152.50	122.10	69.60
1990	352.80	156.50	123.30	73.10
1991	361.20	161.90	124.30	74.90
1992	370.30	161.70	127.80	80.80
1993	365.70	160.50	128.80	76.40
1994	367.60	157.10	129.40	81.20
1995	374.20	155.40	132.40	86.40
1996	381.50	152.20	137.10	92.20
1997	388.70	155.20	138.10	95.30
1998	393.10	154.80	138.60	99.70
1999	396.10	150.30	142.00	103.80
2000	397.60	144.70	134.91	117.99
2001	400.50	133.90	142.30	124.30
2002	413.31	121.38	153.85	138.08
2003	438.96	119.91	163.93	155.12
2004	458.81	113.98	180.63	164.20
2005	471.03	104.48	196.80	169.75
2006	490.10	102.97	209.83	177.30
2007	505.80	102.30	217.80	185.70
2008	513.80	102.40	220.80	190.60
2009	525.71	105.65	220.33	199.73
2010	540.34	105.16	223.85	211.33
2011	551.18	106.02	227.08	218.08
2012	559.88	104.95	229.79	225.14
2013	571.47	107.59	232.17	231.71
2014	588.97	108.45	229.91	250.61

3-2 主要年份全市单位从业人员人数

MAJOR YEAR'S NUMBER OF EMPLOYED PERSONS IN ALL UNITS OF THE CITY

单位:万人(10 000 persons)

年份 Year	合计 Total	#市区 Urban Area	#国有单位 State-owned Units	#集体单位 Collective-owned Units	其他所有制单位 Other Ownership Units
1949	14.8	13.4	9.3	5.5	
1952	23.4	20.1	18.3	5.1	
1957	29.7	24.5	24.1	5.6	
1962	32.3	26.8	24.5	7.8	
1965	36.7	30.6	26.8	9.9	
1970	45.6	37.4	32.2	13.4	
1975	53.4	43.5	38.0	15.4	
1978	70.7	54.5	49.2	21.5	
1980	79.2	61.5	55.0	24.2	
1985	88.8	66.7	59.8	28.9	0.1
1988	98.2	70.0	66.7	31.2	0.3
1989	99.2	70.4	67.7	31.0	0.5
1990	103.2	70.6	69.5	32.9	0.8
1991	105.4	78.4	71.5	32.5	1.4
1992	108.2	80.4	73.6	32.8	1.8
1993	109.4	80.8	75.3	29.5	4.6
1994	110.1	80.2	72.4	28.3	9.4
1995	111.6	80.2	72.4	27.5	11.7
1996	118.4	81.1	71.6	26.0	20.8
1997	117.1	78.1	69.0	22.6	25.5
1998	116.2	75.6	64.2	19.0	33.0
1999	119.0	78.3	60.4	16.6	42.0
2000	118.3	76.6	57.6	14.2	46.5
2001	117.5	75.1	53.2	12.2	52.1
2002	119.1	75.2	49.5	10.3	59.3
2003	118.0	74.3	47.2	8.9	61.9
2004	207.1	111.1	43.7	18.0	145.4
2005	224.3	122.3	43.9	18.2	162.2
2006	243.2	133.7	41.7	16.2	185.3
2007	249.8	137.3	45.1	17.9	186.8
2008	254.1	140.9	44.4	15.4	194.3
2009	260.5	145.6	44.4	14.6	201.5
2010	269.4	151.1	44.6	15.1	209.7
2011	275.9	156.5	44.3	14.7	216.9
2012	283.2	162.1	44.0	13.8	225.4
2013	293.7	184.1	37.8	5.4	250.5
2014	303.0	191.4	36.7	4.9	261.4

注:1. 2004 年以前为城镇单位职工人数。

2. 2013 年统计口径变化,国有单位、集体单位数据与上年不可比。

Note:1. Before 2004, the data refer to number of staff and workers in urban units.

2. Because of the adjustment about the statistics system, the data of State-owned Units and Collective-owned Units since 2013 are not fully comparable with historical statistics.

3-3 全市单位国民经济各行业从业人员人数(2014年)

NUMBER OF EMPLOYED PERSONS IN ALL UNITS OF THE CITY BY SECTOR(2014)

单位:万人(10 000 persons)

		2014		2013	
		合计 Total	女性 Female	合计 Total	女性 Female
总计	**Total**	**303.0**	**122.1**	**293.7**	**109.8**
1. 农、林、牧、渔业	Farming, Forestry, Animal Husbandry and Fishery	1.3	0.6	0.7	0.2
2. 采矿业	Mining	0.2		0.4	
3. 制造业	Manufacturing	146.3	61.7	146.1	58.1
4. 电力、热力、燃气及水生产和供应业	The Electricity, Heat, Gas and Water Production and Supply Industry	2.9	0.7	2.5	0.6
5. 建筑业	Construction	25.2	3.5	28.8	4.6
6. 批发和零售业	Wholesale and Retail Trade	40.8	18.7	37.2	15.0
7. 交通运输、仓储和邮政业	Transport, Storage and Post	13.0	3.9	13.8	4.0
8. 住宿和餐饮业	Hotels and Catering Services	5.7	3.2	5.2	2.6
9. 信息传输、软件和信息技术服务业	Information Transmission Computer Services and Software	4.2	1.3	3.8	1.4
10. 金融业	Financial Intermediation	5.5	2.9	4.1	2.1
11. 房地产业	Real Estate	7.3	2.8	5.5	2.2
12. 租赁和商务服务业	Leasing and Business Services	10.5	3.8	7.3	2.4
13. 科学研究和技术服务业	Scientific Research and Technical Services	5.0	1.8	4.2	1.3
14. 水利、环境和公共设施管理业	Management of Water Conservancy, Environment and Public Facilities	2.9	1.0	2.3	0.7
15. 居民服务、修理和其他服务业	Residents Service, Repair and Other Services	2.1	1.1	2.8	0.8
16. 教育	Education	12.9	7.3	13.0	6.9
17. 卫生和社会工作	Health and Social Welfare	6.3	4.3	5.8	3.9
18. 文化、体育和娱乐业	Culture, Sports and Entertainment	1.5	0.7	1.5	0.6
19. 公共管理、社会保障和社会组织	Public Management, Social Security and Social Organization	9.4	2.8	8.7	2.4

3－4 全市单位分市、区国民经济各行业从业人员人数(2014 年)

NUMBER OF EMPLOYED PERSONS IN ALL UNITS OF THE CITY BY REGION AND SECTOR (2014)

市、区名称	Region	合计 Total	农林牧渔业 Farming, Forestry, Animal Husbandry and Fishery	采矿业 Mining	制造业 Manufacturing	电力热力燃气及水生产和供应业 The Electricity, Heat, Gas and Water Production and Supply Industry
全市	**Whole Municipality**	**303.0**	**1.3**	**0.2**	**146.3**	**2.9**
市内三区	The Three Districts of Qingdao City	73.8	0.04		14.4	0.9
崂山区	Laoshan District	22.7	0		6.8	0.1
黄岛区	Huangdao District	53.7	0.49		25.0	0.6
城阳区	Chengyang District	36.1	0.15		24.4	0.1
即墨市	Jimo	34.9	0.06		24.6	0.2
胶州市	Jiaozhou	33.7			21.1	0.2
平度市	Pingdu	19.3	0.14	0.1	12.4	0.5
莱西市	Laixi	23.7	0.44	0.1	13.7	0.3
红岛经济区	Qingdao National High-tech Industrial Development Zone	3.2			2.8	
保税港区	Qingdao Free Trade Port Area of China	1.9			1.1	

单位:万人(10 000 persons)

建筑业 Construction	批发和零售业 Wholesale and Retail Trade	交通运输仓储及邮政业 Transport, Storage and Post	住宿和餐饮业 Hotels and Catering Services	信息传输软件和信息技术服务业 Information Transmission Computer Services and Software
25.2	**40.8**	**13.0**	**5.7**	**4.2**
5.7	14.9	6.7	3.2	2.7
4.3	4.0	0.7	0.5	0.6
5.4	6.9	3.3	0.9	0.9
1.5	3.1	1.2	0.5	
2.5	2.5	0.2	0.3	
3.2	4.0	0.4	0.1	
0.8	1.5	0.1	0.1	
1.8	3.3	0.2	0.1	
0.0				
0.0	0.6	0.2		

3-4 续表
Continued

市、区名称	Region	金融业 Financial Intermediation	房地产业 Real Estate	租赁和商务服务业 Leasing and Business Services	科学研究和技术服务业 Scientific Research and Technical Services	水利环境和公共设施管理业 Management of Water Conservancy, Environment and Public Facilities
全市	**Whole Municipality**	**5.5**	**7.3**	**10.5**	**5.0**	**2.9**
市内三区	The Three Districts of Qingdao City	3.9	2.1	5.0	2.0	1.3
崂山区	Laoshan District	0.1	1.1	1.1	1.0	0.1
黄岛区	Huangdao District	0.3	1.4	1.8	1.0	0.3
城阳区	Chengyang District	0.4	0.5	1.7	0.1	0.2
即墨市	Jimo	0.3	0.4	0.3	0.1	0.4
胶州市	Jiaozhou	0.3	0.8	0.4	0.2	0.1
平度市	Pingdu	0.1	0.3		0.4	0.3
莱西市	Laixi	0.1	0.6	0.1	0.2	0.2
红岛经济区	Qingdao National High-tech Industrial Development Zone		0.1	0.1		
保税港区	Qingdao Free Trade Port Area of China					

单位:万人(10 000 persons)

居民服务其他服务业 Services to Households and Other Services	教育 Education	卫生和社会工作 Health and Social Welfare	文化体育和娱乐业 Culture, Sports and Entertainment	公共管理社会保障和社会组织 Public Management, Social Security and Social Organization	国际组织 International Organization
2.1	**12.9**	**6.3**	**1.5**	**9.4**	
0.3	3.9	3.1	0.6	3.1	
0.5	0.6	0.2	0.3	0.7	
0.5	2.5	0.7	0.2	1.5	
0.2	0.9	0.4	0.1	0.6	
	1.3	0.5	0.1	1.1	
	1.5	0.6	0.1	0.7	
	1.4	0.4		0.8	
0.6	0.8	0.4		0.8	
			0.1	0.1	

3-5 全市单位分市、区全部从业人员人数(2014年底)

NUMBER OF EMPLOYED PERSONS IN ALL UNITS OF THE CITY BY REGION(END OF 2014)

单位:万人(10 000 persons)

市、区名称	Region	年末人数 Year-end Population	国有单位 State-owned Units	集体单位 Collective-owned Units	其他经济类型单位 Units in Other Types of Economy
全市	**Whole Municipality**	**303.0**	**36.7**	**4.9**	**261.4**
市内三区	The Three Districts of Qingdao City	73.8	15.3	0.9	57.6
崂山区	Laoshan District	22.7	3.1	2.2	17.4
黄岛区	Huangdao District	53.7	5.2	0.4	48.1
城阳区	Chengyang District	36.1	2.0	0.1	34.0
即墨市	Jimo	34.9	2.5	0.7	31.7
胶州市	Jiaozhou	33.7	3.1	0.3	30.3
平度市	Pingdu	19.3	2.8	0.2	16.3
莱西市	Laixi	23.7	2.4	0.1	21.2
红岛经济区	Qingdao National High-tech Industrial Development Zone	3.2	0.2		3.0
保税港区	Qingdao Free Trade Port Area of Chin	1.9	0.1		1.8

3-6 全市在岗职工工资总额、平均工资(1978-2014年)

TOTAL WAGE BILL AND AVERAGE WAGE OF EMPLOYED STAFF AND WORKERS(1978-2014)

年份 Year	工资总额(亿元) Total Wage Bill(100 million yuan)		平均工资(元) Average Wage(yuan)	
	全社会单位 All Units	其中:非私营单位 of which:Non-private Units	全社会单位 All Units	其中:非私营单位 of which:Non-private Units
1978		4.0		584
1979		4.8		662
1980		6.0		782
1981		6.3		778
1982		6.6		785
1983		6.9		809
1984		9.0		1 041
1985		9.6		1 103
1986		11.8		1 311
1987		14.2		1 519
1988		18.0		1 862
1989		20.7		2 120
1990		24.4		2 400
1991		26.4		2 553
1992		31.8		2 970
1993		40.4		3 694
1994		59.5		5 455
1995		68.3		6 164
1996		78.2		6 640
1997		82.5		7 030
1998		87.2		7 518
1999		100.1		8 405
2000		120.4		10 072
2001		135.8		11 426
2002		153.8		12 839
2003	225.6	160.3	12 597	15 335
2004	280.5	193.4	13 932	17 190
2005	359.5	242.8	16 015	20 022
2006	445.6	292.0	18 574	23 457
2007	518.1	338.6	21 419	27 083
2008	578.7	371.9	23 296	30 233
2009	638.1	393.2	25 396	33 258
2010	738.0	446.8	28 549	37 805
2011	877.5	522.0	32 763	43 077
2012	1 044.3	613.1	37 399	49 052
2013	1 251.7	785.7	42 688	55 363
2014	1 456.0	890.5	48 453	62 104

注:2003年以前为职工工资总额、平均工资。

Note:The data before 2003 refer to the total wage bill and average wage of staff and workers.

3－7 全市在岗职工工资总额、平均工资指数(1978－2014年)

INDEXES OF TOTAL WAGE BILL AND AVERAGE WAGE OF EMPLOYED STAFF AND WORKERS(1978－2014)

年份 Year	工资总额指数 Total Wage Bill Indexes		平均工资指数 Average Wage Indexes	
	全社会单位 All Units	其中:非私营单位 of which:Non-private Units	全社会单位 All Units	其中:非私营单位 of which:Non-private Units
1978		120.80		104.66
1979		119.53		113.36
1980		123.95		118.13
1981		106.71		99.49
1982		103.80		100.90
1983		104.14		103.06
1984		130.64		128.68
1985		107.11		105.96
1986		123.22		118.86
1987		120.10		115.87
1988		126.48		122.58
1989		115.29		113.86
1990		117.66		113.21
1991		108.28		106.38
1992		120.26		116.33
1993		127.09		124.38
1994		147.46		147.67
1995		114.76		113.00
1996		114.54		107.72
1997		105.50		105.87
1998		105.64		106.94
1999		114.81		111.80
2000		120.29		119.83
2001		112.77		113.44
2002		113.31		112.37
2003		108.84		110.30
2004	124.34	120.65	110.60	112.10
2005	128.16	125.54	114.95	116.47
2006	123.95	120.26	115.98	117.16
2007	116.27	115.96	115.32	115.46
2008	111.70	109.83	108.76	111.63
2009	110.26	105.73	109.01	110.01
2010	115.66	113.63	112.42	113.67
2011	118.90	116.83	114.76	113.95
2012	119.01	117.45	114.15	113.87
2013	119.86	128.15	114.14	112.87
2014	116.32	113.34	113.50	112.18

注:2004年以前为职工工资总额、平均工资指数。

Note:The data before 2004 refer to the indexes of total wage bill and average wage of staff and workers.

3-8 分行业在岗职工平均工资(2014年)
AVERAGE WAGE OF EMPLOYED STAFF AND WORKERS BY SECTOR(2014)

行业	Sector	非私营单位(元) Non-private Units (yuan)	私营单位(元) Private Units (yuan)
总 计	**Total**	**62 104**	**38 070**
(一)农、林、牧、渔业	Farming, Forestry, Animal Husbandry and Fishery	40 272	33 950
(二)采矿业	Mining	44 975	41 479
(三)制造业	Manufacturing	49 492	38 565
(四)电力、热力、燃气及水生产和供应业	The Electricity, Heat, Gas and Water Production and Supply Industry	70 809	38 142
(五)建筑业	Construction	54 790	37 146
(六)批发和零售业	Wholesale and Retail Trade	48 272	36 507
(七)交通运输、仓储和邮政业	Transport, Storage and Post	68 718	40 708
(八)住宿和餐饮业	Hotels and Catering Services	46 334	32 649
(九)信息传输、软件和信息技术服务业	Information Transmission Computer Services and Software	97 472	47 046
(十)金融业	Financial Intermediation	148 864	48 180
(十一)房地产业	Real Estate	65 644	37 074
(十二)租赁和商务服务业	Leasing and Business Services	59 993	39 589
(十三)科学研究和技术服务业	Scientific Research and Technical Services	86 012	36 844
(十四)水利、环境和公共设施管理业	Management of Water Conservancy, Environment and Public Facilities	49 620	39 626
(十五)居民服务、修理和其他服务业	Residents Service, Repair and Other Services	48 229	35 520
(十六)教育	Education	81 270	28 446
(十七)卫生和社会工作	Health and Social Welfare	78 208	39 646
(十八)文化、体育和娱乐业	Culture, Sports and Entertainment	67 043	42 895
(十九)公共管理、社会保障和社会组织	Public Management, Social Security and Social Organization	87 796	

3-9 分市、区在岗职工工资总额(2014年)
TOTAL WAGE BILL OF EMPLOYED STAFF AND WORKERS BY REGION(2014)

单位:亿元(100 million yuan)

市、区名称	Region	合计 Total	国有单位 State-owned Units	集体单位 Collective-owned Units	其他所有制单位 Other Ownership Units
全市	**Whole Municipality**	**1 456.0**	**297.4**	**32.6**	**1 126.0**
市内三区	The Three Districts of Qingdao City	420.2	134.0	3.6	282.6
崂山区	Laoshan District	117.0	25.9	17.2	73.9
黄岛区	Huangdao District	264.6	45.2	1.8	217.6
城阳区	Chengyang District	176.0	17.6	1.2	157.2
即墨市	Jimo	137.9	16.4	5.0	116.5
胶州市	Jiaozhou	151.8	22.1	1.7	128.0
平度市	Pingdu	73.5	18.7	1.3	53.5
莱西市	Laixi	89.2	16.1	0.8	72.3
红岛经济区	Qingdao National High-tech Industrial Development Zone	16.2	1.0		15.2
保税港区	Qingdao Free Trade Port Area of China	9.6	0.4		9.2

3-10 分市、区在岗职工平均工资(2014 年)

AVERAGE WAGE OF EMPLOYED STAFF AND WORKERS BY REGION(2014)

单位:元/年(yuan/year)

市、区名称	Region	合计 Total	国有单位 State-owned Units	集体单位 Collective-owned Units	其他所有制单位 Other Ownership Units
全市	**Whole Municipality**	**48 453**	**83 311**	**65 901**	**44 810**
市内三区	The Three Districts of Qingdao City	59 539	89 260	49 770	51 530
崂山区	Laoshan District	56 222	88 927	73 253	47 533
黄岛区	Huangdao District	50 287	89 028	46 078	46 146
城阳区	Chengyang District	49 607	90 420	85 268	47 081
即墨市	Jimo	40 849	67 287	67 331	38 110
胶州市	Jiaozhou	45 880	73 182	64 043	42 955
平度市	Pingdu	39 705	68 310	61 680	34 368
莱西市	Laixi	40 642	68 451	65 646	37 131
红岛经济区	Qingdao National High-tech Industrial Development Zone	50 618	70 139	70 375	49 647
保税港区	Qingdao Free Trade Port Area of China	50 987	64 144		50 534

注:2014 年红岛经济区、保税港区统计范围变化,数据与上年不可比。

Note:There was a change in the statistical range for the Hongdao Economic Zone and the bonded port area for 2014 and the numbers are not comparable to the previous year.

主要统计指标解释

社会从业人员 指从事一定社会劳动并取得劳动报酬或经营收入的全部劳动力。这一指标反映了一定时期内全部劳动力资源的实际利用情况,是研究我国基本国情国力的重要指标。各单位的从业人员是指在各级国家机关、政党机关、社会团体及企业、事业单位中工作,并取得劳动报酬的全部人员。包括在岗职工、再就业的离退休人员、民办教师以及在各单位工作的外方人员和港、澳、台方人员等。

职工 指在内资(国有、集体、股份合作、联营、有限责任公司、股份有限公司)单位、港澳台商投资单位和外商投资单位及其附属机构工作,并由其支付工资的在岗人员以及不在岗但劳动关系仍在本单位的离岗人员。

在岗职工 指在本单位工作并由单位支付工资的人员,以及有工作岗位,但由于学习、病伤产假等原因暂未工作,仍由单位支付工资的人员。

职工工资总额 指各单位在一定时期内直接支付给本单位全部职工的劳动报酬总额,即在岗职工工资总额和离岗职工生活费两部分。工资总额的计算原则应以直接支付给职工的全部劳动报酬为根据。各单位支付给职工的劳动报酬以及其他根据有关规定支付的工资,不论是计入成本的还是不计入成本的,不论是按国家规定列入计征奖金税项目的,还是未列入计征奖金税项目的,不论是以货币形式支付的还是以实物形式支付的,均包括在工资总额内。

职工平均工资 指各单位一定时期内平均每人所得的工资。它表明一定时期职工工资收入的高低程度,是反映职工工资水平的主要指标。

全社会单位 包括:国有经济、集体经济、联营经济、股份制经济、外商和港、澳、台投资经济、私营经济、其他内资。

非私营单位 包括:国有经济、集体经济、联营经济、股份制经济、外商和港、澳、台投资经济。

Explanatory Notes on Main Statistical Indicators

Social Employment refers to the persons who are engaged in social working and receive remuneration payment or earn business income. This indicator reflects the actual utilization of total labour force during a certain period of time and is often used for the research on China's economic situation and national power. Persons Employed in Various Units refers to all the persons working in government agencies of various levels, political and party organizations, social organizations, enterprises and institutions, and receiving wages or other forms of payment. They include fully employed staff and workers, re-employed retirees, teachers in schools run by the local people, foreigners and Chinese compatriots from Hong Kong, Macao, and Taiwan working in various units.

Staff and Workers refer to persons working in, and receive payment from units of state ownership, collective ownership, joint ownership, share holding ownership, foreign ownership, and ownership by entrepreneurs from Hong Kong, Macao, and Taiwan, and other types of ownership and their affiliated units.

Employed Staff and Workers refers to persons who work in, and receive wages from their working units, as well as persons who have their work posts, but are temporarily absent from work for reasons of study or on sick, injury or maternal leave and still receive wages from their working units.

Total Wage Bill refer to the total remuneration payment to staff and workers in various units during a certain period of time. The calculation of total wages is based on the total remuneration payment to the staff and workers. Therefore, all the wages and salaries and other payments to staff and workers are included in the total wages regardless of their sources, category, and forms (in kind or cash). (Total wages of staff and workers in this yearbook include only total wages of fully employed staff and workers, excluding the living allowances distributed to those who have left their working units while keeping their labour contract/employment relation unchanged).

Average Wage refers to the average wage in money terms per person during a certain period of time for staff and workers in enterprises, institutions, and government agencies, which reflects the general level of wage income during a certain period of time.

All Units include state ownership, collective ownership, joint ownership, share holding ownership, foreign ownership, ownership by entrepreneurs from Hong Kong, Macao and Taiwan, private ownership, and domestic ownership.

Non-private Units include state ownership, collective ownership, joint ownership, share holding ownership, foreign ownership, and ownership by entrepreneurs from Hong Kong, Macao and Taiwan.

4 固定资产投资

INVESTMENT IN FIXED ASSETS

简 要 说 明

一、本篇资料的主要内容

本篇资料主要反映了全市固定资产投资及房地产开发方面的情况，主要包括固定资产投资的规模、结构、资金来源和房地产开发投资、施竣工及销售情况等方面的资料。

二、本篇资料的来源

本篇资料来源于固定资产投资及房地产开发投资统计年报，由市统计局固定资产投资统计处整理提供。

Brief Introduction

I. Main Content

Data in this chapter show the basic conditions of investment in fixed assets and real estate development of the whole city, mainly including the total investment in fixed assets, the structure of investment, the resources of investment and investment in real estate development, construction, completion, sales, etc.

II. Source of Data

Data in this chapter are based on the annual report on investment in fixed assets and real estate development, and provided by the Division of Investment and Construction Statistics of Qingdao Municipal Bureau of Statistics.

4-1 主要年份固定资产投资
MAJOR YEAR'S INVESTMENT IN FIXED ASSETS

单位:万元(10 000 yuan)

年 份 Year	规模以上固定资产投资总额 Investment in Fixed Assets above Designated Size	按用途分 Grouped by Use 生产性投资 Productive Investment	非生产性投资 Non- Productive Investment	#住宅投资 Investment in Residential Buildings
1949	16	12	4	3
1952	3 097	1 368	1 729	1 007
1957	5 923	3 947	1 976	1 151
1962	2 747	2 049	698	192
1965	5 481	4 155	1 326	375
1970	6 100	5 813	287	154
1975	15 839	13 548	2 381	1 064
1978	29 660	23 499	6 161	3 203
1980	47 499	33 865	13 634	9 335
1985	107 421	60 643	73 424	19 058
1989	262 214	190 950	71 264	26 592
1990	284 576	210 453	74 123	38 898
1991	349 031	256 633	92 398	51 898
1992	583 068	420 748	162 320	83 844
1993	953 274	511 684	441 590	162 419
1994	1 329 716	728 532	601 184	324 094
1995	1 648 281	925 194	723 087	390 206
1996	1 610 562	972 398	638 164	285 412
1997	1 611 902	932 207	679 695	278 951
1998	1 909 711	1 125 821	783 890	316 999
1999	2 205 891	1 246 328	959 563	421 151
2000	2 426 820	1 311 538	1 115 282	470 963
2001	2 934 728	1 487 762	1 446 966	729 181
2002	3 683 623	1 962 588	1 721 035	765 030
2003	5 475 526	3 023 930	2 451 596	1 038 304
2004	9 845 646	6 336 279	3 509 367	1 608 738
2005	14 032 960	9 172 206	4 860 754	1 841 644
2006	14 856 894	9 214 578	5 642 316	2 222 733
2007	16 353 636	10 231 673	6 121 963	2 720 970
2008	20 190 098	12 443 179	7 746 919	3 315 538
2009	24 588 889	13 852 653	10 736 236	3 831 976
2010	30 224 785	16 207 885	14 016 900	5 609 189
2011	35 025 382	18 622 819	16 402 563	5 707 625
2012	41 539 146	24 246 803	17 292 343	6 689 114
2013	50 278 649	30 996 768	19 281 881	7 220 432
2014	57 660 308	32 913 906	24 746 402	7 311 090

注:1. 规模以上固定资产投资数据2003年以前为城镇以上统计范围。
2. 因2004年以来数据有调整,故表中数据不可比。

Note:1. The data of investment above designated size refer to investment above city and town level before 2003.
2. The data since 2004 are not comparable with other data because of the adjustment.

4－1 续表
continued

单位:万元(10 000 yuan)

年 份 Year	按构成分 Grouped by Composition of Funds			按资金来源分 Grouped by Sources of Funds			
	建筑安装工程 Construction and Installation	设备工器具购置 Purchase of Equipment and Instruments	其他费用 Others	国家投资 State Investment	国内贷款 Domestic Loans	利用外资 Foreign Investment	自筹及其他 Self-raising Fund and Others
1949	11	3	2	16			
1952	2 146	870	81	1 512			1 585
1957	2 853	2 773	297	3 816			2 107
1962	1 631	984	132	2 205			542
1965	3 346	1 859	276	4 451			1 030
1970	3 136	2 835	129	2 721			3 379
1975	7 489	8 133	217	9 378	1 362		5 099
1978	19 968	9 124	568	16 828	1 601		11 231
1980	30 993	15 541	965	10 371	12 925	1 420	22 783
1985	64 665	35 100	7 656	17 377	35 888	1 136	53 020
1989	141 821	95 333	17 269	38 747	79 999	25 081	114 939
1990	167 731	91 305	25 540	24 687	91 895	23 688	144 306
1991	196 212	108 929	43 890	22 615	131 676	38 325	156 415
1992	304 060	208 384	70 624	22 660	213 217	89 130	258 061
1993	600 011	225 555	127 708	23 736	208 672	94 469	626 397
1994	842 809	272 126	214 781	26 062	318 334	221 265	764 055
1995	1 020 484	385 934	241 863	25 683	379 198	328 124	915 276
1996	929 735	458 284	222 543	35 639	444 443	310 722	819 758
1997	875 057	485 122	251 723	27 928	297 089	363 789	923 096
1998	1 034 500	574 852	300 359	67 762	491 812	170 709	1 179 428
1999	1 456 473	459 596	289 822	128 603	584 120	145 589	1 347 579
2000	1 476 397	652 640	297 783	75 978	489 697	164 175	1 806 238
2001	1 781 235	744 549	408 944	93 491	620 562	217 526	2 157 787
2002	2 328 492	796 685	558 446	78 775	719 677	411 704	2 831 288
2003	3 544 790	1 133 333	797 403	127 861	989 178	722 644	4 237 643
2004	6 413 046	2 312 139	1 120 461	85 549	1 100 297	1 016 145	8 245 272
2005	8 949 231	3 141 732	1 941 997	136 632	1 250 343	1 850 921	11 540 604
2006	8 818 614	3 668 191	2 370 089	391 315	2 126 523	1 662 897	11 856 506
2007	9 981 666	4 171 878	2 200 092	215 649	2 427 031	1 788 056	13 109 824
2008	11 795 435	5 907 195	2 487 468	322 484	3 309 471	1 951 468	15 855 082
2009	14 911 874	5 869 214	3 807 801	778 090	4 217 265	1 593 287	21 555 685
2010	18 725 922	6 362 880	5 135 983	1 305 737	5 881 886	2 135 736	27 898 294
2011	22 865 421	7 521 441	4 638 520	1 640 702	5 871 709	1 766 278	33 579 182
2012	26 080 239	8 601 282	6 857 625	1 324 159	5 484 459	1 561 597	37 356 847
2013	33 237 368	9 969 777	7 071 504	1 959 340	8 154 829	1 528 585	49 552 883
2014	39 006 113	11 640 126	3 764 630	1 404 667	7 452 983	1 181 541	55 024 776

4-2 主要年份固定资产投资构成(以投资总额为100)

COMPOSITION OF MAJOR YEAR'S INVESTMENT IN FIXED ASSETS(TOTAL INVESTMENT = 100)

年份 Year	按用途分 Grouped by Use		
	生产性投资 Productive Investment	非生产性投资 Non-Productive Investment	#住宅投资占非生产性比重 Percentage of Investment in Residential Buildings to Non-Productive Investment
1949	75.00	25.00	75.00
1952	44.17	55.83	58.24
1957	66.64	33.36	58.25
1962	74.59	25.41	27.51
1965	75.81	24.19	28.28
1970	95.30	4.70	53.66
1975	84.97	15.03	44.69
1978	79.23	20.77	51.99
1980	71.30	28.70	68.47
1985	56.45	43.55	40.74
1989	72.82	27.18	37.30
1990	73.95	26.05	52.50
1991	73.53	26.47	56.17
1992	72.16	27.84	51.65
1993	53.68	46.32	36.78
1994	54.79	45.21	53.91
1995	56.10	43.90	54.00
1996	60.40	39.60	44.70
1997	57.80	42.20	41.00
1998	59.00	41.00	16.60
1999	56.50	43.50	19.10
2000	54.00	46.00	19.40
2001	50.70	49.30	50.40
2002	53.30	46.70	44.50
2003	55.20	44.80	42.40
2004	64.40	35.60	45.80
2005	65.40	34.60	37.90
2006	62.00	38.00	39.40
2007	62.60	37.40	44.40
2008	61.60	38.40	42.80
2009	56.30	43.70	35.70
2010	53.62	46.38	40.02
2011	53.17	46.83	34.80
2012	58.37	41.63	38.68
2013	61.65	38.35	37.45
2014	57.08	42.92	29.54

4-2 续表

continued

年份 Year	按构成分 Grouped by Composition of Funds			按资金来源分 Grouped by Sources of Funds			
	建筑安装工程 Construction and Installation	设备工器具购置 Purchase of Equipment and Instruction	其他费用 Others	国家投资 State Investment	国内贷款 Domestic Loans	利用外资 Foreign Investment	自筹及其他 Self-raising Fund and Others
1949	68.75	18.75	12.5	100			
1952	69.29	28.09	2.62	48.82			51.18
1957	48.17	46.82	5.01	64.43			35.57
1962	59.37	35.82	4.81	80.27			19.73
1965	61.05	33.92	5.03	81.21			18.79
1970	51.41	46.48	2.11	44.61			55.39
1975	47.28	51.35	1.37	59.21	8.60		32.19
1978	67.32	30.76	1.92	56.74	5.40		37.86
1980	65.25	32.72	2.03	21.83	27.21	2.99	47.97
1985	60.20	32.68	7.12	16.18	33.41	1.06	49.35
1989	54.08	36.36	6.59	14.78	30.51	9.56	45.15
1990	58.94	32.08	8.98	8.68	32.29	8.32	50.71
1991	56.22	31.21	12.57	6.48	37.73	10.98	44.81
1992	52.15	35.74	12.11	3.89	36.56	15.29	44.26
1993	62.94	23.66	13.40	2.49	21.89	9.91	65.71
1994	63.38	20.46	16.16	1.96	23.94	16.64	57.46
1995	61.9	23.4	14.7	1.6	23.0	19.9	55.5
1996	57.7	28.5	13.8	2.2	27.6	19.3	50.9
1997	54.3	30.1	15.6	1.7	18.4	22.6	57.3
1998	54.2	20.8	15.7	3.5	25.8	8.9	61.8
1999	66.0	20.8	13.2	5.8	26.5	6.6	61.1
2000	60.8	26.9	12.3	3.1	20.2	6.8	74.4
2001	60.7	25.4	13.9	3.0	20.1	7.0	69.9
2002	63.2	21.6	15.2	1.9	17.8	10.2	70.1
2003	64.7	20.7	14.6	2.1	16.3	11.9	69.7
2004	65.1	23.5	11.4	0.8	10.6	9.7	78.9
2005	63.8	22.4	13.8	0.9	8.5	12.5	78.1
2006	59.4	24.7	15.9	2.4	13.3	10.4	73.9
2007	61.0	25.5	13.5	1.2	13.8	10.2	74.8
2008	58.4	29.3	12.3	1.5	15.4	9.1	74.0
2009	60.6	23.9	15.5	2.8	15.0	5.6	76.6
2010	62.0	21.0	17.0	3.5	15.8	5.7	75.0
2011	65.3	21.5	13.2	3.8	13.7	4.1	78.4
2012	62.8	20.7	16.5	2.9	12.0	3.4	81.7
2013	66.1	19.8	14.1	3.2	13.3	2.5	81.0
2014	71.7	21.4	6.9	2.2	11.5	1.8	84.6

4-3 按三次产业分规模以上固定资产投资(2014 年)
INVESTMENT IN FIXED ASSETS ABOVE DESIGNATED SIZE BY THREE STRATA OF INDUSTRY(2014)

单位:万元(10 000 yuan)

指　标	Indicator	2014
总　计	**Total**	**57 660 308**
第一产业	Primary Industry	1 046 850
第二产业	Secondary Industry	28 179 187
#工业	Industry	27 281 980
第三产业	Tertiary Industry	28 434 271

4-4 分市、区固定资产投资额(2014 年)
INVESTMENT IN FIXED ASSETS BY REGION(2014)

单位:万元(10 000 yuan)

市、区名称	Region	规模以上固定资产投资额 Investment in Fixed Assets above Designated Size	#房地产开发 Investment in Real Estate Development
全市	**Whole Municipality**	**57 660 308**	**11 177 297**
市南区	Shinan District	1 485 505	969 027
市北区	Shibei District	3 244 808	2 438 495
李沧区	Licang District	3 723 405	1 862 488
崂山区	Laoshan District	2 021 241	964 469
黄岛区	Huangdao District	14 404 856	2 281 124
保税港区	Qingdao Free Trade Port Area of China	35 908	
城阳区	Chengyang District	5 224 928	1 136 115
即墨市	Jimo	7 679 652	513 025
胶州市	Jiaozhou	7 655 697	350 828
平度市	Pingdu	5 813 598	350 242
莱西市	Laixi	5 167 821	142 171
红岛经济区	Qingdao National High-tech Industrial Development Zone	1 184 889	169 313

4-5 规模以上固定资产投资(2014 年)
INVESTMENT IN FIXED ASSETS ABOVE DESIGNATED SIZE(2014)

单位:万元(10 000 yuan)

项　目	Item	合计 Total	#房地产开发 Investment in Real Estate Development
一、本年施工项目(个)	**Projects Under Construction This Year(unit)**	**4 580**	
#本年新开工(个)	of which:Newly Started(unit)	3 568	
二、本年建成投产项目(个)	**Projects Completed and Put into Use This Year(unit)**	**3 632**	
三、本年完成投资	**Investment Completed This Year**	**57 660 308**	**11 177 297**
1.按构成分	Grouped by Composition		
#建筑工程	Construction Projects	34 527 974	6 687 339
安装工程	Installation Projects	4 478 139	1 240 519
设备工器具购置	Purchase of Equipment and Instruments	11 640 126	128 120
#用于更新的设备	Equipment Used in Updates	3 713 465	
2.按建设性质分	Grouped by Type of Construction		
#新　建	New Construction	25 220 948	
扩　建	Expansion	6 850 689	
改　建	Reconstruction	11 764 548	
3.按隶属关系分	Grouped by Subordination Relation		
中央单位	Central Units	1 412 471	628 651
地方单位	Local Units	56 247 837	10 548 646
4.按国民经济行业分	Grouped by Economic Sector		
(1)农、林、牧、渔业	Farming,Forestry,Animal Husbandry and Fishery	1 046 850	
农　业	Farming	481 428	
林　业	Forestry	66 204	
畜牧业	Animal Husbandry	57 695	
渔　业	Fishery	344 640	
农、林、牧、渔服务业	Farming,Forestry,Animal Husbandry and Fishery Services	96 883	
(2)采矿业	Mining	135 922	
煤炭开采和洗选业	Mining and Washing of Coal		
石油和天然气开采业	Extraction of Petroleum and Natural Gas		
黑色金属矿采选业	Mining of Ferrous Metal Ores	5 615	
有色金属矿采选业	Mining of Non-ferrous Metal Ores	44 183	
非金属矿采选业	Mining and Processing of Nonmetal Ores	81 401	
开采辅助活动	Auxiliary Activities of Mining	4 723	
其他采矿业	Mining of Other Ores		

4－5 续表1
continued

单位：万元（10 000 yuan）

项　目	Item	合计 Total	#房地产开发 Investment in Real Estate Development
（3）制造业	Manufacturing	26 662 980	
农副食品加工业	Processing of Food from Agricultural Products	1 627 279	
食品制造业	Manufacture of Foods	525 416	
酒、饮料和精制茶制造业	Manufacture of Liquor, Beverage and Refind Tea	302 065	
烟草制品业	Manufacture of Tobacco	2 790	
纺织业	Manufacture of Textile	685 013	
纺织服装、服饰业	Manufacture of Textile Wearing Apparel	979 125	
皮革、毛皮、羽毛及其制品和制鞋业	Manufacture of Leather, Fur, Feather & Its Products Footwear	374 000	
木材加工和木、竹、藤、棕、草制品业	Processing of Timbers, Manufacture of Wood, Bamboo, Rattan, Palm and Straw Products	263 664	
家具制造业	Manufacture of Furniture	394 001	
造纸和纸制品业	Manufacture of Paper and Paper Products	351 258	
印刷和记录媒介复制业	Printing, Reproduction of Recording Media	401 410	
文教、工美、体育和娱乐用品制造业	Manufacture of Articles for Culture, Arts & Crafts, Sports and Entertainment	715 964	
石油加工、炼焦和核燃料加工业	Processing of Petroleum, Coking, Processing of Nucleus Fuel	640 311	
化学原料和化学制品制造业	Manufacture of Chemical Raw Material and Chemical Products	1 485 581	
医药制造业	Manufacture of Medicines	373 418	
化学纤维制造业	Manufacture of Chemical Fiber	23 537	
橡胶和塑料制品业	Manufacture of Rubber and Plastic	1 229 940	
非金属矿物制品业	Manufacture of Non-metallic Mineral Products	1 597 557	
黑色金属冶炼和压延加工业	Smelting and Pressing of Ferrous Metals	392 381	
有色金属冶炼和压延加工业	Smelting and Pressing of Non-ferrous Metals	227 702	
金属制品业	Manufacture of Metal Products	2 429 005	
通用设备制造业	Manufacture of General Purpose Machinery	3 287 122	
专用设备制造业	Manufacture of Special Purpose Machinery	2 611 280	
汽车制造业	Manufacture of Vehicle	1 176 180	
铁路、船舶、航空航天和其他运输设备制造业	Manufacture of Transport Equipment for Railway, Shipping, Aerospace and other uses	1 977 966	
电气机械和器材制造业	Manufacture of Electrical Machinery & Equipment	1 324 085	
计算机、通信和其他电子设备制造业	Manufacture of Computer, Communication Equipment and Other Electronic Equipment	753 514	
仪器仪表制造业	Manufacture of Measuring Instrument	258 685	
其他制造业	Manufacture of Other Products	136 716	
废弃资源综合利用业	Recycling and Disposal of Waste Resources	65 633	
金属制品、机械和设备修理业	Maintenance of Metal Products, Machinery and Equipment	50 382	

4-5 续表2
continued

单位:万元(10 000 yuan)

项　目	Item	合计 Total	#房地产开发 Investment in Real Estate Development
(4)电力、燃气及水的生产和供应业	Production and Supply of Electricity Gas and Water	483 078	
电力、热力的生产和供应业	Production and Supply of Electric Power and Heat Power	335 546	
燃气生产和供应业	Production and Supply of Gas	86 299	
水的生产和供应业	Production and Supply of Water	61 233	
(5)建筑业	Construction	897 207	
(6)交通运输、仓储及邮政业	Transport Storage and Post	3 140 053	
铁路运输业	Railway Transport	316 683	
道路运输业	Road Transport	1 664 609	
水上运输业	Water Transport	546 542	
航空运输业	Air Transport		
管道运输业	Pipeline Transport	28 849	
装卸搬运和运输代理业	Handing,Corrying and Transportation Agent	106 775	
仓储业	Ware houses and Storage	466 120	
邮政业	Post	10 475	
(7)信息传输、软件和信息技术服务业	Information Transmission Computer Services and Software	334 723	
(8)批发和零售业	Wholesale and Retail Trade	2 393 611	
(9)住宿和餐饮业	Hotels and Catering Services	547 816	
(10)金融业	Financial Intermediation	92 616	
(11)房地产业	Financial Intermediation	13 467 924	11 177 297

4-5 续表3
continued

单位:万元(10 000 yuan)

项　目	Item	合计 Total	#房地产开发 Investment in Real Estate Development
(12)租赁和商务服务业	Leasing and Business Services	1 797 331	
(13)科学研究、技术服务和地质勘察业	Scientific Research, Technical Service and Geologic Prospecting	646 760	
(14)水利、环境和公共设施管理业	Management of Water Conservancy, Environment and Public Facilities	2 546 114	
水利管理业	Management of Water Conservancy	135 330	
环境管理业	Environmental Management	68 396	
公共设施管理业	Management of Public Facilities	2 342 388	
(15)居民服务和其他服务业	Services to Households and Other Services	146 512	
居民服务业	Services to Households	115 746	
机动车、电子产品和日用产品修理业	Maintenance of Vehicle, Electronic Products and Daily Articles	30 766	
其他服务业	Other Services		
(16)教育	Education	735 221	
(17)卫生和社会工作	Health and Social Work	125 439	
卫生	Health	55 846	
(18)文化、体育和娱乐业	Culture, Sports and Entertainment	1 938 578	
新闻出版业	Journalism and Publishing Activities		
广播、电视、体育和音像业	Broadcasting, Movies, Televisions and Audiovisual Activities	1 461 802	
文化艺术业	Cultural and Art Activities	225 621	
体育	Sports Activities	36 809	
娱乐业	Entertainment	214 346	
(19)公共管理、社会保障和社会组织	Public Management, Social Security and Social Organization	521 573	
中国共产党机关	Communist Party of China		
国家机构	Government Agencies	310 477	
人民政协、民主党派	People's Political Consultatioe Conference, Democratic Party		
社会保障	Social Security		
群众团体、社会团体和其他成员组织	Non-Governmental Institutions, Social Organizations and Other Organizations	21 199	
基层群众自治组织	Local People Self-government Organization	189 897	
(20)国际组织	International Organization		

4－5 续表4
continued

单位:万元(10 000 yuan)

项目	Item	合计 Total	#房地产开发 Investment in Real Estate Development
四、本年新增固定资产	**Newly Increased Fixed Assets This Year**		
(1)农、林、牧、渔业	Farming, Forestry, Animal Husbandry and Fishery	660 878	
(2)采矿业	Mining	65 314	
(3)制造业	Manufacturing	20 575 821	
(4)电力、燃气及水的生产和供应业	Production and Supply of Electricty, Gas and Water	396 146	
(5)建筑业	Construction	617 591	
(6)交通运输、仓储和邮政业	Transport, Storage and Post	1 827 470	
(7)信息传输、计算机服务和软件业	Information Transmission, Computer Services and Software	167 853	
(8)批发和零售业	Wholesale and Retail Trade	2 145 850	
(9)住宿和餐饮业	Hotels and Catering Services	462 494	
(10)金融业	Financial Intermediation	81 722	
(11)房地产业	Real Estate	6 943 982	4 654 461
(12)租赁和商务服务业	Leasing and Business Services	743 294	
(13)科学研究、技术服务	Scientific Research and Technical Services	394 551	
(14)水利、环境和公共设施管理业	Management of Water Conservancy, Environment and Public Facilities	1 725 191	
(15)居民服务、修理和其他服务业	Services to Households, Repair and Other Services	105 820	
(16)教育	Education	498 319	
(17)卫生和社会工作	Health and Social Work	141 937	
(18)文化、体育和娱乐业	Culture, Sports and Entertainment	167 620	
(19)公共管理、社会保障和社会组织	Public Management, Social Security and Social Organization	410 762	
(20)国际组织	International Organization		
五、本年资金来源合计	**Total Funds This Year**	**75 349 229**	**20 372 152**
上年末结余资金	Balance of Last Year	10 285 262	5 716 879
本年资金来源小计	Sub-total Funds This Year	65 063 967	14 655 273
国家预算内资金	State Budget	1 404 667	
国内贷款	Domestic Loans	7 452 983	3 632 322
债券	State Treasury Bond		
利用外资	Foreign Investment	1 181 541	50 496
自筹资金	Self-raising Funds	48 850 925	5 047 351
其他资金来源	Others	6 173 851	5 925 104

4-6 主要年份房地产开发投资
MAJOR YEAR'S INVESTMENT IN REAL ESTATE DEVELOPMENT

单位:万元、万平方米(10 000 yuan,10 000 sq. m)

年份 Year	房地产开发投资额 Investment in Real Estate Development	房屋施工面积 Floor Space Under Construction	房屋竣工面积 Floor Space Completed	房屋实际销售面积 Floor Space of Buildings Sold	房屋实际销售额 Sale of Buildings
1995	562 861	1 008	240	103	185 384
1996	455 765	748	203	80	125 150
1997	426 570	675	237	113	216 311
1998	438 059	742	259	178	351 805
1999	629 717	900	474	240	430 123
2000	675 142	1 047	352	301	550 401
2001	925 153	1 374	532	406	802 364
2002	1 036 476	1 417	537	427	933 031
2003	1 277 969	1 765	552	469	1 121 885
2004	1 626 965	2 101	635	516	1 530 964
2005	2 238 370	2 363	811	740	2 666 738
2006	2 683 631	2 751	654	719	3 054 907
2007	3 223 547	3 224	641	833	4 333 566
2008	3 805 652	3 773	672	770	3 924 175
2009	4 594 829	4 310	814	1 262	7 036 744
2010	6 024 387	5 058	1 020	1 360	8 952 942
2011	7 827 193	5 693	925	1 026	7 702 379
2012	9 301 099	6 474	1 212	951	7 660 684
2013	10 485 229	7 073	957	1 160	9 786 176
2014	11 177 297	8 171	1 136	1 164	9 708 984

4-7 房地产开发投资情况(2014 年)
INVESTMENT IN REAL ESTATE DEVELOPMENT(2014)

单位:万元(10 000 yuan)

指标名称	Indicator	合计 Total	按经济类型分 Grouped by Economic Types 国有经济 State-owned	集体经济 Collective-owned	其他经济 Others
本年完成投资额	**Investment Completed This Year**	**11 177 297**	**308 153**	**12 313**	**10 856 831**
1. 住宅	Residential Buildings	7 311 090	249 829	700	7 060 561
2. 办公楼	Office Buildings	978 669	161	4 351	974 157
3. 商业营业用房	Houses for Business Use	1 327 878	33 274	4 461	1 290 143
4. 其他	Others	1 559 660	24 889	2 801	1 531 970

4-7 续表
continued

单位:万元(10 000 yuan)

指标名称	Indicator	按资质等级分 Grouped by Qualification Criteria 一级 First Grade	二级 Second Grade	三级 Third Grade	四级 Fourth Grade	暂定 Provisional	其他 Others
本年完成投资额	**Investment Completed This Year**	**230 034**	**475 329**	**709 615**	**108 819**	**8 869 424**	**784 076**
1. 住宅	Residential Buildings	147 436	375 979	563 551	45 843	5 567 338	610 943
2. 办公楼	Office Buildings	6 050	4 413	12 189	36 071	864 726	55 220
3. 商业营业用房	Houses for Business Use	10 190	40 997	52 339	15 119	1 137 101	72 132
4. 其他	Others	66 358	53 940	81 536	11 786	1 300 259	45 781

4-8 房地产施工、竣工面积及竣工价值(2014年)

FLOOR SPACE UNDER CONSTRUCTION AND COMPLETED AND COMPLETED VALUE OF REAL ESTATE(2014)

单位:万平方米(10 000 sq. m)

施工、竣工房屋面积及竣工价值	Indicator	施工面积 Floor Space Under Construction	#新开工 Newly Started	竣工面积 Floor Space Completed	竣工房屋价值(万元) Completed Value (10 000 yuan)
房屋建筑面积总计	**Floor Space of Buildings**	**8 171**	**2 044**	**1 136**	**3 248 069**
住　宅	Residential Buildings	5 333	1 334	810	2 241 077
办公楼	Office Buildings	541	159	62	202 193
商业营业用房	Houses for Business Use	1 019	216	91	267 139
其　他	Others	1 278	335	173	537 660

4-9 商品房屋销售情况(2014年)

BASIC STATISTICS ON SALES OF COMMERCIALIZED BUILDINGS(2014)

单位:万平方米(10 000 sq. m)

商品房屋销售情况	Sales and Rental of Commercialized Buildings	实际销售 Actual Sales	实际销售额(万元) Actual Sales Volume (10 000 yuan)	待售面积 Area for Sale
房屋面积总计	**Floor Space of Buildings**	**1 164**	**9 708 984**	**505**
住　宅	Residential Buildings	1 022	8 030 189	331
办公楼	Office Buildings	43	651 168	31
商业营业用房	Houses for Business Use	72	846 798	98
其　他	Others	27	180 829	45

主要统计指标解释

固定资产投资 是以货币形式表现的在一定时期内全社会建造和购置固定资产的工作量以及与此有关的费用的总称。该指标是反映固定资产投资规模、结构和发展速度的综合性指标,又是观察工程进度和考核投资效果的重要依据。全社会固定资产投资按登记注册类型可分为国有、集体、个体、联营、股份制、外商、港澳台商、其他等。

城镇固定资产投资 是指城镇各种登记注册类型的企业、事业、行政单位及个体户进行的计划总投资(或实际需要总投资)500万元及500万元以上的建设项目投资、房地产开发投资、城镇和工矿区私人建房投资。县城及以上区域内发生的投资,县及县以上各级政府及主管部门直接领导、管理的建设项目和企业事业单位的投资均为城镇固定资产投资。

固定资产投资 包括城镇、农村500万元以上投资项目。

房地产开发投资 指各种登记注册类型的房地产开发公司、商品房建设公司及其他房地产开发法人单位和附属于其他法人单位实际从事房地产开发或经营活动的单位统一开发的包括统代建、拆迁还建的住宅、厂房、仓库、饭店、宾馆、度假村、写字楼、办公楼等房屋建筑物和配套的服务设施,土地开发工程(如道路、给水、排水、供电、供热、通讯、平整场地等基础设施工程)的投资;不包括单纯的土地交易活动。

固定资产投资的资金来源根 据固定资产投资的资金来源不同,分为国家预算内资金、国内贷款、利用外资、自筹资金和其他资金。

固定资产投资 按国民经济行业分根据建设项目建成投产后的主要产品或主要用途及社会经济活动性质来确定国民经济行业。一般情况下,一个建设项目或一个企业、事业单位只能属于一种国民经济行业。

固定资产投资 按建设性质分建设项目的性质一般分为新建、扩建、改建和技术改造、迁建、恢复。

固定资产投资 按构成分固定资产投资活动按其工作内容和实现方式分为建筑安装工程,设备、工具、器具购置,其他费用三个部分。

施工项目 指报告期内进行过建筑或安装施工活动的项目。凡是报告期内施过工的建设项目,不论施工时间长短,均作为施工项目统计。

新增生产能力(或工程效益) 指通过固定资产投资活动而增加的设计能力(或工程效益),它是以实物形态表现的固定资产投资成果。

新增生产能力(或工程效益) 一般有以下几种表现形式:

(1)以建设项目或单项工程建成后的年产能力表示,如煤炭开采,石油开采等。

(2)以建设项目或单项工程建成后处理原料的能力表示,如选矿工程的年处理矿石能力,城市污水处理能力等。

(3)以新增加的主要设备的数量或容量表示,如新增棉布织机、电机组容量等。

(4)用建筑物容积、容量、面积、长度表示,如新建公路、水库容量、学校学生席位等。

房屋施工面积 是指报告期内施工的全部房屋建筑面积。包括本期新开工的面积和上期开工跨入本期继续施工的房屋面积,以及上期已停缓建在本期恢复施工的房屋面积。本期竣工和本期施工后又停缓建的房屋,其建筑面积仍计入本期房屋施工面积中。

房屋竣工面积 是指在报告期内房屋建筑按照设计要求全部完工,达到住人和使用条件,经验收鉴定合格(或达到竣工验收标准),正式移交使用单位的各栋房屋建筑面积的总和。

新增固定资产又称交付使用的固定资产 是指已经完成建造和购置过程,并已交付生产或使用单位的固定资产价值。新增固定资产是表示固定资产投资成果的价值量指标,也是反映建设进度、计算固定资产投资效果的必要数据。

固定资产交付使用率 指一定时期新增固定资产与同期完成投资额的比率。该指标是反映固定资产动用速度,衡量建设过程中宏观投资效果的综合指标。由于新增固定资产是较长时期内形成的结果,而投资额则是当年完成的,因此,该指标一般适宜于反映较长时期内固定资产的动用情况。

Explanatory Notes on Main Statistical Indicators

Investment in Fixed Assets referss to the volume of activities in construction and purchases of fixed assets and related fees, expressed in monetary terms. It is a comprehensive indicator which shows the size, structure and growth of the investment in fixed assets, providing basis for observing the progress of construction projects and evaluating results of investment. Total investment in fixed assets in the whole country includes, by type of ownership, the investment by the state-owned units, collective units, individuals, joint ownership units, share-holding units, as well as investment by businessmen from foreign countries and from Hong Kong, Macau and Taiwan, and by other units.

Urban Investment in Fixed Assets refers to construction projects involving a total planned (or required) investment of 5,000,000 yuan and over by urban enterprises and institutions of various types of ownership, by administrative units and by individuals, investment in real estate development, and housing investment by individuals in urban areas and in industrial and mining areas. In other words, all investments that take place in county towns and urban areas, investment in construction projects under the direct leadership and management of government agencies at and above county levels and investments by enterprises and institutions at and above county levels are covered in urban investment in fixed assets.

Investment in Fixed Assets includes construction projects involving an urban or rural investment of 5,000,000 yuan and over.

Investment in Real Estate Development refers to the investment by the real estate development companies, commercial buildings construction companies and other real estate development units of various types of ownership in the construction of house buildings, such as residential buildings, factory buildings, warehouses, hotels, guesthouses, holiday villages, office buildings, and the complementary service facilities and land development projects, such as roads, water supply, water drainage, power supply, heating, telecommunications, land leveling and other projects of infrastructure. It excludes the activities in pure land transactions.

Sources of Funds for Investment in Fixed Assets include fund from state budget, domestic loans, foreign investment, self-raised funds, and others depending on the source of investment.

Investment in Fixed Assets by SectorThe classification of construction projects by sector is determined by the major products or the purpose of the projects when they are put into production or use, and by the nature of their social economic activities. In general, one project or one enterprise or institution can only be classified into one sector.

Investment in Fixed Assets by Type of ConstructionThe construction projects in general can be classified, by the type of construction, into new construction, expansion, reconstruction and technical transformation, moving and restoration. However, investment by type of construction is not applied to investment by real-estate development units, investment in rural areas and investment in housing by urban individuals.

Investment in Fixed Assets by StructureBy their contents, investment activities are classified into 3 categories, i. e. construction and installation, purchase of equipment and instrument, and other expenses.

Projects under Construction refer to projects with construction and installation activities undertaken in the reference period. All projects that have construction activities undertaken during the reference period are reported as projects under construction irrespective of the length of construction work.

Newly Increased Production Capacity (or Project Efficiency) refers to the increase of designed capacity (or project efficiency) through investment in fixed assets, which reflects the accomplishment of investment in fixed assets in kind.

The newly increased production capacity (project efficiency) are usually expressed in one of the following forms:

(1) output of products, i. e. the output that the project can produce during a given period (usually a year). For instance, the capacity in coal mining is expressed in 10,000 tons/year, the capacity in producing chemical pesticides expressed in ton/year, the capacity in producing tractors in tractor/year, etc. For some chemical products where the effective contents differ significantly, the production capacity is expressed as the designed effective content equivalent, such as in the case of sulphuric acid, soda ash, caustic soda, etc;

(2) raw materials processing capacity, i. e. the volume of raw materials that could be processed by the project per day (or per hour), such as tons of materials processed per day by a sugar refining project or edible vegetable oil project, or tons of urban sewage processed per day;

(3) number or capacity of major equipment increased, such as number of cotton or silk looms increased, wool spindles increased, or capacity (in kilowatts) of power generators increased;

(4) physical measures (volume, capacity, area, and length) of construction, which is typical for non-industrial projects, for instance, the length of railways put into operation, the length of highways, the capacity of reservoirs, the capacity of warehouses, the floor space of housing projects, capacity for new students in schools or beds in hospitals, areas under new irrigation project, etc.

Floor Space of Buildings under Construction refers to total floor space of all buildings under construction during the reference period, including floor space of newly started buildings during the reference period, floor space of construction extended from the previous period to the current period, and floor space of construction suspended during the previous period and resumed in the current period. Floor space of construction completed in the current period, and floor space of construction started and then suspended in the current period are also included in the floor space under construction of the current year.

Floor Space of Buildings Completed refers to the floor space of all buildings completed in the reference period, which have been appraised and accepted (or come up to the designed standards) and have been transferred to the owners for use.

Newly Increased Fixed Assets refer to the newly increased value of fixed assets constructed or purchased, that have been transferred to the investors. This is an indicator that demonstrates the results of investment in fixed assets in monetary terms, and an important indicator to reflect the speed of construction and to calculate the efficiency of investment.

Rate of Projects of Fixed Assets Completed and Put into Operation refers to the ratio of the newly increased fixed assets to the total investment made in the same period. This is a comprehensive indicator reflecting the speed of the employment of fixed assets and the investment efficiency at the macro-level. As the newly increase fixed assets is the result of a long period while the investment is completed in the current year, this indicator is expected to be used to reflect the employment of fixed assets over a long period of time.

5 对外经济贸易 FOREIGN TRADE

简要说明

一、本篇资料的主要内容

本篇资料主要反映了全市外经外贸和外资企业的基本情况，主要包括外贸进出口、利用外资、对外投资与经济合作情况等方面的资料。

二、本篇资料的来源

1、口岸进出口数据来源于青岛海关。

2、进出口、利用外资、对外投资与经济合作等资料来源于市商务局。

本篇资料由市统计局外经贸易统计处整理提供。

Brief Introduction

I. Main Content

Data in this chapter show the basic conditions of foreign trade and foreign-funded enterprises, mainly including imports and exports, utilization of foreign capitals, production and operation condition of foreign-funded enterprises, etc.

II. Source of Data

(1)Data on imports and exports of Qingdao port are provided by Office of Qingdao Port Administration.

(2)Data on imports & exports and utilization of foreign capitals are provided by Qingdao Municipal Commerce Bureau.

Data in this chapter are prepared and compiled by the Division of Trade and External Economic Relations Statistics of Qingdao Municipal Bureau of Statistics.

5-1 青岛口岸进出口总额(1985-2014年)

TOTAL VALUE OF IMPORTS AND EXPORTS OF QINGDAO PORT(1985-2014)

单位:万美元(10000 USD)

年份 Year	青岛口岸进出口总额 Total Value of Imports and Exports of Qingdao Port	#出口 Exports	进口 Imports
1985	414 448	234 652	179 796
1986	382 840	191 926	190 914
1987	445 090	259 458	185 632
1988	474 516	259 176	215 340
1989	506 152	268 397	237 755
1990	477 117	304 011	173 106
1991	519 273	332 949	186 324
1992	581 495	350 163	231 332
1993	678 013	360 297	317 716
1994	888 574	510 760	377 814
1995	1 307 508	705 245	602 263
1996	1 391 323	760 566	629 757
1997	1 542 284	936 142	609 142
1998	1 463 718	933 392	530 326
1999	1 696 514	1 063 768	632 746
2000	2 520 420	1 423 266	1 097 154
2001	2 797 085	1 636 888	1 160 197
2002	3 128 048	1 889 612	1 238 436
2003	4 088 096	2 366 046	1 722 050
2004	5 677 570	3 197 697	2 479 873
2005	6 932 944	3 959 947	2 972 997
2006	8 019 198	4 495 731	3 523 467
2007	9 257 099	5 263 539	3 993 560
2008	11 558 079	5 953 501	5 604 578
2009	9 049 699	4 694 832	4 354 867
2010	11 912 702	5 988 254	5 924 448
2011	15 095 088	7 294 226	7 800 862
2012	14 888 716	7 120 813	7 767 903
2013	15 662 732	7 696 141	7 966 591
2014	16 489 966	8 736 358	7 753 608

5-2 进出口总额(1988-2014年)

TOTAL VALUE OF IMPORTS AND EXPORTS(1988-2014)

单位:万美元(10000 USD)

年份 Year	进出口总额(含中央、省驻青公司) Total Value of Imports and Exports (including central and provincial companies)	#出口 Exports	进口 Imports	进出口总额(不含中央、省驻青公司) Total Value of Imports and Exports (excluding central and provincial companies)	#出口 Exports	进口 Imports
1988				28 097	21 731	6 366
1989				39 327	27 797	11 530
1990				41 649	33 529	8 120
1991				54 624	44 746	9 878
1992				88 600	66 291	22 309
1993	517 643	346 288	171 355	139 048	100 201	38 847
1994	633 213	434 102	199 111	234 978	164 135	70 843
1995	858 560	536 386	322 174	376 372	245 072	131 300
1996	863 521	516 317	347 204	461 950	287 123	174 827
1997	916 269	579 261	377 008	521 967	338 535	183 432
1998	882 042	573 020	309 022	595 826	382 657	213 169
1999	1 009 885	631 072	378 813	775 565	446 260	329 305
2000	1 353 222	826 891	526 331	1 083 133	611 426	471 707
2001	1 541 564	950 160	591 404	1 235 781	712 024	523 757
2002	1 692 567	1 057 141	635 426	1 409 598	850 420	559 178
2003	2 065 912	1 239 199	826 713	1 784 556	1 035 528	749 028
2004	2 698 781	1 578 167	1 120 614	2 433 188	1 391 171	1 042 017
2005	3 302 230	1 942 242	1 359 988	3 045 542	1 758 834	1 286 708
2006	3 911 543	2 346 552	1 564 991	3 655 737	2 164 541	1 491 196
2007	4 572 534	2 831 004	1 741 530	4 360 499	2 677 596	1 682 903
2008	5 363 659	3 262 476	2 101 183	5 215 886	3 146 246	2 069 640
2009	4 485 115	2 729 865	1 755 250	4 398 639	2 692 197	1 706 442
2010	5 705 963	3 391 560	2 314 403	5 614 928	3 335 141	2 279 787
2011	7 215 217	4 061 309	3 153 908	7 126 310	4 005 572	3 120 738
2012				7 320 781	4 081 968	3 238 813
2013				7 791 217	4 198 605	3 592 612
2014				7 988 833	4 577 696	3 411 137

注:2012年起,中央、省驻青公司外贸统计划归青岛,取消含中央、省驻青公司统计口径。

Note:Since 2012,the statistical calibre including central and provincial companies has been cancled.

5-3 分国别外贸出口总额

TOTLA VALUE OF EXPORTS BY COUNTRIES OR REGIONS

单位:万美元(10000 USD)

国别(地区)	Country(Region)	2014	2014年比2013年±% 2014/2013(±%)	占比%
总　计	**Total**	**4 577 331**	**9.0**	**100.0**
亚洲	Asia	2 014 053	8.1	44.0
香港	Hong Kong	144 131	25.7	3.1
日本	Japan	599 448	-5.0	13.1
韩国	Korea	476 944	17.7	10.4
台湾	Taiwan	52 432	9.7	1.1
非洲	Africa	244 738	14.1	5.3
南非	South Africa	36 048	0.3	0.8
欧洲	Europe	939 486	9.2	20.5
欧盟	EU	822 515	8.7	18.0
南美洲	South America	317 609	7.2	6.9
北美洲	North America	931 839	14.2	20.4
美国	United States	834 484	14.9	18.2
大洋洲	Oceanica	129 606	-11.8	2.8
澳大利亚	Australia	111 741	-15.3	2.4

5-4 外贸出口商品分类
EXPORT COMMODITIES BY CATEGORY

单位:万美元(10000 USD)

项目	Item	2014	2014年比2013年±% 2014/2013(±%)	占比%
合计	**Total**	**4 577 696**	**9.1**	**100.0**
按企业性质划分	By Enterprises Nature			
国有企业	State-owned Enterprises	507 316	3.2	11.1
外商投资企业	Foreign Funded Enterprises	1 728 865	4.0	37.8
其他企业	Other Enterprises	2 341 880	14.6	51.2
按贸易方式划分	By Customs Regime			
一般贸易	Ordinary Trade	2 740 654	12.3	59.9
加工贸易	Processing Trade	1 613 026	5.5	35.2
其他贸易	Others	224 381	-2.0	4.9
按大类商品划分	By Category of Commodities			
纺织服装	Textile Garments	771 068	1.9	16.8
农产品	Agricultural Products	520 038	3.5	11.4
机电产品	Mechanical and Electrical Products	1 792 744	17.6	39.2
高新技术产品	High-tech Products	380 564	42.1	8.3

5-5 二十大出口商品出口情况
INFORMATION ON THE EXPORTATION OF TOP 20 PRODUCTS

单位:万美元(10000 USD)

商品名称	Name	2014	2014年比2013年±% 2014/2013(±%)	占比%
合　计	**Total**	**3 858 716**	**14.1**	**100.0**
机械设备	Machinery and Equipment	586 398	21.0	15.2
服装	Garments	511 838	0.6	13.3
电器及电子类产品	Electric Appliance and Electronic Products	474 371	25.4	12.3
运输工具	Transport Tools	379 729	23.1	9.8
计算机与通信技术	Computer and Communication Technology	310 762	49.1	8.1
纺织品	Textile Products	259 230	4.4	6.7
金属制品	Metal Products	246 316	-6.2	6.4
轮胎	Tyre	178 632	2.9	4.6
水海产品	Aquatic and Seawater Products	142 881	3.4	3.7
电话机	Telephone Sets	115 514	72.1	3.0
钢材	Rolled Steel	106 771	15.1	2.8
鞋类	Shoes	103 862	5.6	2.7
家具及其零件	Furniture	103 535	12.9	2.7
箱包	Luggage and Bags	87 645	-2.5	2.3
蔬菜	Vegetables	85 611	6.2	2.2
塑料制品	Plastic Articles	80 645	9.3	2.1
汽车零件	Parts of Motor Vehicles	58 500	16.8	1.5
空调	Air Conditioner	25 970	3.8	0.7
游戏机	Game Console	453	99.7	
铁合金	Ferroalloy	53		

5-6 利用外资情况(2000-2014年)

UTILIZATION OF FOREIGN CAPITAL(2000-2014)

项目	Item	单位	Unit	2000	2005
批准企业(项目)个数	**Number of Enterprises (Projects) Approved**	**个**	**unit**	**1 132**	**2 530**
一、外商直接投资	Foreign Direct Investments	个	unit	1 128	2 530
中外合资企业	Sino-foreign Joint Ventures	个	unit	303	274
中外合作企业	Sino-foreign Cooperative Enterprises	个	unit	57	18
外商独资企业	Foreign-owned Enterprises	个	unit	76	2 236
其它	Others	个	unit	1	2
二、外商其他投资	Other Foreign Investments	个	unit	4	
合同外资金额	**Total Amount of Contracted Foreign Investment**	**万美元**	**10000 USD**	**269 081**	**954 486**
一、外商直接投资	Foreign Direct Investments	万美元	10000 USD	266 221	954 486
中外合资企业	Sino-foreign Joint Ventures	万美元	10000 USD	69 889	112 777
中外合作企业	Sino-foreign Cooperative Enterprises	万美元	10000 USD	26 835	17 588
外商独资企业	Foreign-owned Enterprises	万美元	10000 USD	169 370	813 485
其它	Others	万美元	10000 USD	127	10 636
二、外商其他投资	Other Foreign Investments	万美元	10000 USD	2 860	
实际利用外资金额	**Total Amount of Foreign Investment Actually Utilized**	**万美元**	**10000 USD**	**128 171**	**365 625**
一、外商直接投资	Foreign Direct Investments	万美元	10000 USD	126 132	365 625
中外合资企业	Sino-foreign Joint Ventures	万美元	10000 USD	39 224	77 636
中外合作企业	Sino-foreign Cooperative Enterprises	万美元	10000 USD	3 886	5 654
外商独资企业	Foreign-owned Enterprises	万美元	10000 USD	82 992	280 130
其它	Others	万美元	10000 USD	30	2 205
二、外商其他投资	Other Foreign Investments	万美元	10000 USD	2 039	

单位:万美元(10000 USD)

2006	2007	2008	2009	2010	2011	2012	2013	2014
1 397	**1 068**	**640**	**647**	**731**	**707**	**553**	**645**	**619**
1 397	1 068	640	647	731	707	553	645	619
267	165	99	99	153	158	113	165	140
13	11	4	2	4	4	2	2	1
1 117	892	537	545	574	544	438	478	475
			1		1			3
311 697	**382 500**	**304 505**	**271 504**	**475 723**	**528 501**	**600 231**	**758 063**	**638 637**
311 697	382 500	304 505	271 504	475 723	528 501	600 231	758 063	638 637
31 368	51 821	81 796	61 734	124 148	142 535	102 252	191 172	126 878
6 883	13 878	367	4 531	9 179	15 173	122	4 765	-849
273 446	316 187	221 759	204 187	341 977	369 425	490 764	562 208	506 271
	614	583	1 052	419	1 368	7 093	-82	6 337
365 815	**380 652**	**264 295**	**186 397**	**284 281**	**363 350**	**460 027**	**552 227**	**608 100**
365 815	380 652	264 295	186 397	284 281	363 350	460 027	552 227	608 100
49 240	46 370	43 810	46 856	84 920	100 699	169 469	159 424	172 180
7 123	15 490	2 945	3 971	3 567	2 759	6 262	2 355	128
309 452	318 578	217 540	135 026	194 500	255 763	275 579	390 210	435 102
	214		544	1 294	4 129	8 717	238	690

5-7 当年外商直接投资项目数和投资额(2014 年)
NUMBER OF PROJECTS AND TOTAL AMOUNT OF FOREIGN DIRECT INVESTMENT(2014)

项目	Item	批准企业项目数(个) Number of Projects Approved (unit)	合同外资金额(万美元) Total Amount of Contracted Foreign Investment(10000 USD)	实际利用外资金额(万美元) Total Amount of Foreign Investment Actually Utilized(10000 USD)
外商直接投资	**Foreign Direct Investments**	**619**	**638 637**	**608 100**
一、按投资方式分	**Grouped by Investment Form**			
#中外合资企业	Sino-foreign Joint Ventures	140	126 878	172 180
中外合作企业	Sino-foreign Cooperative Enterprises	1	-849	128
外商独资企业	Foreign-owned Enterprises	475	506 271	435 102
二、按主要行业分	**Grouped by Sector**			
#农、林、牧、渔业	Farming, Forestry, Animal Husbandry and Fishery	12	25 890	20 734
制造业	Manufacturing	203	277 990	305 733
电力、燃气及水的生产和供应业	Production and Supply of Electricity, Gas and Water	2	4 900	6 503
建筑业	Construction	5	111	2 378
交通运输、仓储和邮政业	Transport, Storage and Post	12	46 471	49 549
批发和零售业	Wholesale and Retail Trades	223	109 374	57 261
住宿和餐饮业	Hotels and Catering Services	24	2 019	6 966
房地产业	Real Estate	10	16 486	58 659
租赁和商务服务业	Leasing and Business Services	66	64 541	34 086
三、按主要国别(地区)分	**Grouped by Countries(Regions)**			
#韩国	Korea	248	113 622	75 677
香港	Hong Kong	134	327 500	271 439
日本	Japan	42	28 922	35 321
美国	United States	38	69 741	81 560
台湾省	Taiwan	25	19 896	33 499
新加坡	Singapore	23	28 218	25 842
德国	Germany	13	1 679	1 261

5 -8 对外投资与经济合作
OUTBOUND INVESTMENT AND INTERNATIONAL ECONOMIC COOPERATION

名 称	Name	计算单位	Unit	2014	2014 年比 2013 年 ± % 2014/2013(± %)
对外投资项目数	Number of Outbound Investment Projects	个	unit	145	101.0
对外投资中方投资额	The Amount of Investment by Chinese Sides in Outbound Investment	万美元	10000 USD	146 983	24.6
对外承包工程新签合同额	The Amount of New Contracts for Foreign Contracted Projects	万美元	10000 USD	227 540	-27.1
对外承包工程完成营业额	The Completed Turnover of Foreign Contracted Projects	万美元	10000 USD	359 106	2.4
对外劳务合作派出人数	Number of Persons Sent Overseas for International Labor Service Cooperation	人	person	13 107	18.5

5 -9 对外投资分国别(地区)情况表(2014 年)
INFORMATION ON OUTBOUND INVESTMENT BY COUNTRY/REGION FOR(2014)

国别(地区)	Country(Region)	项目数量(个) Number of Projects (unit)	2014 年比 2013 年 ± % 2014/2013(± %)	中方投资额(万美元) Amount of Investment by Chinese Sides (10000 USD)	2014 年比 2013 年 ± % 2014/2013(± %)
总 计	**Total**	**145**	**101**	**146 983**	**24.6**
亚洲	Asia	74	76.2	77 920	23.1
香港	Hong Kong	30	50.0	22 009	8.2
韩国	Korea	14	366.7	2 993	-69.6
印度尼西亚	Indonesia	6	200.0	19 412	90.6
马来西亚	Malaysia	5	400.0	10 820	1 832.1
日本	Japan	4	100.0	330	621.4
泰国	Thailand	3	200.0	8 553	1 374.6
柬埔寨	Cambodia	3	200.0	1 700	70.0
巴基斯坦	Pakistan	2		285	
新加坡	Singapore	2		1 278	-84.2
越南	Vietnam	2	-33.3	680	-25.3
台湾省	Taiwan	1		780	

5 -9 续表
continued

国别(地区)	Country(Region)	项目数量(个) Number of Projects (unit)	2014 年比 2013 年 ± % 2014/2013(±%)	中方投资额(万美元) Amount of Investment by Chinese Sides (10000 USD)	2014 年比 2013 年 ± % 2014/2013(±%)
蒙古	Mongolia	1	-50.0	9 080	558.0
孟加拉	Bangladesh	1			-100.0
非洲	Africa	11	22.2	26 409	643.8
南非	South Africa	2	100.0	300	-45.5
尼日利亚	Nigeria	2		600	
赞比亚	Zambia	1		5 000	
安哥拉	Angola	1	-50.0	100	-93.5
坦桑尼亚	Tanzania	1		60	
塞舌尔	Seychelles	1		49	
毛里求斯	Mauritius	1		9 800	
津巴布韦	Zimbabwe	1		800	
科特迪瓦	Cote d'Ivoire	1		9 700	
欧洲	Europe	7	16.7	9 871	-64.3
德国	Germany	3	200.0	7 012	40.2
俄罗斯联邦	Russian Federation	2		1 250	
比利时	Belgium	1		1 500	
法国	France	1		102	-99.1
荷兰	Netherlands	增资		7	
拉丁美洲	Latin America	2		6 193	2 562.5
英属维尔京群岛	Virgin Islands(E)	1		1 193	
开曼群岛	The Cayman Islands	1		5 000	
北美洲	North America	45	246.2	13 782	-38.5
美国	United States	40	344.4	7 452	-53.4
加拿大	Canada	5	25.0	6 330	-1.9
大洋洲	Oceanica	6		12 806	1 248.0
澳大利亚	Australia	6		12 806	1 248.0

主要统计指标解释

批准企业(项目)个数 是指外商直接投资中批准设立的外商投资企业个数、批准的合作开发项目个数。

合同外资金额 是指批准外商投资企业的合同、章程中规定的外国投资者认缴的出资额和企业投资总额内的应由外方投资者以自己的境外自有资金直接向企业提供的贷款。包括新批准企业合同外资和原有企业的增资减资,增资减资不对企业(项目)个数进行调整。

实际使用外资金额 是指合同外资金额的实际执行金额。

外商直接投资 是指外国企业和经济组织或个人(包括华侨、港澳台胞以及我国在境外注册的企业)按我国有关政策、法规,用现汇、实物、技术等在我国境内开办外商独资企业、与我国境内的企业或经济组织共同举办中外合资经营企业、合作经营企业或合作开发资源的投资(包括外商投资收益的再投资)以及经政府有关部门批准的项目投资总额内,企业从境外借入的资金。

外商其它投资 是指除外商直接投资以外其他方式吸收的外资。

进出口总额 是指实际进出我国国境的货物总金额。包括对外贸易实际进出口货物,来料加工装配进出口货物,国家间、联合国及国际组织无偿援助物资和赠送品,华侨、港澳台同胞和外籍华人捐赠品,租赁期满归承租人所有的租赁货物,进料加工进出口货物,边境地方贸易及边境地区小额贸易进出口货物(边民互市贸易除外),中外合资企业、中外合作经营企业、外商独资经营企业进出口货物和公用物品,到、离岸价格在规定限额以上的进出口货样和广告品(无商业价值、无使用价值和免费提供出口的除外),从保税仓库提取在中国境内销售的进口货物,以及其他进出口货物。

对外投资 是指在中华人民共和国境内依法设立的企业通过新设、并购及其他方式在境外拥有非金融企业或取得既有非金融企业所有权、控制权、经营管理权及其他权益的行为。

对外承包工程 是指中国的企业或其他单位承包境外建设工程的活动。

对外劳务合作 是指组织劳务人员赴其他国家或地区为国外的企业或机构工作的经营性活动。

Explanatory Notes on Main Statistical Indicators

Enterprises(Projects) Permitted refers to number of foreign invested enterprises and developed projects under cooperation through the permission.

Contracted Foreign Investment refers to expenditure promised by the foreign investor and loan stemed from broad innate fund of the foreign investor,according to the contract and regulation approved of enterprise invested by foreigner.

Actual Utilization of Foreign Investment refers to actual usage of contracted foreign investment,including cash,investment in kind and incorporeal agreed by the both sides as part of the investment,such as services and technology.

Foreign Direct Investment refers to the investments by foreign enterprises and economic organizations or individuals(including overseas Chinese,compatriots from Hong dong, Macao and Taiwan,and Chinese enterprises registered abroad),following the relevant policies and laws of China,for the establishment of ventures and cooperative enterprises or cooperative exploration of resources with enterprises or economic organizations in China,lt includes the reinvestment of the foreign entrepreneurs with the profits gained from the investment and the funds that enterprises borrow from aboard in the total investment of projects which are approved by the relevant department of the government.

Other Investment by Foreign Entrepreneurs refers to all forms of utilization of foreign capitals other than foreign direct investment.

Total Imports and Exports refers to the real value of commodities imported into and exported from the boundary of China. They include the actual imports and exports through foreign trade, imported and exported goods under the processing and assembling trades and materials, supplies and gifts as aid given gratis between governments and by the United Nations and other international organizations, and contributions donated by overseas Chinese, compatriots in Hong Kong and Macao and Chinese with foreign citizenship, leasing commodities owned by tenant at the expiration of leasing period, the imported and exported commodities processed with imported materials, commodities trading in border areas (excluding mutual exchange goods), the imported and exported commodities and articles for public use of the Sino-foreign joint ventures, cooperative enterprises and ventures exclusively with foreign own investment. Also included are import or export of samples and advertising goods for whose CIF or FOB value are beyond the permitted ceiling (excluding goods of no trading or use value and free commodities for export), imported goods sold in China from bonded warehouses and other imported or exported goods.

Outbound investment refers to such actions as to own a non-financial business or acquire the ownership, control or management of a established non-financial business and other rights and interests outside the People's Republic of China by incorporation, merger and acquisition and/or other means by an enterprise incorporated in the People's Republic of China by law.

Foreign engineering contracting refers to the activities of Chinese enterprises or other units involved in contracting construction projects outside the People's Republic of China.

Foreign labor service cooperation refers to the business activities of organizing and sending labor service personnel to other countries or regions to work for the businesses or institutions in foreign countries.

6 城市建设、环境保护 CITY CONSTRUCTION AND ENVIRONMENT PROTECTION

简要说明

一、本篇资料的主要内容

本篇资料主要反映了全市城市基础设施基本情况，包括市政设施、供水、供电、公共交通、园林绿化、燃气供热、城市环卫、环境保护及工业“三废”排放情况等方面的资料。

二、本篇资料的来源

1、本篇资料中市政设施、供水、公共交通、园林绿化、燃气供热、城市环卫相关资料来源于市建设委员会的城市建设统计年报，由市统计局固定资产投资统计处整理提供。

2、本篇资料中供电资料来源于青岛供电公司，由市统计局能源统计处整理提供。

3、本篇资料中环境保护、环境质量及工业“三废”排放情况来源于市环境保护局，由市统计局能源统计处整理提供。

Brief Introduction

I. Main Content

Data in this chapter show the basic conditions of public facilities of the whole city, including urban construction and infrastructure, water supply, electricity supply, public communications, urban greenery, gas and heating, urban sanitation, environmental protection and discharge conditions of industrial waste water, waste gas and solid waste, etc.

II. Source of Data

(1)Data on conditions of urban construction and infrastructure,watersupply,public communications, urban greenery, gas and heating, urban sanitation are based on the annual report of city construction provided by Qingdao Municipal Construction Commission, and compiled by the Division of Investment and Construction Statistics of Qingdao Municipal Bureau of Statistics.

(2)Data on electricity supply are provided by Qingdao Power Corporation, and compiled by the Division of Energy Statistics of Qingdao Municipal Bureau of Statistics.

(3)Data on environmental protection, environmental conditions and discharge conditions of industrial waste water, waste gas and solid waste are provided by Qingdao Municipal Bureau of Environmental Protection ,and compiled by the Division of Energy Statistics of Qingdao Municipal Bureau of Statistics.

6－1 主要年份城市建设和公用事业

MAJOR YEAR'S CITY CONSTRUCTION AND PUBLIC UTILITIES

年 份 Year	建成区面积 (平方公里) Developed Areas(sq. km)	年末道路长度 (公里) Length of Roads at Year-end(km)	年末道路面积 (万平方米) Area of Roads at Year-end (10000 sq. m)	公共汽车、电车线路网长度(公里) Network Length of Bus and Trolley Bus(km)
1949	27	243	206	26.4
1952	29	245	213	124.4
1957	36	248	217	232.3
1962	55	266	235	252.8
1965	57	266	235	308.1
1970	59	374	346	358.5
1975	63	392	355	389.3
1978	66	408	368	422.1
1980	72	408	377	474.1
1985	79	462	464	611.3
1987	81	578	575	581
1989	92.5	541	583	661
1990	94.3	667	786	777
1991	94.7	673	826	922
1992	95.4	683	840	988
1993	99.9	764	944	1 094
1994	103.9	811	985	1 372
1995	106	936	1 177	1 101
1996	110	991	1 339	1 211
1997	112	1 047	1 436	1 492
1998	114	1 106	1 436	1 859
1999	116	1 171	1 698	2 339
2000	119.1	1 192	1 789	2 711
2001	123	1 248	2 169	2 521
2002	133	1 426	2 594	896
2003	145.9	1 595	2 816	973
2004	154.8	1 755	3 254	1 185
2005	178.8	1 862	3 547	1 159
2006	227.5	3 160	5 218	1 362
2007	250.7	3 288	5 411	1 480
2008	267.1	3 318	5 596	1 470
2009	272.9	3 402	5 763	1 216
2010	282.3	3 409	5 893	1 383
2011	291.5	3 705	6 605	1 719
2012	374.6	4 281	7 528	1 978
2013	469.6	4 334	7 859	2 002
2014	490.7	4 393	7 908	2 023

注:1. 自 2002 年起人均公共绿地面积按辖区内全部人口计算。

2. 2005 年以前所用园林绿地面积;公共绿地面积;人均公共绿地面积;公园、动物园个数;公园、动物园面积指标分别改为现在的绿地面积;公共绿地面积;人均公园绿地面积;公园个数;公园面积。

3. 2012 年城市建设数据由建委提供,包括范围:市南区、市北区、李沧区、崂山区、黄岛区、城阳区。黄岛区包含开发区、保税区和原胶南划入的 6 个街道办事处的数据。与以前年度范围不同,数据不可比。

Note:1. Per capita public green areas is calculated at total population in the area under jurisdiction since 2002.

2. Before 2005, the corresponding indicators of greenbelt area, park greenbelt area, per capita park greenbelt area, coverage rate of greenbelt, number of parks and area of parks were greenland area , public greenbelt area , per capita public greenbelt area, coverage rate of green, number of parks and zoos, area of parks and zoos.

3. In 2012, the data on city construction are provided by Qingdao Urban and Rural Construction Commision, include: Shinan, Shibei, Licang, Laoshan, Huangdao, Chengyang. The statistics of Huangdao include Development Zone. Free Trade Zone and 6 sub-districts to be under the jurisdiction of original Jiaonan. The figures are not comparable with those over the years.

6－1 续表 1

continued

年　份 Year	自来水供水管道长度（公里） Length of Tap Water Pipelines (km)	全年供水总量（万立方米） Annual Volume of Tap Water Supply (10000 cu. m)	#全年售水量（万立方米） Annual Volume of Tap Water Sale (10000 cu. m)	#居民家庭用水 of which: Consumption for Residential Use	用水普及率（%） Coverage Rate of Population with Access to Tap Water (%)	排水管道长度（公里） Length of Sewage Pipes (km)	全年用电量（亿千瓦时） Annual Volume of Electricity Supply (100 million kW·h)	#居民生活用电 of which: Consumption for Residential Use
1949	308	721	456	331	89.0	200	0.88	0.14
1952	341	778	612	310	90.0	227	1.85	0.14
1957	412	1 392	1 296	606	93.0	273	2.61	0.26
1962	483	2 700	2 512	937	98.0	290	3.77	0.57
1965	500	3 220	2 979	929	98.0	295	5.92	0.68
1970	521	4 503	4 106	1 085	99.0	350	9.83	1.02
1975	564	6 726	6 302	1 950	99.0	361	12.41	1.43
1978	572	5 334	4 975	1 314	99.0	382	16.34	1.62
1980	588	8 224	7 874	2 577	99.0	394	21.48	2.78
1985	685	7 557	7 038	2 628	99.9	505	26.39	2.87
1987	749	10 716	9 155	3 691	99.9	569	34.15	4.01
1989	853	10 349	8 606	3 666	97.0	620	38.36	3.38
1990	873	11 896	10 211	4 270	96.9	645	41.08	4.32
1991	908	13 865	11 760	4 990	96.6	649	44.51	5.34
1992	1 035	16 385	13 070	5 931	96.5	672	51.78	6.84
1993	1 123	16 137	14 027	6 124	99.1	734	55.02	7.66
1994	1 124	17 367	14 716	6 405	100	811	60.74	8.78
1995	1 046	22 513	15 810	7 050	100	990	67.23	10.16
1996	1 182	23 277	16 566	7 731	100	1 051	72.87	12.23
1997	1 266	24 130	17 215	8 787	100	1 167	77.82	13.73
1998	1 390	23 845	17 271	9 115	100	1 210	79.65	14.28
1999	1 471	23 849	18 558	10 032	100	1 301	88.12	15.31
2000	1 524	25 414	20 642	11 405	100	1 460	106.80	16.00
2001	1 665	22 225	18 556	10 555	100	1 539	116.10	17.62
2002	1 781	27 662	21 684	10 129	100	1 641	131.44	18.31
2003	2 060	27 594	21 483	10 142	100	1 884	147.68	19.88
2004	2 566	30 877	23 864	11 695	100	2 002	167.95	23.63
2005	2 876	33 265	25 874	12 536	100	2 309	193.81	33.76
2006	3 984	30 524	25 572	10 682	100	3 994	215.35	34.87
2007	4 187	31 533	26 454	11 408	100	4 079	236.42	37.40
2008	4 642	32 675	27 396	11 301	100	4 229	250.07	40.31
2009	4 767	33 490	28 274	12 250	100	4 555	259.42	43.29
2010	4 926	34 909	29 617	12 524	100	4 708	292.97	49.50
2011	5 121	34 109	28 837	10 049	100	5 187	313.44	50.13
2012	5 243	38 945	33 039	12 121	100	6 814	318.36	51.64
2013	5 522	38 331	32 418	11 851	100	6 536	339.27	57.52
2014	6 177	46 649	40 612	14 834	100	6 840	337.82	59.95

6－1 续表2

continued

年 份 Year	公共汽车、电车营运车辆(辆) Number of Bus and Trolley Bus under Operation(unit)	全年客运量(万人次) Annual Passenger Traffic(10000 person-times)	出租汽车(辆) Number of Taxi(unit)	使用液化气、煤气、天然气人数(万人) Population with Access to Gas (10000 persons)	液化气 Liquefied Petroleum	煤 气 Coal Gas	天然气 Natural Gas	液化气供气量(吨) Volume of Liquefied Petroleum Supply(ton)
1949	32	298						
1952	76	932						
1957	112	4 110						
1962	127	4 747						
1965	173	6 092						
1970	224	13 002						
1975	324	14 426		2	2			184.9
1978	409	27 351		17	17			3 246
1980	485	38 981	48	24	24			4 345
1985	621	48 852	219	42.1	42.1			10 619
1987	679	56 102	652	56.4	45.4	11.0		12 947
1989	751	63 212	782	62.5	47.5	15.0		14 503
1990	801	63 495	832	75.0	57.4	17.6		17 512
1991	1 372	67 552	1 070	76.2	57.4	18.8		17 963
1992	1 470	73 529	1 828	82.8	62.0	20.8		19 565
1993	1 875	72 427	4 874	88.4	64.6	23.8		22 224
1994	1 850	78 231	5 806	103.6	77.4	26.2		24 684
1995	1 891	71 867	5 887	116.2	82.9	33.3		32 443
1996	2 012	49 077	6 660	126.0	88.0	38.0		40 651
1997	2 148	55 642	6 861	133.6	92.9	40.7		38 717
1998	2 184	51 042	7 469	146.8	97.8	49.0		45 381
1999	2 470	55 414	7 839	154.9	98.3	56.6		40 537
2000	3 141	59 879	7 933	164.1	93.3	70.8		46 951
2001	3 453	60 167	8 110	168.8	87.5	81.3		45 295
2002	3 681	61 713	8 376	224.2	133.8	90.4		60 123
2003	3 648	58 792	8 109	246.7	138.3	93.1	15.3	67 803
2004	3 848	66 463	8 144	258.4	140.6	78.8	39.0	58 548
2005	4 039	68 776	8 121	265.0	132.6	45.7	86.7	78 000
2006	4 167	73 726	8 146	271.0	112.5	49.5	109.0	97 343
2007	4 524	78 702	8 221	275.6	104.1	12.1	159.4	79 715
2008	4 701	82 460	9 241	276.3	91.9	10.5	173.9	81 987
2009	4 288	81 768	9 316	276.1	59.8	12.3	204.0	96 721
2010	4 664	85 251	9 539	276.3	36.7	12.6	227.0	80 073
2011	5 419	89 614	9 683	277.1	25.8	12.6	238.7	79 812
2012	5 640	97 922	9 693	313.7	36.7	13.1	263.9	54 341
2013	6 179	101 108	9 826	318.9	33.0	无	285.9	41 302
2014	6 515	105 592	9 720	325.4	33.0	无	292.4	39 255

注:1990 年以前公共营运车辆不包括系统外及个体。

Note:Vehicles not belonging to system and individual vehicles are not contained in public operating vehicles before 1990.

6-1 续表3
continued

年 份 Year	煤气供气量（万立方米）Volume of Coal Gas Supply (10000 cu. m)	天然气供气量（万立方米）Volume of Natural Gas Supply (10000 cu. m)	燃气普及率（%）Coverage Rate of Population with Access to Gas(%)	绿地面积（公顷）Area of Green Areas (hectare)	公园绿地面积（公顷）Park Green Areas (hectare)	人均公园绿地面积（平方米）Per Capita Park Green Areas(sq. m)	建成区绿化覆盖率（%）Green Coverage Rate of Developed Areas(%)	公园（个）Number of Parks and Zoos(unit)	公园面积（公顷）Area of Parks and Zoos (hectare)
1949				133	42	0.7	4.9	3	43
1952				134	43	0.7	4.4	4	45
1957				245	132	1.7	6.9	10	122
1962				771	184	2.2	14.0	12	174
1965				777	184	2.1	13.7	12	174
1970				772	184	2.1	13.0	6	117
1975			2.3	465	162	1.8	7.6	5	134
1978			18.6	469	162	1.7	7.6	6	165
1980			24.5	625	206	2.1	10.4	6	152
1985			36.3	1 072	255	2.3	17.3	7	153
1987	491		47.0	1 790	427	3.6	21.8	20	372
1989	2 585		47.3	1 941	459	3.5	21.7	22	381
1990	3 073		56.2	2 120	492	3.7	22.8	26	404
1991	3 439		56.5	2 318	500	3.7	24.4	28	443
1992	3 824		60.0	2 471	515	3.7	25.9	28	417
1993	4 215		63.1	2 488	543	3.9	26.5	31	453
1994	4 116		63.1	2 866	572	4.0	27.9	31	463
1995	4 734		79.2	4 547	771	5.3	30.1	33	675
1996	5 447		83.9	4 679	836	5.6	30.4	33	675
1997	5 920		87.3	4 717	924	6.0	31.3	34	730
1998	5 959		92.5	6 812	1 047	6.6	35.0	35	775
1999	7 319		96.0	7 007	1 186	7.4	35.9	36	791
2000	9 567		98.0	7 439	1 423	8.5	37.0	37	790
2001	11 814		99.0	7 688	1 588	9.3	37.5	39	832
2002	13 500		99.5	7 967	1 791	8.1	36.4	43	926
2003	14 826	1 181	100	8 829	2 305	9.3	37.5	45	1 034
2004	15 503	2 710	100	10 047	2 842	11	38.0	48	1 421
2005	16 573	7 456	100	11 137	3 132	11.8	38.8	47	1 110
2006	9 821	13 876	100	11 756	3 198	11.8	39.2	47	1 188
2007	9 516	18 103	100	15 369	3 661	13.3	37.8	73	1 268
2008	8 691	21 780	100	15 630	4 014	14.5	41.5	77	1 815
2009	7 523	26 948	100	16 003	4 003	14.5	43.4	71	1 897
2010	9 153	35 681	100	16 619	4 027	14.6	43.38	72	1 917
2011	9 137	46 147	100	18 013	4 041	14.6	44.69	74	1 931
2012	8 148	68 397	100	21 471	4 573	14.6	44.7	78	2 112
2013	无	70 918	100	28 007	4 649	14.6	44.7	87	2 698
2014	无	74 823	100	28 805	4 741	14.6	44.7	91	2 988

注：1. 自2002年起人均公共绿地面积按辖区内全部人口计算。
2. 2005年以前所用园林绿地面积；公共绿地面积；人均公共绿地面积；公园、动物园个数；公园、动物园面积指标分别改为现在的绿地面积；公共绿地面积；人均公园绿地面积；公园个数；公园面积。

Note：1. Per capita public green areas is calculated at total population in the area under jurisdiction since 2002.
2. Before 2005, the corresponding indicators of greenbelt area, park greenbelt area, per capita park greenbelt area, coverage rate of greenbelt, number of parks and area of parks were greenland area, public greenbelt area, per capita public greenbelt area, coverage rate of green, number of parks and zoos, area of parks and zoos.

6 -2 全年供电(2014 年)
ANNUAL ELECTRICITY SUPPLY(2014)

全年供电项目	Item	单位	Unit	2014
发电设备总容量	Total Capacity of Generation Equipment	万千瓦	10000 kW	423.83
#青岛电厂	Qingdao Power Plant	万千瓦	10000 kW	179
黄岛电厂	Huangdao Power Plant	万千瓦	10000 kW	122
全年发电量	Annual Electricity Generation	亿千瓦时	100 million kW·h	184.53
#青岛电厂	Qingdao Power Plant	亿千瓦时	100 million kW·h	81.5
黄岛电厂	Huangdao Power Plant	亿千瓦时	100 million kW·h	68.85
全年实际用电量	Annual Electricity Consumption	亿千瓦时	100 million kW·h	337.82
#工业	Industrial Consumption	亿千瓦时	100 million kW·h	205.77
农业	Agricultural Consumption	亿千瓦时	100 million kW·h	1.97
生活	Residential Consumption	亿千瓦时	100 million kW·h	59.95
平均每日用电量	Average Daily Consumption	万千瓦时	10000 kW·h	9 255

6 -3 分行业用电(2014 年)
ELECTRICITY CONSUMPTION BY SECTOR(2014)

单位:万千瓦时(10 000 kW·h)

行业	Sector	2014	2014 年比 2013 年增长(%) Growth Rate in 2014 over 2013(%)
全社会用电总计	**Total Electricity Consumption**	**3 378 197**	**-0.43**
一、农、林、牧、渔业	Farming, Forestry, Animal Husbandryand Fishery	54 170	6.93
二、工业	Industry	2 057 653	1.99
三、建筑业	Construction	56 967	11.42
四、交通运输、仓储和邮政业	Transport, Storage and Post	99 065	-3.55
五、信息传输、计算机服务和软件业	Information Transmission, Computer Services and Software	38 270	5.98
六、商业、住宿和餐饮业	Trade, Hotels and Catering Services	168 287	-9.89
七、金融、房地产、商务及居民服务业	Financial Intermediation, Real Estate and Business Services	172 852	-16.72
八、公共事业及管理组织	Public Management and Social Organization	131 440	-20.41
九、城乡居民生活用电	Household Consumption	599 493	4.23
城镇居民	Urban Area	332 400	4.01
乡村居民	Rural Area	267 093	4.49

6 -4 城市供水(2014 年)
URBAN WATER SUPPLY(2014)

项　目	Item	单位	Unit	2014
自来水供水管道长度	Length of Tap Water Pipelines	公里	km	6 177
综合生产能力	Synthesis Production Capacity	万立方米/日	10000 cu. m/day	170.2
全年供水总量	Annual Volume of Tap Water Supply	万立方米	10000 cu. m	46 649
#售水量	of which: Volume of Tap Water Sale	万立方米	10000 cu. m	40 612
#生产运营用水	of which: Consumption for Production Use	万立方米	10000 cu. m	15 366
公共服务用水	Consumption for Public Services Use	万立方米	10000 cu. m	8 365
居民家庭用水	Consumption for Residential Use	万立方米	10000 cu. m	14 834
其他用水	Consumption for Other Uses	万立方米	10000 cu. m	2 047
平均每日供水量	Daily Volume of Tap Water Supply	万立方米	10000 cu. m	111.3
#生产用	of which: Consumption for Production Use	万立方米	10000 cu. m	42.1
生活用	Consumption for Residential Use	万立方米	10000 cu. m	40.6
用水户数	Households with Access to Water	户	household	1 427 492
用水人口	Population with Access to water	万人	10000 persons	325
工业用水量重复利用率	Recycle Rate of Water for Industrial Use	%	%	87.6

6 –5 城市公共交通(2014 年)
URBAN PUBLIC TRAFFIC(2014)

项　目	Item	单位	Unit	2014
公共汽车、电车线路网长度	Network Length of Bus and Trolley Bus	公里	km	2 023
公共汽车、电车营运车辆	Number of Bus and Trolley Bus under Operation	辆	unit	6 515
#汽车	Bus	辆	unit	5 862
电车	Trolley Bus	辆	unit	653
公共汽车、电车全年客运量	Annual Passenger Traffic of Bus and Trolley Bus	万人次	10000 person-times	105 592
公共汽车、电车平均每日客运量	Daily Passenger Traffic of Bus and Trolley Bus	万人	10000 persons	289
出租汽车数	Number of Taxi	辆	unit	9 720
轮渡运营船数	Number of Ferry Boat under Operation	艘	ship	3
轮渡客运总量	Passenger Traffic of Ferry Boat	万人次	10000 person-times	82
轮渡平均每日客运量	Daily Passenger Traffic of Ferry Boat	万人	10000 persons	0.23

6-6 城市供气(2014年)
URBAN GAS SUPPLY(2014)

项 目	Item	单位	Unit	2014
煤气供应总量	Volume of Coal Gas Supply	万立方米	10000 cu. m	
#家庭用量	Household Consumption	万立方米	10000 cu. m	
煤气用气户数	Households with Access to Coal Gas	户	household	
#家庭用户	Household Users	户	household	
液化石油气供应总量	Volume of Liquefied Petroleum Supply	吨	ton	39 255
#家庭用量	Household Consumption	吨	ton	17 645
液化石油气用气户数	Households with Access to Liquefied Petroleum	户	household	167 503
#家庭用户	Household Users	户	household	165 052
天然气供应总量	Volume of Natural Gas Supply	万立方米	10000 cu. m	74 823
#家庭用量	Household Consumption	万立方米	10000 cu. m	17 865
天然气用气户数	Households with Access to Natural Gas	户	household	1 345 943
#家庭用户	Household Users	户	household	1 339 175
燃气普及率	Coverage Rate of Population with Access to Gas	%	%	100

6-7 城市环境卫生(2014年)
URBAN ENVIRONMENTAL SANITATION(2014)

项　目	Item	单位	Unit	2014
市容环卫专用车辆总数	Number of Special Vehicles for Environmental Sanitation	辆	unit	2 198
生活垃圾清运量	Volume of Garbage Disposal	万吨	10000 tons	156
生活垃圾无害化处理厂(场)数	Number of Bio-safety Disposal Plant of Garbage	座	unit	5
生活垃圾无害化处理能力	Bio-safety Disposal Capacity of Garbage	吨/日	ton/day	4 190
生活垃圾无害化处理量	Bio-safety Disposal Volume of Garbage	万吨	10000 tons	156
道路清扫保洁面积	Area under Cleaning Program	万平方米	10000 sq. m	5 664
#机械化	of which:Mechanization	万平方米	10000 sq. m	2 232
粪便清运量	Volume of Excrement and Urine Disposal	万吨	10000 tons	7.2
粪便无害化处理量	Bio-safety Disposal Volume of Excrement and Urine	万吨	10000 tons	5.96
公共厕所	Public Toilets	个	unit	529

6-8 城市道路、下水道及绿化(2014年)
URBAN ROAD,SEWAGE AND GREEN(2014)

项　目	Item	单位	Unit	2014
道路	**Road**			
年末道路长度	Length of Roads at Year-end	公里	km	4 393
年末道路面积	Area of Roads at Year-end	万平方米	10000 sq. m	7 908
#人行道面积	of which:Area of Pavements	万平方米	10000 sq. m	1 664
排水管道长度	Length of Sewage Pipes	公里	km	6 840
园林绿化	**Greening**			
绿化覆盖面积	Area of Green Coverage Areas	公顷	hectare	31 735
绿地面积	Area of Green Areas	公顷	hectare	28 805
公园绿地面积	Area of Park Green Areas	公顷	hectare	4 741
公园数	Number of Parks and Zoos	个	unit	91
公园面积	Area of Parks and Zoos	公顷	hectare	2 988
游人量	Number of Tourists	万人次	10000 person-times	1 732.0
城市每人平均公园绿地面积	Per Capita Park Green Area	平方米	sq. m	14.6
建成区绿化覆盖率	Green Coverage Rate of Developed Areas	%	%	44.7

6-9 环境保护基本情况(2014 年)
BASIC CONDITIONS OF ENVIRONMENTAL PROTECTION(2014)

项目	Item	单位	Unit	2014	2013	2014 年比 2013 年增(+)减(-)% 2014 Compared to 2013(+/-)
二氧化硫排放总量	Sulphur Dioxide Emission	吨	ton	91 119	96 835.4	-5.90
氮氧化物排放总量	Discharge Amount of Nitrogenoxides	吨	ton	101 657.45	108 797.54	-6.56
烟(粉)尘排放总量	Soot(Dust) Emission	吨	ton	41 474.21	42 058.16	-1.39
工业固体废物排放总量	Industrial Solid Wastes Discharged	吨	ton	0	0	
化学需氧量排放总量	Discharge Amount of Chemical Oxygen Demand	吨	ton	143 690.51	144 279.17	-0.41
氨氮排放总量	Discharge Amount of Ammonia and Nitrogen	吨	ton	12 193.35	12 221.86	-0.23
废水排放总量	Waste Water Discharged	万吨	10 000 tons	50 870.00	47 177.00	7.83

6-10 环境质量状况(2014 年)
ENVIRONMENT CONDITION(2014)

项目	Item	单位	Unit	2014	2013	2014 年比 2013 年增(+)减(-)% 2014 Compared to 2013(+/-)
市区空气质量优良率	The Percentages of Excellent Or Good Air Quality of Urban Area	%	%	71.8	72.9	-1.51
近岸海域功能区达标率	The Reaching Rate of The Offshore Sea Water for Corresponding Functional Regions	%	%	84.4	81.3	3.81
市区区域环境噪声平均等效声级	The Average Equivalent Sound Level of the Urban Regional Environmental Noise	分贝(A)	db(A)	58.2	57.5	1.22
市区道路交通噪声平均等效声级	The Average Equivalent Sound Level of the Urban Road Traffic Noise	分贝(A)	db(A)	67.8	68.9	-1.60

6-11 工业“三废”排放情况(2014年)
DISCHARGE CONDITIONS OF INDUSTRIAL WASTE WATER,WASTE GAS AND SOLID WASTE(2014)

项目	Item	单位	Unit	2014	2013	2014年比2013年增(+)减(-)% 2014 Compared to 2013(+/-)
工业废水排放总量	Industrial Waste Water Discharged	万吨	10000 tons	10 989.4	10 660.1	2.96
废水治理设施数	Number of Facilities for Treatment of Waste Water	套	set	457	478	-4.39
废水治理设施处理能力	Capacity of Facilities for Treatment of Waste Water	万吨/日	10000 tons/day	156.21	158.58	-1.49
进入城市污水处理厂量	Volume Handled by Sewage Treatment Plant	万吨	10000 tons	7 375.49	7 870.92	-6.29
化学需氧量排放量	Discharge Amount of Chemical Oxygen Demand	吨	ton	8 128.42	8 286.19	-1.90
氨氮排放量	Discharge Amount of Ammonia and Nitrogen	吨	ton	693.3	730.37	-5.08
工业废气排放总量	Industrial Waste Air Discharged	万标立方米	10000 cu. m	20 848 600	21 286 831	-2.06
废气治理设施数	Number of Facilities for Treatment of Waste Air	套	set	1 396	1 280	9.06
其中:脱硫设施数	of which:Desulphurization Facilities	套	set	286	300	-4.67
废气治理设施处理能力	Capacity of Facilities for Treatment of Waste Air	万标立方米/时	10000 cu. m/hr	6 978.07	7 238.23	-3.59
其中:脱硫能力	of which:Desulphurization Capacity	千克/时	kg/hr	63 371.99	71 221.07	-11.02
二氧化硫去除量	Sulphur Dioxide Removed	吨	ton	217 848.33	194 654.62	11.92
二氧化硫排放量	Sulphur Dioxide Emission	吨	ton	64 029.23	69 336.78	-7.65
烟(粉)尘排放量	Soot (Dust) Emission	吨	ton	32 196.05	27 802.72	0.34
工业固体废物产生量	Industrial Solid Wastes Producted	万吨	10000 tons	865.57	821.83	5.32
其中:危险废物	of which:Hazardous Wastes	吨	ton	41 808	32 463	28.79
工业固体废物综合利用量	Industrial Solid Wastes Comprehensive Utilized	万吨	10000 tons	842.39	791.15	6.48
工业固体废物排放量	Industrial Solid Wastes Discharged	万吨	10000 tons	0	0	
其中:危险废物	of which:Hazardous Wastes	吨	ton	0	0	
污染治理项目完成投资	Investment in Treatment Projects of Pollution	万元	10000 yuan	76 250.4	21 762	250.38
污染治理项目数	Number of Treatment Projects of Pollution	个	item	21	26	-19.23
当年竣工治理项目数	Number of Completed Treatment Projects in the Year	个	item	17	24	-29.17

主要统计指标解释

供水综合生产能力　指按供水设施取水、净化、送水、出厂输水干管等环节设计能力计算的综合生产能力。

年末供水管道长度　指从送水泵至用户水表之间所有管道的长度。不包括新安装尚未使用的管道。

用水普及率　指城市用水人口数与城市人口总数的比率。计算公式:

$$用水普及率 = \frac{城市用水人口数}{城市人口总数} \times 100\%$$

全年供水总量　指报告期供水企业(单位)供出的全部水量。包括有效供水量和漏损水量。

全年供气总量　指全年燃气企业(单位)向用户供应的燃气数量。包括销售量和损失量。

用气普及率　指报告期末使用燃气的城市人口数与城市人口总数的比率。计算公式为:

$$用气普及率 = \frac{城市用气人口数}{城市人口总数} \times 100\%$$

年末道路长度　指年末道路长度和与道路相通的广场、桥梁、隧道的长度,按车行道中心线计算。在统计时只统计路面宽度在3.5米(含3.5米)以上的各种铺装道路,包括开放型工业区和住宅区道路在内。

工业废气排放量　指报告期内企业厂区内燃料燃烧和生产工艺过程中产生的各种排入大气的含有污染物的气体的总量,以标准状态(273K,101325Pa)计算。

工业废水排放量　指经过企业厂区所有排放口排到企业外部的工业废水量。包括生产废水、外排的直接冷却水、超标排放的矿井地下水和与工业废水混排的厂区生活污水,不包括外排的间接冷却水(清污不分流的间接冷却水应计算在内)。

工业废水排放达标量　指各项指标都达到国家或地方排放标准的外排工业废水量,包括未经处理外排达标的和经过处理后外排达标的和两部分。国家排放标准见GB8978—88。

工业固体废物产生量　指企业在生产过程中产生的固体状、半固体状和高浓度液体状废弃物的总量,包括危险废物、冶炼废渣、粉煤灰、炉渣、煤矸渣、尾矿、放射性废物和其他废物等;不包括矿山开采的剥离废石和掘进废石(煤矸石和呈酸性或碱性的废石除外)酸性或碱性废石是指采掘的废石其流经水、雨淋水的pH值小于4或pH值大于10.5者。

工业粉尘排放量　指企业在生产工艺过程中排放的能在空气中悬浮一定时间的固体颗粒物排放量。如钢铁企业的耐火材料粉尘、焦化企业的筛焦系统粉尘、烧结机的粉尘、石灰窑的粉尘、建材企业的水泥粉尘等。不包括电厂排入大气的烟尘。

化学需氧量(COD)　测量有机和无机物质化学分解所消耗氧的质量浓度的水污染指数。

Explanatory Notes on Main Statistical Indicators

Production Capacity of Water Supply　refers to the designed comprehensive production capacity of water facilities, covering the 4 links of water collection, purification, conveyance, and outflow through trunk pipelines.

Length of Water Supply Pipelines at the Year-end　refers to the total length of all the pipelines between the water pumps and the user water meters, excluding pipelines newly installed but not used yet.

Coverage Rate of Urban Population with Access to Tap Water　refers to the ratio of the urban population with access to tap water to the total urban population. The formula is:

Coverage rate of urban population with access to tap water = (Urban population with access to tap water)/(Urban population) × 100%

Annual Volume of Water Supply refers to the total volume of water supplied by water-works(units) during the reference period, including both the effective water supply and loss during the water supply.

Annual Volume of Gas Supply refers to the total volume of gas provided to users by gas-producing enterprises(units) in a year, including the volume sold and the volume lost.

Coverage Rate of Urban Population with Access to Gas refers to the ratio of the urban population with access to gas to the total urban population at the end of the reference period. The formula is:

Coverage rate of urban population with access to gas = (Urban population with access to gas/Urban population) ×100%

Length of Paved Roads at the Year-end refers to the length of roads with paved surface including squares bridges and tunnels connected with roads by the end of the year. Length of the roads is measured by the central lines for vehicles for paved roads with a width of 3.5 meters and over, including roads in open-ended factory compounds and residential quarters.

Industrial Waste Air Emission refers to discharge into atmosphere of waste air containing pollutants generated from fuel burning and production process in enterprises within a given period of time. It is calculated at standard status(273K, 101325Pa).

Waste Water Discharged by Industry refers to the volume of waste water discharged by industrial enterprises through all their outlets, including waste water from production process, directly cooled water, groundwater from mining wells which does not meet discharge standards and sewage from households mixed with waste water produced by industrial activities, but excluding indirectly cooled water discharged(It should be included if the discharge is not separated with waste water).

Industrial Waste Water Meeting Discharge Standards refers to volume of industrial waste water discharge which, with or without treatment, reaches national or local standards with regard to all pollutants. National Discharge standards see GB8978—88.

Industrial Solid Wastes Produced refers to total volume of solid, semi-solid and high concentration liquid residues produced by industrial enterprises from production process in a given period of time, including hazardous wastes, slag, coal ash, gangue, tailings, radioactive residues and other wastes, but excluding stones stripped or dug out in mining(gangue and acid or alkaline stones not included). A stone is acid or alkaline depending on the pH value of the water below 4 or above 10.5 when the stone is in, or soaked by, the water.

Industrial Dust Emission refers to volume of dust emitted by production process of enterprises and suspended in the air for a given period of time, including dust from refractory material of iron and steel works, dust from coke-screening systems and sintering machines of coke plants, dust from lime kilns and dust from cement production in building material enterprises, but excluding soot and dust emitted from power plants.

Chemical Oxygen Demand(COD) refers to index of water pollution measuring the mass concentration of oxygen consumed by the chemical breakdown of organic and inorganic matter.

7 能 源 消 耗
CONSUMPTION OF ENERGY

简 要 说 明

一、本篇资料的主要内容

本篇资料主要反映了全市规模以上工业主要能源消费与库存情况，主要包括规模以上工业主要能源消费与库存、规模以上工业主要能源分行业消费量、重点耗能工业企业能源加工转换、规模以上工业主要能源工业消费量等方面的资料。

二、本篇资料的来源

本篇资料来源于规模以上工业能源统计年报，由市统计局能源统计处整理提供。

Brief Introduction

I. Main Content

Data in this chapter show the consumption and stock of major energy of industry above designated size, including consumption and stock of major energy of industry above designated size, major energy consumption of industry above designated size grouped by sector, energy conversion of major energy-consuming industrial enterprises and major energy consumption of industry above designated size, etc.

II. Source of Data

Data in this chapter are based on the annual report of energy consumed by industrial enterprises above designated size. The data are provided by the Division of Energy Statistics of Qingdao Municipal Bureau of Statistics.

7－1 规模以上工业主要能源消费与库存(2014 年)
CONSUMPTION AND STOCK OF MAJOR ENERGY OF INDUSTRY ABOVE DESIGNATED SIZE(2014)

名　称	Name	计算单位	Unit	年初库存 Stock at Year-beginning	本年消费 Consumption in the Year	#工 业 Industry	#非工业 Non-industry	年末库存 Stock at Year-end
原　煤	Raw Coal	吨	ton	1 849 816.46	14 038 068.40	14 011 518.59	26 549.81	1 730 578.89
焦　炭	Coke	吨	ton	54 706.74	1 004 450.62	1 004 397.30	53.32	35 799.63
焦炉煤气	Coking Gas	万立方米	10 000 cu. m					
高炉煤气	Blast Furnace Gas	万立方米	10 000 cu. m		18 495.12	18 495.12		
原　油	Crude Oil	吨	ton	530 723.44	15 492 410.95	15 492 410.95		514 807.68
汽　油	Petrol	吨	ton	550.99	130 992.53	110 122.13	20 870.38	254.36
煤　油	Kerosene	吨	ton	58.00	390.82	365.76	25.06	1.64
柴　油	Diesel Oil	吨	ton	2 130.85	121 039.01	106 880.44	14 158.57	2 325.89
燃料油	Fuel Oil	吨	ton	6 919.93	234 589.13	234 257.99	331.14	4 687.93
液化石油气	Liquefied Petroleum Gas	吨	ton	590.96	151 947.28	151 460.29	486.99	499.09
炼厂干气	Refinery Dry Gas	吨	ton		600 795.00	600 795.00		
热　力	Heat	百万千焦	million kJ		27 601 394.10	26 717 173.46	884 220.61	
电　力	Electricity	万千瓦时	10 000 kW · h		2 078 121.04	2 059 632.60	18 488.32	

补充资料:2014 年综合能源消费量 1489.58 万吨标准煤。

Note: In 2014, comprehensive energy consumption is 1489.58 million tons SCE.

7-2 规模以上工业主要能源分行业消费量(2014年)

MAJOR ENERGY CONSUMPTION OF INDUSTRY ABOVE DESIGNATED SIZE BY SECTOR (2014)

名称	Name	原煤（吨）Raw Coal (ton)	焦炭（吨）Coke (ton)	焦炉煤气（万立方米）Coking Gas (10 000 cu. m)	原油（吨）Crude Oil (ton)	汽油（吨）Petrol (ton)
总　计	**Total**	**14 038 068.40**	**1 004 450.62**		**15 492 410.95**	**130 992.53**
采掘业	Mining	858.57				1 590.94
制造业	Manufacturing	3 603 816.05	1 004 450.62		15 492 410.95	126 089.19
电力煤气及水生产供应业	Production and Supply of Electricity, Gas and Water	10 433 393.78				3 312.40

7-2 续表

continued

名称	Name	煤油（吨）Kerosene (ton)	柴油（吨）Diesel Oil (ton)	燃料油（吨）Fuel Oil (ton)	液化石油气（吨）Liquefied Petroleum Gas (ton)	热　力（百万千焦）Heat (million kJ)	电　力（万千瓦时）Electricity (10 000 kW·h)
总　计	**Total**	**390.82**	**121 039.01**	**234 589.13**	**151 947.28**	**27 601 394.10**	**2 078 121.04**
采掘业	Mining		1 404.62				10 926.91
制造业	Manufacturing	390.82	117 372.38	233 235.47	151 945.13	22 978 428.28	1 722 900.46
电力煤气及水生产供应业	Production and Supply of Electricity, Gas and Water		2 262.01	1 353.66	2.15	4 622 965.82	344 293.67

7-3 重点耗能工业企业能源加工转换(2014年)
ENERGY CONVERSION OF MAJOR ENERGY-CONSUMING INDUSTRIAL ENTERPRISES(2014)

名称	Name	单位	Unit	能源消费合计 Total Energy Consumption	#加工转换投入 Conversion Input	火电 Thermal Power	供热 Heating	炼油 Petrolume Refining	制气 Gas Production	能源加工转换产出 Conversion Output of Energy
原煤	Raw Coal	吨	ton	11 658 258.00	11 221 628.84	6 782 572.33	4 439 056.51			
洗精煤	Dressing Coal	吨	ton							
煤制品	Coal Products	吨	ton							
焦炭	Coke	吨	ton	959 611.92						
其他焦化产品	Other Coking Products	吨	ton	109 770.31						
焦炉煤气	Coking Gas	万立方米	10 000 cu. m							
高炉煤气	Blast Furnace Gas	万立方米	10 000 cu. m	18 495.12	18 495.12	0.00	18 495.12			
原油	Raw Oil	吨	ton	15 492 316.25	15 482 307.25			15 482 307.25		
汽油	Petrol	吨	ton	316.37						4 475 077.37
煤油	Kerosene	吨	ton							1 269 391.00
柴油	Diesel Oil	吨	ton	4 030.41						4 656 846.68
燃料油	Fuel Oil	吨	ton	192 455.66	189 920.00	756.00	136.00	189 028.00		308 421.56
液化石油气	Liquefied Petroleum Gas	吨	ton							1 166 765.16
炼厂干气	Refinery Dry Gas	吨	ton	600 795.00	22 728.00	0.00	22 728.00			600 795.00
其他石油制品	Other Petroleum Products	吨	ton	541 242.85	163 226.00			163 226.00		1 075 747.46
热力	Heat	百万千焦	million kJ	11 876 155.00						75 585 927.10
电力	Electricity	万千瓦时	10 000 kW·h	364 391.75						1 688 985.33
其他燃料	Other Fuel	吨标准煤	ton SCE							
能源合计	**Total**	**吨标准煤**	**ton SCE**	**34 935 872.61**	**31 024 192.54**	**4 924 849.30**	**3 482 757.29**	**22 616 585.95**		**27 013 994.27**

7-4 规模以上工业主要能源工业消费量(2014年)

MAJOR ENERGY CONSUMPTION OF INDUSTRY ABOVE DESIGNATED SIZE(2014)

行业	Sector
总　计	**Total**
煤炭开采和洗选业	Mining and Washing of Coal
石油和天然气开采业	Extraction of Petroleum and Natural Gas
黑色金属矿采选业	Mining of Ferrous Metal Ores
有色金属矿采选业	Mining of Non-ferrous Metal Ores
非金属矿采选业	Mining and Processing of Nonmetal Ores
开采辅助活动	Auxiliary Activities of Mining
其他采矿业	Mining of Other Ores
农副食品加工业	Processing of Food from Agricultural Products
食品制造业	Manufacture of Foods
酒、饮料和精制茶制造业	Manufacture of Liquor, Beverage and Refind Tea
烟草制品业	Manufacture of Tobacco
纺织业	Manufacture of Textile
纺织服装、服饰业	Manufacture of Textile Wearing Apparel
皮革、毛皮、羽毛及其制品和制鞋业	Manufacture of Leather, Fur, Feather & Its Products Footwear
木材加工和木、竹、藤、棕、草制品业	Processing of Timbers, Manufacture of Wood, Bamboo, Rattan, Palm and Straw Products
家具制造业	Manufacture of Furniture
造纸和纸制品业	Manufacture of Paper and Paper Products
印刷和记录媒介复制业	Printing, Reproduction of Recording Media
文教、工美、体育和娱乐用品制造业	Manufacture of Articles for Culture, Arts & Crafts, Sports and Entertainment
石油加工、炼焦和核燃料加工业	Processing of Petroleum, Coking, Processing of Nucleus Fuel
化学原料和化学制品制造业	Manufacture of Chemical Raw Material and Chemical Products
医药制造业	Manufacture of Medicines
化学纤维制造业	Manufacture of Chemical Fiber
橡胶和塑料制品业	Manufacture of Rubber and Plastic
非金属矿物制品业	Manufacture of Non-metallic Mineral Products
黑色金属冶炼和压延加工业	Smelting and Pressing of Ferrous Metals
有色金属冶炼和压延加工业	Smelting and Pressing of Non-ferrous Metals
金属制品业	Manufacture of Metal Products
通用设备制造业	Manufacture of General Purpose Machinery
专用设备制造业	Manufacture of Special Purpose Machinery
汽车制造业	Manufacture of Vehicle
铁路、船舶、航空航天和其他运输设备制造业	Manufacture of Transport Equipment for Railway, Shipping, Aerospace and other uses
电气机械和器材制造业	Manufacture of Electrical Machinery & Equipment
计算机、通信和其他电子设备制造业	Manufacture of Computer, Communication Equipment and Other Electronic Equipment
仪器仪表制造业	Manufacture of Measuring Instrument
其他制造业	Manufacture of Other Products
废弃资源综合利用业	Recycling and Disposal of Waste Resources
金属制品、机械和设备修理业	Maintenance of Metal Products, Machinery and Equipment
电力、热力的生产和供应业	Production and Supply of Electric Power and Heat Power
燃气生产和供应业	Production and Supply of Gas
水的生产和供应业	Production and Supply of Water

原煤 （吨） Raw Coal （ton）	洗精煤 （吨） Dressing Coal（ton）	其他洗煤 （吨） Other Dressing Coal（ton）	煤制品 （吨） Coal Products （ton）	焦炭 （吨） Coke （ton）
14 038 068.40	**70 083.23**	**395.00**	**8 607.70**	**1 004 450.62**
90.00				
768.57				
142 574.70	14 269.00		394.00	
24 160.86	539.00	390.00		
56 745.54				
96 559.49			5.00	
151 182.46	38.00			
36 783.77				
7 545.32				
39 635.78				1 596.43
97 877.27			2 956.00	
102 493.84				
103 161.38	147.00			46.62
9 711.00	0.00			
750 843.99	54 902.00		622.00	57 119.92
8 656.72	120.00		1 622.78	
404 975.32	35.00		315.00	
269 933.22			152.02	
446 249.34				905 569.27
7 933.68				
267 649.10	15.00			19 272.57
100 319.50	7.23	5.00	695.00	9 905.49
59 651.19			1 825.00	7 081.32
24 252.43				3 780.00
49 302.29				79.00
308 799.63	11.00			
17 096.65			20.90	
8 494.00				
3 333.62				
659.00				
7 234.96				
10 336 972.78				
96 387.00				
34.00				

7-4 续表1
continued

行业	Sector
总　计	**Total**
煤炭开采和洗选业	Mining and Washing of Coal
石油和天然气开采业	Extraction of Petroleum and Natural Gas
黑色金属矿采选业	Mining of Ferrous Metal Ores
有色金属矿采选业	Mining of Non-ferrous Metal Ores
非金属矿采选业	Mining and Processing of Nonmetal Ores
开采辅助活动	Auxiliary Activities of Mining
其他采矿业	Mining of Other Ores
农副食品加工业	Processing of Food from Agricultural Products
食品制造业	Manufacture of Foods
酒、饮料和精制茶制造业	Manufacture of Liquor, Beverage and Refind Tea
烟草制品业	Manufacture of Tobacco
纺织业	Manufacture of Textile
纺织服装、服饰业	Manufacture of Textile Wearing Apparel
皮革、毛皮、羽毛及其制品和制鞋业	Manufacture of Leather, Fur, Feather & Its Products Footwear
木材加工和木、竹、藤、棕、草制品业	Processing of Timbers, Manufacture of Wood, Bamboo, Rattan, Palm and Straw Products
家具制造业	Manufacture of Furniture
造纸和纸制品业	Manufacture of Paper and Paper Products
印刷和记录媒介复制业	Printing, Reproduction of Recording Media
文教、工美、体育和娱乐用品制造业	Manufacture of Articles for Culture, Arts & Crafts, Sports and Entertainment
石油加工、炼焦和核燃料加工业	Processing of Petroleum, Coking, Processing of Nucleus Fuel
化学原料和化学制品制造业	Manufacture of Chemical Raw Material and Chemical Products
医药制造业	Manufacture of Medicines
化学纤维制造业	Manufacture of Chemical Fiber
橡胶和塑料制品业	Manufacture of Rubber and Plastic
非金属矿物制品业	Manufacture of Non-metallic Mineral Products
黑色金属冶炼和压延加工业	Smelting and Pressing of Ferrous Metals
有色金属冶炼和压延加工业	Smelting and Pressing of Non-ferrous Metals
金属制品业	Manufacture of Metal Products
通用设备制造业	Manufacture of General Purpose Machinery
专用设备制造业	Manufacture of Special Purpose Machinery
汽车制造业	Manufacture of Vehicle
铁路、船舶、航空航天和其他运输设备制造业	Manufacture of Transport Equipment for Railway, Shipping, Aerospace and other uses
电气机械和器材制造业	Manufacture of Electrical Machinery & Equipment
计算机、通信和其他电子设备制造业	Manufacture of Computer, Communication Equipment and Other Electronic Equipment
仪器仪表制造业	Manufacture of Measuring Instrument
其他制造业	Manufacture of Other Products
废弃资源综合利用业	Recycling and Disposal of Waste Resources
金属制品、机械和设备修理业	Maintenance of Metal Products, Machinery and Equipment
电力、热力的生产和供应业	Production and Supply of Electric Power and Heat Power
燃气生产和供应业	Production and Supply of Gas
水的生产和供应业	Production and Supply of Water

焦炉煤气 (万立方米) Coking Gas (10 000 cu. m)	高炉煤气 (万立方米) Blast Furnace Gas (10 000 cu. m)	原油 (吨) Crude Oil(ton)	汽油 (吨) Petrol (ton)	煤油 (吨) Kerosene (ton)
	18 495.12	**15 492 410.95**	**130 992.53**	**390.82**
			1 234.41	
			356.53	
			10 290.03	20.04
			1 621.75	
			1 520.82	
			86.32	
			3 030.30	0.32
		84.70	11 317.50	113.43
			2 780.56	18.00
		8.00	365.95	
			1 821.06	
			916.30	
			6 192.00	2.00
			11 632.48	6.60
		15 492 316.25	304.38	
			4 258.62	
			1 071.26	
			17.11	
			8 200.72	92.00
			8 978.17	
	18 495.12		1 593.60	
			914.12	
			14 785.90	11.23
			9 344.58	108.03
			7 285.75	7.32
			4 887.89	5.03
		2.00	2 668.70	6.20
			5 294.29	0.62
			2 502.38	
			1 500.00	
			148.21	
			166.55	
			591.89	
			2 387.34	
			351.49	
			573.57	

7-4 续表 2
continued

行业	Sector
总 计	**Total**
煤炭开采和洗选业	Mining and Washing of Coal
石油和天然气开采业	Extraction of Petroleum and Natural Gas
黑色金属矿采选业	Mining of Ferrous Metal Ores
有色金属矿采选业	Mining of Non-ferrous Metal Ores
非金属矿采选业	Mining and Processing of Nonmetal Ores
开采辅助活动	Auxiliary Activities of Mining
其他采矿业	Mining of Other Ores
农副食品加工业	Processing of Food from Agricultural Products
食品制造业	Manufacture of Foods
酒、饮料和精制茶制造业	Manufacture of Liquor, Beverage and Refind Tea
烟草制品业	Manufacture of Tobacco
纺织业	Manufacture of Textile
纺织服装、服饰业	Manufacture of Textile Wearing Apparel
皮革、毛皮、羽毛及其制品和制鞋业	Manufacture of Leather, Fur, Feather & Its Products Footwear
木材加工和木、竹、藤、棕、草制品业	Processing of Timbers, Manufacture of Wood, Bamboo, Rattan, Palm and Straw Products
家具制造业	Manufacture of Furniture
造纸和纸制品业	Manufacture of Paper and Paper Products
印刷和记录媒介复制业	Printing, Reproduction of Recording Media
文教、工美、体育和娱乐用品制造业	Manufacture of Articles for Culture, Arts & Crafts, Sports and Entertainment
石油加工、炼焦和核燃料加工业	Processing of Petroleum, Coking, Processing of Nucleus Fuel
化学原料和化学制品制造业	Manufacture of Chemical Raw Material and Chemical Products
医药制造业	Manufacture of Medicines
化学纤维制造业	Manufacture of Chemical Fiber
橡胶和塑料制品业	Manufacture of Rubber and Plastic
非金属矿物制品业	Manufacture of Non-metallic Mineral Products
黑色金属冶炼和压延加工业	Smelting and Pressing of Ferrous Metals
有色金属冶炼和压延加工业	Smelting and Pressing of Non-ferrous Metals
金属制品业	Manufacture of Metal Products
通用设备制造业	Manufacture of General Purpose Machinery
专用设备制造业	Manufacture of Special Purpose Machinery
汽车制造业	Manufacture of Vehicle
铁路、船舶、航空航天和其他运输设备制造业	Manufacture of Transport Equipment for Railway, Shipping, Aerospace and other uses
电气机械和器材制造业	Manufacture of Electrical Machinery & Equipment
计算机、通信和其他电子设备制造业	Manufacture of Computer, Communication Equipment and Other Electronic Equipment
仪器仪表制造业	Manufacture of Measuring Instrument
其他制造业	Manufacture of Other Products
废弃资源综合利用业	Recycling and Disposal of Waste Resources
金属制品、机械和设备修理业	Maintenance of Metal Products, Machinery and Equipment
电力、热力的生产和供应业	Production and Supply of Electric Power and Heat Power
燃气生产和供应业	Production and Supply of Gas
水的生产和供应业	Production and Supply of Water

柴油 (吨) Diesel Oil (ton)	燃料油 (吨) Fuel Oil (ton)	液化石油气 (吨)Liquefied Petroleum Gas(ton)	炼厂干气 (吨) Refinery Dry Gas(ton)
121 039.01	**234 589.13**	**151 947.28**	**600 795.00**
534.54			
870.08			
6 612.47		89.31	
1 016.09		69.22	
1 684.81		367.83	
4.97			
2 701.55	5 410.05	433.00	
5 928.32	0.00	31.00	
1 641.99	122.50		
192.33			
1 845.18			
1 028.29			
3 414.52			
4 869.99	1 257.89	2.15	
162.00	191 421.00		600 795.00
5 780.26	1 687.00	146 936.32	
1 775.18			
3.42			
5 589.04	4 986.00		
30 986.71	28 102.76		
3 279.29	195.00		
1 040.67			
9 289.04	53.27	1 209.15	
7 162.43		0.18	
4 820.36		3.65	
3 329.70		299.77	
4 989.02		4.00	
4 387.71		2 480.46	
1 983.36		19.09	
1 055.22			
179.81			
139.34			
479.31			
1 837.27	1 353.66	2.15	
110.72			
314.02			

7-4 续表3
continued

行业	Sector
总　计	**Total**
煤炭开采和洗选业	Mining and Washing of Coal
石油和天然气开采业	Extraction of Petroleum and Natural Gas
黑色金属矿采选业	Mining of Ferrous Metal Ores
有色金属矿采选业	Mining of Non-ferrous Metal Ores
非金属矿采选业	Mining and Processing of Nonmetal Ores
开采辅助活动	Auxiliary Activities of Mining
其他采矿业	Mining of Other Ores
农副食品加工业	Processing of Food from Agricultural Products
食品制造业	Manufacture of Foods
酒、饮料和精制茶制造业	Manufacture of Liquor, Beverage and Refind Tea
烟草制品业	Manufacture of Tobacco
纺织业	Manufacture of Textile
纺织服装、服饰业	Manufacture of Textile Wearing Apparel
皮革、毛皮、羽毛及其制品和制鞋业	Manufacture of Leather, Fur, Feather & Its Products Footwear
木材加工和木、竹、藤、棕、草制品业	Processing of Timbers, Manufacture of Wood, Bamboo, Rattan, Palm and Straw Products
家具制造业	Manufacture of Furniture
造纸和纸制品业	Manufacture of Paper and Paper Products
印刷和记录媒介复制业	Printing, Reproduction of Recording Media
文教、工美、体育和娱乐用品制造业	Manufacture of Articles for Culture, Arts & Crafts, Sports and Entertainment
石油加工、炼焦和核燃料加工业	Processing of Petroleum, Coking, Processing of Nucleus Fuel
化学原料和化学制品制造业	Manufacture of Chemical Raw Material and Chemical Products
医药制造业	Manufacture of Medicines
化学纤维制造业	Manufacture of Chemical Fiber
橡胶和塑料制品业	Manufacture of Rubber and Plastic
非金属矿物制品业	Manufacture of Non-metallic Mineral Products
黑色金属冶炼和压延加工业	Smelting and Pressing of Ferrous Metals
有色金属冶炼和压延加工业	Smelting and Pressing of Non-ferrous Metals
金属制品业	Manufacture of Metal Products
通用设备制造业	Manufacture of General Purpose Machinery
专用设备制造业	Manufacture of Special Purpose Machinery
汽车制造业	Manufacture of Vehicle
铁路、船舶、航空航天和其他运输设备制造业	Manufacture of Transport Equipment for Railway, Shipping, Aerospace and other uses
电气机械和器材制造业	Manufacture of Electrical Machinery & Equipment
计算机、通信和其他电子设备制造业	Manufacture of Computer, Communication Equipment and Other Electronic Equipment
仪器仪表制造业	Manufacture of Measuring Instrument
其他制造业	Manufacture of Other Products
废弃资源综合利用业	Recycling and Disposal of Waste Resources
金属制品、机械和设备修理业	Maintenance of Metal Products, Machinery and Equipment
电力、热力的生产和供应业	Production and Supply of Electric Power and Heat Power
燃气生产和供应业	Production and Supply of Gas
水的生产和供应业	Production and Supply of Water

其他油制品 （吨） Other Petroleum Products(ton)	热　　力 （百万千焦） Heat (million kJ)	电　　力 （万千瓦时） Electricity (10 000 kW·h)	其他燃料 （吨标准煤） Other Fuel (ton SCE)
544 699.70	**27 601 394.10**	**2 078 121.04**	**1 626.98**
		4 274.33	
		6 652.58	
	566 102.81	122 070.74	
	317 433.03	24 143.85	
	1 860 513.80	21 218.17	
	239 326.00	4 712.44	
2.49	1 542 639.69	44 440.72	
	2 094 965.99	58 145.84	110.00
	238 415.64	25 275.90	
		4 834.24	
	1 886.92	17 051.20	
	966 896.04	20 458.20	
	96 419.22	31 709.87	
	20 700.00	51 718.30	18.69
540 892.00		50 967.20	
3 723.85	11 653 904.17	139 061.12	
	460 048.60	14 303.59	116.49
	16 522.70	10 534.81	
	215 557.90	155 584.57	
	34 294.00	130 978.27	
	127 728.10	179 219.78	
	66 895.63	29 650.97	
7.82	423 677.07	125 160.33	191.00
63.94	102 524.52	104 203.98	
	33 198.65	59 640.32	
	500 948.90	76 782.17	15.00
9.60	292 944.90	64 229.98	1 173.80
	866 289.40	87 431.85	2.00
	152 790.60	57 530.13	
		7 871.62	
	85 804.00	2 157.12	
		349.51	
		1 463.67	
	4 609 059.00	320 773.61	
	13 906.82	3 257.52	
		20 262.54	

主要统计指标解释

工业企业能源消费量 工业企业能源消费包括工业企业在生产过程中作为燃料、动力、原料、辅助材料使用的能源以及工艺用能、非生产用能;作为能源加工转换企业,还要包括能源加工转换的投入量。工业企业能源消费量具体包括:

(1)用于本企业产品生产、工业性作业和其他生产性活动的能源。

(2)用于技术更新改造措施、新技术研究和新产品试制以及科学试验等方面的能源。

(3)用于经营维修、建筑及设备大修理、机电设备和交通运输工具等方面的能源。

(4)用于劳动保护的能源。

(5)其他非生产消费的能源。

不包括:

(1)由仓库发到车间,但在报告期最后一天没有消费的能源。这部分能源应在办理假退料手续后计入库存量。

(2)拨到外单位,委托外单位加工用的能源。

(3)调出本单位或借给外单位的能源。

工业生产能源消费 是指工业企业为进行工业生产活动所使用的能源。主要包括:

1. 用于本企业产品生产、工业性作业的能源,包括用作原料、材料、燃料、动力:作为能源加工转换企业,还包括用作加工转换的能源。

2. 产品生产过程中作为辅助材料使用的能源。

3. 生产工艺过程使用的能源。

4. 新技术研究、新产品试制、科学试验使用的能源。

5. 为了工业生产活动而在进行的各种修理过程中使用的能源。

6. 生产区内的劳动保护用能等。

Explanatory Notes on Main Statistical Indicators

Energy Consumption of Industrial Enterprises include energy in the production process as fuel, power, raw materials, supplementary materials, and for use of technology and non-production. As energy processing and conversion enterprises, also include energy processing and conversion of inputs. These specifically include: (1) Energy for the enterprise product, industrial production operations and other activities. (2) Energy for technical upgrading measures and new technology research and new product production and scientific experiments. (3) Energy for operation maintenance, construction and equipment overhaul, electrical and mechanical equipment and transport, and other aspects. (4) Energy for the protection of labor. (5) Energy for Other non-production and consumption. And these exclude: (1) Energy from the warehouse to the workshop, but out of consumption on the last day of the reporting period. This part of the energy should leave retreat materials handling procedures included stock. (2) Energy transferred to other units, entrusted with the processing. (3) Energy transferred out of the unit or loans to other units.

Energy Consumption for Industrial Production refers to energy for industrial enterprises in industrial production activities. These mainly include: 1. Energy for the enterprise products, industrial operations, including energy as raw materials, materials, fuels, and power. As energy processing and conversion enterprises, also include energy for processing and conversion. 2. Energy as supplementary material in product process. 3. Energy used in production process. 4. Energy for new technologies, new product production, and scientific experiment. 5. Energy in process of repairing for industrial production activities. 6. Energy for labor protection in production areas and so on.

8 财政、金融和保险业

GOVERNMENT FINANCE FINANCIAL INTERMEDIATION AND INSURANCE

简要说明

一、本篇资料的主要内容

本篇资料主要反映了全市财政收支、金融和保险方面的情况，主要包括财政收入、财政支出、金融机构存贷款、保险业务开展等方面的资料。

二、本篇资料的来源

1、财政部分的资料来源于市财政局。

2、金融方面的资料来源于中国人民银行青岛市中心支行。

3、保险方面的资料来源于中国保险监督管理委员会青岛监管局。

本篇资料由市统计局国民经济核算处整理提供。

Brief Introduction

I. Main Content

Data in this chapter show the conditions of local government budgetary finance, banking and insurance,and securities, including government revenue and expenditure, deposits and loans of financial institutions and statistics on insurance companies.

II. Source of Data

(1) Data on local government finance are provided by Qingdao Municipal Finance Bureau.

(2) Data on banking are provided by Qingdao Branch of the People's Bank of China.

(3) Data on insurance are provide by China Insurance Regulatory Commission of Qingdao Bureau.

Data in this chapter are prepared and compiled by the Division of National Accounts of Qingdao Municipal Bureau of Statistics.

8-1 主要年份地方财政收支

MAJOR YEAR'S REVENUE AND EXPENDITURE OF LOCAL GOVERNMENT FINANCE

单位:万元(10 000 yuan)

年份 Year	财政收入 Revenue of Government Finance	财政支出 Expenditure of Government Finance
1949	1 527	306
1952	19 809	2 226
1957	29 875	3 556
1962	32 869	4 327
1965	47 682	6 280
1970	95 778	7 825
1975	90 220	11 966
1978	130 749	19 427
1980	124 835	20 064
1985	165 155	41 996
1988	201 206	93 931
1989	221 183	113 585
1990	242 303	133 875
1991	259 377	137 716
1992	275 589	155 696
1993	182 348	211 938
1994	227 490	277 331
1995	294 771	376 982
1996	379 674	469 569
1997	476 804	564 787
1998	580 434	678 575
1999	680 089	740 937
2000	800 120	878 702
2001	987 080	1 097 848
2002	1 006 616	1 243 880
2003	1 201 398	1 471 747
2004	1 305 136	1 646 214
2005	1 763 412	2 030 622
2006	2 257 663	2 367 875
2007	2 925 798	3 211 777
2008	3 424 359	3 694 111
2009	3 769 896	4 335 754
2010	4 526 138	5 323 888
2011	5 661 400	6 580 605
2012	6 701 820	7 659 801
2013	7 889 313	10 142 273
2014	8 952 450	10 747 138

注:1. 1993 年以后实行新制度,财政收入数与历年不可比。

2. 2002 年以后,财政收入、支出为一般预算数。

Note:1. Since 1993,new regulations have been adopted in calculating revenue of government finance,the figures are not comparable with those over the years.

2. Since 2002,revenue of government finance and expenditure of government finance refer to general budgetary revenue and expenditure.

8 -2 分市、区一般公共预算收入(2014 年)

GENERAL PUBLIC BUDGET REVENUE BY CITY AND DISTRICT(2014)

单位:万元(10 000 yuan)

市、区名称	Region	一般公共预算收入 General Public Budget Revenue	#增值税 Value-added Tax	#营业税 Business Tax	#企业所得税 Enterprise Income Tax
全　市	**Whole Municipality**	**8 952 450**	**1 039 518**	**2 057 076**	**1 050 852**
市南区	Shinan District	1 108 917	182 832	368 951	168 003
市北区	Shibei District	923 017	106 482	257 843	153 731
李沧区	Licang District	508 904	40 974	208 976	34 202
崂山区	Laoshan District	1 037 339	136 521	215 273	195 081
黄岛区	Huangdao District	1 673 004	228 626	379 016	185 629
保税港区	Qingdao Free Trade Port Area of China	80 072	20 884	7 175	24 196
城阳区	Chengyang District	766 267	127 887	214 158	84 242
即墨市	Jimo	790 393	55 757	141 826	35 949
胶州市	Jiaozhou	675 066	61 629	124 964	47 388
平度市	Pingdu	448 202	36 041	68 203	37 692
莱西市	Laixi	419 867	23 638	40 486	15 134
红岛经济区	Qingdao National High-tech Industrial Development Zone	126 018	18 247	30 205	18 989
市本级	Municipal Level	395 384	0	0	50 616

8-2 续表
continued

单位:万元(10 000 yuan)

市、区名称	Region	#个人所得税 Personal Income Tax	#城市维护建设税 Urban Maintenance and Development Tax	#基金预算收入 Funds Budgetary Revenue
全　市	**Whole Municipality**	**301 670**	**437 297**	**5 855 158**
市南区	Shinan District	74 929	48 856	13 911
市北区	Shibei District	28 043	48 035	13 606
李沧区	Licang District	9 672	35 253	13 651
崂山区	Laoshan District	72 522	83 891	390 976
黄岛区	Huangdao District	45 387	91 691	1 398 358
保税港区	Qingdao Free Trade Port Area of China	2 818	5 001	15 472
城阳区	Chengyang District	19 439	47 771	397 882
即墨市	Jimo	8 707	24 859	545 111
胶州市	Jiaozhou	26 581	22 251	292 256
平度市	Pingdu	5 210	14 347	45 786
莱西市	Laixi	4 129	8 897	7 000
红岛经济区	Qingdao National High-tech Industrial Development Zone	4 233	6 445	389 347
市本级	Municipal Level	0	0	2 331 802

8－3 分市、区一般公共预算支出(2014 年)

GENERAL PUBLIC BUDGET EXPENDITURE BY CITY AND DISTRICT(2014)

单位:万元(10 000 yuan)

市、区名称	Region	一般公共预算支出 General Public Budget Expenditure	#一般公共服务支出 General Public Services	#公共安全 Public Security	#教育 Education	#科学技术 Science and Technology	#文化体育与传媒 Culture,Sport and Media
全　市	**Whole Municipality**	**10 747 138**	**1 432 292**	**587 288**	**1 871 258**	**270 133**	**147 612**
市南区	Shinan District	463 281	66 998	15 662	89 249	7 144	3 790
市北区	Shibei District	694 606	124 986	25 569	152 069	22 015	8 818
李沧区	Licang District	315 073	39 815	10 974	92 206	5 427	4 691
崂山区	Laoshan District	654 440	75 967	23 174	128 493	17 638	3 975
黄岛区	Huangdao District	1 555 170	188 606	51 047	301 216	49 718	14 663
保税港区	Qingdao Free Trade Port Area of China	62 249	13 647	1 782	787	80	5
城阳区	Chengyang District	603 448	90 676	18 031	149 050	12 468	6 218
即墨市	Jimo	887 645	252 957	23 239	242 276	2 569	6 337
胶州市	Jiaozhou	788 072	117 358	37 424	186 187	14 556	9 058
平度市	Pingdu	708 989	93 601	25 902	184 582	7 312	5 256
莱西市	Laixi	560 394	64 359	18 223	101 259	1 596	3 196
红岛经济区	Qingdao National High-tech Industrial Development Zone	150 217	16 773	2 168	23 457	15 601	336
市本级	Municipal Level	3 303 554	286 549	334 093	220 427	114 009	81 269

8 -3 续表
continued

单位：万元(10 000 yuan)

市、区名称	Region	#社会保障和就业 Social Security and Employment	#医疗卫生 Health Care	#节能保护 Environment Protection	#城乡社区事务 Urban and Rural Community Affairs	#农林水事务 Affairs of Agiculture, Forest and Irrigation	#基金预算支出 Funds Budgetary Expenditure
全　市	**Whole Municipality**	**859 856**	**584 278**	**126 356**	**1 971 377**	**493 638**	**5 999 794**
市南区	Shinan District	42 209	23 425	775	67 400	1	52 871
市北区	Shibei District	55 259	43 183	1 750	233 681		120 037
李沧区	Licang District	41 553	20 390	1 341	68 609	2 595	248 244
崂山区	Laoshan District	23 293	23 813	2 730	159 568	46 041	322 910
黄岛区	Huangdao District	129 189	81 775	22 798	367 068	77 468	1 387 633
保税港区	Qingdao Free Trade Port Area of China	483	574	20	29 956	552	6 868
城阳区	Chengyang District	29 548	35 296	5 096	117 172	36 115	388 040
即墨市	Jimo	66 442	60 663	4 467	124 222	59 508	565 171
胶州市	Jiaozhou	53 041	57 837	18 486	89 712	80 451	339 399
平度市	Pingdu	87 291	84 457	14 937	112 171	69 130	84 146
莱西市	Laixi	62 649	46 228	9 455	24 669	56 185	67 891
红岛经济区	Qingdao National High-tech Industrial Development Zone	12 311	7 828	793	22 128	9 920	394 255
市本级	Municipal Level	256 588	98 809	43 708	555 021	55 672	2 022 329

8-4 主要年份金融系统人民币存贷款(年末余额)
MAJOR YEAR'S DEPOSITS AND LOANS OF FINANCIAL INSTITUTIONS(YEAR-END BALANCE)

单位:万元(10 000 yuan)

年份 Year	存款合计 Total Deposits	#企业存款 Deposits by Enterprises	#储蓄存款 Savings Deposits	贷款合计 Total Loans
1949	693	239	28	278
1952	9 093	4 308	1 838	3 322
1957	10 372	3 359	4 037	30 690
1962	20 040	8 579	3 279	73 601
1965	27 331	11 830	6 347	64 555
1970	38 264	13 024	7 576	126 382
1975	60 622	22 568	15 637	207 006
1978	66 523	21 004	21 455	297 184
1980	120 644	38 105	38 609	379 666
1985	344 760	99 736	155 604	452 142
1988	754 442	206 541	366 483	955 351
1989	932 430	245 529	481 692	1 174 448
1990	1 235 562	321 542	655 895	1 535 751
1991	1 553 564	411 417	824 428	1 871 462
1992	2 076 667	612 868	1 044 165	2 352 449
1993	2 747 294	835 617	1 372 239	2 940 658
1994	3 769 019	1 399 110	1 918 734	3 610 564
1995	5 324 026	2 030 382	2 687 888	4 777 864
1996	6 991 289	2 630 958	3 499 219	5 941 281
1997	7 385 092	2 885 632	4 060 259	6 508 776
1998	8 183 471	3 018 063	4 591 012	7 239 231
1999	9 160 001	3 454 570	4 978 045	8 945 730
2000	10 560 624	4 386 316	5 353 215	9 564 293
2001	12 323 942	4 955 336	6 187 409	10 798 871
2002	15 225 733	5 819 655	7 449 408	13 044 792
2003	18 920 868	7 027 227	9 084 693	16 783 917
2004	22 462 592	7 924 690	10 894 941	18 472 613
2005	26 975 372	8 226 661	13 431 016	20 394 792
2006	32 453 583	10 144 296	15 676 197	25 779 442
2007	38 915 882	13 213 434	17 020 383	30 970 553
2008	47 353 803	14 641 948	21 233 637	37 483 209
2009	63 019 764	21 001 185	25 278 658	48 735 326
2010	76 592 065	27 271 963	29 123 256	58 862 263
2011	86 384 994	49 189 415	31 985 099	69 477 500
2012	94 348 924	50 978 985	37 576 007	79 465 532
2013	109 695 588	60 367 185	41 405 946	88 607 439
2014	113 703 085	60 791 933	44 358 964	97 200 532

注:自 2011 年起,企业存款指标改为单位存款,口径与以前年度不一致。

Note: Since 2011, "Deposits by Corporate" has been used instead of "Deposits by Enterprises", and the caliber is different from the preoious year.

8-5 金融系统人民币存贷款(年末余额)

DEPOSITS AND LOANS OF FINANCIAL INSTITUTIONS(YEAR-END BALANCE)

单位:万元(10 000 yuan)

项目	Item	2014 年	比年初增减数 Incremental/Reductions Compared to the Beginning of the Year
一、存款总计	**Total Deposits**	**113 703 085**	**4 007 497**
企业存款	Deposits by Enterprises	60 791 933	393 580
储蓄存款	Savings Deposits	44 358 964	2 953 019
二、贷款总计	**Total Loans**	**97 200 532**	**8 400 675**
短期贷款	Short-Term Loans	36 782 757	224 681
#个人贷款及透支	Personal Loans and Line	5 059 477	101 669
单位贷款及透支	Business Loans and Line	27 862 396	748 743
贸易融资	Trade Financing	3 803 884	-571 357
中长期贷款	Medium&Long-term Loans	55 926 866	7 117 170
#个人贷款	Personal Loans	18 377 551	2 067 819
单位贷款	Business Loans	29 600 003	4 266 015
银团贷款	Syndicated Loans	6 229 079	851 914
贸易融资	Trade Financing	1 659 751	-96 656
票据融资	Notes Financing	3 788 135	472 599

8-6 国内保险业务(2000-2014 年)

DOMESTIC INSURANCE BUSINESS(2000-2014)

项目	Item	2000	2005	2006	2007	2008
风险保障金额	**Total domestic insurance Value**	**38 357 485**	**91 691 581**	**119 396 881**	**228 774 417**	**276 989 344**
国内业务收入	**Domestic Business Income**	**220 780**	**495 701**	**605 143**	**776 031**	**1 027 258**
1. 保费收入	Premium Income	218 714	495 701	605 143	776 031	1 027 258
#财产险	Property Insurance	85 161	159 746	199 213	272 664	280 008
农业险	Agriculture Insurance	18	12	19	1 542	3 135
人身险	Personal Insurance	133 535	335 943	405 911	501 825	744 115
国内业务支出	**Domestic Business Expenditure**	**94 877**	**214 148**	**252 477**	**361 183**	**423 743**
1. 赔款支出	Claim Expenditure	62 275	111 385	131 321	171 613	196 318
#财产险	Property Insurance	58 361	92 700	115 214	138 739	164 415
农业险	Agriculture Insurance	5	11	3	53	907
人身险	Personal Insurance	3 909	18 674	16 104	32 821	30 996
2. 给付支出	Mature Payment	27 955	32 739	63 144	95 282	132 621
3. 退保	Surrender	4 647	70 024	58 012	94 288	94 804

注:本表由青岛市保监局提供,风险保障金额 2012 年之前为国内保险总值。

Note:This table was provided by the Qingdao Insurance Regulatory Bureau. The amount of risk protection before 2012 was the total value of domestic insurance.

单位:万元(10 000 yuan)

2009	2010	2011	2012	2013	2014
293 519 697	**309 244 255**	**380 829 634**	**447 476 690**	**491 953 749**	**611 632 799**
1 153 101	1 538 526	1 457 269	1 602 881	1 789 854	2 031 421
1 153 101	1 538 526	1 457 269	1 602 881	1 789 854	2 031 421
339 314	492 190	556 257	644 269	744 470	872 805
4 066	3 261	3 587	5 046	6 824	8 395
809 721	1 043 075	897 425	953 566	1 038 560	1 150 220
476 377	**497 832**	**463 751**	**592 167**	**757 404**	**1 031 415**
219 546	279 019	307 564	360 085	432 494	492 693
188 723	250 966	286 214	328 877	392 860	442 168
3 452	2 808	1 087	1 833	3 820	5 519
27 371	25 245	20 263	29 375	35 814	45 006
123 056	109 318	156 188	154 922	194 592	274 790
133 775	109 496	69 275	77 159	130 318	263 932

主要统计指标解释

财政收入　指国家财政参与社会产品分配所取得的收入，是实现国家职能的财力保证。财政收入所包括的内容几经变化，目前主要包括：

(1)税收收入：包括增值税、营业税、企业所得税、个人所得税、资源税、固定资产投资方向调节税、城市维护建设税、房产税、印花税、城镇土地使用税、土地增值税、车船税、耕地占用税、契税、烟叶税、其他税收收入。

(2)非税收入：包括专项收入、行政事业性收费收入、罚没收入、国有资本经营收入、国有资源有偿使用收入、其他收入。

财政支出　国家财政将筹集起来的资金进行分配使用，以满足经济建设和各项事业的需要，主要包括：

(1)一般公共服务支出：反映政府提供一般公共服务的支出。

(2)公共安全：反映政府维护社会公共安全方面的支出，有关事务包括武装警察、公安、国家安全、检察、法院、司法行政、监狱、劳教、国家保密、缉私警察等。

(3)教育支出：反映政府教育事务支出。有关具体教育事务包括教育行政管理、学前教育、小学教育、初中教育、普通高中教育、普通高等教育、初等职业教育、中专教育、技校教育、职业高中教育、高等职业教育、广播电视教育、留学生教育、特殊教育、干部继续教育、教育机关服务等。

(4)科学技术：反映政府用于科学技术方面的支出。

(5)文化体育与传媒：反映政府在文化、文物、体育、广播电视、新闻出版等方面的支出。

(6)社会保障和就业：反映政府在社会保障与就业方面的支出。有关事项包括社会保障与就业管理事务、民政管理事务、财政对社会保险基金的补助、补充全国社会保障基金、行政事业单位离退休、企业改革补助、就业补助、抚恤、退役安置、社会福利、残疾人事业、城市居民最低生活保障、其他城镇社会救济、农村社会救济、自然灾害生活补助、红十字事务等。

(7)医疗卫生支出：反映政府医疗卫生方面的支出。具体包括医疗卫生管理事务支出、医疗服务支出、医疗保障支出、疾病预防控制支出、卫生监督支出、妇幼保健支出、农村卫生支出等。

(8)环境保护：反映政府环境保护支出。具体包括：环境保护管理事务支出、环境监测与监察支出、污染治理支出、自然生态保护支出、天然林保护工程支出、退耕还林支出、风沙荒漠治理支出、退牧还草支出、已垦草原退耕还草支出。

(9)城乡社区事务：反映政府城乡社区事务支出。具体包括：城乡社区管理事务支出、城乡社区规划与管理支出、城乡社区公共设施支出、城乡社区住宅支出、城乡社区环境卫生支出、建设市场管理与监督支出等。

(10)农林水事务：反映政府农林水事务方面的支出。具体包括农业、林业、水利、扶贫支出、农业综合开发支出等。

存款　指企业、机关、团体或居民根据资金必须收回的原则，把货币资金存入银行或其他信贷机构保管并取得一定利息的一种信用活动形式。根据存款对象或性质的不同可划分为企业存款、财政存款、机关团体存款、基本建设存款、储蓄存款、农村存款、委托存款、其他存款等科目。它是银行信贷资金的主要来源。

贷款　指银行或其他信贷机构根据资金必须归还的原则，按一定利率，为企业、个人等提供资金的一种信用活动形式。我国银行贷款分为短期贷款、中期流动资金贷款、中长期贷款、信托贷款、融资租赁、委托贷款、票据融资、各项垫款等。

承保额　又叫保险金额，指保险人承担赔偿或者给付保险金责任的最高限额。

保费　指投保人为取得保险人在约定范围内所承担赔偿责任而支付给保险人的费用。

Explanatory Notes on Main Statistical Indicators

Government Revenue　refers to the revenue of the government finance by means of participating in the distribution of the social products, which is the financial resources for ensuring the government to function. The contents of government revenue have been changed several times. Now it includes the following main items:

(1) Various tax revenues, including value added tax, business tax, enterprise income tax, personal income tax, resources tax, fixed assets investment direction regulating tax, tax on city maintenance and construction, real estate tax, stamp tax, tax on use of urban land, land value added tax, vehicle and vessel tax, tax on occupancy of cultivated land, property tax, tobacco leaf tax, and other tax revenues.

(2) Non-tax Revenues including special revenues, revenues from Administrative and institutional fees, penalty and confiscatory revenues , revenues from state-owned capital operationg,revenues from paid use of state-owned resources, and other revenues.

Government Expenditure refers to the distribution and use of the funds the government finance has raised, so as to meet the needs of economic construction and various causes. It includes the following main items:

(1) Expenditure for general public services: It reflects the expenditure from the government for general public services.

(2) Expenditure on public security: It reflects the expenditure from the government towards safeguarding the public security, including the related affairs of armed police, public security, state security, procuratorial administration,law court, judicial administration, jail , reeducation through labor, state confidentiality, anti-smuggling Patrol,etc.

(3) Expenditure on education: It reflects the expenditure from the government on education, including the related affairs of educational administration management, preschool education, primary education, junior secondary educate, regular senior secondary educate, regular higher education, primary vocational education, specialized secondary educate, technical educate, vocational senior secondary educate, vocational higher education, radio and television education, foreign student educate, special education, cadre continuing education, education institution services,etc.

(4) Expenditure on science and technology: It reflects the expenditure from the government on science and technology.

(5) Expenditure on culture, sport and media: It reflects the expenditure from the government on culture, cultural relics, sport, radio and television, publication, etc.

(6)Expenditure on social security and employment:It reflects the expenditure from the government on social security and employment, including the related affairs of management of social security and employment, civil administration, subsidies to social insurance funds, supplement to national social security funds, retirees of government agencies and institutions, subsidies to enterprises reform, subsidies to employment, pension, settling down demobilized servicemen,social security, disabled person administration, minimum living allowance in urban area, other social relief in urban area, social relief in rural area, subsidies to natural disaster, Red Cross business,etc.

(7)Expenditure on health care: It reflects the expenditure from the government on health care, including expenditure on management of health care, medical services, medical security, disease control and prevention, public health supervision, rural health care, etc.

(8) Expenditure on environment protection: It reflects the expenditure from the government on environment protection, including expenditure on management of environment protection, environment monitoring and supervisory, pollution government, natural ecological protection, project of natural forest protection, returning farmland to forest, sandstorm and wilderness government, returning grazing land to grassland, returning cultivated grassland to grassland, etc.

(9) Expenditure on urban and rural community affairs: It reflects the expenditure from the government on urban and rural community affairs, including expenditure on management of urban and rural community affairs, plan and management of urban and rural community, public utility of urban and rural community, residential buildings of urban and rural community, environmental sanitation of urban and rural community, management and supervision of markets construction, etc.

(10) Expenditure on agriculture, forest and irrigation: It reflects the expenditure from the government on agriculture, forest and irrigation, including expenditure on agriculture, forest, irrigation, poverty alleviation, comprehensive development of agriculture, etc.

Deposit is a form of credit by which enterprises, institutions, organizations or households can put money into banks and other credit institutions for safekeeping and interest earning under the principle of free withdrawal. According to different depositors, deposits are divided into enterprise deposits, treasury deposits, deposits of government agencies and organizations, capital construction deposits, savings deposits, rural saving deposits, entrusted deposits and other deposits. Deposits are major sources of the credit funds of banks.

Loan is a form of credit by which banks and other credit institutions provide funds at certain interest rate to enterprises and individuals in the light of the principle of unconditional repayment. Loans from Chinese banks include circulating capital loans, fixed assets loans, loans to urban and rural individuals engaged in industrial and commercial business and agricultural loans.

Amount Covered which also is known as amount Insured, refers to the maximum that the insurant will get for the claim of the case insured.

Premium is the fee paid by the insurant to the insurer to obtain the obligation of compensation from the insurance within the agreed terms.

价格指数 9
PRICE

简要说明

一、本篇资料的主要内容

本篇资料主要包括工业生产者出厂、工业生产者购进、固定资产投资、房地产、居民消费、商品零售等价格指数。

二、本篇资料的来源

1、工业生产者出厂、工业生产者购进、固定资产投资、房地产价格指数分别来源于生产、投资、房地产价格统计调查年报，由国家统计局青岛调查队生产投资价格调查处整理提供。

2、居民消费、商品零售价格指数来源于消费价格统计调查年报，由国家统计局青岛调查队消费价格调查处整理提供。

Brief Introduction

I. Main Content

Data in this chapter mainly include producer price indices for manufactured goods, purchasing price indices for industrial producers, price indices of investment in fixed assets, real estate price indices, consumer price indices and retail price indices.

II. Source of Data

(1) Data on producer price indices for manufactured goods, purchasing price indices for industrial producers, price indices of investment in fixed assets, real estate price indices are based on annual report of price survey on production,investment,real estate,and provided by the Division of Production Price Survey of Survey Office of the National Bureau of Statistics in Qingdao.

(2) Data on consumer price indices and retail price indices are based on annual report of consumer price survey, and provided by the Division of Consumer Price Survey of Survey Office of the National Bureau of Statistics in Qingdao.

9-1 主要年份居民消费和商品零售价格指数

MAJOR YEAR'S CONSUMER AND RETAIL PRICE INDEXES

(上年=100) (preceding year = 100)

年份 Year	居民消费价格指数 Consumer Price Index	#食品类 Food	衣着类 Clothing	服务项目价格指数 Services Price Index	商品零售价格指数 Retail Price Index
1951	110.5	105.2	112.4		110.5
1952	99.8	99.6	98.7		99.8
1957	101.4	101.3	101.4	99.3	101.4
1962	102.6	102.0	100.2	99.9	102.6
1965	101.2	101.3	98.8	96.9	101.2
1970	98.9	99.7	100.0	99.5	98.9
1975	100.3	100.1	100.0	100.0	100.3
1978	100.5	100.2	99.8	100.0	100.5
1980	105.2	108.5	100.3	100.6	105.5
1985	110.4	115.2	102.3	102.7	110.9
1987	109.4	112.5	106.8	102.5	109.8
1988	120.7	125.2	117.3	118.3	120.9
1989	115.3	109.2	121.1	130.2	114.4
1990	104.5	103.4	103.4	118.8	103.6
1991	107.0	107.0	112.1	109.6	106.8
1992	111.4	115.1	108.6	119.9	110.8
1993	123.9	120.9	119.0	158.5	119.8
1994	126.9	135.2	130.1	117.9	122.8
1995	116.2	118.1	122.8	123.2	114.2
1996	112.6	110.1	104.3	130.4	106.0
1997	104.0	101.2	102.3	120.8	100.2
1998	100.0	93.7	94.5	136.2	94.9
1999	100.2	96.7	97.1	115.6	96.6
2000	103.3	100.0	108.3	112.0	99.7
2001	101.0	100.6	98.0	108.7	98.9
2002	98.9	97.8	100.2	101.0	99.5
2003	101.4	104.3	98.4	101.7	98.3
2004	102.1	104.0	103.6	104.7	99.0
2005	102.3	102.1	108.3	101.4	99.3
2006	100.9	101.7	99.4	100.8	99.7
2007	104.5	111.6	99.4	102.4	102.7
2008	104.7	111.7	103.9	99.8	103.9
2009	100.5	101.6	101.4	100.6	98.6
2010	102.2	106.4	101.0	100.4	101.4
2011	105.0	111.1	108.2	103.1	104.5
2012	102.7	104.3	106.3	102.1	101.7
2013	102.5	105.3	104.9	100.7	101.4
2014	102.6	104.4	103.2	101.9	102.3

9-2 主要年份居民消费和商品零售价格指数(以1950年价格为100)

MAJOR YEAR'S CONSUMER AND RETAIL PRICE INDEXES (1950 = 100)

年份 Year	居民消费价格指数 Consumer Price Index	#食品类 Food	衣着类 Clothing	服务项目价格指数 Services Price Index	商品零售价格指数 Retail Price Index
1951	110.5	105.2	112.4		110.5
1952	110.3	104.8	110.9		110.3
1957	119.5	120.7	115.3	91.6	119.5
1962	127.4	128.8	115.1	94.2	127.4
1965	133.3	138.7	108.4	81.5	133.3
1970	129.0	137.6	110.3	76.8	129.0
1975	128.8	138.2	110.0	75.7	128.8
1978	129.1	138.7	109.8	75.7	129.1
1980	137.6	154.1	109.3	76.1	138.1
1985	160.8	196.1	103.8	80.5	162.5
1987	185.4	235.8	113.6	85.2	188.2
1988	223.8	295.2	133.2	100.8	227.6
1989	258.1	322.4	161.3	131.3	260.3
1990	269.7	333.3	166.8	155.9	269.7
1991	288.6	356.7	187.0	170.9	288.1
1992	321.5	410.5	203.1	204.9	319.2
1993	398.3	496.3	241.7	324.8	382.4
1994	505.4	671.1	314.4	382.9	469.5
1995	587.3	792.5	386.1	471.8	536.2
1996	661.3	872.6	402.7	615.2	568.4
1997	687.8	883.0	412.0	743.1	569.5
1998	687.8	827.4	389.3	1 012.1	540.5
1999	689.2	800.1	378.0	1 170.0	522.1
2000	711.9	800.1	409.4	1 310.4	520.5
2001	719.0	804.9	401.2	1 424.4	514.8
2002	711.1	787.2	402.0	1 438.7	512.2
2003	721.1	821.0	395.6	1 463.1	503.5
2004	736.2	853.9	409.8	1 531.9	498.5
2005	753.1	871.8	443.8	1 553.4	495.0
2006	759.9	886.6	441.2	1 565.8	493.5
2007	794.1	989.5	438.5	1 603.4	506.8
2008	831.4	1 105.3	455.6	1 600.2	526.6
2009	835.6	1 123.0	462.0	1 609.8	519.2
2010	854.0	1 194.9	466.6	1 616.2	526.5
2011	896.7	1 327.5	504.9	1 666.3	550.2
2012	920.9	1 384.6	536.7	1 701.3	559.6
2013	943.9	1 458.0	563.0	1 713.2	567.4
2014	968.4	1 522.2	581.0	1 745.8	580.5

9 -3 主要年份生产投资价格指数

MAJOR YEAR'S PRICE INDEXES FOR PRODUCTION AND INVESTMENT

(上年 = 100) (preceding year = 100)

年份 Year	工业生产者出厂价格指数 Producer Price Indexes for Industrial Producers	工业生产者购进价格指数 Purchasing Price Indexes for Industrial Producers	房屋销售价格指数 Sales Price Indexes of Houses	房屋租赁价格指数 Renting Price Indexes of Houses	物业管理价格指数 Property Management Price Indexes	固定资产投资价格指数 Price Indexes for Investment in Fixed Assets
1990	104.33	108.64				
1991	101.68	108.10				
1992	105.46	107.13				
1993	115.49	126.91				
1994	121.62	120.30				
1995	112.70	114.25				
1996	103.81	103.25				
1997	100.22	101.93				
1998	94.96	92.77	100.1	94.0		
1999	96.93	95.88	103.7	104.3		
2000	101.89	106.81	102.3	95.8		
2001	98.00	97.81	104.1	107.0		
2002	97.37	96.78	107.6	94.4		
2003	100.97	106.51	114.6	99.4		
2004	102.92	113.62	115.2	98.6		105.8
2005	101.39	106.52	110.9	103.3	100.2	103.1
2006	101.08	105.80	106.9	110.1	99.8	102.6
2007	101.50	106.69	106.5	108.3	100.4	104.1
2008	105.33	115.91	105.1	106.5	102.1	111.0
2009	95.78	90.35	100.3	103.5	100.4	94.6
2010	103.75	112.21		103.0	100.5	104.9
2011	104.90	109.39				107.0
2012	98.61	97.00				100.0
2013	98.82	96.53				100.1
2014	97.46	96.72				99.9

注：自 2011 年工业品出厂价格改为工业生产者出厂价格；主要原材料、燃料、动力购进价格改为工业生产者购进价格。

Note: Since 2011, "Producer Price Indexes for Industrial Producers" has been used in stead of "Producer Price Indexes for Manufactured Goods", "Purchasing Price Indexes for Industrial Producers" has been used in stead of "Purchasing Price Indexes for Raw Material, Fuel and Power".

9-4 工业生产者出厂价格指数
PRODUCER PRICE INDEXES FOR INDUSTRIAL PRODUCERS

(上年=100) (preceding year=100)

类　别	Item	2000	2005	2006	2007	2008	2009	2010	2011	2012	2013	2014
总 指 数	**General Index**	**101.89**	**101.39**	**101.08**	**101.50**	**105.33**	**95.78**	**103.75**	**104.90**	**98.61**	**98.82**	**99.20**
其中:轻工业	Light Industry	98.50	99.78	99.58	100.97	102.93	97.21	100.80	103.46	99.70	99.11	99.62
重工业	Heavy Industry	105.62	104.32	103.94	102.49	109.17	93.45	107.57	105.89	97.87	98.62	98.91
其中:生产资料	**Means of Production**	**105.03**	**103.24**	**102.49**	**102.41**	**108.76**	**94.25**	**106.43**	**105.54**	**97.55**	**98.58**	**98.87**
采掘	Excavation	95.67	114.74	104.73	99.85	115.24	93.44	130.94	132.07	93.35	91.72	100.65
原料	Raw Materials	113.82	106.91	104.05	104.01	108.81	90.67	115.24	111.52	99.05	99.26	98.87
加工	Processing	97.58	101.45	101.86	101.91	108.59	95.34	103.50	103.49	97.20	98.50	98.84
生活资料	**Means of Livelihood**	**98.25**	**99.13**	**99.74**	**100.64**	**101.72**	**97.45**	**99.61**	**103.82**	**100.42**	**99.21**	**99.76**
食品	Food	96.59	98.80	101.52	106.55	108.42	98.21	105.06	109.71	99.91	95.34	98.34
衣着	Clothing	99.37	101.48	102.16	102.46	103.36	102.03	101.56	107.44	102.03	102.74	100.34
一般日用品	Articles for Daily Use	104.52	101.97	101.82	103.21	103.03	99.39	99.96	108.02	101.64	101.42	101.01
耐用消费品	Durable Consumer Goods	97.70	97.43	97.23	96.10	97.13	94.52	93.23	94.34	98.79	98.41	99.65

9-5 工业生产者购进价格指数

PURCHASING PRICE INDEXES FOR INDUSTRIAL PRODUCERS

(上年=100) (preceding year=100)

名称	Item	2000	2005	2006	2007	2008	2009	2010	2011	2012	2013	2014
总指数	**General Index**	**106.81**	**106.52**	**105.8**	**106.69**	**115.91**	**90.35**	**112.21**	**109.39**	**97.00**	**96.53**	**97.40**
燃料、动力类	Fuel and Power	113.82	117.34	117.17	103.14	126.19	90.53	115.43	111.29	100.64	95.18	97.65
黑色金属材料类	Ferrous Metals	102.66	107.84	95.83	109.61	122.19	82.38	111.97	113.08	93.20	93.76	95.81
#钢材	Rolled-steel	105.44	106.57	96.11	108.14	119.10	85.25	108.67	107.95	92.33	92.87	96.87
其他	Others	101.1	112.88	94.91	114.43	132.40	72.73	122.64	129.01	94.64	96.57	92.49
有色金属材料及电线类	Nonferrous Metals and Electric Wire	106.75	108.06	131.58	106.51	93.41	86.24	122.65	108.45	93.64	96.23	96.24
化工原料类	Raw Chemical Materials	106.90	112.47	99.71	111.09	123.00	87.66	111.04	113.79	96.72	96.47	99.51
木材及纸浆类	Timber and Paper Pulp	108.98	103.8	104.29	107.23	103.58	89.16	117.06	103.78	93.12	98.79	102.42
建筑材料及非金属矿类	Building Materials and Nonmetals	99.50	115.54	92.83	95.80	124.52	100.98	107.61	116.71	102.48	100.13	97.36
其他工业原材料及半成品	Other Industrial Raw Materials and Semi-finished Goods	105.32	97.87	103.33	104.43	109.65	92.70	106.41	103.31	98.05	96.65	96.25
农副产品	Agricultural Products	92.73	101.55	110.87	112.49	117.68	88.60	121.30	115.04	98.21	98.54	97.62
纺织原料类	Textile Materials	104.03	98.15	100.15	104.01	101.44	98.69	112.90	111.11	95.61	99.60	97.38

9－6 按工业行业分工业生产者出厂价格指数

PRODUCER PRICE INDEXES FOR INDUSTRIAL PRODUCERS BY SECTOR

(上年＝100)

行　　业	Sector	2005
工业生产者出厂价格指数	**Producer Price Indexes for Manufactured Goods**	**101.39**
煤炭开采和洗选业	Mining and Washing of Coal	
石油和天然气开采业	Extraction of Petroleum and Natural Gas	
黑色金属矿采选业	Mining of Ferrous Metal Ores	100.65
有色金属矿采选业	Mining of Non－ferrous Metal Ores	108.54
非金属矿采选业	Mining and Processing of Nonmetal Ores	117.32
其他采矿业	Mining of Other Ores	
农副食品加工业	Processing of Food from Agricultural Products	97.23
食品制造业	Manufacture of Foods	101.21
饮料制造业	Manufacture of Beverage	100.80
烟草制品业	Manufacture of Tobacco	101.64
纺织业	Manufacture of Textile	
纺织服装、鞋、帽制造业	Manufacture of Textile Wearing Apparel, Footware, and Caps	102.56
皮革、毛皮、羽毛(绒)及其制品业	Manufacture of Leather, Fur, Feather & Its Products	99.38
木材加工及木、竹、藤、棕、草制品业	Processing of Timbers, Manufacture of Wood, Bamboo, Rattan, Palm, and Straw Products	101.46
家具制造业	Manufacture of Furniture	104.29
造纸及纸制品业	Manufacture of Paper and Paper Products	106.98
印刷业和记录媒介的复制	Printing, Reproduction of Recording Media	100.60
文教体育用品制造业	Manufacture of Articles for Culture, Education and Sport Activity	100.25
石油加工、炼焦及核燃料加工业	Processing of Petroleum, Coking, Processing of Nucleus Fuel	113.93
化学原料及化学制品制造业	Manufacture of Chemical Raw Material and Chemical Products	107.20
医药制造业	Manufacture of Medicines	102.19
化学纤维制造业	Manufacture of Chemical Fiber	107.79
橡胶制品业	Manufacture of Rubber	99.82
塑料制品业	Manufacture of Plastic	103.37
非金属矿物制品业	Manufacture of Non－metallic Mineral Products	101.18
黑色金属冶炼及压延加工业	Smelting and Pressing of Ferrous Metals	101.93
有色金属冶炼及压延加工业	Smelting and Pressing of Non－ferrous Metals	100.22
金属制品业	Manufacture of Metal Products	108.47
通用设备制造业	Manufacture of General Purpose Machinery	103.58
专用设备制造业	Manufacture of Special Purpose Machinery	103.47
交通运输设备制造业	Manufacture of Transport Equipment	100.98
电气机械及器材制造业	Manufacture of Electrical Machinery & Equipment	102.28
通信设备、计算机及其他电子设备制造业	Manufacture of Communication Equipment, Computer and Other Electronic Equipment	84.90
仪器仪表及文化、办公用机械制造业	Manufacture of Measuring Instrument and Machinery for Cultural Activity & Office Work	105.75
工艺品及其他制造业	Manufacture of Artwork, Other Manufacture	105.95
废弃资源和废旧材料回收加工业	Recycling and Disposal of Waste	
电力、热力的生产和供应业	Production and Supply of Electric Power and Heat Power	104.92
燃气生产和供应业	Production and Supply of Gas	105.85
水的生产和供应业	Production and Supply of Water	120.28

(preceding year = 100)

2006	2007	2008	2009	2010	2011	2012	2013	2014
101.08	**101.50**	**105.33**	**95.78**	**103.75**	**104.90**	**98.61**	**98.82**	**99.20**
96.10	101.24	99.25	101.67	113.85	104.33	99.93	100.00	99.86
107.57	104.55	110.23	123.38	122.69	111.39	102.48	98.72	95.57
103.80	98.71	116.71	86.15	132.38	145.13	89.33	87.06	102.14
				0.00				
101.38	110.20	111.53	95.8	105.68	111.32	98.69	93.46	97.58
99.71	100.86	113.82	98.52	107.13	112.52	103.11	103.08	101.78
100.20	101.66	104.21	101.63	100.66	104.14	105.89	100.48	98.76
100.00	100.00	100.00	100.00	100.00				
100.67	100.71	104.01	100.22	105.39	105.09	96.15	100.18	100.27
103.20	102.83	102.20	99.51	101.82	105.42	101.52	103.99	101.67
101.63	103.44	100.52	100.56	100.70	102.95	102.62	102.17	98.29
98.54	102.47	102.03	100.54	101.41	108.13	103.21	99.67	100.96
99.84	100.13	106.09	100.47	100.01	101.11	102.00	100.02	100.00
98.92	102.91	111.51	91.37	104.01	105.71	95.59	96.13	101.96
101.11	106.56	115.27	107.72	94.71	110.06	107.10	108.65	96.97
100.60	100.12	103.39	100.3	102.21	99.65	103.56	101.61	99.94
112.84	110.56	118.02	83.82	124.23	114.95	104.26	99.49	97.38
96.74	102.84	107.31	86.37	113.85	114.60	89.61	98.04	99.70
98.65	102.45	103.67	99.71	101.52	107.33	95.05	105.08	127.56
98.92	101.82	95.98	78.75	114.01	123.72	92.56	95.65	96.69
103.49	104.21	105.44	101.5	101.59	118.21	99.41	92.92	93.98
100.33	102.40	103.38	92.05	99.92	108.76	100.73	100.86	99.08
100.96	102.80	108.40	98.21	104.13	108.15	98.38	99.82	100.92
97.31	111.16	133.12	79.23	115.41	110.90	85.57	93.89	93.45
128.45	103.03	91.81	85.30	125.88	108.26	89.14	93.87	94.43
93.02	102.83	112.00	100.08	98.83	102.19	98.13	97.87	96.00
102.09	102.21	108.50	100.32	98.87	100.79	99.95	105.12	99.62
100.15	101.87	102.69	104.70	100.91	101.69	101.26	99.99	99.81
99.44	100.50	101.65	98.51	99.63	99.22	99.31	98.13	101.75
106.64	101.74	100.34	97.15	100.53	103.10	98.40	98.82	99.24
88.78	87.30	93.92	89.41	91.49	84.65	95.43	94.31	98.88
100.44	100.78	98.75	101.55	102.46	101.77	98.69	97.80	98.63
104.84	105.02	104.07	98.39	98.37	100.94	100.38	99.93	100.03
103.25	100.00	103.10	104.95	101.17	101.49	104.36	99.80	99.15
104.33	101.61	104.29	91.66	112.18	107.34	103.32	102.54	109.38
127.90	100.41	99.90	99.83	100.05	100.15	100.25	100.05	100.34

9-7 固定资产投资价格指数
PRICE INDEXES FOR INVESTMENT IN FIXED ASSETS

(上年=100) (preceding year=100)

项目名称	Item	2005	2006	2007	2008	2009	2010	2011	2012	2013	2014
总　计	**Total**	**103.1**	**102.6**	**104.1**	**111.0**	**94.6**	**104.9**	**107.0**	**100.0**	**100.1**	**99.9**
建筑安装、装饰工程	Construction and Installation Project	103.7	103.5	105.4	115.5	92.1	107.5	110.1	99.8	100.0	99.6
其中:人工费	of which:Labor Cost	112.7	110.0	111.0	112.7	104.9	112.0	115.9	110.4	107.8	104.8
材料费	Materials Expenses	101.0	100.7	103.9	120.5	87.5	107.0	109.6	96.7	97.6	97.7
机械使用费	Expenses on Machinery Use	104.2	109.1	107.2	106.9	100.0	104.3	105.0	102.3	101.0	100.8
设备、工器具购置	Purchase of Equipment,Tools and Instruments	99.7	100.6	100.8	102.5	98.0	100.2	101.8	99.2	99.3	99.9
其他费用	Others	105.5	100.9	103.9	105.9	98.5	102.2	103.0	102.0	101.4	101.4

9-8 住宅销售价格指数(2014 年)
SALES PRICE INDEXES FOR RESIDENCE(2014)

(上年=100) (preceding year=100)

项目	Item	2014
新建住宅销售价格指数	**Sales Price Indexes for Newly Constructed Residence**	
一月	January	109.9
二月	February	108.8
三月	March	107.8
四月	April	107.1
五月	May	106.1
六月	June	104.6
七月	July	102.6
八月	August	100.3
九月	September	98.5
十月	October	96.6
十一月	November	95.2
十二月	December	93.8
二手住宅销售价格指数	**Sales Price Indexes for Second-hand Residence**	
一月	January	103.8
二月	February	103.5
三月	March	103.2
四月	April	102.6
五月	May	101.8
六月	June	101.0
七月	July	99.8
八月	August	98.6
九月	September	97.4
十月	October	96.4
十一月	November	95.6
十二月	December	94.8

9-9 居民消费价格分类指数(2014 年)
CONSUMER PRICE INDEXES BY CATEGORY(2014)

(上年 = 100) (preceding year = 100)

项目	Item	指数 Indexes
居民消费价格总指数	**Consumer Price Index**	**102.6**
非食品价格指数	Non-food Price Index	101.9
服务项目价格指数	Services Price Index	101.9
扣除鲜菜鲜果总指数	Price Index Without Fresh Vegetables and Fresh Fruits	102.6
消费品价格指数	Consumer Goods Price Index	102.9
一、食品	**Food**	**104.4**
1. 粮食	Grain	106.5
2. 淀粉及薯类	Starches and Tubers	105.8
3. 干豆类及豆制品	Beans and Bean Products	106.1
4. 油脂	Oil or Fat	93.3
5. 肉禽及其制品	Meat Poultry and Its Products	101.4
6. 蛋类	Eggs	117.2
7. 水产品	Aquatic Products	107.7
8. 菜	Vegetables	94.2
9. 调味品	Flavoring	100.7
10. 糖	Carbohydrate	103.6
11. 茶及饮料	Tea and Beverages	104.3
12. 干鲜瓜果类	Dried and Fresh Melons and Fruits	114.9
13. 糕点饼干面包	Cake,Biscuit and Bread	101.3
14. 液体乳及乳制品	Milk and Its Products	105.2
15. 在外用膳食品	Outward Dinner Food	104.8
16. 其它食品及食品加工服务	Other Foods and Manufacturing Services	98.0
二、烟酒	**Tobacco Liquor**	**100.1**
1. 烟草	Tobacco	99.7
2. 酒	Liquor	100.5

9-9 续表
continued

项　目	Item	指　数 Indexes
三、衣着	**Clothing**	**103.2**
1. 服装	Garments	103.5
2. 衣着材料	Clothing Materials	104.3
3. 鞋袜帽	Footgear and Hats	102.6
4. 衣着加工服务	Clothing Manufacturing Services	104.7
四、家庭设备用品及维修服务	**Household Facilities, Articles and services**	**102.0**
1. 耐用消费品	Durable Consumer Goods	101.7
2. 室内装饰品	Interior Decorations	96.1
3. 床上用品	Bed Articles	99.6
4. 家庭日用杂品	Daily Use Household Articles	102.0
5. 家庭服务及加工维修服务	Household Services and Maintenance and Renovation	109.5
五、医疗保健和个人用品	**Health Care and Personal Articles**	**102.0**
1. 医疗保健	Health Care	102.2
2. 个人用品及服务	Personal Articles and Services	101.7
六、交通和通讯	**Transportation and Communication**	**100.3**
1. 交通	Transportation	100.7
2. 通讯	Communication	99.5
七、娱乐教育文化用品及服务	**Recreation, Education and Culture Articles and Services**	**101.4**
1. 文娱用耐用消费品及服务	Durable Consumer Goods for Cultural and Recreational Use and Services	96.6
2. 教育	Education	102.9
3. 文化娱乐用品	Cultural and Recreational Articles	101.7
4. 旅游及外出	Touring and Outing	100.7
八、居住	**Residence**	**102.2**
1. 建房及装修材料	Building and Building Decoration Materials	101.4
2. 租房	Renting	101.8
3. 自有住房	Private Housing	102.0
4. 水、电、燃料	Water, Electricity and Fuels	102.7

9-10 商品零售价格分类指数(2014年)
RETAIL PRICE INDEXES BY CATEGORY(2014)

(上年=100) (preceding year=100)

项　目	Item	指　数 Indexes
商品零售价格总指数	**Retail Price Index**	**102.3**
一、食品	**Food**	**104.1**
1.粮食	Grain	104.1
2.淀粉及薯类	Starches and Tubers	105.8
3.干豆类及豆制品	Beans and Bean Products	105.7
4.油脂	Oil or Fat	93.4
5.肉禽及其制品	Meat Poultry and Its Products	101.9
6.蛋	Eggs	117.0
7.水产品	Aquatic Products	108.0
8.菜	Vegetables	94.2
9.调味品	Flavoring	101.0
10.糖	Carbohydrate	103.4
11.干鲜瓜果	Dried and Fresh Melons and Fruits	114.6
12.糕点饼干面包	Cake,Biscuit and Bread	101.3
13.液体乳及乳制品	Milk and Its Products	104.9
14.在外用膳食品	Outward Dinner Food	104.6
15.其他食品	Other Foods	98.0
二、饮料、烟酒	**Beverages,Tobacco and Liquor**	**101.1**
1.茶及饮料	Tea and Beverages	104.3
2.烟草	Tobacco	99.7
3.酒	Liquor	100.5
三、服装、鞋帽类	**Clothing**	**103.0**
1.服装	Garments	103.5
2.鞋袜帽	Footgear and Hats	102.5
3.其他	Others	97.7
四、纺织品类	**Textiles**	**99.8**
1.衣着材料	Cotton Cloth	104.3
2.床上用品	Blend Cloth	99.0
五、家用电器及音像器材	**Household Appliances,Music and Video Equipment**	**98.7**
1.家庭设备	Household Facilities	101.1
2.文娱用耐用消费品	Durable Consumer Goods for Cultural and Recreational Use and Services	95.0
3.音像器材类	Music and Video Equipment	99.6

9－10 续表
continued

项　目	Item	指 数 Indexes
六、文化办公用品	**Culture and office Articles**	**99.2**
七、日用品	**Articles for Daily Use**	**101.5**
1. 日用百货	General Merchandise for Daily Use	104.2
2. 日用杂品	Miscellaneous for Daily Use	102.4
3. 洗涤用品	Cleaning Products	104.2
4. 其他日用品	Other Articles for Daily Use	96.6
八、体育娱乐用品	**Sports and Recreation Articles**	**102.0**
1. 体育用品	Sports Articles	102.9
2. 娱乐用品	Recreation Articles	101.5
九、交通、通信用品	**Transportation and Communication Appliances**	**100.6**
1. 交通运输机械	Transportation Machines	101.7
2. 通讯器材类	Communication Equipment	95.8
十、家具	**Furniture**	**103.6**
十一、化妆品类	**Cosmetics**	**100.9**
十二、金银珠宝类	**Gold, Silver and Jewelry**	**95.0**
十三、中西药品及医疗保健用品	**Traditional Chinese and Western Medicals and Health Care Articles**	**102.8**
1. 医疗器具及用品	Medical Apparatus and Articles	105.4
2. 中药材及中成药	Traditional Chinese Medicinal Materials and Medicines	103.7
3. 西药	Western Medicines	100.2
4. 保健器具及用品	Health Care Articles	107.3
十四、书报杂志及电子出版物	**Books, Newspapers, Magazines and Electronic Publications**	**104.6**
1. 教材及参考书	Teaching Material and Reference Books	104.8
2. 书报杂志	Books, Newspapers and Magazines	103.0
3. 电子音像制品	Electronic Music and Video Products	109.2
十五、燃料类	**Fuels**	**104.4**
1. 煤炭及制品类	Coal and Its Products	100.0
2. 石油及制品类	Petroleum and Its Products	104.8
十六、建筑材料及五金电料类	**Building Materials and Hardware**	**100.4**
1. 建筑装璜材料	Building Decoration Materials	100.9
2. 五金电料类	Hardware	99.7

主要统计指标解释

居民消费价格指数 是反映一定时期内城乡居民所购买的生活消费品价格和服务项目价格变动趋势和程度的相对数,是对城市居民消费价格指数和农村居民消费价格指数进行综合汇总计算的结果。该指数可以观察和分析消费品的零售价格和服务价格变动对城乡居民实际生活费支出的影响程度。

商品零售价格指数 是反映一定时期内城乡商品零售价格变动趋势和程度的相对数。商品零售价格的变动直接影响到城乡居民的生活支出和国家的财政收入,影响居民购买力和市场供需的平衡,影响到消费与积累的比例关系。因此,该指数可以从一个侧面对上述经济活动进行观察和分析。

工业生产者出厂价格指数 是反映一定时期内全部工业产品出厂价格总水平的变动趋势和程度的相对数,包括工业企业售给本企业以外所有单位的各种产品和直接售给居民用于生活消费的产品。该指数可以观察出厂价格变动对工业总产值及增加值的影响。

工业生产者购进价格指数 是反映工业企业作为生产投入,而从物资交易市场和能源、原材料生产企业购买原材料、燃料和动力产品时,所支付的价格水平变动趋势和程度的统计指标,是扣除工业企业物质消耗成本中的价格变动影响的重要依据。

房地产价格指数 是反映一定时期内房地产价格变动趋势和程度的相对数,包括新建住宅销售价格指数、二手住宅销售价格指数。

Explanatory Notes on Main Statistical Indicators

Consumer Price Indices reflect the trend and degree of changes in prices of consumer goods and services purchased by urban and rural households during a given period. They are obtained by combining the Urban Consumer Price Indices and the Rural Consumer Price Indices. The Indices enable the observation and analysis of the degree of impact of the changes in the prices of retailed goods and services on the actual living expenses of urban and rural residents.

Retail Price Indices reflect the trend and degree of change in retail prices of commodities during a given period. The change in retail prices of commodities directly affect the living expenditure of urban and rural residents, government revenue, purchasing power of residents and the equilibrium of market supply and demand, and the ratio of consumption to accumulation. Therefore, the retail price indices are useful to analyze the changes of the above economic activities.

Producer Price Indices for Industrial Producers reflect the trend and degree of changes in general ex-factory prices of all industrial products during a given period, including sales of industrial products by an industrial enterprise to all units outside the enterprise, as well as sales of consumer goods to residents. It can be used to analyze the impact of ex-factory prices on gross output value and value-added of the industrial sector.

Purchasing Price Indices for Industrial Producers reflect changes in the level and degree of prices paid by industrial enterprises when they purchase production input such as raw materials, fuels and power from the market or from other energy or raw materials producing enterprises. These indices provide important basis for measuring the material consumption of industrial enterprises after removing influence of price changes.

Price Indices for Real Estate reflect the trend and degree of changes in prices of real estate during a given period, including sales price indices for newly constructed residential buildings and secondhand residential buildings.

10 人民生活

PEOPLE S LIVING CONDITIONS

简要说明

一、本篇资料的主要内容

本篇资料主要反映了全市城市、农村居民的家庭收支、就业、居住、耐用消费品拥有量、生产和生活等方面的情况。

二、本篇资料的来源

1、本篇资料中城市居民家庭相关资料来源于城市住户调查年报。由于2013年城乡一体化住户调查采用新的制度及数据处理方式，新老制度的数据在口径范围上有较大差别，目前暂不公布分组数据。因此,本年鉴中缺分组数据及部分数据。由国家统计局青岛调查队城镇住户调查处整理提供。

2、本篇资料中农村居民家庭相关资料来源于农村住户调查年报，由市统计局农村统计处整理提供。

3、人民生活基本情况由市统计局国民经济综合统计处加工整理。

Brief Introduction

I. Main Content

Data in this chapter show the basic conditions of the people's livelihood of the whole city, including income and expenditure of the households, employment, housing condition, consumption and possession of the major consumer goods, etc.

II. Source of Data

(1) Data on conditions of urban households are based on the annual report of sample survey on urban households and compiled by the Division of Urban Household Survey of Survey Office of the National Bureau of Statistics in Qingdao. As a new statistics system and data processing method were used in the household survey in urban and rural area in 2013, there was a significant statistic difference between the new and old systems. Therefore, the statistics of the median income and the five equal income groups of urban residents are not included herein.

(2) Data on conditions of rural households are based on the annual report of sample survey on rural households and compiled by the Division of Countryside Statistics of Qingdao Municipal Bureau of Statistics.

(3) Data on basic statistics on people's living conditions are compiled by the Division of Comprehensive Statistics of Qingdao Municipal Bureau of Statistics.

10－1 人民生活基本情况(2000－2014年)
BASIC STATISTICS ON PEOPLE'S LIVING CONDITIONS(2000－2014)

		单位	Unit	2000	2005	2006	2007	2008
一、城乡居民收入	**Income of Urban and Rural Households**							
城市居民年人均可支配收入	Annual Per Capita Disposable Income of Urban Households	元	yuan	8 016	12 920	15 328	17 856	20 464
农民年人均纯收入	Annual Per Capita Net Income of Rural Households	元	yuan	3 637	5 806	6 546	7 477	8 509
二、城乡居民消费	**Expenditure of Urban and Rural Households**							
城市居民人均消费支出	Per Capita Consumption Expenditure of Urban Households	元	yuan	6 677	9 883	11 945	13 376	14 999
农村居民人均生活消费支出	Per Capita Consumption Expenditure of Rural Households	元	yuan	2 380	3 737	4 203	4 736	5 303
三、城市居民人均现住房建筑面积	**Per Capita Building Space in Urban Areas**	**平方米**	**sq. m**	**20.76**	**22.96**	**23.73**	**23.72**	**26.83**
农村居民人均居住面积	Per Capita Living Space in Rural Areas	平方米	sq. m	25.88	29.54	30.82	30.95	30.73
四、城乡居民人民币储蓄余额	**Savings Deposit of Urban and Rural Households at Year-end(RMB)**	**亿元**	**100 million yuan**	**535.32**	**1 343.10**	**1 567.62**	**1 702.04**	**2 123.36**
人均人民币储蓄余额	Per Capita Savings Deposit at Year-end (RMB)	元	yuan	7 575	18 248	21 038	22 455	27 882
五、学龄儿童入学率	**Attendance Rate of School Age Children**	**%**	**%**	**99.99**	**99.99**	**99.99**	**99.99**	**99.99**
每万人口中大学在校学生	Students Enrollment of University Per 10000 Population	人	person	65	324	347	349	354
六、城市每百户拥有彩色电视机	**Color TV Per 100 Urban Households**	**台**	**set**	**120.00**	**118.25**	**124.5**	**121.84**	**116.00**
城市每百户拥有电冰箱	Refrigerators Per 100 Urban Households	台	set	94.30	94.50	98.5	106.70	102.75
七、每万人口拥有医疗床位	**Hospital Beds Per 10 000 Population**	**张**	**bed**	**34.5**	**41.3**	**38.3**	**39.7**	**42.5**
每万人口拥有医生	Doctors Per 10000 Population	人	person	21.0	20.3	20.6	19.8	21.4
八、城市每一就业者负担人数(包括本人)	**Number of Dependents Per Employee of Urban Household(including the employee himself or herself)**	**人**	**person**	**1.82**	**1.97**	**1.79**	**1.79**	**1.77**
农村每一就业者负担人数(包括本人)	Number of Dependents Per Employee of Rural Household (including the employee himself or herself)	人	person	1.33	1.33	1.34	1.33	1.33
九、农民、城市居民人均年收入对比	**Contrast of Rural and Urban Residents in Annual Per Capita Income**			**1:2.2**	**1:2.2**	**1:2.34**	**1:2.39**	**1:2.41**
农民、城市居民人均年生活费支出对比	Contrast of Rural and Urban Residents in Annual Per Capita Living Expenditure			1:2.8	1:2.6	1:2.84	1:2.82	1:2.83

注：1. 自2002年起城市居民年人均可支配收入为新口径。农民与城市居民人均年收入对比,农民以纯收入,城市居民以可支配收入计算。
2. 城乡居民住房面积分别根据城乡住户抽样调查取得。
3. 2013年农村居民人均居住面积为农村居民人均拥有住房面积。

Note: 1. Since 2002, new calibre has been adopted in per capita annual disposable income of urban households. The calculation of contrast of rural and urban residents in per capita annual income is using net income of rural residents and disposable income of urban residents.
2. Figures relating to floor space among urban and rural dwellers were based on a survey.
3. Since 2013, data on per capita living space in rural areas means per capita construction area of building in rural.

10-1 续表
continued

		单位	Unit	2009	2010	2011	2012	2013	2014
一、城乡居民收入	**Income of Urban and Rural Households**								
城市居民年人均可支配收入	Annual Per Capita Disposable Income of Urban Households	元	yuan	22 368	24 998	28 567	32 145	35 227	38 294
农民年人均纯收入	Annual Per Capita Net Income of Rural Households	元	yuan	9 249	10 550	12 370	13 990	15 731	17 461
二、城乡居民消费	**Expenditure of Urban and Rural Households**								
城市居民人均消费支出	Per Capita Consumption Expenditure of Urban Households	元	yuan	16 080	17 531	19 297	20 391	22 060	24 016
农村居民人均生活消费支出	Per Capita Consumption Expenditure of Rural Households	元	yuan	5 832	6 662	7 661	8 653	9 786	10 808
三、城市居民人均现住房建筑面积	**Per Capita Building Space in Urban Areas**	**平方米**	**sq. m**	**26.71**	**27.42**	**27.67**	**27.86**	**29.12**	**29.8**
农村居民人均居住面积	Per Capita Living Space in Rural Areas	平方米	sq. m	31.39	30.97	31.73	32.32	33.50	34.2
四、城乡居民人民币储蓄余额	**Savings Deposit of Urban and Rural Households at Year-end (RMB)**	**亿元**	**100 million yuan**	**2 527.87**	**2 912.33**	**3 198.51**	**3 757.60**	**4 141**	**4 436**
人均人民币储蓄余额	Per Capita Savings Deposit at Year-end(RMB)	元	yuan	33 134	38 137	41 736	48 828	53 524	56 826
五、学龄儿童入学率	**Attendance Rate of School Age Children**	**%**	**%**	**99.99**	**99.99**	**99.99**	**99.99**	**99.99**	**99.99**
每万人口中大学在校学生	Students Enrollment of University Per 10000 Population	人	person	361	373	380	386	388	402
六、城市每百户拥有彩色电视机	**Color TV Per 100 Urban Households**	**台**	**set**	**117.50**	**118.5**	**117.25**	**115.00**	**118.00**	**109**
城市每百户拥有电冰箱	Refrigerators Per 100 Urban Households	台	set	105.00	106.75	108.25	118.00	107.00	105
七、每万人口拥有医疗床位	**Hospital Beds Per 10 000 Population**	**张**	**bed**	**43.0**	**47.2**	**52.2**	**61.4**	**58.0**	**60.3**
每万人口拥有医生	Doctors Per 10000 Population	人	person	21.9	23.2	23.9	28.1	31.2	32
八、城市每一就业者负担人数(包括本人)	**Number of Dependents Per Employee of Urban Household (including the employee himself or herself)**	**人**	**person**	**1.73**	**1.75**	**1.71**	**1.69**		
农村每一就业者负担人数(包括本人)	Number of Dependents Per Employee of Rural Household (including the employee himself or herself)	人	person	1.34	1.33	1.48	1.46	1.48	
九、农民、城市居民人均年收入对比	**Contrast of Rural and Urban Residents in Annual Per Capita Income**			**1:2.42**	**1:2.37**	**1:2.31**	**1:2.30**	**1:2.24**	**1:2.19**
农民、城市居民人均年生活费支出对比	Contrast of Rural and Urban Residents in Annual Per Capita Living Expenditure			1:2.76	1:2.63	1:2.52	1:2.36	1:2.25	1:2.22

10－2 城市居民家庭基本情况（2014 年）

BASIC CONDITIONS OF URBAN HOUSEHOLDS(2014)

单位：元(yuan)

指标名称	Name	2014	2013	2014 年比 2013 年增长(±%) 2014/2013(±%)
人均家庭总收入	**Per Capita Total Income of Household**	**42 213**	**38 616**	**9.3**
其中：人均可支配收入	of which：Per Capita Disposable Income	38 294	35 227	8.7
（一）工资性收入	Income from Wages and Salaries	27 965	25 343	10.3
（二）经营性净收入	Net Income from Household Operations	3 388	3 182	6.5
（三）财产性收入	Income from Properties	1 273	1 204	5.8
（四）转移性收入	Income from Transfers	9 587	8 887	7.9
人均消费性支出	**Per Capita Consumption Expenditure**	**24 016**	**22 060**	**8.9**
（一）食品	Food	8 571	8 052	6.4
（二）衣着	Clothing	2 907	2 792	4.1
（三）居住	Residence	2 104	2 005	4.9
（四）家庭设备用品及服务	Household Facilities，Articles and Services	1 734	1 545	12.2
（五）医疗保健	Health Care and Medical Services	1 764	1 560	13.1
（六）交通和通讯	Transportation and Communication	3 159	2 762	14.4
（七）教育文化娱乐服务	Education，Cultural and Recreation Services	2 482	2 183	13.7
（八）其他商品和服务	Other Goods and Services	1 295	1 160	11.6

10 -3 农村居民家庭基本情况(2000 -2014 年)
BASIC CONDITIONS OF RURAL HOUSEHOLDS(2000 - 2014)

项　目	Item
调查户数(户)	**Number of Households Surveyed(household)**
常住人口(人)	Number of Permanent Residents(person)
平均每户常住人口(人)	Average Number of Permanent Residents Per Household(person)
平均每户整半劳力(人)	Average Number of Full/Semi Labour Force Per Household(person)
平均每个劳动力负担人口(含本人)(人)	Average Number of Dependents Per Labour Force(including the labour force himself or herself)(person)
总收入(元)	**Total Income(yuan)**
工资性收入	Income from Wages and Salaries
家庭经营收入	Income from Household Operations
财产性收入	Income from Properties
转移性收入	Income from Transfers
现金收入(元)	**Cash Income(yuan)**
工资性收入	Income from Wages and Salaries
家庭经营收入	Income from Household Operations
财产性收入	Income from Properties
转移性收入	Income from Transfers
总支出(元)	**Total Expenditure(yuan)**
家庭经营费用支出	Expenditure for Household Operations
购置生产性固定资产	Purchase of Productive Fixed Assets
税费支出	Taxes and Fees
生活消费支出	Expenditure on Household Consumption
转移性和财产性支出	Expenditure on Properties and Transfers
现金支出(元)	**Cash Expenditure(yuan)**
家庭经营费用支出	Expenditure for Household Operations
购买生产性固定资产	Purchase of Productive Fixed Assets
税费支出	Taxes and Fees
生活消费支出	Expenditure on Household Consumption
转移性和财产性支出	Expenditure on Properties and Transfers
平均每人年纯收入(元)	**Per Capita Annual Net Income(yuan)**
工资性收入	Income from Wages and Salaries
家庭经营纯收入	Income from Household Operations
财产性收入	Income from Properties
转移性收入	Income from Transfers

2000	2005	2006	2007	2008	2009	2010	2011	2012	2013	2014
820	**860**	**900**	**900**	**900**	**900**	**900**	**680**	**680**	**680**	
2 856	2 964	3 073	3 066	3 077	3 069	3 061	2 263	2 223	2 220	
3.48	3.45	3.41	3.41	3.42	3.41	3.40	3.33	3.27	3.26	
2.61	2.59	2.58	2.58	2.59	2.56	2.58	2.37	2.37	2.37	
1.33	1.33	1.32	1.32	1.32	1.33	1.32	1.40	1.38	1.38	
5 394	**8 370**	**9 464**	**10 881**	**12 381**	**13 299**	**14 993**	**17 156**	**19 567**	**21 689**	
1 481	2 402	2 783	3 178	3 518	3 820	4 361	5 418	6 308	7 195	
3 802	5 565	6 297	7 230	8 257	8 778	9 840	10 840	12 216	13 292	
32	236	192	226	293	334	364	281	309	350	
79	167	192	247	314	367	427	617	734	852	
4 554	**7 403**	**8 633**	**10 188**	**11 487**	**12 668**	**14 090**	**15 589**	**18 112**	**20 581**	
1 479	2 400	2 775	3 177	3 512	3 819	4 361	5 367	6 282	7 168	
2 428	4 603	5 460	6 544	7 395	8 203	8 882	9 420	10 857	12 323	
24	233	212	226	270	288	425	222	284	298	
135	167	186	241	309	358	422	580	689	792	
4 223	**6 363**	**7 198**	**8 144**	**9 144**	**9 871**	**11 031**	**13 192**	**14 832**	**16 449**	
1 536	2 244	2 560	2 937	3 401	3 570	3 931	4 222	4 919	5 294	
144	192	148	121	98	108	104	280	310	289	
103	27	14	12	9	9	7	8	8	3	
2 380	3 737	4 203	4 736	5 303	5 832	6 662	7 661	8 653	9 786	
60	162	271	333	329	351	327	1 019	936	1 072	
3 883	**5 700**	**6 737**	**7 851**	**8 771**	**9 474**	**10 655**	**12 779**	**14 462**	**16 135**	
941	1 833	2 279	2 809	3 245	3 482	3 812	4 095	4 797	5 239	
144	192	148	121	98	108	104	280	310	289	
96	27	13	9	9	8	6	8	8	3	
2 080	3 486	4 026	4 575	5 088	5 524	6 406	7 389	8 420	9 546	
117	162	269	332	329	351	327	1 006	922	1 053	
3 637	**5 806**	**6 546**	**7 477**	**8 509**	**9 249**	**10 550**	**12 370**	**13 990**	**15 731**	**17 461**
1 481	2 402	2 783	3 178	3 518	3 820	4 361	5 418	6 308	7 195	8 004
2 059	3 026	3 406	3 859	4 419	4 775	5 453	6 122	6 718	7 408	8 205
32	236	192	226	293	334	364	281	309	350	382
65	142	165	214	280	319	372	549	656	777	870

10-4 城市住户每百户家庭主要耐用品拥有量(1980-2014 年)
OWNERSHIP OF MAJOR DURABLE CONSUMER GOODS PER 100 URBAN HOUSEHOLDS(1980-2014)

年 份 Year	家用电脑(台) Computer (set)	钢琴(架) Piano (set)	空调器(台) Air Conditioner (set)	淋浴热水器(台) Water Heater (set)	洗衣机(台) Washing Machine (set)	电冰箱(台) Refrigerator (set)	家用汽车(辆) Automobile (unit)	彩色电视机(台) Color TV (set)	移动电话(部) Cell Phone (unit)	照相机(架) Camera (set)
1980										2.0
1981					12.0			1.0		2.0
1982					22.0			2.0		4.0
1983					27.0	1.0		6.0		6.0
1984					30.0	2.0		8.0		8.0
1985					35.5	3.5		17.5		13.5
1986					40.0	4.5		24.5		15.0
1987					51.5	18.0		33.5		17.5
1988					60.5	33.0		47.0		20.5
1989					67.0	50.0		59.0		22.0
1990					66.0	62.0		68.0		26.0
1991					70.0	76.0		82.0		33.0
1992		1.0		12.5	72.5	83.0		81.0		38.5
1993		2.0	0.5	18.0	82.5	85.5		87.5		49.5
1994		4.0	1.0	17.0	81.0	88.5		92.0		51.0
1995		4.0	3.0	33.5	81.5	89.0		100.0		60.5
1996		4.5	6.5	39.5	83.0	91.5		105.0		63.0
1997	1.0	4.5	9.0	46.5	83.0	93.0		110.5	2.5	63.0
1998	8.3	5.3	16.5	53.0	83.0	91.8		110.8	6.8	69.4
1999	10.5	3.8	21.8	61.3	83.0	93.5		117.3	15.0	68.5
2000	19.3	2.0	24.5	65.8	83.3	94.3		120.0	30.3	69.5
2001	20.0	2.3	24.3	65.8	84.0	92.8		127.5	36.0	68.5
2002	31.5	2.3	38.3	75.3	89.3	93.0	0.5	123.3	80.0	72.8
2003	40.8	3.3	47.5	76.3	90.5	92.8	0.3	124.8	105.5	70.0
2004	46.0	3.0	55.0	79.0	92.5	92.5	2.0	123.5	128.0	68.3
2005	55.0	4.3	69.3	83.8	91.8	94.8	3.8	118.3	152.8	72.3
2006	71.3	7.8	89.3	88.0	97.3	98.5	6.3	124.5	187.0	81.8
2007	75.4	7.4	98.3	93.3	99.8	106.7	7.9	121.8	193.8	82.9
2008	75.0	5.0	93.8	90.3	94.5	102.8	12.8	116.0	190.8	67.0
2009	81.8	6.5	98.3	90.5	96.3	105.0	18.0	117.5	199.0	70.8
2010	86.0	7.5	99.3	90.8	97.3	106.8	20.3	118.5	207.5	71.0
2011	95.0	8.0	103.0	91.5	98.0	108.3	22.0	117.3	218.8	76.5
2012	100.8	9.0	103.5	92.8	97.5	108.0	28.5	115.0	230.5	78.8
2013	105.0	10.0	104.0	93.0	98.0	107.0	32.0	118.0	232.0	79.0
2014	105.0	10.0	104.0	98.0	99.0	105.0	34.0	109.0	235.0	79.0

10－5 城市居民家庭居住情况
HOUSING CONDITIONS OF URBAN HOUSEHOLDS

类别	Category	2005	2006	2007	2008	2009	2010	2011	2012	2013	2014
现住房总建筑面积（平方米/人）	**Floor Space of Houses (sq. m/person)**	**22.96**	**23.73**	**23.71**	**26.83**	**26.71**	**27.42**	**27.67**	**27.86**	**29.12**	**29.8**
房屋产权（合计）	**Housing Property**	**100.00**	**100.00**	**100.00**	**100.00**	**100.00**	**100.00**	**100.00**	**100.00**		
租赁公房（%）	Leasehold of Public Housing (%)	11.00	11.00	7.50	2.25	1.75	2.00	5.25	5.25		
租赁私房（%）	Leasehold of Private Housing (%)	1.75	2.00	2.25	3.75	3.25	3.00	2.25	2.50		
原有私房（%）	Original Private Housing(%)	17.50	14.00	3.75	12.00	14.25	14.00	9.50	6.75		
房改私房（%）	Private Housing After Housing Reform(%)	59.25	52.25	53.75	53.25	51.00	52.25	49.50	46.25		
商品房（%）	Condominium(%)	10.00	20.00	32.00	27.75	29.00	27.75	32.00	37.00		
借用房（%）	Borrowed Housing								2.00		
其它（%）	Others(%)	0.50	0.75	0.75	1.00	0.75	1.00	1.50	0.25		
住宅建筑式样（合计）	**Style of Residential Building**	**100.00**	**100.00**	**100.00**	**100.00**	**100.00**	**100.00**	**100.00**	**100.00**		
单栋住宅（%）	Monomer House(%)	1.75	1.75	0.25	2.50	3.00	2.75	0.75	0.25		
四居室（%）	Four Bedrooms Department (%)	1.50	2.00	3.50	1.00	1.75	2.75	3.75	2.75		
三居室（%）	Three Bedrooms Department (%)	16.75	19.75	20.00	26.00	25.75	26.50	29.00	27.50		
二居室（%）	Two Bedrooms Department(%)	64.75	63.25	60.50	55.75	55.25	53.75	51.75	56.00		
一居室（%）	One Bedroom Department(%)	5.75	5.75	3.25	2.25	2.25	2.25	3.00	3.50		
普通楼房（%）	Ordinary Building(%)	5.75	5.25	9.50	10.00	8.00	8.00	9.75	7.75		

10-5 续表
continued

类　别	Category	2005	2006	2007	2008	2009	2010	2011	2012
平房及其它(%)	Bungalow and Others(%)	3.75	2.25	3.00	2.50	4.00	4.00	2.00	2.25
卫生设备(合计)	**Sanitary Equipment**	**100.00**	**100.00**	**100.00**	**100.00**	**100.00**	**100.00**	**100.00**	**100.00**
无卫生设备(%)	No Sanitary Equipment(%)			0.25	0.25				
有厕所浴室(%)	Having Toilet and Bathroom(%)	89.00	92.75	92.50	89.00	89.75	89.75	90.75	91.5
有厕所无浴室(%)	Having Toilet but No Bathroom (%)	6.50	3.25	3.25	8.75	8.25	8.00	5.75	4.75
公用(%)	Public Sanitary Equipment(%)	4.50	4.00	4.00	2.00	2.00	2.25	3.50	3.75
取暖设备(合计)	**Heating Equipment**	**100.00**	**100.00**	**100.00**	**100.00**	**100.00**	**100.00**	**100.00**	**100.00**
无取暖设备(%)	No Heating Equipment(%)	2.75	2.50	3.25	6.00	2.75	2.75	2.75	1.75
空调设备(%)	Having Air Conditioner(%)	41.75	43.25	35.25	24.00	25.50	25.50	22.00	14.75
暖气(%)	Having Heater(%)	36.00	43.50	46.25	57.50	60.75	62.00	68.00	77.5
其它(%)	Others(%)	19.50	10.75	15.25	12.50	11.00	9.75	7.25	6.00
炊用燃料使用情况(合计)	**Conditions of Cooking Fuel**	**100.00**	**100.00**	**100.00**	**100.00**	**100.00**	**100.00**	**100.00**	**100.00**
管道煤气(%)	Tap Gas(%)	55.00	61.00	61.25	58.50	61.50	61.75	67.50	76.96
液化石油气(%)	Liquid Natural Gas(%)	42.75	36.50	37.25	36.75	35.50	36.25	31.00	22.3
煤(%)	Coal(%)	2.25	2.00	0.75	4.50	2.75	1.75	1.25	0.74
其他(%)	Others(%)		0.50	0.75	0.25	0.25	0.25	0.25	

10－6 城市居民家庭消费构成
COMPOSITION OF URBAN HOUSEHOLDS CONSUMPTION

项　　目	Item	2014		2013	
		年人均支出金额(元) Per Capita Annual Expenditure(yuan)	占消费支出的比重(%) Percentage to Consumption Expenditure(%)	年人均支出金额(元) Per Capita Annual Expenditure(yuan)	占消费支出的比重(%) Percentage to Consumption Expenditure(%)
消费支出	**Consumption Expenditure**	**24 016**	**100**	**22 060**	**100**
一、食　品	**Food**	**8 571**	**35.7**	**8 052**	**36.5**
#1.粮　食	Grain				
2.油　脂	Oil or Fat				
3.肉禽及其制品	Meat,Poultry and Processed Products				
4.蛋　类	Eggs				
5.水产品	Aquatic Products				
6.菜　类	Vegetables				
7.烟　草	Tobacco				
8.酒和饮料	Liquor and Beverages				
9.干鲜果品	Dried and Fresh Melons and Fruits				
10.奶及奶制品	Milk and Its Products				
二、衣　着	**Clothing**	**2 907**	**12.1**	**2 792**	**12.6**
#1.服装	Garments				
2.衣着材料	Clothing Materials				
三、家庭设备用品及服务	**Household Facilities, Articles and Services**	**1 734**	**7.2**	**1 545**	**7.0**
#日用耐用消费品	Daily Use Durable Consumer Goods				
四、医疗保健	**Health Care and Medical Sevices**	**1 764**	**7.3**	**1 560**	**7.1**
五、交通与通讯	**Transportation and Communication**	**3 159**	**13.2**	**2 762**	**12.5**
六、娱乐教育文化服务	**Education, Cultural and Recreation Services**	**2 482**	**10.3**	**2 183**	**9.9**
1.文化娱乐用品	Cultural and Recreational Articles				
2.文化娱乐服务	Cultural and Recreational Services				
3.教育	Education				
七、居住	**Residence**	**2 104**	**8.8**	**2 005**	**9.1**
八、杂项商品与服务	**Miscellaneous Goods and Services**	**1 295**	**5.4**	**1 160**	**5.3**

10-7 农村住户基本情况(2005-2013年)
BASIC CONDITIONS OF RURAL HOUSEHOLDS(2005-2013)

项 目	Item	单位	Unit
调查户数	**Number of Households Surveyed**	**户**	**household**
常住人口	**Number of Permanent Residents**	**人**	**person**
一、平均每户常住人口	**Average Number of Permanent Residents Per Household**	**人**	**person**
1. 年龄结构	Age Distribution	人	person
(1)6岁及以下	6 Year-old and Under	人	person
(2)7-15岁	Between 7 and 15 Year-old	人	person
(3)16-60岁	Between 16 and 60 Year-old	人	person
(4)61岁及以上	61 Year-old and Above	人	person
2. 在校学生人数	Students Enrollment	人	person
其中:7-15岁在校学生人数	of which:Between 7 and 15 Year-old	人	person
3. 平均每户整半劳动力	Average Number of Full/Semi Labour Force Per Household	人	person
(1)整劳动力	Full Labour Force	人	person
(2)半劳动力	Semi Labour Force	人	person
整半劳动力占常住人口的比重	Percentage of Full/Semi Labour Force to Permanent Residents	%	%
平均每个劳动力负担人口	Average Number of Dependents Per Labour Force	人	person
二、平均每百个劳动力中	**Among Per 100 Labour Force**		
文盲半文盲人数	Illiterate and Semiliterate	人	person
小学程度人数	Primary School	人	person
初中程度人数	Junior High School	人	person
高中程度人数	Senior High School	人	person
中专程度人数	Secondary School	人	person
大专程度人数	Junior College	人	person
三、经营耕地面积(人均)	**Area of Cultivated Land under Management(per capita)**	**亩**	**mu**
#承包耕地面积	Area of Cultivated Land Contracted	亩	mu
占经营耕地面积的比重	Percentage to Area of Cultivated Land under Management	%	%
四、平均每户年末生产性固定资产原值	**Productive Original Value of Fixed Assets Per Household(year-end)**	**元**	**yuan**
1. 役畜、产品畜	Draught Animal and Commodity Animal	元	yuan
2. 大中型铁木农具	Large and Medium Iron and Wooden Farm Tools	元	yuan
3. 农林牧渔业机械	Agricultural Machinery	元	yuan
4. 工业机械	Industrial Machinery	元	yuan
5. 运输机械	Transport Machinery	元	yuan
6. 生产用房	Buildings for Production	元	yuan
7. 其他	Others	元	yuan
五、平均每户年末拥有汽车	**Ownership of Automobiles Per Household(year-end)**	**辆**	**set**
大中型拖拉机	Large and Medium Tractors	台	set
小型和手扶拖拉机	Small and Walking Tractors	台	set

注:平均每百个劳动力中文化程度人数,2010年及以前为整半劳动力文化程度,2011年为就业劳动力文化程度。

Note:In the education attainment statistics among per 100 labour force,the labour force refers to full/semi labour force before 2010,and refers to employed labour force since 2011.

2005	2006	2007	2008	2009	2010	2011	2012	2013
860	**900**	**900**	**900**	**900**	**900**	**680**	**680**	**680**
2 964	**3 073**	**3 066**	**3 077**	**3 069**	**3 061**	**2 263**	**2 222**	**2 220**
3.45	**3.41**	**3.41**	**3.42**	**3.41**	**3.40**	**3.33**	**3.27**	**3.26**
0.15	0.15	0.14	0.12	0.12	0.11	0.15	0.17	0.17
0.33	0.35	0.35	0.35	0.35	0.31	0.36	0.36	0.36
2.74	2.73	2.69	2.71	2.69	2.70	2.50	2.44	2.43
0.23	0.19	0.23	0.24	0.25	0.28	0.30	0.30	0.30
0.60	0.60	0.59	0.60	0.60	0.58	0.56	0.51	0.53
0.33	0.35	0.35	0.35	0.34	0.30	0.36	0.37	0.37
2.59	2.58	2.58	2.59	2.56	2.58	2.37	2.38	2.39
1.73	1.76	1.72	1.66	1.57	1.51	1.52	1.54	1.55
0.86	0.82	0.86	0.93	0.99	1.06	0.85	0.84	0.84
75.1	75.6	75.67	75.63	75.20	75.76	71.24	72.70	73.21
1.33	1.32	1.32	1.32	1.33	1.30	1.40	1.38	1.37
2.07	1.46	1.64	1.68	1.60	1.38	1.65	1.62	1.59
15.72	12.78	12.24	12.46	12.52	9.36	13.45	13.46	13.25
54.04	54.43	53.10	53.89	56.63	58.52	60.59	59.06	58.61
21.61	24.01	24.48	23.12	19.89	20.53	16.53	17.39	17.62
4.27	4.69	5.30	5.20	5.24	5.56	2.70	3.20	3.45
2.29	2.62	3.23	3.65	4.12	4.66	5.07	5.27	5.48
1.40	**1.31**	**1.26**	**1.27**	**1.30**	**1.47**	**1.38**	**1.60**	**1.66**
1.40	1.31	1.26	1.27	1.30	1.30	1.30	1.52	1.59
100.00	100.00	100.00	100.00	100.00	88.44	94.20	95.00	95.78
13 845	**16 191**	**21 568**	**21 993**	**21 626**	**22 950**	**24 349**	**27 949**	**28 721**
1 103	871	1 264	1 320	1 358	1 333	1 037	1 527	1 560
217	275	435	299	265	293	140	143	144
3 204	2 912	4 261	4 658	4 062	4 118	4 153	5 167	4 959
1 247	1 759	1 899	1 710	1 718	2 008	2 899	3 452	3 107
1 623	1 169	1 768	1 110	1 138	1 234	2 421	3 434	3 503
3 746	4 479	7 247	7 079	6 372	7 238	8 042	9 548	10 330
315	482	739	774	858	819	1 112	1 339	1 479
0.04	**0.05**	**0.07**	**0.06**	**0.07**	**0.08**	**0.09**	**0.08**	**0.09**
0.05	0.03	0.03	0.04	0.05	0.05	0.05	0.06	0.06
0.31	0.34	0.29	0.30	0.30	0.30	0.22	0.23	0.23

10－8 农村住户居住情况(2005－2013 年)
HOUSING CONDITIONS OF RURAL HOUSEHOLDS(2005－2013)

类 别	Category	单位	Unit
一、期末住房情况	**Housing Conditions at Term-end**		
(一)住房面积	Floor Space of Houses	平方米/人	sq. m/person
(二)住房价值	Value of Houses	元/平方米	yuan/sq. m
(三)住房类型	Type of Houses		
1. 楼房面积	Floor Space of Apartment	平方米/人	sq. m/person
2. 砖瓦平房面积	Floor Space of Brick Bungalow	平方米/人	sq. m/person
3. 其他	Others	平方米/人	sq. m/person
(四)住房结构	Structure of Houses		
1. 钢筋混泥土结构面积	Reinforced Concrete Structure	平方米/人	sq. m/person
2. 砖木结构面积	Brick and Wood Structure	平方米/人	sq. m/person
3. 其他	Others	平方米/人	sq. m/person
二、期内新建(购)住房情况	**Conditions of Houses Newly Built (Bought) This Term**		
(一)新建(购)住房面积	Floor Space of Houses Newly Built (Bought)	平方米/人	sq. m/person
(二)新建(购)住房价值	Value of Houses Newly Built (Bought)	元/平方米	yuan/sq. m
(三)新建(购)住房类型	Type of Houses Newly Built (Bought)		
1. 楼房面积	Floor Space of Apartment	平方米/人	sq. m/person
2. 砖瓦平房面积	Floor Space of Brick Bungalow	平方米/人	sq. m/person
3. 其他	Others	平方米/人	sq. m/person
(四)新建(购)住房结构	Structure of Newly Building Housing		
1. 钢筋混泥土结构面积	Reinforced Concrete Structure	平方米/人	sq. m/person
2. 砖木结构面积	Brick and Wood Structure	平方米/人	sq. m/person
3. 其他	Residental Buildings	平方米/人	sq. m/person

2005	2006	2007	2008	2009	2010	2011	2012	2013
29.54	30.82	30.95	30.73	31.39	32.06	31.73	32.32	32.67
394	537	676	732	750	880	1 345	1 369	1 407
3.42	7.04	6.08	5.96	6.34	6.33	4.15	4.13	4.36
25.85	23.48	24.52	24.54	24.81	24.58	27.57	28.18	28.32
0.26	0.30	0.35	0.23	0.24	0.47			
6.53	7.94	5.37	6.05	6.71	6.57	5.26	4.8	5.06
23	22.77	25.47	24.58	24.56	24.71	26.47	27.52	27.61
	0.11	0.11	0.11	0.12	0.1			
0.99	0.72	0.23	0.3	0.43	0.16	0.55	0.19	0.23
521	549	545	708	930	1 221	1 199	1 927	1 747
0.29	0.38		0.07	0.11	0.08	0.16	0.05	0.05
0.70	0.34	0.23	0.23	0.32	0.08	0.39	0.14	0.17
0.67	0.42	0.08	0.11	0.18	0.08	0.2	0.13	0.16
0.31	0.3	0.15	0.19	0.25	0.08	0.35	0.06	0.06

10 -8 续表
continued

类 别	Category	单位	Unit
三、居住条件	**Living Condition**		
(一)住房卫生设备使用情况	Condition of Health Equipment		
1. 使用水冲式厕所的户数	Having Flushing Toilet	户/百户	household/100 households
2. 使用旱厕的户数	Having Old Toilet	户/百户	household/100 households
3. 无厕所的户数	No Toilet	户/百户	household/100 households
(二)取暖设备使用情况	Condition of Heating Equipment		
1. 使用空调的户数	Having Air Conditioner	户/百户	household/100 households
2. 使用暖气的户数	Having Heater	户/百户	household/100 households
3. 使用火炕的户数	Having Kang	户/百户	household/100 households
4. 无取暖设备的户数	No Heating Equipment	户/百户	household/100 households
(三)炊事使用的主要能源	Major Source of Cooking		
1. 使用液化气的户数	Liquid Natural Gas	户/百户	household/100 households
2. 使用煤炭的户数	Coal	户/百户	household/100 households
3. 使用柴草的户数	Fuelwood	户/百户	household/100 households
4. 使用电的户数	Electricity	户/百户	household/100 households
5. 使用其他燃料的户数	Other Fuels	户/百户	household/100 households
(四)饮用水来源情况	Source of Drinking Water		
1. 饮用自来水的户数	Tap Water	户/百户	household/100 households
2. 饮用深井水的户数	Deep Well Water	户/百户	household/100 households
3. 饮用浅井水的户数	Other Water	户/百户	household/100 households
(五)住宅外道路路面状况	Condition of Road Near Residential		
1. 水泥或柏油路面的户数	Cement or Asphalt	户/百户	household/100 households
2. 沙石或石板等硬质路面的户数	Stone, Sand and Gravel or Other Hard Materials	户/百户	household/100 households
3. 其他路面的户数	Others	户/百户	household/100 households

2005	2006	2007	2008	2009	2010	2011	2012	2013
40	42	45	46	46	46	51	50	51
60	58	55	54	54	54	49	51	50
7	8	6	7	6	6	9	9	10
23	18	21	22	22	22	19	20	20
70	73	71	69	69	69	60	61	60
						11	11	11
60	62	82	82	83	83	66	65	65
	1							
40	37	16	16	16	16	35	29	28
	1	1	1	1	1	1	7	7
77	85	92	95	95	95	94	97	97
21	15	7	5	5	5	5	2	2
1						2	2	2
54	40	54	62	71	75	81	84	84
32	53	42	34	25	22	13	12	12
13	7	5	4	3	3	6	5	5

10－9 农村住户人均生活消费支出(2014 年)
PER CAPITA EXPENDITURE ON HOUSEHOLD CONSUMPUTION OF RURAL HOUSEHOLDS (2014)

单位:元(yuan)

项 目	Item	金额 Sum
生活消费支出	**Expenditure on Household Consumption**	**10 808**
(一)食品	Food	3 651
购买食品支出	Buying Food	
食品消费服务性支出	Services of Food Consumption	
(二)衣着	Clothing	979
购买衣着支出	Buying Clothing	
衣着消费服务性支出	Services ofClothing Consumption	
(三)居住	Residence	1 989
1. 购买居住消费品支出	Buying Residential Consumption	
2. 居住消费服务性支出	Services for Residential Consumption	
(四)家庭设备、用品及服务	Household Facilities, Articles and Services	655
1. 购买家庭设备、用品支出	Buying Household Facilities and Articles	
2. 家庭设备服务消费支出	Services for Household Facilities	
(五)交通和通讯	Transportation and Communication	1 798
1. 购买交通和通讯用品支出	Buying Traffic and Communications Articles	
2. 交通和通讯服务消费支出	Services for Traffic and Communications	
(六)文化教育、娱乐用品及服务	Culture, Education and Recreation Articles and Services	842
1. 购买文化教育、娱乐用品	Culture, Education and Recreation Articles	
2. 教育服务消费	Services for Education	
3. 文化体育、娱乐服务消费	Services for Culture, Sports and Recreation	
(七)医疗保健	Health Care and Medical Services	657
1. 购买医疗保健用品	Buying Articles of Medicines and Medical Services	
2. 医疗保健服务消费支出	Services for Health care	
(八)其他商品和服务	Other Goods and Services	237
1. 购买其他商品支出	Goods	
2. 其他消费服务支出	Services	

10 -10 农村住户每百户家庭主要耐用品拥有量(1985 -2014 年)

OWNERSHIP OF MAJOR DURABLE CONSUMER GOODS PER 100 RURAL HOUSEHOLDS(1985 -2014)

年份 Year	家用电脑(台) Computer (unit)	空调器(台) Air Conditioner (unit)	热水器(台) Water Heater (unit)	自行车(辆) Bicycle (unit)	洗衣机(台) Washing Machine (unit)	电冰箱(台) Household Refrigerator (unit)	彩色电视机(台) Color TV Set (unit)	移动电话(部) Cell Phone (unit)	照相机(架) Camera (unit)	家用汽车(辆) Automobile (unit)
1985				147	0.3		3		1	
1986				165	1.1	0.3	4.5		1	
1987				148	2.4	0.5	7		2	
1988				154	2.4	1	9		2	
1989				170	3	1	12		2	
1990				164	4	2	13		2	
1991				173	5	4	16		2	
1992				178	5	7	20		2	
1993				203	7	14	26		2	
1994				204	9	21	35		7	
1995				203	16	28	43		6	
1996				198	13	33	46		8	
1997				191	15	36	56		13	
1998				184	17	39	63		15	
1999				185	20	42	74		10	
2000				165	28	47	86		13	
2001				153	28	53	92		13	
2002				152	36	58	98		16	
2003	6	5	33	137	39	60	100	45	16	2
2004	8	8	39	142	48	68	105	68	21	2
2005	14	14	53	138	57	77	109	91	21	5
2006	17	15	54	116	63	87	112	114	14	7
2007	19	19	63	118	70	94	113	132	17	8
2008	25	23	68	124	76	97	114	148	19	9
2009	28	25	71	127	79	99	115	160	21	11
2010	34	30	75	128	82	102	117	170	21	12
2011	44	32	76	114	85	100	112	202	18	15
2012	55	37	85	119	91	102	114	216	21	16
2013	61	45	88	111	93	105	116	221	26	23
2014	61	49	85		93	102	106	225	24	26

10－11 农村住户人均主要食品消费量(2000－2013年)

PER CAPITA CONSUMPTIONS OF MAJOR COMMODITIES OF RURAL HOUSEHOLDS(2000－2013)

项目	Item	单位	Unit	2000	2005	2006	2007
1. 粮食	Grain	千克	kg	216.45	155.79	144.16	116.52
2. 蔬菜	Vegetables	千克	kg	103.98	69.51	68.81	56.79
3. 食用油	Edible Oil	千克	kg	9.03	6.01	6.05	5.36
(1)植物油	Vegetable Oil	千克	kg	8.93	5.95	6.04	5.33
(2)动物油	Animal Fats	千克	kg	0.07	0.06	0.01	0.04
4. 肉类	Meat	千克	kg	12.36	23.53	25.32	26.05
(1)猪肉	Pork	千克	kg	11.85	12.82	13.86	12.87
(2)牛羊肉	Beef and Mutton	千克	kg	0.51	0.76	1	1.13
5. 牛羊奶	Milk	千克	kg	1.79	8.29	14.87	14.4
6. 家禽	Poultry	千克	kg	2.55	3.81	2.08	2.75
7. 蛋类	Eggs	千克	kg	14.41	11.52	12.75	11.03
8. 水产品	Aquatic Products	千克	kg	12.7	14.28	18.2	17.89
9. 食糖	Carbohydrate	千克	kg	0.86	0.52	0.63	0.74
10. 卷烟	Cigarette	盒	case	23.18	24.36	26.94	26.63
11. 酒	Liquor	千克	kg	22.81	20.13	21.86	20.56
12. 茶叶	Tea	千克	kg	0.06	0.51	0.6	0.65
13. 糖果	Sweet	千克	kg	0.52	0.41	0.50	0.53
14. 糕点	Cake	千克	kg	4.51	3.1	3.63	3.89
15. 水果及水果制品	Fruits and Fruit Products	千克	kg	39.73	20.11	24.25	22.5

注：抽样调查资料。

Note: The data is from sampling.

2008	2009	2010	2011	2012	2013
133.16	141.91	127.63	133.03	124.04	135.64
59.21	58.78	55.51	71.00	66.16	65.56
6.03	6.58	6.31	7.56	7.67	9.19
6.01	6.55	6.29	7.55	7.65	9.16
0.02	0.03	0.03	0.01	0.02	0.02
23.93	25.86	26.33	23.97	26.58	27.12
11.92	12.73	12.04	12.45	13.47	13.65
0.92	1.04	1.00	0.83	0.87	0.92
12.12	10.51	11.8	10.26	11.18	11.19
2.7	2.48	2.19	2.52	2.75	2.87
12.25	12.78	11.26	10.10	11.34	12.25
20.46	22.06	23.72	17.88	17.17	18.99
0.75	0.61	0.79	0.63	0.74	0.63
25.61	26.78	26.96	25.67	26.60	27.87
19.41	20.21	19.47	17.92	18.6	18.79
0.76	0.64	0.88	0.83	0.59	1.09
0.17	0.76	0.78	1.25	1.03	0.95
0.81	3.88	2.13	3.83	4.49	4.03
22.16	21.88	21.16	24.31	29.30	28.63

主要统计指标解释

城市家庭人口 指居住在一起,经济上合在一起共同生活的家庭成员。凡计算为家庭人口的成员其全部收支都包括在本家庭中。

城市就业者负担人数 指家庭人口与就业人口之比。

城市居民家庭总收入、可支配收入 城市居民家庭总收入指生活在一起的所有家庭成员得到的工资性收入、经营净收入、财产性收入、转移性收入之和,不包括出售财务收入和借贷收入。城市居民家庭可支配收入指家庭成员得到可用于最终消费支出和其他非义务性支出以及储蓄的总和,即居民家庭可以用来自由支配的收入。它是家庭总收入扣除交纳的个人所得税、个人交纳的社会保障费以及记账补贴后的收入。计算公式为:

可支配收入 = 家庭总收入—交纳个人所得税—个人交纳的社会保障支出—记账补贴

城市居民消费性支出 指被调查的城市居民家庭用于日常生活的全部支出,包括购买商品支出和文化生活、服务等支出。包括用于赠送的商品或服务。不包括罚没、丢失款和缴纳的各种税款(如个人所得税、牌照税、房产税等),也不包括个体劳动者生产经营过程中发生的各项费用。

农村居民家庭整、半劳动力整劳动力 指男子18周岁到50周岁,女子18周岁到45周岁;半劳动力指男子16周岁到17周岁,51周岁到60周岁;女子16周岁到17周岁,46周岁到55周岁,同时具有劳动能力的人。虽然在劳动年龄之内,但已丧失劳动能力的人,不应算为劳动力;超过劳动年龄,但能经常参加劳动,计入半劳动力数内。常住人口中的职工,若这些职工为劳动力,就包括在本户的整半劳动力中。

农村居民家庭总收入、纯收入农村居民家庭总收入 指调查期内农村住户和住户成员从各种来源渠道得到的收入总和。按收入的性质划分为工资性收入、家庭经营收入、财产性收入和转移性收入。农民人均纯收入指按人口平均的纯收入水平,反映的是一个地区或一个农户农村居民的平均收入水平。纯收入指农村住户当年从各个来源得到的总收入相应地扣除所发生的费用后的收入总和。纯收入主要用于再生产投入和当年生活消费支出,也可用于储蓄和各种非义务性支出。计算方法:

纯收入 = 总收入 - 家庭经营费用支出 - 税费支出 - 生产性固定资产折旧 - 赠送农村外部亲友支出

农村居民家庭生活消费支出 指农村常住居民家庭用于日常生活的全部开支,是反映和研究农民家庭实际生活消费水平高低的重要指标。

Explanatory Notes on Main Statistical Indicators

Population of Urban Households refer to members of the household living and sharing economically together. All income and expenditure of the population of the household are included in the income and expenditure of the household.

Number of Dependents per Urban Employee refers to the ratio between number of persons in urban households and the number of dependents.

Total Income and Disposable Income of Urban Households Total Income of Urban Households refers to the sum of wage income, net business income, income from properties, and income from transfers of members of the households, excluding income from selling of properties and income from borrowings. Disposable Income of Urban Households refers to the actual income at the disposal of members of the households which can be used for final consumption, other non-compulsory expenditure and savings. This equals to total income minus income tax, personal contribution to social security and sample household subsidy for keeping dairies. Following formula is used:

Disposable income = total income - income tax - personal contribution to social security - sample household subsidy for keeping dairies.

Consumption Expenditure of Urban Households refers to total expenditure of the sample households for consumption in daily life, including expenditure for various commodities and expenses for non-commodity items such as culture and service, including commodities and service give the other person as a present, but excluding fines and confiscation, loss, tax payments (such as income tax, real estates tax, etc,) and various expenses by individual laborers for business purposes.

Rural Full/Semi Labour ForceFull labour force refers to persons capable of work, aged 18-50 for males and 18-45 for females. Semi labour force refers to persons capable of work, aged 16-17 and 51-60 for males and 16-17 and 46-55 for females. Persons at their working ages but not capable of work are not to be included as labour force. Persons not at working ages but participating regularly in work are included in semi labour force. For staff and workers as resident population of the household, they are included as full or semi labour force of the household if they are in the labour force.

Total Income and Net Income of Rural Households Total Income of Rural Households refers to the sum of income earned from various sources by the rural households and their members during the reference period, and is classified as income from wages and salaries, income from from household operations, income from properties and income from transfers.

Net Income of Rural Households refers to the total income of rural households from all sources minus all corresponding expenses. the formula for calculation is an follows:

Net income = total income household operation expenses taxes and fees depreciation of fixed assets for production subsidy for participating in household survey gifts to non rural relatives.

Consumption Expenditure of Rural Households refers to total expenses of rural households on daily life. This indicator is used to show the actual consumption level of peasants.

11 农 业 AGRICULTURE

简要说明

一、本篇资料的主要内容

本篇资料主要反映了全市农业生产和农村经济的基本情况，主要包括农林牧渔业总产值、中间消耗、增加值、农村劳动力、耕地、主要农产品产量、农业机械年末拥有量、农业机械化和电气化以及农田水利建设等方面的资料。

二、本篇资料的来源

1、本篇资料中耕地面积资料来源于市国土资源房屋管理局。

2、水产品产量等相关资料来源于市海洋与渔业局。

3、农业机械化等相关资料来源于市农机局。

4、农田水利灌溉等相关资料来源于市水利局。

5、植树造林等相关资料来源于市林业局。

本篇资料由市统计局农村统计处、国家统计局青岛调查队农村调查处整理提供。

Brief Introduction

I. Main Content

Data in this chapter show the basic conditions of agricultural production and rural economy, mainly including agricultural output, intermediate consumption, value added, rural labor force, cultivated land, output of main agricultural produces, agricultural machinery and electrification in rural areas and basic construction on irrigation and drainage.

II. Source of Data

(1)Data on area of cultivated land are provided by Qingdao Municipal Bureau of Land Resources and Housing Management.

(2)Data on output of aquatic products are provided by Qingdao Municipal Bureau of Ocean and Fishery.

(3)Data on Agricultural machinery are provided by Qingdao Municipal Bureau of Agricultural Machinery.

(4)Data on farmland water conservancy are provided by Qingdao Municipal Bureau of Water Conservancy.

(5)Data on forest planting are provided by Qingdao Municipal Forestry Bureau.

Data in this chapter are compiled by the Division of Countryside Statistics of Qingdao Municipal Bureau of Statistics and Division of Rural Household Survey of Survey Office of the National Bureau of Statistics in Qingdao.

11－1 农村基本情况(2000－2014年)
BASIC STATISTICS ON RURAL AREA(2000－2014)

项目	Item	单位	Unit	2000	2005	2006	2007	2008	2009
一、乡村户数、人口、劳动力	**Rural Households, Population and Labor Force**								
乡村户数	Rural Households	万户	10000 households	148.20	151.06	151.1	151.19	151.75	152.37
乡村人口	Rural Population	万人	10000 persons	483.39	478.78	478.32	478.06	480.22	484.81
乡村劳动力	Rural Labor Force	万人	10000 persons	254.62	257.87	264.7	268.31	270.71	274.74
男劳动力	Male	万人	10000 persons	137.09	137.66	141.27	144.04	144.36	146.20
女劳动力	Female	万人	10000 persons	117.53	120.21	123.43	124.27	126.35	128.54
二、年末实有耕地面积	**Year-end Area of Cultivated Land**	**万公顷**	**10000 hectares**	**47.75**	**42.1**	**41.29**	**41.31**	**41.79**	**41.87**
三、农用机械总动力	**Total Agricultural Machinery Power**	**万千瓦**	**10000 kW**	**459.21**	**619.69**	**650.65**	**680.16**	**697.38**	**719.33**
拖拉机	Tractors	台	unit	126 981	163 032	171 155	173 326	176 156	180 171
四、农村用电量	**Electricity Consumed in Rural Areas**	**万千瓦时**	**10000 kW·h**	**189 651**	**372 645**	**413 762**	**425 715**	**424 292**	**426 306**
五、农用化肥施用量(折纯)	**Consumption of Chemical Fertilizer (convert to pure amount)**	**万吨**	**10000 tons**	**32.53**	**33.01**	**32.64**	**33.89**	**31.05**	**30.17**
六、有效灌溉面积	**Irrigated Area**	**万公顷**	**10000 hectares**	**29.52**	**29.65**	**30.31**	**30.58**	**31.39**	**32.27**

11 –1 续表
continued

项目	Item	单位	Unit	2010	2011	2012	2013	2014
一、乡村户数、人口、劳动力	**Rural Households, Population and Labor Force**							
乡村户数	Rural Households	万户	10000 households	154.92	154.91	155.66	155.22	157.00
乡村人口	Rural Population	万人	10000 persons	487.04	488.67	491.1	491.39	494.26
乡村劳动力	Rural Labor Force	万人	10000 persons	276.03	277.24	276.97	277.32	276.90
男劳动力	Male	万人	10000 persons	147.09	146.67	146.48	146.57	146.63
女劳动力	Female	万人	10000 persons	128.94	130.57	130.49	130.75	130.27
二、年末实有耕地面积	**Year-end Area of Cultivated Land**	**万公顷**	**10000 hectares**	**42.04**	**41.98**	**52.81**	**52.55**	**52.42**
三、农用机械总动力	**Total Agricultural Machinery Power**	**万千瓦**	**10000 kW**	**763.61**	**784.06**	**797.71**	**809.31**	**826.93**
拖拉机	Tractors	台	unit	200 208	202 022	206 290	206 300	205 065
四、农村用电量	**Electricity Consumed in Rural Areas**	**万千瓦时**	**10000 kW·h**	**426 819**	**431 646**	**426 815**	**359 139**	**404 380**
五、农用化肥施用量（折纯）	**Consumption of Chemical Fertilizer (convert to pure amount)**	**万吨**	**10000 tons**	**29.89**	**29.37**	**29.09**	**29.12**	**28.94**
六、有效灌溉面积	**Irrigated Area**	**万公顷**	**10000 hectares**	**32.9**	**33.17**	**33.39**	**30.28**	**32.17**

11-2 农村劳动力(1985-2014年)

RURAL LABOR FORCE(1985-2014)

单位:万人(10 000 persons)

年份 Year	合计 Total	农林牧渔业 Farming, Forestry, Animal Husbandry and Fishery	工业 Industry	建筑业 Construction
1985	225.09	147.89	32.92	15.62
1988	238.93	146.00	44.46	17.51
1989	242.70	151.16	44.65	16.46
1990	247.29	155.20	44.48	16.17
1991	253.01	160.31	45.49	15.87
1992	258.23	160.04	47.00	17.25
1993	259.18	159.22	44.04	20.20
1994	258.34	155.74	43.70	21.52
1995	258.66	154.08	44.06	22.33
1996	256.34	151.10	43.08	21.80
1997	258.60	153.07	41.66	22.02
1998	258.50	152.79	40.79	21.68
1999	256.82	149.11	42.18	22.32
2000	254.62	143.59	42.76	22.99
2001	253.98	132.46	47.76	24.66
2002	254.08	119.98	53.66	26.52
2003	257.67	118.27	55.65	26.65
2004	258.91	112.05	60.32	28.36
2005	257.87	103.03	65.59	29.03
2006	264.70	102.28	71.46	28.16
2007	268.31	100.63	74.70	30.97
2008	270.71	100.90	74.82	30.87
2009	274.74	102.64	75.42	31.23
2010	276.04	102.45	76.32	32.10
2011	277.24	102.73	76.87	32.57
2012	276.97	102.24	76.82	32.36
2013	277.32	104.48	76.42	31.15
2014	276.90			

11－2 续表
continued

单位:万人(10 000 persons)

年　份 Year	交通运输仓储和邮政业 Transport, Postal and Telecommunication Services	批发零售贸易、餐饮业 Wholesale and Retail Trades and Catering Services	金融保险业 Finance and Insurance	其他劳动力 Other Labor Force
1985	5.23	0.06	19.76	3.61
1988	5.89	0.09	20.40	4.58
1989	6.00	0.12	19.95	4.36
1990	6.11	0.12	20.71	4.50
1991	6.09	0.13	20.52	4.60
1992	7.02	0.16	21.74	5.02
1993	8.93	0.16	20.65	5.98
1994	6.48	10.10		20.80
1995	7.11	10.71		20.37
1996	7.33	11.78		21.25
1997	7.62	12.40		21.83
1998	8.02	13.32		21.90
1999	8.19	14.03		20.99
2000	8.39	16.10		20.79
2001	9.02	17.80		22.28
2002	10.00	20.07		23.85
2003	9.96	20.60		26.54
2004	10.20	24.08		22.96
2005	10.70	25.88		22.34
2006	11.66	25.31		24.37
2007	11.61	27.61		21.16
2008	11.06	28.76		22.09
2009	11.40	29.03		22.75
2010	11.78	28.85		22.01
2011	11.89	29.34		21.02
2012	11.96	29.56		21.11
2013	11.92	29.48		20.33
2014				

11－3 分市、区乡村户数、人口、劳动力(2014 年)

RURAL HOUSEHOLDS, POPULATION AND LABOR FORCE BY REGION(2014)

市、区名称	Region	乡村户数(万户) Rural Households (10000 households)	乡村人口(万人) Rural Population (10000 persons)	乡村劳动力(万人) Labor Force of Village (10000 persons)	男劳动力 Male Laborer	女劳动力 Female Laborer	#种植业 Planting
全　市	**Whole Municipality**	**157.00**	**494.26**	**276.90**	**146.63**	**130.27**	**82.33**
崂山区	Laoshan District	6.71	15.76	9.18	5.13	4.05	1.28
黄岛区	Original Huangdao District	27.11	88.51	46.39	24.82	21.56	10.15
城阳区	Chengyang District	15.53	41.75	22.41	11.64	10.77	1.59
即墨市	Jimo	29.56	97.50	52.93	28.17	24.75	14.14
胶州市	Jiaozhou	19.76	63.43	36.98	19.37	17.60	9.61
平度市	Pingdu	37.66	123.27	71.14	37.61	33.53	28.20
莱西市	Laixi	20.68	64.03	37.88	19.89	17.99	17.36

11－4 主要年份农、林、牧、渔业总产值(按现价计算)

MAJOR YEAR'S GROSS OUTPUT VALUE OF FARMING, FORESTRY, ANIMAL HUSBANDRY AND FISHERY (CURRENT PRICE)

单位:万元(10 000 yuan)

年 份 Year	农、林、牧、渔业总产值 Gross Output Value of Farming, Forestry, Animal Husbandry and Fishery	农业产值 Farming	林业产值 Forestry	牧业产值 Animal Husbandry	渔业产值 Fishery
1949	16 511	14 755	325	1 200	231
1952	24 428	21 353	479	1 888	708
1957	26 189	22 717	644	2 218	610
1962	15 356	13 257	230	1 243	626
1965	25 123	21 488	854	2 110	671
1970	44 078	36 889	1 851	3 817	1 521
1975	93 213	79 208	2 144	7 923	3 938
1978	121 497	94 397	3 112	17 293	6 695
1980	149 436	117 547	2 953	22 215	6 721
1985	299 139	215 729	8 986	53 894	20 530
1987	378 981	263 066	5 949	73 271	36 695
1989	463 952	303 679	19 134	91 885	49 254
1990	579 877	381 287	13 801	119 208	65 581
1991	664 779	417 111	12 875	144 909	89 884
1992	703 433	400 471	15 252	150 942	136 768
1993	989 763	509 601	20 845	232 143	227 174
1994	1 424 074	763 366	23 101	356 734	280 873
1995	1 923 771	1 021 413	26 765	503 999	371 594
1996	2 317 434	1 145 399	29 100	692 362	450 573
1997	2 047 712	939 922	24 052	578 443	505 295
1998	2 386 303	1 198 043	16 760	633 735	537 765
1999	2 382 320	1 169 596	17 122	618 020	577 582
2000	2 483 256	1 116 397	19 102	692 782	654 975
2001	2 615 228	1 135 816	20 433	758 313	700 666
2002	2 688 532	1 110 671	23 157	796 007	758 697
2003	2 759 692	1 062 576	36 183	859 915	801 018
2004	2 967 389	1 181 009	32 831	937 494	816 055
2005	3 205 057	1 265 695	25 246	1 070 831	843 285
2006	3 396 096	1 360 755	23 546	1 076 254	855 131
2007	3 429 877	1 483 733	20 842	975 032	830 479
2008	4 008 540	1 778 404	24 452	1 214 648	856 227
2009	4 086 146	1 856 753	22 264	1 160 558	898 608
2010	4 831 806	2 339 238	19 241	1 264 028	1 051 452
2011	5 359 343	2 365 300	19 237	1 560 108	1 232 720
2012	5 665 217	2 492 493	20 461	1 582 549	1 370 622
2013	6 118 581	2 841 323	22 178	1 640 755	1 394 753
2014	6 300 421	2 998 853	22 620	1 657 075	1 372 771

11－5 分市、区农、林、牧、渔业总产值(2014 年,现价)
GROSS OUTPUT VALUE OF FARMING,FORESTRY,ANIMAL HUSBANDRY AND FISHERY BY REGION(2014,CURRENT PRICE)

单位:万元(10 000 yuan)

市、区名称	Region	农、林、牧、渔业总产值 Gross Output Value of Farming, Forestry, Animal Husbandry and Fishery	农 业 Farming	林 业 Forestry	牧 业 Animal Husbandry	渔 业 Fishery	服务业 Services
全 市	**Whole Municipality**	**6 300 421**	**2 998 853**	**22 620**	**1 657 075**	**1 372 771**	**249 102**
崂山区	Laoshan District	100 248	9 947	218	5 873	72 665	11 546
黄岛区	Original Huangdao District	1 057 492	330 048	3 261	194 619	482 737	46 827
城阳区	Chengyang District	267 723	24 918	978	28 205	211 409	2 212
即墨市	Jimo	1 069 765	423 420	4 502	225 726	354 365	61 752
胶州市	Jiaozhou	888 743	410 831	3 964	210 871	221 122	41 955
平度市	Pingdu	1 797 074	1 225 642	5 160	500 896	17 376	48 000
莱西市	Laixi	1 119 376	574 047	4 537	490 885	13 097	36 810

注:本表按当年价格计算。
Note:Data in this form are calculated at current price.

11 -6 农、林、牧、渔业总产值、增加值(2014 年)

VALUE-ADDED OF FARMING,FORESTRY,ANIMAL HUSBANDRY AND FISHERY(2014)

单位:万元(10 000 yuan)

		总 计 Total	农 业 Farming	林 业 Forestry	牧 业 Animal Husbandry	渔 业 Fishery	服务业 Services
总产值	**Gross Output Value**	**6 300 422**	**2 998 853**	**22 620**	**1 657 076**	**1 372 771**	**249 102**
中间消耗	**Intermediate Expenditure**	**2 674 818**	**1 164 065**	**10 871**	**882 668**	**497 527**	**119 687**
中间物质消耗	Intermediate Expenditure of Matter	1 916 976	872 632	7 452	608 680	365 930	62 282
对非农生产部门的劳动支出	Expenditure of Labor Services to Nonagricultural Production Development	757 842	291 433	3 419	273 988	131 597	57 405

11 -7 分市、区农、林、牧、渔业增加值(2014 年)

VALUE-ADDED OF FARMING,FORESTRY,
ANIMAL HUSBANDRY FISHERY BY REGION(2014)

单位:亿元(100 million yuan)

市、区名称	Region	增加值 Added Value	农 业 Farming	林 业 Forestry	牧 业 Animal Husbandry	渔 业 Fishery	服务业 Services
全 市	**Whole Municipality**	**362.6**	**183.5**	**1.2**	**77.4**	**87.5**	**12.9**
崂山区	Laoshan District	6.1	0.6		0.3	4.6	0.6
黄岛区	Original Huangdao District	62.7	20.2	0.2	9.1	30.8	2.4
城阳区	Chengyang District	16.5	1.5	0.1	1.3	13.5	0.1
即墨市	Jimo	62.5	25.9	0.2	10.5	22.6	3.2
胶州市	Jiaozhou	51.5	25.1	0.2	9.9	14.1	2.2
平度市	Pingdu	102.3	75.0	0.3	23.4	1.1	2.5
莱西市	Laixi	61.0	35.1	0.2	22.9	0.8	1.9

11－8 主要年份耕地面积与播种面积

MAJOR YEAR'S CULTIVATED AND SOWN AREA

单位:万公顷(10 000 hectares)

年份 Year	年末实有耕地面积 Year－end Area of Cultivated Land	农作物播种面积 Sown Area of Farm Crops	#粮食作物 Grain Crops	经济作物 Economic Crops
1949		93.47	84.00	7.20
1952		97.53	85.07	10.80
1957		97.87	87.07	10.53
1962		81.47	72.53	5.80
1965		82.80	71.80	8.33
1970		80.73	68.27	10.07
1975		79.82	65.84	11.01
1978		77.60	63.60	10.40
1980		75.87	60.33	12.00
1985		78.27	57.33	15.73
1987		76.67	55.87	15.93
1989		74.78	54.28	16.06
1990		76.85	56.99	15.53
1991		76.98	56.89	15.69
1992		76.96	56.37	15.64
1993	56.90	77.75	56.22	15.71
1994		76.61	54.08	16.20
1995		76.54	53.71	15.65
1996	55.01	77.26	54.81	14.90
1997		75.04	52.32	14.40
1998		77.18	53.05	14.54
1999		77.56	50.61	13.24
2000		76.47	45.07	13.98
2001		73.69	41.91	14.54
2002		72.32	40.83	13.95
2003	53.20	67.82	36.05	14.50
2004	52.23	71.33	41.40	14.11
2005	50.90	75.02	49.93	11.89
2006	51.19	74.86	49.79	11.75
2007	51.25	72.79	47.56	12.11
2008	51.31	74.09	51.06	11.29
2009	53.50	75.00	52.92	11.34
2010		75.39	53.56	11.00
2011		75.70	54.56	10.69
2012	52.81	74.96	54.08	10.69
2013	52.55	70.99	50.04	10.83
2014	52.42	69.96	49.55	9.92

11－9 分市、区耕地面积(2014 年)
AREA OF CULTIVATED LAND BY REGION(2014)

单位:万公顷(10 000 hectares)

市、区名称	Region	年末耕地面积 Year-end Area of Cultivated Land	当年增加的耕地 Area of Cultivated Land Increased in the Year		
			#旱田 Dry Farmland	当年增加的耕地 Area of Cultivated Land Increased in the Year	#新开荒地 Wasteland Newly Opened up
全　市	**Whole Municipality**	**52.42**			
崂山区	Laoshan District	0.09			
黄岛区	Original Huangdao District	7.57			
城阳区	Chengyang District	0.70			
即墨市	Jimo	10.10			
胶州市	Jiaozhou	6.47			
平度市	Pingdu	18.49			
莱西市	Laixi	8.99			

11－9 续表
continued

单位:公顷(hectare)

市、区名称	Region	当年减少的耕地 Area of Cultivated Land Decreased in the Year	国家基建占地 Government Capital Construction	乡镇集体基建占地 Rural Capital Construction	农民个人建房占地 Private Building
全　市	**Whole Municipality**				
崂山区	Laoshan District				
黄岛区	Original Huangdao District				
城阳区	Chengyang District				
即墨市	Jimo				
胶州市	Jiaozhou				
平度市	Pingdu				
莱西市	Laixi				

11-10 分市、区农作物播种面积(2014年)
SOWN AREA OF FARM CROPS BY REGION(2014)

单位:万公顷(10 000 hectares)

市、区名称	Region	总播种面积 Total Sown Area	#粮 食 Grain	#棉 花 Cotton	#花 生 Peanut	#烟 叶 Tobacco	#蔬 菜 Vegetable
全 市	**Whole Municipality**	**69.96**	**49.55**	**0.15**	**8.86**	**0.03**	**10.48**
崂山区	Laoshan District	0.07	0.02		0.02		0.03
黄岛区	Original Huangdao District	8.10	5.19		1.95	0.02	0.88
城阳区	Chengyang District	0.66	0.46		0.01		0.18
即墨市	Jimo	10.88	8.05		1.76		0.99
胶州市	Jiaozhou	9.93	6.81		0.87		2.20
平度市	Pingdu	27.35	20.05	0.14	2.41		4.38
莱西市	Laixi	12.96	8.96		1.84		1.82

11－11 分市、区部分农作物产量(2014 年)
OUTPUT OF FARM CROPS BY REGION(2014)

单位:吨(ton)

市、区名称	Region	粮 食 Grain	棉 花 Cotton	花 生 Peanut	烟 叶 Tobacco	蔬 菜 Vegetable
全 市	**Whole Municipality**	**3 230 238**	**2 467**	**398 028**	**782**	**5 953 466**
崂山区	Laoshan District	1 294		548		11 701
黄岛区	Original Huangdao District	276 064	4	88 442	673	428 702
城阳区	Chengyang District	22 221		132		76 341
即墨市	Jimo	479 437	185	72 522		585 082
胶州市	Jiaozhou	412 797	96	40 711		1 193 427
平度市	Pingdu	1 442 561	2 182	110 326	109	2 511 685
莱西市	Laixi	595 865		85 347		1 146 527

11－12 分市、区部分农作物播公顷单产量(2014 年)

OUTPUT OF FARM CROPS PER HECTARE BY REGION(2014)

单位:千克(kg)

市、区名称	Region	粮食 Grain	棉花 Cotton	花生 Peanut	烟叶 Tobacco	蔬菜 Vegetable
全　市	**Whole Municipality**	**6 520**	**1 670**	**4 490**	**2 744**	**56 790**
崂山区	Laoshan District	6 972		2 850		43 147
黄岛区	Original Huangdao District	5 314	1 800	4 530	2 700	48 645
城阳区	Chengyang District	4 796		2 444		41 663
即墨市	Jimo	5 954	4 950	4 110		59 249
胶州市	Jiaozhou	6 065	2 105	4 689		54 310
平度市	Pingdu	7 196	1 568	4 572	3 050	57 300
莱西市	Laixi	6 648		4 635		62 879

11－13 主要年份农作物总产量
MAJOR YEAR'S OUTPUT OF FARM CROPS

单位:吨(ton)

年份 Year	粮食 Grain	#小麦 Wheat	#玉米 Corn	棉花 Cotton	花生 Peanut	水果 Fruit	蔬菜 Vegetable
1949	723 190	158 815	25 810	1 280	71 080	9 955	356 015
1952	967 640	200 380	58 130	6 025	115 585	13 468	284 050
1957	921 920	210 690	141 540	3 520	90 445	18 869	625 220
1962	628 930	104 340	53 010	1 280	35 470	8 366	524 455
1965	917 635	180 610	135 595	6 090	88 390	16 034	465 850
1970	1 175 985	243 945	244 530	16 490	96 280	33 907	541 145
1975	1 899 540	430 135	420 095	15 390	98 495	59 206	693 970
1978	1 900 850	514 570	510 635	8 720	114 370	82 819	921 140
1980	2 164 415	520 045	819 930	19 630	160 670	80 840	996 565
1985	2 331 060	961 055	739 455	19 335	475 270	200 515	1 253 075
1987	2 626 029	996 165	1 030 926	13 819	394 296	249 655	1 489 250
1989	2 654 334	993 406	1 084 441	14 638	391 782	288 757	1 664 238
1990	2 998 246	1 265 157	1 210 687	17 490	413 636	292 366	1 786 041
1991	3 180 893	1 421 143	1 285 043	25 965	446 880	294 349	1 837 265
1992	2 675 641	1 235 755	981 490	8 160	321 145	341 415	2 030 327
1993	3 164 812	1 463 759	1 248 780	15 344	419 109	383 368	2 705 349
1994	3 106 562	1 392 977	1 252 952	8 326	494 827	423 024	3 002 318
1995	3 291 587	1 480 385	1 365 167	8 177	510 662	478 685	3 221 507
1996	3 390 033	1 513 479	1 466 668	4 001	486 574	505 711	3 405 056
1997	2 523 064	1 584 478	743 199	2 000	308 233	438 398	3 333 181
1998	3 469 821	1 627 261	1 484 182	4 159	546 786	529 592	4 036 992
1999	3 331 124	1 501 182	1 499 775	3 668	572 941	606 800	5 459 140
2000	2 780 481	1 353 445	1 169 649	2 077	534 174	651 591	6 649 322
2001	2 539 257	1 143 679	1 178 851	3 409	579 441	675 244	6 250 361
2002	2 383 802	1 085 936	1 094 731	3 755	557 714	579 703	6 847 570
2003	2 221 697	931 787	1 117 704	5 324	568 798	677 361	7 305 618
2004	2 650 952	1 301 791	1 202 063	7 216	580 290	748 516	6 720 886
2005	3 150 203	1 535 471	1 478 616	4 042	503 941	737 300	5 792 110
2006	3 039 266	1 548 928	1 372 166	3 954	471 853	827 755	6 051 239
2007	3 007 443	1 395 643	1 497 343	4 330	495 972	793 859	6 157 471
2008	3 336 643	1 620 734	1 620 910	4 173	471 447	806 815	6 118 876
2009	3 539 075	1 727 966	1 723 279	4 529	468 022	820 887	5 679 434
2010	3 514 081	1 646 745	1 795 187	3 952	441 443	803 092	5 807 761
2011	3 630 046	1 653 376	1 906 374	3 917	443 713	805 192	5 838 183
2012	3 699 600			4 301	459 464	798 685	5 697 564
2013	3 223 879	1 518 351	1 658 129	3 429	443 909	749 501	5 754 180
2014	3 230 238	1 520 990	1 667 630	2 467	398 028	751 757	5 953 466

11－14 分市、区大牲畜头数(2014 年)
NUMBER OF LARGE LIVESTOCK BY REGION(2014)

单位:万头(10 000 head)

市、区名称	Region	年末大牲畜头数 Number of Large Livestock (year-end)	牛 Cattle and Buffaloes	#奶　牛 Cows	马 Horses	驴 Donkeys	骡 Mules
全　市	**Whole Municipality**	**22.69**	**22.66**	**11.32**	**0.02**	**0.01**	
崂山区	Laoshan District	0.02	0.02	0.02			
黄岛区	Original Huangdao District	1.49	1.48	0.09		0.01	
城阳区	Chengyang District	0.53	0.53	0.52			
即墨市	Jimo	2.10	2.10	1.47			
胶州市	Jiaozhou	2.02	2.02	0.46			
平度市	Pingdu	6.45	6.44	0.77			
莱西市	Laixi	10.09	10.07	8.00	0.02		

11－15 分市、区猪、羊及家禽存养量(2014 年)
HOGS, SHEEP, GOATS AND POULTRY IN STOCK BY REGION(2014)

单位:万只(10 000 head)

市、区名称	Region	年末生猪存养量 Hogs in Stock (year-end)	年末羊存养量 Sheep and Goats in Stock (year-end)	#山　羊 Goats	#绵　羊 Sheep	家　禽 Poultry
全　市	**Whole Municipality**	**212.04**	**20.32**	**13.95**	**6.37**	**5 287.90**
崂山区	Laoshan District	0.33	0.09	0.09		50.52
黄岛区	Original Huangdao District	40.46	4.98	4.45	0.53	290.39
城阳区	Chengyang District	4.60	0.22	0.19	0.03	140.10
即墨市	Jimo	25.77	1.30	0.91	0.40	934.30
胶州市	Jiaozhou	31.90	3.58	2.76	0.81	382.09
平度市	Pingdu	64.77	7.06	2.84	4.22	1 572.94
莱西市	Laixi	44.20	3.09	2.70	0.39	1 917.56

11－16 分市、区肉、蛋、奶、蜂蜜产量(2014年)

OUTPUT OF MEAT,EGGS AND MILK BY REGION(2014)

单位:万吨(10 000 tons)

市、区名称	Region	肉类产量 Output of Meat	#猪肉 Pork	#牛肉 Beef	#羊肉 Mutton	#禽肉 Poultry Meat	禽蛋 Poultry Eggs	牛羊奶 Milk
全 市	**Whole Municipality**	**59.6**	**27.4**	**1.0**	**0.2**	**30.4**	**19.1**	**37.5**
崂山区	Laoshan District	0.2	0.1			0.2	0.4	0.1
黄岛区	Original Huangdao District	7.0	5.0	0.1	0.1	1.3	1.7	1.5
城阳区	Chengyang District	0.7	0.5			0.3	1.5	1.5
即墨市	Jimo	7.6	3.3	0.1		4.1	5.0	4.4
胶州市	Jiaozhou	5.7	4.4	0.1		1.2	3.2	2.1
平度市	Pingdu	18.9	8.4	0.3	0.1	10.1	3.9	3.0
莱西市	Laixi	19.4	5.7	0.4		13.3	3.4	24.9

11－17 分市、区渔业养殖面积

AQUACULTURE AREA BY REGION

单位:公顷(hectare)

市、区名称	Region	2014			2013		
		养殖面积 Aquaculture Area	#海水 Seawater	#淡水 Fresh Water	养殖面积 Aquaculture Area	#海水 Seawater	#淡水 Fresh Water
全 市	**Whole Municipality**	**50 088**	**33 829**	**16 259**	**51 155**	**35 030**	**16 125**
崂山区	Laoshan District	1 600	1 600		1 600	1 600	
黄岛区	Original Huangdao District	13 927	11 518	2 409	13 418	11 132	2 286
城阳区	Chengyang District	9 690	7 934	1 756	10 092	8 331	1 761
即墨市	Jimo	12 063	10 889	1 174	13 253	12 079	1 174
胶州市	Jiaozhou	4 332	1 888	2 444	4 288	1 888	2 400
平度市	Pingdu	3 800		3 800	3 800		3 800
莱西市	Laixi	4 676		4 676	4 704		4 704

11－18 分市、区水产品总产量(2014 年)

OUTPUT OF AQUATIC PRODUCTS BY REGION(2014)

单位:吨(ton)

市、区名称	Region	水产品总产量 Output of Aquatic Products	#养殖产量 Aquaculture Outpu	鱼 类 Fish	甲壳类 Crust	贝 类 Shellfish	藻 类 Algae
全 市	**Whole Municipality**	**1 094 459**	**826 703**	**79 998**	**27 378**	**690 944**	**14 471**
崂山区	Laoshan District	73 002	22 785	422	160	18 542	3 561
黄岛区	Original Huangdao District	347 712	265 098	43 310	11 525	194 299	4 000
城阳区	Chengyang District	245 955	204 523	1 878	7 395	187 965	6 650
即墨市	Jimo	298 190	233 142	2 036	4 551	225 103	260
胶州市	Jiaozhou	108 057	79 612	10 858	3 719	65 035	
平度市	Pingdu	11 006	11 006	10 974	28		
莱西市	Laixi	10 537	10 537	10 520			

11－19 分市、区植树及造林面积(2014 年)

AREA OF FORESTATION AND AFFORESTATION BY REGION(2014)

市、区名称	Region	当年造林面积(公顷) Area of Afforestation in the Year(hectare)	本年新增育苗面积(公顷) Nursery Garden Area(hectare)	未成林抚育作业面积(公顷) Laid out Area of Young Trees(hectare)	成林抚育面积(公顷) Laid out Area of Grown-up Trees (hectare)	零星(四旁)植树(万株) Surrounding Tree Planting(10 000 trees)
全 市	**Whole Municipality**	**10 402**	**1 426**	**6 340**	**22 504**	**422**
崂山区	Laoshan District	35	13		1 467	2
黄岛区	Original Huangdao District	1 667	187		667	11
城阳区	Chengyang District	135	12		367	15
即墨市	Jimo	1 653	400		2 577	80
胶州市	Jiaozhou	1 833	100		333	8
平度市	Pingdu	2 279	441		7 886	136
莱西市	Laixi	2 533	273	6 340	9 207	170
市直属单位		267				

11－20 分市、区果园面积、水果总产量(2014 年)
AREA OF ORCHARDS AND OUTPUT OF FRUITS BY REGION(2014)

单位:吨(ton)

市、区名称	Region	果园总面积(公顷) Area of Orchards (hectare)	水果总产量(吨) Output of Fruits(ton)	#苹果 Apple	#梨 Pear	#桃 Peach	#葡萄 Grape	#杏 Apricot	#山楂 Hawthorn
全　市	**Whole Municipality**	**28 472**	**751 757**	**459 301**	**74 434**	**59 967**	**115 396**	**59 967**	**3 602**
崂山区	Laoshan District	660	6 031	400	325	1 926	16	1 926	10
黄岛区	Original Huangdao District	6 009	103 132	75 181	7 517	10 544	483	10 544	316
城阳区	Chengyang District	929	12 022	233	17	5 448	3 004	5 448	
即墨市	Jimo	627	15 591	4 576	548	2 501	1 054	2 501	250
胶州市	Jiaozhou	1 534	46 191	17 744	4 440	14 216	3 748	14 216	63
平度市	Pingdu	10 666	344 585	220 200	15 287	20 176	77 948	20 176	756
莱西市	Laixi	8 046	224 206	140 967	46 299	5 156	29 143	5 156	2 207

11－21 分市、区茶园、桑园面积和茶叶、蚕茧产量(2014 年)
AREA OF TEA AND MULBERRY PLANTATIONS AND OUTPUT OF TEA AND SILKWORM COCOONS BY REGION(2014)

市、区名称	Region	茶园面积(公顷) Area of Tea Plantations(hectare)	茶叶产量(吨) Output of Tea(ton)	蚕茧产量(吨) Output of Silkworm Cocoons(ton)
全　市	**Whole Municipality**	**4 482**	**2 043**	**229**
崂山区	Laoshan District	1 205	1 104.8	
黄岛区	Original HuangdaoDistrict	2 945	555.6	3.1
城阳区	Chengyang District	111	18.0	
即墨市	Jimo	220	364.7	
胶州市	Jiaozhou			
平度市	Pingdu			117.8
莱西市	Laixi			108.1

11－22 主要年份主要农业机械拥有量
MAJOR YEAR'S OWNERSHIP OF AGRICULTURAL MACHINERY

年 份 Year	农业机械总动力(万千瓦) Total Agricultural Machinery Power (10 000 kW)	农用拖拉机 Agricultural Tractors		大、中型机引农具(万台) Large and Medium Towing Farm Machinery(10 000 sets)	农用汽车(辆) Agricultural Automobiles (vehicle)	排灌机械 Drainage and Irrigation Machinery	
		混合台 set	千 瓦 kW			台 set	万千瓦 10 000 kW
1949							
1952					1		
1957	0.22	59	2.2	0.01	2		
1962	2.47	254	11.47	0.06	13		
1965	3.49	296	13.2	0.08	15		
1970	10.40	602	7 963	0.07	12		
1975	43.94	6 447	103 476	0.48	90		
1978	75.45	15 576	309 287	1.02	261		
1980	110.44	24 278	502 731	1.72	728		
1985	174.76	33 097	506 217	1.71	2 645	67 794	54.92
1987	228.00	50 904	649 340	1.91	3 961	86 314	62.90
1989	241.00	53 556	661 400	1.96	3 982	93 437	70.46
1990	253.52	55 363	680 903	2.03	3 880	105 574	74.63
1991	250.58	57 404	691 332	2.20	3 706	134 900	73.77
1992	253.94	57 182	684 182	2.28	3 948	124 800	82.68
1993	261.24	56 335	678 161	2.34	4 378	144 460	78.96
1994	278.41	58 698	688 886	2.39	5 474	147 259	80.81
1995	289.23	56 391	657 025	2.28	6 314	138 625	73.98
1996	303.57	59 698	680 447	2.32	7 263	148 313	81.53
1997	326.72	66 841	744 424	2.42	8 085	155 629	88.09
1998	364.21	87 226	894 985	2.48	8 409	156 565	86.68
1999	411.44	105 743	1 075 907	3.06	9 363	170 875	96.20
2000	459.21	126 981	1 253 210	3.30	9 613	182 646	108.26
2001	496.27	141 409	1 394 114	4.33	10 212	178 437	104.18
2002	534.92	152 920	1 537 544	4.79	10 411	182 799	107.35
2003	560.94	160 676	1 666 185	5.07	11 201	192 930	109.44
2004	598.87	168 061	1 818 276	5.31	11 085	192 144	110.38
2005	619.69	163 032	1 757 177	5.66	11 552	188 689	112.16
2006	650.65	171 155	1 890 402	6.20	11 098	192 010	116.08
2007	680.16	173 326	1 958 047	6.57	11 408	195 050	118.22
2008	697.38	176 156	2 034 453	7.98	11 408	208 711	134.10
2009	719.33	180 171	2 266 697	8.60	11 408	207 648	133.99
2010	763.61	200 208	2 331 867	9.80		190 770	123.33
2011	784.06	202 022	2 649 283	9.77		189 834	127.16
2012	797.71	206 290	2 759 004	9.91		190 134	127.34
2013	809.31	206 309	2 968 332	9.97		190 433	127.42
2014	826.93	205 065	2 960 438	10.05		190 584	128.00

11-23 主要年份农业机械化、用电量、化肥施用量

MAJOR YEAR'S MECHANIZATION, ELECTRICITY AND CHEMICAL FERTILIZER CONSUMPTION

年份 Year	有效灌溉面积(公顷) Irrigated Area (hectare)	配套机电井(眼) Number of Electromechanical Well (well)	机耕面积(公顷) Area of Motorized Cultivation (hectare)	机播面积(公顷) Area of Motorized Planting (hectare)	机收面积(公顷) Area of Motorized Harvesting (hectare)	农村用电量(万千瓦时) Electricity Consumption in Rural Area (10 000 kW·h)	化肥施用量(折纯万吨) Chemical Fertilizer Consumption (convert to 10 000 tons)
1949	8 340						
1952	14 980						
1957	59 353		12 800	13			0.19
1962	55 213	191	65 680	927	927	55	0.10
1965	80 000	125	11 433	573	247	128	0.55
1970	147 613	3 947	143 700	2 527	133	1 208	1.76
1975	233 980	12 820	248 867	54 507	953	2 522	2.77
1978	276 660	21 017	329 213	178 533	15 060	13 975	3.64
1980	296 606	22 472	444 800	187 980	55 333	20 492	12.06
1985	302 647	42 925	366 786	148 433	56 447	41 524	11.66
1987	260 800	48 497	410 820	187 680	104 240	58 280	13.87
1989	267 440	61 570	540 413	208 527	107 320	62 859	17.91
1990	274 680	56 821	426 680	220 593	143 133	67 616	20.47
1991	281 500	58 987	431 293	254 266	192 946	81 200	22.53
1992	281 610	62 100	438 533	270 453	207 780	88 024	22.60
1993	284 080	63 954	439 300	260 287	225 807	102 501	28.04
1994	286 750	64 877	436 820	262 846	238 693	121 307	28.73
1995	287 020	64 651	435 213	271 707	250 267	134 284	31.45
1996	289 320	65 237	438 947	280 480	235 933	143 740	31.36
1997	292 130	66 783	442 213	308 267	266 147	150 971	28.99
1998	294 120	64 109	442 920	359 447	285 513	153 113	31.95
1999	294 790	64 734	440 967	396 180	286 367	169 337	32.58
2000	295 190	65 179	439 980	346 480	292 787	189 651	32.53
2001	296 980	65 547	436 576	382 870	265 730	228 069	31.73
2002	294 310	65 588	433 660	364 680	267 690	256 453	31.07
2003	292 410	65 406	415 790	404 980	256 600	299 425	31.89
2004	292 520	65 501	415 220	454 800	314 680	330 609	32.45
2005	296 450	65 303	409 610	493 240	367 740	372 644	33.01
2006	303 070	65 981	403 980	493 750	398 700	413 762	32.64
2007	305 760	66 400	400 480	499 590	429 630	425 715	33.89
2008	313 920	66 828	404 080	517 540	455 120	424 292	31.05
2009	322 710	67 027	404 080	538 220	481 176	426 306	30.17
2010	328 960	67 242		558 611	499 248	426 819	29.89
2011	331 690	62 104		567 947	547 108	431 646	29.37
2012	333 850	62 112	410 440	627 701	566 653	426 815	29.09
2013	302 790	170 008	410 601	627 701	566 653	359 138	29.12
2014	321 670	169 491	411 355	590 798	545 360	404 380	28.94

11－24 分市、区农业机械化和电气化(2014 年)

MECHANIZATION AND ELECTRIFICATION IN AGRICULTURE BY REGION(2014)

市、区名称	Region	机耕作业面积 Area of Motorized Cultivation		机播地面积 Area of Motorized Planting	
		面积(公顷) Area(hectare)	占播种面积比重(%) Percentage to Area of Cultivated Land(%)	面积(公顷) Area(hectare)	占播种面积比重(%) Percentage to Sown Area(%)
全 市	**Whole Municipality**	**411 355**	**96.7**	**590 798**	**84.4**
崂山区	Laoshan District				
黄岛区	Original Huangdao District	49 732		55 747	68.8
城阳区	Chengyang District	4 639		6 389	96.5
即墨市	Jimo	73 581		103 058	94.7
胶州市	Jiaozhou	59 777		90 448	91.1
平度市	Pingdu	164 330		226 665	82.9
莱西市	Laixi	59 296		108 491	83.7

11－24 续表

continued

市、区名称	Region	机收面积 Area of Motorized Harvesting		农村用电量(万千瓦小时) Electricity Consumed in Rural Areas(10 000 kW·h)
		面积(公顷) Area(hectare)	占播种面积比重(%) Percentage to Sown Area(%)	
全 市	**Whole Municipality**	**545 360**	**77.9**	**404 380**
崂山区	Laoshan District			12 731
黄岛区	Original Huangdao District	51 640	63.8	54 657
城阳区	Chengyang District	4 305	65.0	47 311
即墨市	Jimo	94 164	86.5	70 812
胶州市	Jiaozhou	83 677	84.3	94 499
平度市	Pingdu	216 795	79.3	86 787
莱西市	Laixi	94 779	73.1	37 584

11－25 分市、区农用化肥施用量(2014 年)
CONSUMPTION OF CHEMICAL FERTILIZERS BY REGION(2014)

单位:折纯吨(ton converted to pure amount)

市、区名称	Region	农用化肥施用量 Consumption of Chemical Fertilizers	氮　肥 Nitrogenous Fertilizer	磷　肥 Phosphate Fertilizer	钾　肥 Potash Fertilizer	复合肥 Compound Fertilizer	附:平均每公顷耕地施用化肥量(＊) Annotation:Consumption of Chemical Fertilizer Per Hectare
全　市	**Whole Municipality**	**289 374**	**52 360**	**13 495**	**16 736**	**206 784**	**552**
崂山区	Laoshan District	1 026	205	55	57	708	1 130
黄岛区	Original Huangdao District	35 554	9 173	3 322	4 657	18 402	470
城阳区	Chengyang District	1 371	319	112	93	847	195
即墨市	Jimo	38 638	15 576	2 615	1 219	19 229	382
胶州市	Jiaozhou	38 097	6 440	992	4 466	26 198	589
平度市	Pingdu	120 807	8 777	2 123	5 967	103 940	653
莱西市	Laixi	53 881	11 870	4 275	277	37 460	599

注:(＊)单位为[折纯千克]
Note:The(＊)mark refers to kilogram converted to pure amount.

11－26 分市、区农田水利(2014 年)
FARMLAND WATER CONSERVANCY BY REGION(2014)

市、区名称	Region	有效灌溉面积(公顷) Irrigated Area (hectare)	有效灌溉面积占耕地面积比重(%) Percentage of Irrigated Area to Area of Cultivated Land(%)	农业排灌机械拥有量(万台/万千瓦) Ownership of Drainage and Irrigation Machinery (10 000 sets/10 000 kW)	农用水泵(万台) Agricultural Pump (10 000 sets)	喷灌机械(万套) Spraying Irrigation Machinery (10 000 sets)	机电井数(眼) Number of Electromechanical Well (well)
全　市	**Whole Municipality**	**321 670**	**61.4**	**19.1/127.6**	**14.3**	**8.9**	**169 491**
崂山区	Laoshan District	520	57.3				1 307
黄岛区	Original Huangdao District	41 890	55.3	0.7/6	1.2	0.9	22 381
城阳区	Chengyang District	3 670	52.1	0.6/4.5	0.4	0.3	868
即墨市	Jimo	58 880	58.3	2.1/14.9	2.1	1.9	35 135
胶州市	Jiaozhou	37 570	58.1	1.4/10.9	0.8	1.4	17 505
平度市	Pingdu	127 420	68.9	12.5/80.5	7.4	1.8	66 146
莱西市	Laixi	51 720	57.5	1.8/10.8	2.4	2.7	26 138

11－27 分市、区主要农业机械拥有量(2014 年)
OWNERSHIP OF MAJOR AGRICULTURAL MACHINERY BY REGION(2014)

市、区名称	Region	农业机械总动力(万千瓦) Agricultural Machinery Power (10 000 kW)	平均每公顷耕地拥有量(千瓦) Power Per Hectare of Cultivated Land(kW)	大中型拖拉机 Large and Medium Tractors		小型拖拉机 Small Tractors	
				台 set	千 瓦 kW	台 set	千 瓦 kW
全 市	**Whole Municipality**	**826.9**	**15.8**	**41 537**	**1 587 842**	**163 528**	**1 372 596**
崂山区	Laoshan District						
黄岛区	Original Huangdao District	91.0	12.0	3 602	100 686	43 406	287 556
城阳区	Chengyang District	34.3	48.7	436	14 321	1 547	10 639
即墨市	Jimo	129.2	12.8	7 151	229 061	31 454	259 664
胶州市	Jiaozhou	117.5	18.2	5 125	254 427	18 377	257 278
平度市	Pingdu	323.5	17.5	19 165	779 866	33 722	320 356
莱西市	Laixi	131.5	14.6	6 058	209 481	35 022	237 103

11－27 续表 1
continued

市、区名称	Region	大、中、小播种机(部) Large, Medium and Small Seeders(set)	机引犁(部) Towing Ploughs(unit)	机引耙(部) Towing Rakes(unit)	脱粒机(部) Threshers(unit)
全　市	**Whole Municipality**	**58 821**	**125 605**	**28 866**	**34 564**
崂山区	Laoshan District				
黄岛区	Original Huangdao District	1 260	32 905	1 000	7 300
城阳区	Chengyang District	772	1 200	207	
即墨市	Jimo	12 624	19 952	1 680	6 574
胶州市	Jiaozhou	9 014	15 092	5 240	3 390
平度市	Pingdu	26 850	21 845	16 500	12 000
莱西市	Laixi	8 301	34 611	4 239	5 300

11 -27 续表2
continued

市、区名称	Region	粮食加工机械（台）Grain Processing Machinery(unit)	棉花加工机械（部）Cotton Processing Machinery(unit)	油料加工机械（部）Oil Processing Machinery(unit)	饲料粉碎机（部）Pulverizers (unit)
全　市	**Whole Municipality**	**25 677**	**132**	**9 132**	**23 001**
崂山区	Laoshan District				
黄岛区	Original Huangdao District	1 112		255	3 544
城阳区	Chengyang District	1 605	17	520	338
即墨市	Jimo	3 259		1 472	1 449
胶州市	Jiaozhou	3 050		2 125	3 570
平度市	Pingdu	4 371	6	1 410	7 510
莱西市	Laixi	12 280	109	3 350	6 590

主要统计指标解释

农业总产值 是以货币表现的农、林、牧、渔业全部产品的总量,它反映一定时期内农业生产的总规模和总成果。

农、林、牧、渔业的统计范围是:

(1)农业包括农作物种植业和其他农业。

农作物种植业包括谷物、豆类、薯类、棉、油料、糖料、麻类、烟叶、蔬菜、药材、瓜类和其他农作物的种植,以及茶园、桑园、果园的生产经营。其他农业包括采集野生植物的果实、纤维、树胶、树脂、油料以及柴草、野生药材、菌类等及农民家庭兼营的商品性工业。

(2)林业包括林木的栽培(不包括茶园、桑园和果园的栽培、管理和收获等活动)、林产品的采集和村及村以下合作经济组织和农户的竹木采伐。

(3)牧业包括除渔业养殖以外的一切动物饲养和放牧,以及野生动物的捕猎和饲养。

(4)渔业包括水生动物和海藻类植物的养殖和捕捞。

粮食产量 指稻谷、小麦、玉米、高粱等谷物及薯类和豆类的全社会产量。包括国有经济经营的、集体统一经营的和农民家庭经营的粮食产量,还包括工矿企业办的农场和其他生产单位的产量。其产量计算方法,豆类按去豆荚后的干豆计算;薯类(包括甘薯和马铃薯,不包括芋头和木薯)按5公斤鲜薯折1公斤粮食计算。城市郊区作为蔬菜的薯类(如马铃薯等)按鲜品计算,并且不作粮食统计。其他粮食一律按脱粒后的原粮计算。

水产品产量 指人工养殖的水产品和天然生长的水产品的捕捞量.包括海水的鱼类、虾蟹类、贝类和藻类以及内陆水域的鱼类、虾蟹类和贝类,不包括淡水生植物。

猪、牛、羊肉产量 指当年出栏并已屠宰、除去头蹄下水后带骨头肉(即胴体重)的重量。其统计范围为全社会。

农用化肥施用量 指本年内实际用于农业生产的化肥数量,包括氮肥、磷肥、钾肥和复合肥。化肥施用量要求按折纯量计算数量。折纯量是指把氮肥、磷肥、钾肥分别按含氮、含五氧化二磷、含氧化钾的百分之百成分进行折算后的数量。复合肥按其所含主要成分折算。

公式:折纯量 = 实物量 × 某种化肥有效成分含量的百分比

农业机械总动力 指用于农、林、牧、渔业生产的各种动力机械的动力总和。动力机械包括耕作、排灌、种植、植物保护、收获、农产品加工、运输、畜牧、渔业、农田水利等各种机械。不包括专门用于乡办工业、基本建设、非农业运输、科学试验和教学等非农业生产方面用的动力机械与作业机械的数量。

Explanatory Notes on Main Statistical Indicators

Gross Output Value of Agriculture refers to the total volume of products of farming, forestry, animal husbandry, and fishery expressed in the monetary terms. It reflects the overall scale and achievements of agricultural production during a given period of time.

The scope of statistics on farming, forestry, animal husbandry, and fishery are as follows:

(1) Farming includes cultivation of farm crops and other agricultural activities.

Cultivation of farm crops include cultivation of grain crops, legume crops, tuber-crops, cotton, oil-bearing crops, sugar crops, and cultivation and management of tea plantations, mulberry fields and orchards.

Other agricultural activities include harvesting wild fruits, fiber, tree gum, resin, oil-bearing plants, firewood, wild medicinal herbs, fungus, and rural-household commodity industries.

(2) Forestry refers to planting trees of various kinds (excluding tea plantations, mulberry fields and orchards), collection of forestry products and cutting and felling of bamboo and trees by villages and other cooperative organizations under village level.

(3) Animal husbandry refers to raising and grazing of all kinds of farm animals except fishing and aquatic cultivating, and hunting and rising of wild animals.

(4) Fishery refers to cultivation and catching of fish and other aquatic products and cultivation and collection of seaweed and other aquatic plants.

Grain Output refers to the total output of rice, wheat, corn, sorghum, millet and other miscellaneous grains as well as tubers and bean in the whole country including grains produced by states farms, collective unit, industrial enterprises and mines, output of beans refers to dry beans without pods, the output of tubers (sweet potatoes and potatoes, excluding taros and cassava) was converted into that of grain at the ratio 5: 1, i. e. 5 kilograms of fresh tubers was equivalent to 1 kilogram of grain, tubers supplies as vegetable (such as potatoes) in cities and suburbs are calculated as fresh vegetables and their output is not included in the output of grain output of all other grains refers to husked grain.

Output of Aquatic Products refers to catches of both artificially cultured and naturally grown aquatic products, including fish, shrimps, crabs and shellfish in sea and inland water as well as seaweed. Freshwater plants are not included.

Output of Pork, Beef, and Mutton refers to the meat of slaughtered hogs, cattle, sheep and goats with head, feet, and offal taken away. Data refers to the production of the whole country.

Consumption of Chemical Fertilizers in Agriculture refers to the quantity of chemical fertilizers applied in agriculture in the year, including nitrogenous fertilizer, phosphate fertilizer, potash fertilizer, and compound fertilizer. The consumption of chemical fertilizers is required in calculation to convert the gross weight into weight containing 100% effective component (e. g. 100% nitrogen content in nitrogenous fertilizer, 100% phosphorous pent oxide contents in phosphate fertilizer, 100% potassium oxide contents in potash fertilizer). Compound fertilizer is converted with its major component. The formula is:

Volume of effective component = physical quantity × effective component of certain chemical fertilizer (%)

Total Power of Agriculture Machinery Refers to the total mechanical power of machinery used in farming forestry animal husbandry and fishery, including machines used for ploughing, irrigation and drainage, crop growing, plant protection, harvesting, farm product processing, transport, stock breeding, fishery and water conservancy, Machinery employed for non agricultural purposes such as township industry, capital construction, non-agricultural transport, scientific experiments and for teaching is excluded.

工　业 12
INDUSTRY

简要说明

一、本篇资料的主要内容

本篇资料主要反映了全市工业生产和基本效益情况，主要包括工业企业单位数、历年工业总产值、规模以上工业、国有控股工业、国有工业、集体工业、外商投资和港澳台投资工业、大中型工业企业的主要经济指标、相关的财务分析指标和主要工业产品产量等方面的内容。

二、本篇资料的来源

1、本篇中规模以上工业资料来源于工业统计年报，由市统计局工业统计处整理提供。

2、规模以下工业资料产值与单位数均来源于抽样调查推算，工业单位数除普查年度外无分市（区）数据，由国家统计局青岛调查队工业与投资建筑业调查处整理提供。

Brief Introduction

I. Main Content

Data in this chapter show the basic condition of industrial production and benefit in Qingdao, mainly including the number of industrial enterprises, gross industrial output value and indices, the output of major industrial products and major economic and relevant financial indicators of industrial enterprises. Industrial enterprises include enterprises above designated size, state share-holding enterprises, state owned enterprises, collective owned enterprises, foreign funded enterprises, enterprises with funds from Hong Kong, Macao and Taiwan, large and medium sized enterprises.

II. Source of Data

(1)Data on industry above designated size are based on the annual report of industrial statistics, and prepared by the Division of Industry Statistics of Qingdao Municipal Bureau of Statistics.

(2)Data on output value and unit number of industry below designated size are based on the sample survey, and there is no data on number of enterprises by region except census year. The Data are complied by the Division of Industry, Investment and Construction Survey of Survey Office of the National Bureau of Statistics in Qingdao.

12 -1 规模以上工业企业单位数

NUMBER OF INDUSTRIAL ENTERPRISES ABOVE DESIGNATEO SIZE

单位:个(unit)

项　目	Item	1985	1990	1995	2000	2005	2006
总　计	**Total**	**2 411**	**2 997**	**4 987**	**1 504**	**3 697**	**4 567**
一、按隶属关系分	**Grouped by Subordination**						
中央工业	Central Industry	24	16	102	18	26	17
省属工业	Provincial Industry	26	22	64	7	37	33
地方工业	Local Industry	2 361	2 959	4 821	1 479	3 634	4 517
二、按经济类型分	Grouped by Economic Types						
国有企业	State-owned	502	568	1 084	179	76	74
集体企业	Collective-owned	1 907	2 386	2 731	226	87	72
其他经济类型企业	Other Economic Types	2	43	1 172	1 099	3 534	4 421
#外商及港澳台商投资企业	Foreign Funded Enterprises and Enterprises with Funds from Hong Kong, Macao and Taiwan		35	1 027	593	1 658	1 952
三、按轻重工业分	Grouped by Light and Heavy Industries						
轻工业	Light Industry	1 398	1 730	2 858	891	1 942	2 313
重工业	Heavy Industry	1 013	1 267	2 129	613	1 755	2 254
四、按企业规模分	Grouped by Size of Enterprises						
大型企业	Large	26	42	89	202	51	51
中型企业	Medium	80	168	216	229	441	469
小型企业	Small	2 305	2 787	4 480	1 073	3 205	4 047
五、按行业分	Grouped by Sectors						
黑色金属矿采选业	Mining of Ferrous Metal Ores		4	6	1	2	5
有色金属矿采选业	Mining of Non-ferrous Metal Ores	2	7	9	7	5	5
非金属矿采选业	Mining and Processing of Nonmetal Ores	43	70	87	29	34	31
食品制造业	Manufacture of Foods	244	324	437	170	121	137
#粮食及饲料加工	Processing of Grain and Feed	62	57	60	27		
饮料制造业	Manufacture of Beverage	31	44	74	23	29	28
#饮料酒	Beverage Liquor	20	28	27	19	20	25

注：1. 规模以上工业企业为年主营业务收入2000万元及以上的工业法人企业。

2. 2010年以前为国有及年主营业务收入500万元以上的非国有工业企业。

3. 本表1998年以前为乡及乡以上工业企业单位数 。

4. 2012年行业分类按2011年发布的《国民经济行业分类》(GB/T4754 -2011)重新划分。

Note:1. Industrial enterprises above designated size refers to industrial enterprises with revenue from principal business over 20 million yuan.

2. Before 2010, industrial enterprises above designated size refered to all the state-owned enterprises and non-state enterprises with revenue from principal business over 5 million yuan.

3. Before 1998, the number of industial enterprises refer to those at and above county level.

4. The sectors are grouped by "Classification and Code of the Sectors of the National Economy" (GB/T4754 -2011) in 2012.

12－1 续表 1

项　目	Item	2007	2008	2009	2010	2011
总　计	**Total**	**5 032**	**5 628**	**5 895**	**5 674**	**4 727**
一、按隶属关系分	**Grouped by Subordination**					
中央工业	Central Industry	9	40	44	31	31
省属工业	Provincial Industry	34	28	25	25	17
地方工业	Local Industry	4 989	5 560	5 826	5 618	4 679
二、按经济类型分	Grouped by Economic Types					
国有企业	State-owned	63	65	163	61	147
集体企业	Collective-owned	72	61	59	53	31
其他经济类型企业	Other Economic Types	4 897	5 502	5 673	5 560	4 549
#外商及港澳台商投资企业	Foreign Funded Enterprises and Enterprises with Funds from Hong Kong, Macao and Taiwan	2 091	2 217	2 244	2 037	1 618
三、按轻重工业分	Grouped by Light and Heavy Industries					
轻工业	Light Industry	2 489	2 704	2 805	2 635	2 131
重工业	Heavy Industry	2 543	2 924	3 090	3 039	2 596
四、按企业规模分	Grouped by Size of Enterprises					
大型企业	Large	53	48	50	52	50
中型企业	Medium	489	519	502	525	516
小型企业	Small	4 490	5 061	5 343	5 097	4 161
五、按行业分	Grouped by Sectors					
黑色金属矿采选业	Mining of Ferrous Metal Ores	7	23	22	12	12
有色金属矿采选业	Mining of Non-ferrous Metal Ores	5	6	6	4	
非金属矿采选业	Mining and Processing of Nonmetal Ores	33	30	26	26	23
食品制造业	Manufacture of Foods	156	158	174	167	127
#粮食及饲料加工	Processing of Grain and Feed					
饮料制造业	Manufacture of Beverage	33	40	42	42	36
#饮料酒	Beverage Liquor					

12－1 续表2
continued

单位：个(unit)

项　目	Item	1985	1990	1995	2000	2005	2006
烟草制品业	Manufacture of Tobacco	2	2	5	3	2	2
纺织业	Manufacture of Textile	169	225	330	132	300	327
纺织服装、鞋、帽制造业	Manufacture of Textile Wearing Apparel, Footware and Caps	171	194	322	95	272	339
皮革、毛皮、羽毛(绒)及其制品业	Manufacture of Leather, Fur, Feather and Related Products	56	64	161	64	167	194
木材加工制品业	Processing of Wood and Wood Products	71	89	116	19	40	53
家具制造业	Manufacture of Furniture	61	72	88	10	72	103
造纸及纸制品业	Manufacture of Paper and Paper Products	66	74	110	56	102	128
印刷业和记录媒介的复制	Printing, Reproduction of Recording Media	61	81	215	23	44	59
文教体育用品制造业	Manufacture of Articles For Culture, Education and Sport Activities	31	27	93	48	89	91
石油加工、炼焦及核燃料加工业	Processing of Petroleum, Coking, Processing of Nuclear Fuel	2	3	13	5	10	6
化学原料及制品	Manufacture of Raw Chemical Materials and Chemical Products	106	156	278	81	178	233
医药制造业	Manufacture of Medicines	16	14	39	20	30	46
化学纤维制造业	Manufacture of Chemical Fibers	2	4	26	15	14	13
橡胶制品业	Manufacture of Rubber	53	57	143	48	116	170
塑料制品业	Manufacture of Plastics	103	131	237	64	153	179
非金属矿物制品业	Manufacture of Non-metallic Mineral Products	230	245	275	62	161	218
黑色金属压延加工业	Smelting and Pressing of Ferrous Metals	11	13	31	15	41	45
有色金属压延加工业	Smelting and Pressing of Non-ferrous Metals	6	8	19	9	28	40
金属制品业	Manufacture of Metal Products	161	186	372	88	186	250
通用设备制造业	Manufacture of General Purpose Machinery	320	398	320	94	299	397
交通运输制造业	Manufacture of Transport Equipment	104	114	358	52	151	194
电气机械及器材制造业	Manufacture of Electrical Machinery and Equipment	86	96	211	79	214	249
通信设备、计算机及其他电子设备制造业	Manufacture of Communication Equipment, Computers and Other Electronic Equipment	32	31	79	34	123	140
仪器仪表及文化、办公用机械制造业	Manufacture of Measuring Instruments and Machinery for Cultural Activity and Office Work	28	33	70	20	40	44
水的生产和供应业	Production and Supply of Water	8	12	12	8	10	10
电力、热力的生产和供应业	Production and Supply of Electric Power and Heat Power	10	16	20	17	27	32
燃气生产和供应业	Production and Supply of Gas	1	4	3	2	5	6
其他工业	Other Industrial Sectors	46	48	209	63	166	534

12 -1 续表3
continued

单位:个(unit)

项　目	Item	2007	2008	2009	2010	2011
烟草制品业	Manufacture of Tobacco	2	2	2	1	1
纺织业	Manufacture of Textile	340	330	322	287	229
纺织服装、鞋、帽制造业	Manufacture of Textile Wearing Apparel, Footware and Caps	362	418	434	392	295
皮革、毛皮、羽毛(绒)及其制品业	Manufacture of Leather, Fur, Feather and Related Products	197	209	210	211	160
木材加工制品业	Processing of Wood and Wood Products	64	66	68	68	49
家具制造业	Manufacture of Furniture	119	130	133	117	97
造纸及纸制品业	Manufacture of Paper and Paper Products	126	133	133	138	101
印刷业和记录媒介的复制	Printing, Reproduction of Recording Media	63	74	79	92	58
文教体育用品制造业	Manufacture of Articles For Culture, Education and Sport Activities	97	96	99	90	75
石油加工、炼焦及核燃料加工业	Processing of Petroleum, Coking, Processing of Nuclear Fuel	7	7	9	8	7
化学原料及制品	Manufacture of Raw Chemical Materials and Chemical Products	261	276	275	262	231
医药制造业	Manufacture of Medicines	48	49	56	52	44
化学纤维制造业	Manufacture of Chemical Fibers	12	13	14	12	10
橡胶制品业	Manufacture of Rubber	183	211	214	196	187
塑料制品业	Manufacture of Plastics	199	227	234	233	169
非金属矿物制品业	Manufacture of Non-metallic Mineral Products	259	311	320	327	303
黑色金属压延加工业	Smelting and Pressing of Ferrous Metals	39	24	27	31	29
有色金属压延加工业	Smelting and Pressing of Non-ferrous Metals	40	41	40	35	34
金属制品业	Manufacture of Metal Products	271	347	376	361	294
通用设备制造业	Manufacture of General Purpose Machinery	473	535	592	597	521
交通运输制造业	Manufacture of Transport Equipment	217	264	290	296	263
电气机械及器材制造业	Manufacture of Electrical Machinery and Equipment	274	303	300	281	230
通信设备、计算机及其他电子设备制造业	Manufacture of Communication Equipment, Computers and Other Electronic Equipment	152	163	168	167	124
仪器仪表及文化、办公用机械制造业	Manufacture of Measuring Instruments and Machinery for Cultural Activity and Office Work	47	47	55	54	39
水的生产和供应业	Production and Supply of Water	10	13	14	14	11
电力、热力的生产和供应业	Production and Supply of Electric Power and Heat Power	34	36	39	38	36
燃气生产和供应业	Production and Supply of Gas	7	13	13	14	11
其他工业	Other Industrial Sectors	895	1 033	1 109	1 049	921

12－1 续表 4
continued

单位：个(unit)

项　目	Item	2012 年	2013 年	2014 年
总　计	**Total**	**4 817**	**4917**	**4 790**
一、按隶属关系分	**Grouped by Subordination Relation**			
中央工业	Central Industry	15	30	28
省属工业	Provincial Industry	18	16	15
地方工业	Local Industry	4 784	4 871	4 747
二、按经济类型分	**Grouped by Economic Types**			
国有企业	State-owned	144	140	132
集体企业	Collective-owned	28	24	19
其他经济类型企业	Other Economic Types	4 645	4 753	4 639
#外商及港澳台商投资企业	Foreign Funded Enterprises and Enterprises with Funds from Hong Kong, Macao and Taiwan	1 599	1 551	1 445
三、按轻重工业分	**Grouped by Light and Heavy Industries**			
轻工业	Light Industry	2 153	2 190	2 080
重工业	Heavy Industry	2 664	2 727	2 710
四、按企业规模分	**Grouped by Size of Enterprises**			
大型企业	Large	98	97	91
中型企业	Medium	596	599	568
小型企业	Small	4 123	4 221	4 131
五、按行业分	**Grouped by Sectors**			
黑色金属矿采选业	Mining of Ferrous Metal Ores	10	11	8
非金属矿采选业	Mining and Processing of Nonmetal Ores	14	13	7
农副食品加工业	Processing of Food from Agricultural Products	454	468	444
食品制造业	Manufacture of Foods	129	123	109
酒、饮料和精制茶制造业	Manufacture of Liquor, Beverage and Refind Tea	34	35	34
烟草制品业	Manufacture of Tobacco	1	1	1
纺织业	Manufacture of Textile	181	175	146
纺织服装、服饰业	Manufacture of Textile Wearing Apparel	312	283	249
皮革、毛皮、羽毛及其制品和制鞋业	Manufacture of Leather, Fur, Feather & Its Products Footwear	177	148	124

12 -1 续表 5
continued

单位:个(unit)

项 目	Item	2012 年	2013 年	2014 年
木材加工和木、竹、藤、棕、草制品业	Processing of Timbers, Manufacture of Wood, Bamboo, Rattan, Palm and Straw Products	34	40	32
家具制造业	Manufacture of Furniture	103	107	96
造纸和纸制品业	Manufacture of Paper and Paper Products	100	71	54
印刷和记录媒介复制业	Printing, Reproduction of Recording Media	80	121	150
文教、工美、体育和娱乐用品制造业	Manufacture of Articles for Culture, Arts & Crafts, Sports and Entertainment	263	335	348
石油加工、炼焦和核燃料加工业	Processing of Petroleum, Coking, Processing of Nucleus Fuel	8	8	9
化学原料和化学制品制造业	Manufacture of Chemical Raw Material and Chemical Products	224	240	246
医药制造业	Manufacture of Medicines	45	49	50
化学纤维制造业	Manufacture of Chemical Fiber	9	8	8
橡胶和塑料制品业	Manufacture of Rubber and Plastic	350	345	331
非金属矿物制品业	Manufacture of Non-metallic Mineral Products	325	333	330
黑色金属冶炼和压延加工业	Smelting and Pressing of Ferrous Metals	105	93	87
有色金属冶炼和压延加工业	Smelting and Pressing of Non-ferrous Metals	37	36	38
金属制品业	Manufacture of Metal Products	399	389	380
通用设备制造业	Manufacture of General Purpose Machinery	362	382	395
专用设备制造业	Manufacture of Special Purpose Machinery	312	322	314
汽车制造业	Manufacture of Vehicle	136	141	145
铁路、船舶、航空航天和其他运输设备制造业	Manufacture of Transport Equipment for Railway, Shipping, Aerospace and other uses	145	146	152
电气机械和器材制造业	Manufacture of Electrical Machinery & Equipment	202	212	217
计算机、通信和其他电子设备制造业	Manufacture of Computer, Communication Equipment and Other Electronic Equipment	137	136	141
仪器仪表制造业	Manufacture of Measuring Instrument	41	49	52
其他制造业	Manufacture of Other Products	18	17	13
废弃资源综合利用业	Recycling and Disposal of Waste Resources	4	6	6
金属制品、机械和设备修理业	Maintenance of Metal Products, Machinery and Equipment	7	7	7
电力、热力的生产和供应业	Production and Supply of Electric Power and Heat Power	36	39	40
燃气生产和供应业	Production and Supply of Gas	12	13	12
水的生产和供应业	Production and Supply of Water	11	15	15

12 –2 分市、区全部工业企业单位数(2014 年)

NUMBER OF ALL INDUSTRIAL ENTERPRISES BY REGION(2014)

单位:个(unit)

市、区名称	Region	合计 Total	规模以上 Above Designated Size	按轻重工业分 Grouped by Light and Heavy Industries		按企业规模分 Grouped by Size of Enterprises		
				轻工业 Light Industry	重工业 Heavy Industry	大型企业 Large	中型企业 Medium	小型企业 Small
全　市	**Total**	**25 104**	**4 790**	**2 080**	**2 710**	**91**	**568**	**4 131**
市内三区	Three Districts in Urban Area	1 749	157	46	111	8	32	117
崂山区	Laoshan District	1 037	104	42	62	8	20	76
黄岛区	Huangdao District	4 225	846	253	593	23	99	724
保税港区	Qingdao Free Trade Port Area of China	23	23	7	16	1	5	17
城阳区	Chengyang District	4 666	462	219	243	11	80	371
即墨市	Jimo	5 195	822	439	383	15	89	718
胶州市	Jiaozhou	3 915	952	397	555	9	119	824
平度市	Pingdu	2 163	678	290	388	8	60	610
莱西市	Laixi	1 805	659	358	301	5	47	607
红岛经济区	Qingdao National High-tech Industrial Development Zone	326	87	29	58	3	17	67

注:2014 年分市、区全部工业企业数不含个体。

Note:Total number of industrial enterprises (excluding the self – employed) by city and district for 2014.

12 –2 续表

continued

单位:个(unit)

市、区名称	Region	按经济类型分 Grouped by Economic Types				规模以下 Below Designated Size
		国有企业 State-owned	集体企业 Collective-owned	其他经济 Others	#外资及港澳台商企业 Foreign Funded Enterprises and Enterprises with Funds from Hong Kong, Macao and Taiwan	
全　市	**Total**	**132**	**19**	**4 639**	**1 445**	**20 314**
市内三区	Three Districts in Urban Area	31	1	125	52	1 592
崂山区	Laoshan District	8	2	94	33	933
黄岛区	Huangdao District	36	3	807	245	3 379
保税港区	Qingdao Free Trade Port Area of China			23	12	
城阳区	Chengyang District	11	1	450	241	4 204
即墨市	Jimo	12	2	808	233	4 373
胶州市	Jiaozhou	8	1	943	227	2 963
平度市	Pingdu	13	4	661	181	1 485
莱西市	Laixi	6	5	648	181	1 146
红岛经济区	Qingdao National High-tech Industrial Development Zone	7		80	40	239

12 -3 历年全部工业总产值
GROSS INDUSTRIAL OUTPUT VALUE OVER THE YEARS

单位:万元(10 000 yuan)

年 份 Year	工业总产值 Gross Industrial Output Value	轻工业产值 Light Industry	重工业产值 Heavy Industry
1949	21 605	18 494	3 111
1950	34 010	28 720	5 290
1951	53 538	44 600	8 938
1952	84 295	69 258	15 037
1953	115 222	74 716	40 506
1954	126 064	80 604	45 460
1955	118 935	86 956	31 979
1956	144 833	93 809	51 024
1957	142 920	101 202	41 718
1958	217 648	92 407	125 241
1959	282 610	84 376	198 234
1960	291 451	77 043	214 408
1962	120 738	64 233	56 505
1963	139 542	83 630	55 912
1964	177 273	108 884	68 389
1965	215 536	141 765	73 771
1966	252 896	152 304	100 592
1967	287 739	163 627	124 112
1968	299 814	175 791	123 489
1969	296 814	188 860	107 954
1970	345 212	202 903	142 309

注:本表按当年价格计算,1995 年开始工业总产值按新规定计算。

Note:The data in this form are calculated at current price. Since 1995, new regulations have been adopted in calculating gross industrial output value.

12 -3 续表 1
continued

单位:万元(10 000 yuan)

年　份 Year	工业总产值 Gross Industrial Output Value	轻工业产值 Light Industry	重工业产值 Heavy Industry
1971	365 770	216 172	149 598
1972	378 266	230 309	147 957
1973	377 943	245 371	132 572
1974	237 219	154 054	83 165
1975	402 541	261 418	141 123
1976	439 793	278 514	161 279
1977	490 669	296 728	193 941
1978	565 503	336 817	228 686
1979	625 227	379 276	245 951
1980	677 690	442 078	235 612
1981	707 434	479 954	227 480
1982	732 705	474 767	257 938
1983	816 793	513 759	303 034
1984	918 364	569 080	349 284
1985	1 113 891	699 524	414 367
1986	1 316 230	833 864	482 366
1987	1 703 830	1 065 873	637 957
1988	2 481 594	1 451 215	1 030 379
1989	3 191 643	1 857 019	1 334 624
1990	3 571 845	2 057 968	1 513 878
1991	3 986 427	2 318 257	1 668 170

12-3 续表 2
continued

单位：万元(10 000 yuan)

年 份	Year	工业总产值 Gross Industrial Output Value	轻工业产值 Light Industry	重工业产值 Heavy Industry
1992	1992	4 826 834	2 835 728	1 991 106
1993	1993	5 929 236	3 422 107	2 507 129
1994	1994	8 456 974	4 931 262	3 525 712
1995	1995	9 412 635	5 579 637	3 832 998
1996	1996	11 173 672	6 793 007	4 380 665
1997	1997	13 704 735	8 620 710	5 084 025
1998	1998	15 794 106	10 153 634	5 640 472
1999	1999	16 822 436	10 918 827	5 903 609
2000	2000	19 408 338	12 433 214	6 975 124
2001	2001	22 398 464	14 368 582	8 029 882
2002	2002	25 794 324	14 811 106	10 983 218
2003	2003	31 195 595	17 306 539	13 889 056
2004	2004	39 590 783	21 473 202	18 117 581
2005	2005	50 017 829	24 697 792	25 320 037
2006	2006	59 188 120	28 686 826	30 501 294
2007	2007	74 306 364	33 463 071	40 843 293
2008	2008	89 467 300	37 871 227	51 596 073
2009	2009	102 556 155	42 715 781	59 840 374
2010	2010	116 148 345	44 954 630	71 193 715
2011	2011	132 779 629	50 854 938	81 924 691
2012	2012	153 102 565	60 521 444	92 581 121
2013	2013	168 971 805	66 799 317	102 172 488
2014	2014	174 442 125	67 683 545	106 758 580
“一五”时期合计	“First Five-Year Plan” Period	647 974	437 287	210 687
“二五”时期合计	“Second Five-Year Plan” Period	1 077 075	388 406	688 669
1963-1965 年合计	1963-1965	532 351	334 279	198 072
“三五”时期合计	“Third Five-Year Plan” Period	1 481 941	883 485	598 456
“四五”时期合计	“Fourth Five-Year Plan” Period	1 761 739	1 107 324	654 415
“五五”时期合计	“Fifth Five-Year Plan” Period	2 798 882	1 733 413	1 065 469
“六五”时期合计	“Sixth Five-Year Plan” Period	4 289 187	2 737 084	1 552 103
“七五”时期合计	“Seventh Five-Year Plan” Period	12 265 142	7 265 939	4 999 204
“八五”时期合计	“Eighth Five-Year Plan” Period	32 612 106	19 087 323	13 524 783
“九五”时期合计	“Ninth Five-Year Plan” Period	76 903 287	48 919 392	27 983 895
“十五”时期合计	“Tenth Five-Year Plan” Period	168 996 995	92 657 221	76 339 774
“十一五”时期合计	“Eleventh Five-Year Plan” Period	175 336 465	73 641 456	101 695 009

12 -4 分市、区全部工业总产值(2014 年)
GROSS INDUSTRIAL OUTPUT VALUE BY REGION(2014)

单位:万元(10 000 yuan)

市、区名称	Region	工业总产值 Gross Industrial Output Value	规模以上 Above Designated Size	#外商及港澳台商投资企业 Foreign Funded Enterprises and Enterprises with Funds from Hong Kong, Macao and Taiwan	规模以下 Below Designated Size
全　　市	**Whole Municipality**	**174 442 125**	**159 557 125**	**42 110 461**	**14 885 000**
市内三区	The Three Districts of Qingdao City	18 158 230	17 373 030	2 126 467	785 200
崂山区	Laoshan District	5 111 112	4 548 612	771 071	562 500
黄岛区	Huangdao District	48 926 354	46 318 054	12 196 100	2 608 300
保税港区	Qingdao Free Trade Port Area of China	424 445	424 445	329 401	
城阳区	Chengyang District	17 631 192	15 293 192	5 565 100	2 338 000
即墨市	Jimo	28 064 757	25 404 757	7 894 961	2 660 000
胶州市	Jiaozhou	24 768 465	22 646 465	4 793 642	2 122 000
平度市	Pingdu	16 851 518	14 891 518	4 052 951	1 960 000
莱西市	Laixi	12 098 245	10 392 645	3 050 192	1 705 600
红岛经济区	Qingdao National High-tech Industrial Development Zone	2 407 807	2 264 407	1 330 576	143 400

12-5 分市、区规模以上工业总产值(2014年)

GROSS INDUSTRIAL OUTPUT VALUE ABOVE DESIGNATED SIZE BY REGION(2014)

指　标	Indicator	总计 Total	市内三区 The Three Districts of Qingdao City	崂山区 Laoshan District	黄岛区 Huangdao District
总　计	**Total**	**159 557 125**	**17 373 030**	**4 548 612**	**46 318 054**
按隶属关系分	**Grouped by Subordination**				
中央	Centrality	16 927 414	3 594 971	240 546	7 958 939
省(自治区、直辖市)	Province(Autonomous Region, Municipality)	3 526 098	1 893 641	1 155 742	210 098
市(地级)	Municipality(local level)	19 334 798	9 576 131	1 334 761	6 573 430
县级市(区)	Municipality at County Level(District)	4 800 028	243 045	281 053	1 208 020
镇、街道	Town and Subdistrict Office	5 455 111	23 033	44 763	1 413 294
乡	Country	84 721			
其它	Others	109 428 955	2 042 206	1 491 748	28 954 272
按登记注册类型分	**Grouped by Status of Registration**				
国有经济	State-owned	33 501 013	8 649 186	1 305 778	16 841 136
集体经济	Collective-owned	8 388 201	4 940 021	969 699	1 967 560
其他经济	Others	117 667 911	3 783 823	2 273 135	27 509 358
#外资与港澳台企业	Foreign Funded Enterprises and Enterprises with Funds from Hong Kong, Macao and Taiwan	42 110 461	2 126 467	771 071	12 196 100
按轻重工业分	**Grouped by Light and Heavy Industries**				
轻工业	Light Industry	61 852 839	7 962 751	2 753 443	13 133 050
重工业	Heavy Industry	97 704 287	9 410 278	1 795 170	33 185 004
按企业规模分	**Grouped by Size of Enterprises**				
大型企业	Large	44 125 484	12 283 338	2 063 100	15 286 314
中型企业	Medium	36 466 543	1 391 495	657 307	14 462 998
小型企业	Small	78 965 099	3 698 200	1 828 204	16 568 742

注:部分数据因四舍五入的原因,存在着分项合计不等的情况。

Note: Some of the data are unequal to subtotal due to rounding.

单位:万元(10 000 yuan)

保税港区 Qingdao Free Trade Port Area of China	城阳区 Chengyang District	即墨市 Jimo	胶州市 Jiaozhou	平度市 Pingdu	莱西市 Laixi	红岛经济区 Qingdao National High-tech Industrial Development Zone
424 445	**15 293 192**	**25 404 757**	**22 646 465**	**14 891 518**	**10 392 645**	**2 264 407**
	4 632 748	5 762	204 899	181 762		107 787
	16 572	240 055		9 990		
4 911	844 612	270 486	143 017	181 001	113 653	292 796
	932 707	1 257 760	265 848	403 774	204 115	3 706
	817 411	632 532	2 016 049	403 573	68 978	35 478
					84 721	
419 535	8 049 143	22 998 162	20 016 652	13 711 417	9 921 179	1 824 641
	4 773 989	512 969	398 940	419 009	187 168	412 838
	44 451	217 195	37 599	134 213	77 463	
424 445	10 474 752	24 674 593	22 209 926	14 338 296	10 128 014	1 851 569
329 401	5 565 100	7 894 961	4 793 642	4 052 951	3 050 192	1 330 576
156 469	3 968 042	12 954 009	7 961 392	6 060 806	6 022 440	880 437
267 977	11 325 150	12 450 748	14 685 073	8 830 712	4 370 205	1 383 970
125 944	7 007 590	3 464 569	1 001 714	580 614	1 819 988	492 313
128 461	4 057 872	5 908 022	5 101 464	2 599 431	1 321 982	837 511
170 040	4 227 729	16 032 166	16 543 286	11 711 474	7 250 675	934 583

12－5 续表
continued

指　标	Indicator	总计 Total	市内三区 The Three Districts of Qingdao City
按行业分	**Grouped by Industrial Sector**	**159 557 125**	**17 373 030**
煤炭开采和洗选业	Mining and Washing of Coal		
石油和天然气开采业	Extraction of Petroleum and Natural Gas		
黑色金属矿采选业	Mining of Ferrous Metal Ores	155 313	
有色金属矿采选业	Mining of Non-ferrous Metal Ores		
非金属矿采选业	Mining and Processing of Nonmetal Ores	162 813	
开采辅助活动	Auxiliary Activities of Mining		
其他采矿业	Mining of Other Ores		
农副食品加工业	Processing of Food from Agricultural Products	12 316 973	311 413
食品制造业	Manufacture of Foods	2 927 930	32 558
酒、饮料和精制茶制造业	Manufacture of Liquor, Beverage and Refind Tea	1 768 183	864 881
烟草制品业	Manufacture of Tobacco	1 155 742	
纺织业	Manufacture of Textile	2 520 602	115 318
纺织服装、服饰业	Manufacture of Textile Wearing Apparel	5 363 224	40 066
皮革、毛皮、羽毛及其制品和制鞋业	Manufacture of Leather, Fur, Feather & Its Products Footwear	2 395 334	19 209
木材加工和木、竹、藤、棕、草制品业	Processing of Timbers, Manufacture of Wood, Bamboo, Rattan, Palm, and Straw Products	595 862	
家具制造业	Manufacture of Furniture	1 632 455	26 479
造纸和纸制品业	Manufacture of Paper and Paper Products	930 890	4 027
印刷和记录媒介复制业	Printing, Reproduction of Recording Media	3 233 006	99 864
文教、工美、体育和娱乐用品制造业	Manufacture of Articles for Culture, Arts & Crafts, Sports and Entertainment	6 028 458	89 792
石油加工、炼焦和核燃料加工业	Processing of Petroleum, Coking, Processing of Nucleus Fuel	8 782 322	1 722 510
化学原料和化学制品制造业	Manufacture of Chemical Raw Material and Chemical Products	7 584 389	1 110 907
医药制造业	Manufacture of Medicines	1 531 436	28 740
化学纤维制造业	Manufacture of Chemical Fiber	168 003	23 009
橡胶和塑料制品业	Manufacture of Rubber and Plastic	8 675 967	47 358
非金属矿物制品业	Manufacture of Non-metallic Mineral Products	6 048 576	136 479
黑色金属冶炼和压延加工业	Smelting and Pressing of Ferrous Metals	4 018 722	1 396 274
有色金属冶炼和压延加工业	Smelting and Pressing of Non-ferrous Metals	1 384 394	
金属制品业	Manufacture of Metal Products	11 622 065	16 603
通用设备制造业	Manufacture of General Purpose Machinery	11 144 910	391 836
专用设备制造业	Manufacture of Special Purpose Machinery	7 544 061	65 040
汽车制造业	Manufacture of Vehicle	7 311 898	1 278 238
铁路、船舶、航空航天和其他运输设备制造业	Manufacture of Transport Equipment for Railway, Shipping, Aerospace and other uses	10 497 679	567 950
电气机械和器材制造业	Manufacture of Electrical Machinery & Equipment	17 002 133	5 279 375
计算机、通信和其他电子设备制造业	Manufacture of Computer, Communication Equipment and Other Electronic Equipment	8 800 160	1 153 941
仪器仪表制造业	Manufacture of Measuring Instrument	1 237 859	26 964
其他制造业	Manufacture of Other Products	196 224	14 318
废弃资源综合利用业	Recycling and Disposal of Waste Resources	83 889	1
金属制品、机械和设备修理业	Maintenance of Metal Products, Machinery and Equipment	168 073	
电力、热力生产和供应业	Production and Supply of Electric Power and Heat Power	3 968 964	2 380 838
燃气生产和供应业	Production and Supply of Gas	451 340	60 064
水的生产和供应业	Production and Supply of Water	147 276	68 966

单位:万元(10 000 yuan)

崂山区 Laoshan District	黄岛区 Huangdao District	保税区 Qingdao Free Trade Port Area of China	城阳区 Chengyang District	即墨市 Jimo	胶州市 Jiaozhou	平度市 Pingdu	莱西市 Laixi	红岛经济区 Qingdao National High-tech Industrial Development Zone
4 548 612	**46 318 054**	**424 445**	**15 293 192**	**25 404 757**	**22 646 465**	**14 891 518**	**10 392 645**	**2 264 407**
						102 975	52 339	
				3 613		102 320	56 881	
42 301	2 075 933	11 315	941 777	1 366 991	1 804 420	2 422 330	3 162 896	177 597
107 789	1 063 022	83 131	239 075	112 684	523 584	284 096	464 991	17 000
197 733	317 145		5 295	175 463	14 859	154 211	38 596	
1 155 742								
4 976	107 744	22 176	220 648	816 306	580 762	254 601	398 071	
15 615	546 508		296 631	3 525 686	287 868	335 496	290 165	25 189
8 571	310 689		165 919	886 299	467 562	53 921	483 164	
	144 042			20 559	250 875	50 800	129 587	
4 214	105 307		260 908	77 204	886 485	168 989	95 075	7 794
24 963	364 285		118 520	4 016	150 767	212 830	51 482	
	807 540		317 092	1 660 428	210 925	9 240	85 179	42 738
10 779	439 723	15 255	330 333	1 248 403	1 864 773	1 487 982	534 738	6 680
70 269	6 442 210		531 225	2 238	9 864	4 006		
19 001	2 429 823	3 571	403 458	1 047 031	1 117 611	676 452	498 032	278 503
157 226	276 619		125 226	307 199	330 396	102 392	120 939	82 699
	31 689		19 039		94 266			
65 048	4 581 169	21 422	374 579	943 777	878 214	1 015 373	650 915	98 112
89 548	1 103 403	16 748	535 037	194 559	963 673	1 671 244	1 320 880	17 005
	1 226 052		10 168	186 887	238 136	938 464	22 741	
	142 515		22 856	209 400	344 566	523 682		141 376
8 226	1 544 569	25 220	563 822	5 846 026	2 806 907	409 183	331 512	69 997
27 299	3 613 684		552 023	1 072 300	3 486 495	1 444 743	342 036	214 494
74 579	3 092 889	42 943	918 213	741 029	1 581 333	719 458	266 330	42 247
19 569	3 993 913	4 043	691 595	320 975	350 064	304 671	127 543	221 287
150 920	3 176 012		5 047 026	325 169	530 596	296 678	146 513	256 815
1 705 576	3 881 776	8 156	476 569	3 307 850	1 974 840	57 190	276 404	34 397
185 047	3 459 503	163 043	1 990 715	439 775	204 186	571 251	158 489	474 210
369 572	146 735	7 424	56 339	26 210	332 679	196 998	25 285	49 653
7 045			22 686	32 226	44 240	50 002	19 092	6 615
	17 901						65 987	
	89 645			78 428				
27 005	676 994		6 478	286 624	203 538	261 524	125 963	
	84 385		45 623	123 912	108 018	2 424	26 914	
	24 630		4 317	15 492	3 967	5 995	23 909	

12 -6 规模以上工业企业主要指标(2014 年)
MAIN INDICATORS OF INDUSTRIAL ENTERPRISES ABOVE DESIGNATED SIZE(2014)

项　目	Indicator	企业单位数(个) Number of Enterprises (unit)
总　计	**Total**	**4 790**
按注册登记类型分	**Grouped by Status of Registration**	
国有及国有控股企业	State-owned and State-holding Enterprises	132
集体企业	Collective-owned Enterprises	19
股份有限公司	Share-holding Corporations Ltd	100
外商投资企业	Foreign Funded Enterprises	1 165
港澳台商投资企业	Invested by HongKong, Macao and Taiwan	280
按轻重工业分	**Grouped by Light and Heavy Industries**	
轻工业	Light Industry	2 080
重工业	Heavy Industry	2 710
按企业规模分	**Grouped by Size of Enterprises**	
大型企业	Large	91
中型企业	Medium	568
小型企业	Small	4 131
按所在地分	**Grouped by Location**	
市　区	Urban Area	1 592
#崂山区	Laoshan District	104
黄岛区	Huangdao District	846
保税港区	Qingdao Free Trade Port Area of China	23
城阳区	Chengyang District	462
即墨市	Jimo	822
胶州市	Jiaozhou	952
平度市	Pingdu	678
莱西市	Laixi	659
红岛经济区	Qingdao National High-tech Industrial Development Zone	87
按行业分	**Grouped by Sector**	
煤炭开采和洗选业	Mining and Washing of Coal	
石油和天然气开采业	Extraction of Petroleum and Natural Gas	
黑色金属矿采选业	Mining of Ferrous Metal Ores	8
有色金属矿采选业	Mining of Non-ferrous Metal Ores	
非金属矿采选业	Mining and Processing of Nonmetal Ores	7
开采辅助活动	Auxiliary Activities of Mining	
其他采矿业	Mining of Other Ores	

单位:万元(10 000 yuan)

工业总产值 Gross Industrial Output Value	资产合计 Total Assets	流动资产合计 Total Current Assets	固定资产净值 Net Value of Fixed Assets
159 557 125	**109 624 603**	**61 883 820**	**30 769 033**
33 501 013	27 044 238	16 525 905	6 862 592
8 388 201	14 815 232	11 814 930	1 022 294
10 929 191	10 381 976	7 329 341	1 372 787
32 948 196	29 691 257	16 101 992	9 994 144
9 162 265	4 825 806	2 967 864	1 291 412
61 852 839	48 330 308	28 227 906	12 513 514
97 704 287	61 294 295	33 655 914	18 255 518
44 125 484	47 368 803	32 289 447	7 200 415
36 466 543	23 637 444	12 107 670	8 128 615
78 965 098	38 618 356	17 486 703	15 440 003
83 957 333	75 957 007	47 247 227	16 597 135
4 548 612	5 160 199	3 635 220	675 783
46 318 054	27 542 228	16 654 529	6 639 363
424 445	1 172 232	761 201	120 242
15 293 192	20 773 846	12 670 907	5 472 722
25 404 757	8 587 300	4 097 955	2 520 996
22 646 465	12 282 115	4 645 060	6 459 510
14 891 518	5 478 803	2 468 444	2 229 325
10 392 645	4 704 930	1 921 864	2 150 487
2 264 407	2 614 448	1 503 270	811 580
155 313	28 090	4 953	17 370
162 813	44 340	15 947	18 918

12－6 续表 1
continued

项　目	Indicator	主营业务收入 Revenue from Principal Business
总　计	**Total**	**155 927 458**
按注册登记类型分	**Grouped by Status of Registration**	
国有及国有控股企业	State-owned and State-holding Enterprises	31 291 554
集体企业	Collective-owned Enterprises	10 787 293
股份有限公司	Share-holding Corporations Ltd	10 648 490
外商投资企业	Foreign Funded Enterprises	31 524 426
港澳台商投资企业	Invested by HongKong Macao and Taiwan	8 855 007
按轻重工业分	**Grouped by Light and Heavy Industries**	
轻工业	Light Industry	63 434 714
重工业	Heavy Industry	92 492 744
按企业规模分	**Grouped by size of Enterprises**	
大型企业	Large	47 254 240
中型企业	Medium	35 571 849
小型企业	Small	72 117 971
按所在地分	**Grouped by Location**	
市　区	Urban Area	81 962 050
#崂山区	Laoshan District	3 885 171
黄岛区	Huangdao District	44 707 871
保税港区	Qingdao Free Trade Port Area of China	454 833
城阳区	Chengyang District	13 712 889
即墨市	Jimo	24 547 884
胶州市	Pingdu	22 194 228
平度市	Pingdu	14 752 453
莱西市	Pingdu	10 220 821
红岛经济区	Qingdao National High－tech Industrial Development Zone	2 250 022
按行业分	**Grouped by Sector**	
煤炭开采和洗选业	Mining and Washing of Coal	
石油和天然气开采业	Extraction of Petroleum and Natural Gas	
黑色金属矿采选业	Mining of Ferrous Metal Ores	154 992
有色金属矿采选业	Mining of Non-ferrous Metal Ores	
非金属矿采选业	Mining and Processing of Nonmetal Ores	160 272
开采辅助活动	Auxiliary Activities of Mining	
其他采矿业	Mining of Other Ores	

单位:万元(10 000 yuan)

主营业务成本 Cost of Principal Business	主营业务税金及附加 Taxes and Extra Charges on Principal Business	利润总额 Total Profits	本年应交增值税 Value-added Tax Payable	全部从业人员年平均人数(人) Annual Average Employed Persons(person)
132 832 944	**2 603 271**	**8 433 193**	**5 034 158**	**1 065 374**
27 091 378	1 204 677	1 106 921	1 069 463	122 568
8 017 826	69 614	766 565	196 634	32 436
9 053 074	62 796	571 965	277 640	71 403
26 736 931	397 029	1 831 214	955 753	320 083
7 744 259	64 842	442 954	232 398	64 233
52 905 642	627 745	3 967 936	1 963 275	526 390
79 927 302	1 975 526	4 465 257	3 070 884	538 984
39 637 777	590 248	2 528 045	913 544	284 440
30 689 669	991 018	1 297 884	1 341 958	304 028
61 659 558	1 014 174	4 547 280	2 743 193	468 131
69 939 903	1 740 848	3 731 022	2 292 811	460 550
2 971 623	23 799	313 570	110 856	34 455
38 831 710	1 244 974	1 903 871	1 517 463	69 027
329 992	2 258	57 370	13 005	10 844
11 863 198	80 536	660 621	293 141	121 326
21 610 713	317 552	1 534 490	903 234	186 492
17 942 801	404 489	1 545 162	1 015 641	174 713
12 607 071	110 856	918 880	620 696	105 464
8 866 949	24 641	593 140	169 558	112 155
1 865 507	4 885	110 499	32 218	26 000
126 424	2 137	14 210	2 985	1 002
127 060	2 894	8 978	6 458	1 140

12 -6 续表 2
continued

项　目	Indicator	企业单位数(个) Number of Enterprises (unit)
农副食品加工业	Processing of Food from Agricultural Products	444
食品制造业	Manufacture of Foods	109
酒、饮料和精制茶制造业	Manufacture of Liquor, Beverage and Refind Tea	34
烟草制品业	Manufacture of Tobacco	1
纺织业	Manufacture of Textile	146
纺织服装、服饰业	Manufacture of Textile Wearing Apparel	249
皮革、毛皮、羽毛及其制品和制鞋业	Manufacture of Leather, Fur, Feather & Its Products Footwear	124
木材加工和木、竹、藤、棕、草制品业	Processing of Timbers, Manufacture of Wood, Bamboo, Rattan, Palm, and Straw Products	32
家具制造业	Manufacture of Furniture	96
造纸和纸制品业	Manufacture of Paper and Paper Products	54
印刷和记录媒介复制业	Printing, Reproduction of Recording Media	150
文教、工美、体育和娱乐用品制造业	Manufacture of Articles for Culture, Arts & Crafts, Sports and Entertainment	348
石油加工、炼焦和核燃料加工业	Processing of Petroleum, Coking, Processing of Nucleus Fuel	9
化学原料和化学制品制造业	Manufacture of Chemical Raw Material and Chemical Products	246
医药制造业	Manufacture of Medicines	50
化学纤维制造业	Manufacture of Chemical Fiber	8
橡胶和塑料制品业	Manufacture of Rubber and Plastic	331
非金属矿物制品业	Manufacture of Non-metallic Mineral Products	330
黑色金属冶炼和压延加工业	Smelting and Pressing of Ferrous Metals	87
有色金属冶炼和压延加工业	Smelting and Pressing of Non-ferrous Metals	38
金属制品业	Manufacture of Metal Products	380
通用设备制造业	Manufacture of General Purpose Machinery	395
专用设备制造业	Manufacture of Special Purpose Machinery	314
汽车制造业	Manufacture of Vehicle	145
铁路、船舶、航空航天和其他运输设备制造业	Manufacture of Transport Equipment for Railway, Shipping, Aerospace and other uses	152
电气机械和器材制造业	Manufacture of Electrical Machinery & Equipment	217
计算机、通信和其他电子设备制造业	Manufacture of Computer, Communication Equipment and Other Electronic Equipment	141
仪器仪表制造业	Manufacture of Measuring Instrument	52
其他制造业	Manufacture of Other Products	13
废弃资源综合利用业	Recycling and Disposal of Waste Resources	6
金属制品、机械和设备修理业	Maintenance of Metal Products, Machinery and Equipment	7
电力、热力生产和供应业	Production and Supply of Electric Power and Heat Power	40
燃气生产和供应业	Production and Supply of Gas	12
水的生产和供应业	Production and Supply of Water	15

单位:万元(10 000 yuan)

工业总产值 Gross Industrial Output Value	资产合计 Total Assets	流动资产合计 Total Current Assets	固定资产净值 Net Value of Fixed Assets
12 316 973	5 738 927	2 663 185	2 136 127
2 927 930	1 721 860	1 036 343	472 880
1 768 183	2 102 124	571 565	350 290
1 155 742			
2 520 602	1 028 582	468 415	343 810
5 363 224	2 900 252	1 505 819	771 811
2 395 334	835 910	436 042	265 024
595 862	236 806	64 125	138 795
1 632 455	673 244	266 677	328 740
930 890	529 288	304 325	154 124
3 233 006	1 159 999	495 722	512 680
6 028 458	2 072 825	841 451	990 722
8 782 322	2 857 718	1 056 904	1 217 977
7 584 389	5 138 324	2 514 326	1 723 015
1 531 436	1 318 958	621 594	365 706
168 003	151 052	87 861	49 181
8 675 967	4 647 309	2 106 182	1 628 780
6 048 576	3 537 428	1 855 630	1 244 838
4 018 722	3 129 096	1 616 432	964 258
1 384 394	660 378	290 932	283 922
11 622 065	4 602 951	2 110 047	1 767 423
11 144 910	5 533 572	2 963 466	1 790 395
7 544 061	9 942 048	4 589 391	4 202 472
7 311 898	7 139 488	5 306 805	1 201 057
10 497 679	10 365 175	7 419 309	1 773 781
17 002 133	19 623 429	14 505 455	2 123 322
8 800 160	6 071 682	3 923 455	1 039 533
1 237 859	1 314 958	881 386	248 309
196 224	129 074	74 164	44 306
83 889	78 336	34 190	27 998
168 073	53 212	33 185	13 355
3 968 964	3 042 699	849 897	1 904 063
451 340	363 615	127 631	186 819
147 276	851 855	241 012	467 233

12-6 续表3
continued

项　目	Indicator	主营业务收入 Revenue from Principal Business
农副食品加工业	Processing of Food from Agricultural Products	12 146 208
食品制造业	Manufacture of Foods	2 959 751
酒、饮料和精制茶制造业	Manufacture of Liquor, Beverage and Refind Tea	2 411 050
烟草制品业	Manufacture of Tobacco	
纺织业	Manufacture of Textile	2 483 403
纺织服装、服饰业	Manufacture of Textile Wearing Apparel	5 199 542
皮革、毛皮、羽毛及其制品和制鞋业	Manufacture of Leather, Fur, Feather & Its Products Footwear	2 296 910
木材加工和木、竹、藤、棕、草制品业	Processing of Timbers, Manufacture of Wood, Bamboo, Rattan, Palm, and Straw Products	580 648
家具制造业	Manufacture of Furniture	1 607 780
造纸和纸制品业	Manufacture of Paper and Paper Products	867 836
印刷和记录媒介复制业	Printing, Reproduction of Recording Media	3 021 315
文教、工美、体育和娱乐用品制造业	Manufacture of Articles for Culture, Arts & Crafts, Sports and Entertainment	5 803 039
石油加工、炼焦和核燃料加工业	Processing of Petroleum, Coking, Processing of Nucleus Fuel	8 717 758
化学原料和化学制品制造业	Manufacture of Chemical Raw Material and Chemical Products	7 489 899
医药制造业	Manufacture of Medicines	1 434 098
化学纤维制造业	Manufacture of Chemical Fiber	165 363
橡胶和塑料制品业	Manufacture of Rubber and Plastic	8 473 868
非金属矿物制品业	Manufacture of Non-metallic Mineral Products	5 926 041
黑色金属冶炼和压延加工业	Smelting and Pressing of Ferrous Metals	4 709 329
有色金属冶炼和压延加工业	Smelting and Pressing of Non-ferrous Metals	1 364 254
金属制品业	Manufacture of Metal Products	11 184 062
通用设备制造业	Manufacture of General Purpose Machinery	10 666 453
专用设备制造业	Manufacture of Special Purpose Machinery	7 019 415
汽车制造业	Manufacture of Vehicle	6 302 840
铁路、船舶、航空航天和其他运输设备制造业	Manufacture of Transport Equipment for Railway, Shipping, Aerospace and other uses	10 086 378
电气机械和器材制造业	Manufacture of Electrical Machinery & Equipment	19 250 464
计算机、通信和其他电子设备制造业	Manufacture of Computer, Communication Equipment and Other Electronic Equipment	9 096 575
仪器仪表制造业	Manufacture of Measuring Instrument	1 199 931
其他制造业	Manufacture of Other Products	194 836
废弃资源综合利用业	Recycling and Disposal of Waste Resources	67 873
金属制品、机械和设备修理业	Maintenance of Metal Products, Machinery and Equipment	126 804
电力、热力生产和供应业	Production and Supply of Electric Power and Heat Power	2 152 843
燃气生产和供应业	Production and Supply of Gas	448 601
水的生产和供应业	Production and Supply of Water	157 029

单位:万元(10 000 yuan)

主营业务成本 Cost of Principal Business	主营业务税金及附加 Taxes and Extra Charges on Principal Business	利润总额 Total Profits	本年应交增值税 Value-added Tax Payable	全部从业人员年平均人数(人) Annual Average Employed Persons(person)
10 706 349	104 082	577 657	305 187	101 575
2 251 118	36 206	215 723	101 918	18 399
1 850 560	64 038	240 459	87 427	18 277
				1 441
2 135 484	26 575	153 301	103 903	25 668
4 454 282	53 422	341 084	184 215	94 805
1 932 493	24 139	157 543	88 020	50 090
486 582	8 283	43 834	26 208	4 524
1 348 057	21 971	104 079	67 339	17 358
755 871	9 778	38 171	35 503	8 162
2 587 495	41 614	199 033	133 127	18 089
4 945 142	84 177	415 790	242 719	59 276
7 540 038	1 072 324	-61 469	560 823	3 582
6 572 211	73 852	202 699	202 289	38 629
1 046 590	13 681	153 011	71 686	11 694
140 391	1 788	2 720	5 165	1 312
7 488 688	83 920	398 728	236 287	60 474
5 039 310	54 742	368 286	203 488	39 835
4 251 310	22 770	125 450	74 372	19 032
1 192 010	9 503	54 666	40 709	6 256
9 826 079	166 614	615 731	401 749	64 802
9 046 319	109 511	630 425	376 439	69 178
5 859 194	125 876	481 936	277 597	47 924
5 391 494	89 993	404 993	148 473	43 890
8 586 678	66 269	687 863	244 413	51 839
15 449 234	150 265	1 170 806	434 499	74 437
7 939 058	52 113	419 941	212 404	58 460
966 280	12 933	84 804	55 316	13 407
159 312	3 216	15 095	5 999	3 265
67 727	426	7 549	748	868
104 065	1 206	10 241	7 085	550
1 887 369	9 531	144 975	75 459	16 527
404 367	2 369	14 029	9 464	1 737
168 304	1 055	-9 146	4 687	3 688

12-7 按行业分国有及国有控股工业企业主要指标（2014年）
MAIN INDICATORS OF STATE-OWNED AND STATE-HOLDING INDUSTRIAL ENTERPRISES BY INDUSTRIAL SECTOR(2014)

项 目	Indicator	企业单位数(个) Number of Enterprises(unit)
总 计	**Total**	**132**
煤炭开采和洗选业	Mining and Washing of Coal	
石油和天然气开采业	Extraction of Petroleum and Natural Gas	
黑色金属矿采选业	Mining of Ferrous Metal Ores	
有色金属矿采选业	Mining of Non-ferrous Metal Ores	
非金属矿采选业	Mining and Processing of Nonmetal Ores	1
开采辅助活动	Auxiliary Activities of Mining	
其他采矿业	Mining of Other Ores	
农副食品加工业	Processing of Food from Agricultural Products	2
食品制造业	Manufacture of Foods	1
酒、饮料和精制茶制造业	Manufacture of Liquor, Beverage and Refind Tea	3
烟草制品业	Manufacture of Tobacco	1
纺织业	Manufacture of Textile	
纺织服装、服饰业	Manufacture of Textile Wearing Apparel	3
皮革、毛皮、羽毛及其制品和制鞋业	Manufacture of Leather, Fur, Feather & Its Products Footwear	1
木材加工和木、竹、藤、棕、草制品业	Processing of Timbers, Manufacture of Wood, Bamboo, Rattan, Palm, and Straw Products	
家具制造业	Manufacture of Furniture	
造纸和纸制品业	Manufacture of Paper and Paper Products	1
印刷和记录媒介复制业	Printing, Reproduction of Recording Media	1
文教、工美、体育和娱乐用品制造业	Manufacture of Articles for Culture, Arts & Crafts, Sports and Entertainment	
石油加工、炼焦和核燃料加工业	Processing of Petroleum, Coking, Processing of Nucleus Fuel	4
化学原料和化学制品制造业	Manufacture of Chemical Raw Material and Chemical Products	13
医药制造业	Manufacture of Medicines	2
化学纤维制造业	Manufacture of Chemical Fiber	
橡胶和塑料制品业	Manufacture of Rubber and Plastic	4
非金属矿物制品业	Manufacture of Non-metallic Mineral Products	9
黑色金属冶炼和压延加工业	Smelting and Pressing of Ferrous Metals	3
有色金属冶炼和压延加工业	Smelting and Pressing of Non-ferrous Metals	3
金属制品业	Manufacture of Metal Products	1
通用设备制造业	Manufacture of General Purpose Machinery	9
专用设备制造业	Manufacture of Special Purpose Machinery	4
汽车制造业	Manufacture of Vehicle	5
铁路、船舶、航空航天和其他运输设备制造业	Manufacture of Transport Equipment for Railway, Shipping, Aerospace and other uses	15
电气机械和器材制造业	Manufacture of Electrical Machinery & Equipment	4
计算机、通信和其他电子设备制造业	Manufacture of Computer, Communication Equipment and Other Electronic E-quipment	1
仪器仪表制造业	Manufacture of Measuring Instrument	1
其他制造业	Manufacture of Other Products	1
废弃资源综合利用业	Recycling and Disposal of Waste Resources	
金属制品、机械和设备修理业	Maintenance of Metal Products, Machinery and Equipment	
电力、热力生产和供应业	Production and Supply of Electric Power and Heat Power	29
燃气生产和供应业	Production and Supply of Gas	
水的生产和供应业	Production and Supply of Water	10

单位:万元(10 000 yuan)

工业总产值 Gross Industrial Output Value	资产合计 Total Assets	流动资产合计 Total Current Assets	固定资产净值 Net Value of Fixed Assets
33 501 013	**27 044 238**	**16 525 905**	**6 862 592**
6 196	9 494	5 891	1 605
94 197	32 319	4 118	23 561
6 478	6 868	5 353	1 307
290 977	150 616	90 864	38 773
1 155 742			
26 411	29 607	20 177	7 934
14 160	12 056	8 239	2 102
142 898	74 764	35 920	22 198
4 839	10 251	2 648	6 887
8 695 946	2 778 218	1 026 285	1 198 902
645 353	1 173 033	484 398	304 263
165 657	160 280	82 368	52 409
476 315	643 851	326 396	178 163
201 786	241 814	175 209	37 985
1 660 284	2 043 453	1 048 744	526 704
37 122	170 023	19 335	89 915
7 217	43 686	19 769	20 091
482 804	482 849	288 126	144 288
207 729	298 534	242 720	49 047
3 995 111	4 177 535	3 579 543	461 685
6 547 958	6 742 813	5 005 468	1 029 057
649 313	833 242	558 689	101 902
4 003 187	3 244 716	2 477 105	308 085
6 931	4 290	4 131	158
14 318	24 480	20 944	1 782
3 846 711	2 854 271	779 630	1 803 624
115 375	801 176	213 835	450 163

12 -7 续表
continued

项 目	Indicator	主营业务收入 Revenue from Principal Business
总 计	**Total**	**31 291 554**
煤炭开采和洗选业	Mining and Washing of Coal	
石油和天然气开采业	Extraction of Petroleum and Natural Gas	
黑色金属矿采选业	Mining of Ferrous Metal Ores	
有色金属矿采选业	Mining of Non-ferrous Metal Ores	
非金属矿采选业	Mining and Processing of Nonmetal Ores	8 443
开采辅助活动	Auxiliary Activities of Mining	
其他采矿业	Mining of Other Ores	
农副食品加工业	Processing of Food from Agricultural Products	97 195
食品制造业	Manufacture of Foods	6 478
酒、饮料和精制茶制造业	Manufacture of Liquor, Beverage and Refind Tea	227 552
烟草制品业	Manufacture of Tobacco	
纺织业	Manufacture of Textile	
纺织服装、服饰业	Manufacture of Textile Wearing Apparel	27 155
皮革、毛皮、羽毛及其制品和制鞋业	Manufacture of Leather, Fur, Feather & Its Products Footwear	12 129
木材加工和木、竹、藤、棕、草制品业	Processing of Timbers, Manufacture of Wood, Bamboo, Rattan, Palm, and Straw Products	
家具制造业	Manufacture of Furniture	
造纸和纸制品业	Manufacture of Paper and Paper Products	126 338
印刷和记录媒介复制业	Printing, Reproduction of Recording Media	4 348
文教、工美、体育和娱乐用品制造业	Manufacture of Articles for Culture, Arts & Crafts, Sports and Entertainment	
石油加工、炼焦和核燃料加工业	Processing of Petroleum, Coking, Processing of Nucleus Fuel	8 632 584
化学原料和化学制品制造业	Manufacture of Chemical Raw Material and Chemical Products	645 721
医药制造业	Manufacture of Medicines	144 202
化学纤维制造业	Manufacture of Chemical Fiber	
橡胶和塑料制品业	Manufacture of Rubber and Plastic	418 720
非金属矿物制品业	Manufacture of Non-metallic Mineral Products	208 440
黑色金属冶炼和压延加工业	Smelting and Pressing of Ferrous Metals	2 592 121
有色金属冶炼和压延加工业	Smelting and Pressing of Non-ferrous Metals	35 557
金属制品业	Manufacture of Metal Products	7 111
通用设备制造业	Manufacture of General Purpose Machinery	445 550
专用设备制造业	Manufacture of Special Purpose Machinery	189 269
汽车制造业	Manufacture of Vehicle	3 257 748
铁路、船舶、航空航天和其他运输设备制造业	Manufacture of Transport Equipment for Railway, Shipping, Aerospace and other uses	6 364 923
电气机械和器材制造业	Manufacture of Electrical Machinery & Equipment	938 558
计算机、通信和其他电子设备制造业	Manufacture of Computer, Communication Equipment and Other Electronic Equipment	4 718 912
仪器仪表制造业	Manufacture of Measuring Instrument	6 001
其他制造业	Manufacture of Other Products	18 600
废弃资源综合利用业	Recycling and Disposal of Waste Resources	
金属制品、机械和设备修理业	Maintenance of Metal Products, Machinery and Equipment	
电力、热力生产和供应业	Production and Supply of Electric Power and Heat Power	2 033 663
燃气生产和供应业	Production and Supply of Gas	
水的生产和供应业	Production and Supply of Water	124 237

单位:万元(10 000 yuan)

主营业务成本 Cost of Principal Business	主营业务 税金及附加 Taxes and Extra Charges on Principal Business	利润总额 Total Profits	本年应 交增值税 Value-added Tax Payable	全部从业人员 年平均人数(人) Annual Average Employed Persons(person)
27 091 378	**1 204 677**	**1 106 921**	**1 069 463**	**116 930**
6 677	442	201	560	203
82 693	749	2 212	1 071	393
4 831	60	1 229	594	352
185 308	4 117	42 464	7 058	2 164
				1 441
25 844	400	-1 475	711	1 367
9 644	44	752	369	179
120 320	192	1 300	1 919	1 240
2 871	51	102	393	155
7 478 728	1 071 230	-71 145	557 474	2 981
523 636	7 505	26 122	21 665	6 420
71 507	1 037	22 033	8 554	1 300
367 602	1 405	5 672	7 545	6 925
175 663	624	14 464	4 919	1 660
2 473 142	1 106	8 798	6 755	8 892
22 072	92	2 271	691	1 189
5 764	119	151	293	200
407 147	2 923	3 546	5 225	4 294
159 337	1 119	-20 900	8 492	2 160
2 780 076	57 206	256 870	75 181	9 223
5 415 759	23 265	399 955	132 248	21 208
825 627	3 026	17 342	16 566	7 685
4 005 633	18 024	262 473	133 122	17 231
3 266	65	556	549	80
17 167	156	381	415	127
1 778 992	8 873	143 278	72 669	14 553
142 071	849	-11 730	4 425	3 308

12－8 按行业分规模以上外商投资和港澳台商投资工业企业主要指标（2014年）

MAIN INDICATORS OF FOREIGN FUNDED ENTERPRISES AND ENTERPRISES WITH FUNDS FROM HONG KONG, MACAO AND TAIWAN ABOVE DESIGNATED SIZE BY INDUSTRIAL SECTOR(2014)

项　目	Indicator	企业单位数(个) Number of Enterprises(unit)
总　计	**Total**	**1 445**
煤炭开采和洗选业	Mining and Washing of Coal	
石油和天然气开采业	Extraction of Petroleum and Natural Gas	
黑色金属矿采选业	Mining of Ferrous Metal Ores	1
有色金属矿采选业	Mining of Non-ferrous Metal Ores	
非金属矿采选业	Mining and Processing of Nonmetal Ores	
开采辅助活动	Auxiliary Activities of Mining	
其他采矿业	Mining of Other Ores	
农副食品加工业	Processing of Food from Agricultural Products	147
食品制造业	Manufacture of Foods	51
酒、饮料和精制茶制造业	Manufacture of Liquor, Beverage and Refind Tea	10
烟草制品业	Manufacture of Tobacco	
纺织业	Manufacture of Textile	58
纺织服装、服饰业	Manufacture of Textile Wearing Apparel	126
皮革、毛皮、羽毛及其制品和制鞋业	Manufacture of Leather, Fur, Feather & Its Products Footwear	71
木材加工和木、竹、藤、棕、草制品业	Processing of Timbers, Manufacture of Wood, Bamboo, Rattan, Palm, and Straw Products	3
家具制造业	Manufacture of Furniture	30
造纸和纸制品业	Manufacture of Paper and Paper Products	17
印刷和记录媒介复制业	Printing, Reproduction of Recording Media	35
文教、工美、体育和娱乐用品制造业	Manufacture of Articles for Culture, Arts & Crafts, Sports and Entertainment	151
石油加工、炼焦和核燃料加工业	Processing of Petroleum, Coking, Processing of Nucleus Fuel	1
化学原料和化学制品制造业	Manufacture of Chemical Raw Material and Chemical Products	75
医药制造业	Manufacture of Medicines	9
化学纤维制造业	Manufacture of Chemical Fiber	5
橡胶和塑料制品业	Manufacture of Rubber and Plastic	80
非金属矿物制品业	Manufacture of Non-metallic Mineral Products	56
黑色金属冶炼和压延加工业	Smelting and Pressing of Ferrous Metals	16
有色金属冶炼和压延加工业	Smelting and Pressing of Non-ferrous Metals	6
金属制品业	Manufacture of Metal Products	98
通用设备制造业	Manufacture of General Purpose Machinery	77
专用设备制造业	Manufacture of Special Purpose Machinery	52
汽车制造业	Manufacture of Vehicle	50
铁路、船舶、航空航天和其他运输设备制造业	Manufacture of Transport Equipment for Railway, Shipping, Aerospace and other uses	37
电气机械和器材制造业	Manufacture of Electrical Machinery & Equipment	60
计算机、通信和其他电子设备制造业	Manufacture of Transport Equipment for Railway, Shipping, Aerospace and other uses	87
仪器仪表制造业	Manufacture of Measuring Instrument	17
其他制造业	Manufacture of Other Products	4
废弃资源综合利用业	Recycling and Disposal of Waste Resources	1
金属制品、机械和设备修理业	Maintenance of Metal Products, Machinery and Equipment	3
电力、热力生产和供应业	Production and Supply of Electric Power and Heat Power	2
燃气生产和供应业	Production and Supply of Gas	7
水的生产和供应业	Production and Supply of Water	2

单位:万元(10 000 yuan)

工业总产值 Gross Industrial Output Value	资产合计 Total Assets	流动资产合计 Total Current Assets	固定资产净值 Net Value of Fixed Assets
42 110 461	**34 517 063**	**19 069 855**	**11 285 555**
74 956	10 246	863	8 386
4 145 419	2 431 422	1 311 024	962 828
1 956 238	1 302 412	841 706	333 806
1 138 625	1 835 079	433 918	269 354
996 172	565 317	244 183	183 158
1 780 060	960 593	491 560	270 016
1 275 027	421 957	242 504	128 827
67 435	53 802	3 448	43 885
442 664	193 024	90 478	75 844
370 960	253 875	173 580	66 445
1 172 477	536 410	262 952	222 228
2 336 210	888 835	428 314	358 381
70 269	41 735	20 973	9 795
2 796 972	2 363 156	1 305 391	844 284
482 805	135 761	75 074	33 443
73 738	119 918	79 680	26 227
1 513 763	1 066 286	488 682	495 430
1 041 191	715 520	371 967	266 856
693 114	619 486	360 866	250 188
295 244	110 220	61 924	45 810
4 351 013	1 786 296	883 573	658 554
2 361 690	1 526 292	880 973	517 428
1 123 786	6 543 206	2 871 878	3 359 096
3 906 272	4 110 020	3 554 661	498 478
1 352 167	1 863 089	1 543 128	213 454
1 579 061	1 100 642	518 489	331 977
3 807 827	2 311 330	1 142 339	595 701
383 496	320 234	235 710	76 183
62 995	47 250	32 517	12 846
18 189	11 266	4 073	7 193
26 553	18 102	13 064	4 598
37 386	42 478	2 979	33 165
358 593	187 674	92 240	65 395
18 096	24 133	5 147	16 299

12 -8 续表
continued

项　　目	Indicator	主营业务收入 Revenue from Principal Business
总　　计	**Total**	**40 379 432**
煤炭开采和洗选业	Mining and Washing of Coal	
石油和天然气开采业	Extraction of Petroleum and Natural Gas	
黑色金属矿采选业	Mining of Ferrous Metal Ores	74 956
有色金属矿采选业	Mining of Non-ferrous Metal Ores	
非金属矿采选业	Mining and Processing of Nonmetal Ores	
开采辅助活动	Auxiliary Activities of Mining	
其他采矿业	Mining of Other Ores	
农副食品加工业	Processing of Food from Agricultural Products	4 302 219
食品制造业	Manufacture of Foods	1 998 975
酒、饮料和精制茶制造业	Manufacture of Liquor, Beverage and Refind Tea	1 858 323
烟草制品业	Manufacture of Tobacco	
纺织业	Manufacture of Textile	995 127
纺织服装、服饰业	Manufacture of Textile Wearing Apparel	1 721 895
皮革、毛皮、羽毛及其制品和制鞋业	Manufacture of Leather, Fur, Feather & Its Products Footwear	1 198 802
木材加工和木、竹、藤、棕、草制品业	Processing of Timbers, Manufacture of Wood, Bamboo, Rattan, Palm, and Straw Products	67 765
家具制造业	Manufacture of Furniture	436 389
造纸和纸制品业	Manufacture of Paper and Paper Products	331 836
印刷和记录媒介复制业	Printing, Reproduction of Recording Media	1 096 211
文教、工美、体育和娱乐用品制造业	Manufacture of Articles for Culture, Arts & Crafts, Sports and Entertainment	2 230 594
石油加工、炼焦和核燃料加工业	Processing of Petroleum, Coking, Processing of Nucleus Fuel	69 662
化学原料和化学制品制造业	Manufacture of Chemical Raw Material and Chemical Products	2 727 778
医药制造业	Manufacture of Medicines	425 674
化学纤维制造业	Manufacture of Chemical Fiber	74 462
橡胶和塑料制品业	Manufacture of Rubber and Plastic	1 464 313
非金属矿物制品业	Manufacture of Non-metallic Mineral Products	1 026 013
黑色金属冶炼和压延加工业	Smelting and Pressing of Ferrous Metals	544 216
有色金属冶炼和压延加工业	Smelting and Pressing of Non-ferrous Metals	294 466
金属制品业	Manufacture of Metal Products	4 168 111
通用设备制造业	Manufacture of General Purpose Machinery	2 311 483
专用设备制造业	Manufacture of Special Purpose Machinery	946 958
汽车制造业	Manufacture of Vehicle	2 987 183
铁路、船舶、航空航天和其他运输设备制造业	Manufacture of Transport Equipment for Railway, Shipping, Aerospace and other uses	1 164 326
电气机械和器材制造业	Manufacture of Electrical Machinery & Equipment	1 518 140
计算机、通信和其他电子设备制造业	Manufacture of Computer, Communication Equipment and Other Electronic E-quipment	3 452 274
仪器仪表制造业	Manufacture of Measuring Instrument	379 128
其他制造业	Manufacture of Other Products	57 612
废弃资源综合利用业	Recycling and Disposal of Waste Resources	18 082
金属制品、机械和设备修理业	Maintenance of Metal Products, Machinery and Equipment	25 043
电力、热力生产和供应业	Production and Supply of Electric Power and Heat Power	35 748
燃气生产和供应业	Production and Supply of Gas	357 573
水的生产和供应业	Production and Supply of Water	18 096

单位：万元(10 000 yuan)

主营业务成本 Cost of Principal Business	主营业务 税金及附加 Taxes and Extra Charges on Principal Business	利润总额 Total Profits	本年应 交增值税 Value-added Tax Payable	全部从业人员 年平均人数(人) Annual Average Employed Persons(person)
34 481 190	**461 870**	**2 274 168**	**1 785 848**	**380 354**
63 418	1 043	6 652	1 240	295
3 859 461	36 973	180 712	150 277	36 447
1 434 756	26 272	155 275	53 083	9 687
1 400 111	54 079	171 508	47 420	13 626
867 322	10 432	48 824	51 332	12 562
1 487 401	19 838	100 875	160 596	42 469
1 039 700	16 287	52 282	136 278	34 256
57 167	766	5 452	1 242	297
368 410	5 189	24 335	22 109	5 540
292 904	2 038	12 332	9 658	2 658
950 235	8 962	60 384	33 514	6 785
1 920 865	27 107	144 934	123 617	30 678
49 630	908	8 149	4 053	426
2 438 134	19 013	-34 759	75 243	12 822
348 918	3 255	31 589	8 782	1 775
65 495	293	-3 436	4 416	962
1 211 957	15 560	87 595	80 982	17 127
861 029	6 931	53 175	40 694	7 910
487 353	2 353	13 478	15 436	2 780
244 210	1 269	18 149	9 295	1 163
3 734 958	53 500	201 032	135 195	24 266
1 986 008	16 407	121 329	135 570	19 236
787 375	11 647	62 247	47 384	7 867
2 391 030	61 967	336 842	100 477	20 064
916 615	13 144	156 417	54 845	10 072
1 343 214	18 518	62 811	72 925	16 435
3 138 232	21 470	115 096	163 040	32 793
281 284	4 255	50 255	26 824	5 579
52 466	168	642	8 829	2 159
15 341		2 091	1 010	248
21 319	115	1 566	1 242	241
28 315	125	3 852	90	22
324 889	1 878	19 550	5 769	844
11 668	108	2 934	3 379	263

12－9 按行业分大中型工业企业主要指标（2014 年）
MAIN INDICATORS OF LARGE AND MEDIUM-SIZED INDUSTRIAL ENTERPRISES BY INDUSTRIAL SECTOR(2014)

项　目	Indicator	企业单位数(个) Number of Enterprises(unit)
总　计	**Total**	**659**
煤炭开采和洗选业	Mining and Washing of Coal	
石油和天然气开采业	Extraction of Petroleum and Natural Gas	
黑色金属矿采选业	Mining of Ferrous Metal Ores	
有色金属矿采选业	Mining of Non-ferrous Metal Ores	
非金属矿采选业	Mining and Processing of Nonmetal Ores	1
开采辅助活动	Auxiliary Activities of Mining	
其他采矿业	Mining of Other Ores	
农副食品加工业	Processing of Food from Agricultural Products	59
食品制造业	Manufacture of Foods	17
酒、饮料和精制茶制造业	Manufacture of Liquor, Beverage and Refind Tea	6
烟草制品业	Manufacture of Tobacco	
纺织业	Manufacture of Textile	17
纺织服装、服饰业	Manufacture of Textile Wearing Apparel	56
皮革、毛皮、羽毛及其制品和制鞋业	Manufacture of Leather, Fur, Feather & Its Products Footwear	31
木材加工和木、竹、藤、棕、草制品业	Processing of Timbers, Manufacture of Wood, Bamboo, Rattan, Palm, and Straw Products	2
家具制造业	Manufacture of Furniture	12
造纸和纸制品业	Manufacture of Paper and Paper Products	2
印刷和记录媒介复制业	Printing, Reproduction of Recording Media	7
文教、工美、体育和娱乐用品制造业	Manufacture of Articles for Culture, Arts & Crafts, Sports and Entertainment	46
石油加工、炼焦和核燃料加工业	Processing of Petroleum, Coking, Processing of Nucleus Fuel	4
化学原料和化学制品制造业	Manufacture of Chemical Raw Material and Chemical Products	25
医药制造业	Manufacture of Medicines	10
化学纤维制造业	Manufacture of Chemical Fiber	2
橡胶和塑料制品业	Manufacture of Rubber and Plastic	38
非金属矿物制品业	Manufacture of Non-metallic Mineral Products	18
黑色金属冶炼和压延加工业	Smelting and Pressing of Ferrous Metals	6
有色金属冶炼和压延加工业	Smelting and Pressing of Non-ferrous Metals	6
金属制品业	Manufacture of Metal Products	49
通用设备制造业	Manufacture of General Purpose Machinery	46
专用设备制造业	Manufacture of Special Purpose Machinery	29
汽车制造业	Manufacture of Vehicle	33
铁路、船舶、航空航天和其他运输设备制造业	Manufacture of Transport Equipment for Railway, Shipping, Aerospace and other uses	27
电气机械和器材制造业	Manufacture of Electrical Machinery & Equipment	43
计算机、通信和其他电子设备制造业	Manufacture of Computer, Communication Equipment and Other Electronic Equipment	35
仪器仪表制造业	Manufacture of Measuring Instrument	9
其他制造业	Manufacture of Other Products	2
废弃资源综合利用业	Recycling and Disposal of Waste Resources	
金属制品、机械和设备修理业	Maintenance of Metal Products, Machinery and Equipment	
电力、热力生产和供应业	Production and Supply of Electric Power and Heat Power	17
燃气生产和供应业	Production and Supply of Gas	1
水的生产和供应业	Production and Supply of Water	3

单位:万元(10 000 yuan)

工业总产值 Gross Industrial Output Value	资产合计 Total Assets	流动资产合计 Total Current Assets	固定资产净值 Net Value of Fixed Assets
80 592 027	**71 006 247**	**44 397 117**	**15 329 030**
40 925	8 727	1 862	6 864
5 638 301	3 086 750	1 331 053	1 188 250
1 149 708	844 295	537 141	200 995
1 368 251	1 863 531	448 466	276 659
718 452	254 485	133 595	97 488
3 069 293	1 893 473	1 078 326	424 417
1 282 770	489 309	270 450	151 761
83 769	42 951	9 484	33 468
447 236	200 751	96 455	80 951
149 622	94 289	53 427	23 829
323 379	205 203	118 902	75 940
1 104 038	488 475	219 607	218 336
8 563 530	2 740 378	1 025 372	1 169 792
2 393 445	2 652 021	1 302 960	786 027
499 124	986 245	488 078	236 716
44 463	72 184	51 222	13 498
4 283 065	2 927 169	1 336 457	985 756
852 947	1 161 982	672 845	342 133
1 841 201	2 103 486	1 084 928	548 722
382 172	358 923	136 138	146 264
3 652 707	2 277 797	1 066 714	902 672
4 642 660	2 620 309	1 754 713	560 217
2 051 056	1 888 419	1 216 231	333 092
5 847 263	6 203 114	4 813 148	905 506
8 196 573	9 085 791	6 761 138	1 391 155
12 159 688	17 391 921	13 560 332	1 387 852
7 121 876	5 053 792	3 364 752	720 864
675 195	887 213	634 358	123 253
58 367	43 969	29 657	12 515
1 829 926	2 476 098	690 681	1 577 987
60 064	155 789	27 609	110 406
60 960	447 410	81 018	295 648

12 -9 续表
continued

项　目	Indicator	主营业务收入 Revenue from Principal Business
总　计	**Total**	**82 826 089**
煤炭开采和洗选业	Mining and Washing of Coal	
石油和天然气开采业	Extraction of Petroleum and Natural Gas	
黑色金属矿采选业	Mining of Ferrous Metal Ores	
有色金属矿采选业	Mining of Non-ferrous Metal Ores	
非金属矿采选业	Mining and Processing of Nonmetal Ores	40 598
开采辅助活动	Auxiliary Activities of Mining	
其他采矿业	Mining of Other Ores	
农副食品加工业	Processing of Food from Agricultural Products	5 549 534
食品制造业	Manufacture of Foods	1 178 868
酒、饮料和精制茶制造业	Manufacture of Liquor, Beverage and Refind Tea	1 992 252
烟草制品业	Manufacture of Tobacco	
纺织业	Manufacture of Textile	747 414
纺织服装、服饰业	Manufacture of Textile Wearing Apparel	2 996 515
皮革、毛皮、羽毛及其制品和制鞋业	Manufacture of Leather, Fur, Feather & Its Products Footwear	1 249 878
木材加工和木、竹、藤、棕、草制品业	Processing of Timbers, Manufacture of Wood, Bamboo, Rattan, Palm, and Straw Products	81 151
家具制造业	Manufacture of Furniture	444 380
造纸和纸制品业	Manufacture of Paper and Paper Products	137 348
印刷和记录媒介复制业	Printing, Reproduction of Recording Media	320 582
文教、工美、体育和娱乐用品制造业	Manufacture of Articles for Culture, Arts & Crafts, Sports and Entertainment	1 049 684
石油加工、炼焦和核燃料加工业	Processing of Petroleum, Coking, Processing of Nucleus Fuel	8 551 634
化学原料和化学制品制造业	Manufacture of Chemical Raw Material and Chemical Products	2 465 705
医药制造业	Manufacture of Medicines	474 138
化学纤维制造业	Manufacture of Chemical Fiber	45 251
橡胶和塑料制品业	Manufacture of Rubber and Plastic	4 142 567
非金属矿物制品业	Manufacture of Non-metallic Mineral Products	834 202
黑色金属冶炼和压延加工业	Smelting and Pressing of Ferrous Metals	2 644 776
有色金属冶炼和压延加工业	Smelting and Pressing of Non-ferrous Metals	369 598
金属制品业	Manufacture of Metal Products	3 504 127
通用设备制造业	Manufacture of General Purpose Machinery	4 468 569
专用设备制造业	Manufacture of Special Purpose Machinery	1 864 730
汽车制造业	Manufacture of Vehicle	4 846 378
铁路、船舶、航空航天和其他运输设备制造业	Manufacture of Transport Equipment for Railway, Shipping, Aerospace and other uses	7 897 616
电气机械和器材制造业	Manufacture of Electrical Machinery & Equipment	14 799 135
计算机、通信和其他电子设备制造业	Manufacture of Computer, Communication Equipment and Other Electronic Equipment	7 499 001
仪器仪表制造业	Manufacture of Measuring Instrument	617 050
其他制造业	Manufacture of Other Products	52 984
废弃资源综合利用业	Recycling and Disposal of Waste Resources	
金属制品、机械和设备修理业	Maintenance of Metal Products, Machinery and Equipment	
电力、热力生产和供应业	Production and Supply of Electric Power and Heat Power	1 840 511
燃气生产和供应业	Production and Supply of Gas	60 064
水的生产和供应业	Production and Supply of Water	59 850

单位：万元(10 000 yuan)

主营业务成本 Cost of Principal Business	主营业务税金及附加 Taxes and Extra Charges on Principal Business	利润总额 Total Profits	本年应交增值税 Value-added Tax Payable	全部从业人员年平均人数(人) Annual Average Employed Persons (person)
70 327 446	**1 581 266**	**3 825 929**	**2 255 502**	**576 900**
25 828	380	3 369	528	429
5 016 306	36 742	169 533	93 824	57 355
731 851	10 575	101 688	47 519	7 303
1 521 899	56 768	213 294	69 465	15 551
636 131	4 992	48 633	20 066	9 862
2 553 831	19 327	189 617	88 564	68 555
1 041 376	7 460	87 188	47 007	36 062
67 531	1 075	7 825	3 165	967
387 258	3 444	14 044	11 062	7 154
129 071	262	648	2 382	1 541
272 573	1 496	22 009	12 021	3 201
895 202	14 281	73 752	40 035	23 328
7 386 425	1 058 080	-54 143	542 420	3 220
2 247 569	14 291	-69 196	53 445	16 355
260 878	4 121	83 429	32 350	6 580
42 821	116	-3 264	79	838
3 748 098	13 277	140 356	56 310	29 371
716 607	6 505	52 451	24 375	10 034
2 511 829	2 069	8 348	11 987	10 370
327 059	274	1 329	5 169	2 844
3 063 406	42 040	169 781	97 884	28 390
3 923 251	29 226	188 265	95 345	28 535
1 527 423	11 799	132 611	74 197	17 351
4 144 814	71 084	326 646	108 244	30 400
6 751 491	33 104	501 484	168 941	38 715
11 578 219	89 897	914 499	278 954	52 814
6 533 179	35 332	356 421	169 089	43 656
484 627	4 611	38 932	31 209	8 201
48 332	155	759	219	2 032
1 608 191	8 085	123 616	66 340	13 119
54 274	74	-7 717	567	617
90 097	327	-10 276	2 741	2 150

12-10 按行业分规模以上工业企业主要经济效益指标（2014年）
MAIN INDICATORS ON ECONOMIC BENEFIT OF INDUSTRIAL ENTERPRISES ABOVE DESIGNATED SIZE BY INDUSTRIAL SECTOR(2014)

行　业	Sector	总资产贡献率(%) Ratio of Total Assets to Industrial Output Value(%)
总　计	**Total**	**15.45**
按轻重工业分	**Grouped by Light and Heavy Industries**	
轻工业	Light Industry	14.23
重工业	Heavy Industry	16.42
按行业分	**Grouped by Sector**	
煤炭开采和洗选业	Mining and Washing of Coal	
石油和天然气开采业	Extraction of Petroleum and Natural Gas	
黑色金属矿采选业	Mining of Ferrous Metal Ores	69.5
有色金属矿采选业	Mining of Non-ferrous Metal Ores	
非金属矿采选业	Mining and Processing of Nonmetal Ores	41.89
开采辅助活动	Auxiliary Activities of Mining	
其他采矿业	Mining of Other Ores	
农副食品加工业	Processing of Food from Agricultural Products	18.38
食品制造业	Manufacture of Foods	21.49
酒、饮料和精制茶制造业	Manufacture of Liquor, Beverage and Refind Tea	18.71
烟草制品业	Manufacture of Tobacco	
纺织业	Manufacture of Textile	29.47
纺织服装、服饰业	Manufacture of Textile Wearing Apparel	21.06
皮革、毛皮、羽毛及其制品和制鞋业	Manufacture of Leather, Fur, Feather & Its Products Footwear	33.33
木材加工和木、竹、藤、棕、草制品业	Processing of Timbers, Manufacture of Wood, Bamboo, Rattan, Palm, and Straw Products	34.44
家具制造业	Manufacture of Furniture	31.35
造纸和纸制品业	Manufacture of Paper and Paper Products	17
印刷和记录媒介复制业	Printing, Reproduction of Recording Media	36.67
文教、工美、体育和娱乐用品制造业	Manufacture of Articles for Culture, Arts & Crafts, Sports and Entertainment	37.46
石油加工、炼焦和核燃料加工业	Processing of Petroleum, Coking, Processing of Nucleus Fuel	56.86
化学原料和化学制品制造业	Manufacture of Chemical Raw Material and Chemical Products	10.05
医药制造业	Manufacture of Medicines	19.08
化学纤维制造业	Manufacture of Chemical Fiber	8.11
橡胶和塑料制品业	Manufacture of Rubber and Plastic	16.81
非金属矿物制品业	Manufacture of Non-metallic Mineral Products	18.82
黑色金属冶炼和压延加工业	Smelting and Pressing of Ferrous Metals	8.92
有色金属冶炼和压延加工业	Smelting and Pressing of Non-ferrous Metals	17.91
金属制品业	Manufacture of Metal Products	26.72
通用设备制造业	Manufacture of General Purpose Machinery	21.18
专用设备制造业	Manufacture of Special Purpose Machinery	9.43
汽车制造业	Manufacture of Vehicle	9.31
铁路、船舶、航空航天和其他运输设备制造业	Manufacture of Transport Equipment for Railway, Shipping, Aerospace and other uses	9.79
电气机械和器材制造业	Manufacture of Electrical Machinery & Equipment	9.31
计算机、通信和其他电子设备制造业	Manufacture of Computer, Communication Equipment and Other Electronic Equipment	11.17
仪器仪表制造业	Manufacture of Measuring Instrument	12.08
其他制造业	Manufacture of Other Products	19.88
废弃资源综合利用业	Recycling and Disposal of Waste Resources	11.14
金属制品、机械和设备修理业	Maintenance of Metal Products, Machinery and Equipment	37.65
电力、热力生产和供应业	Production and Supply of Electric Power and Heat Power	9.3
燃气生产和供应业	Production and Supply of Gas	8.49
水的生产和供应业	Production and Supply of Water	0.62

资产负债率 (%) Assets-Liability Ratio(%)	流动资产周转次数(次/年) Number of Times of Annualof Turnover Current Assets(time/year)	工业成本费用利润率(%) Ratio of Profits to Industrial Costs(%)	产品销售率 (%) Ratio of Sales to Output(%)
56.67	**2.56**	**5.67**	**98.74**
56.27	2.29	6.52	99.92
56.98	2.79	5.08	97.99
23.21	31.29	10.25	98.88
49.91	10.06	6.15	96.68
50.79	4.63	4.96	97.51
42.99	2.91	8.25	99.33
34.64	4.46	9.81	133.17
			100.75
53.51	5.32	6.57	98.38
44.6	3.49	6.9	98.59
48.58	5.27	7.38	98.3
39.59	9.06	8.29	97.82
50.73	6.03	7	97.53
45.34	2.9	4.59	97.64
43.6	6.2	7.06	98.43
41.37	6.91	7.75	97.79
82.14	8.5	-0.77	99.14
56.88	3.03	2.74	96.24
39.47	2.31	11.73	97.09
56.69	2.07	1.55	102.99
53.46	4.06	4.9	98.83
55.71	3.21	6.65	98.21
64.33	2.93	2.74	98.68
52.71	4.7	4.23	97.68
45.19	5.31	5.68	96.95
49.1	3.69	6.27	98.08
39.78	1.55	7.29	96.48
58.89	1.23	6.76	99.5
66.92	1.37	7.27	98.02
71.48	1.33	6.41	98.75
52.24	2.5	4.45	102.53
57.63	1.38	7.57	97
51.38	2.66	8.5	96.15
65.04	1.99	9.95	98.53
49.62	3.86	8.18	89.67
64.65	2.64	6.65	99.22
64.57	3.68	3.05	99.96
62.97	0.76	-4.08	99.1

12－11 按行业分国有控股工业企业主要经济效益指标(2014 年)
MAIN INDICATORS ON ECONOMIC BENEFIT OF STATE-OWNED AND STATE-HOLDING INDUSTRIAL ENTERPRISES BY INDUSTRIAL SECTOR(2014)

行　业	Sector	总资产贡献率(%) Ratio of Total Assets to Industrial Output Value(%)
总　计	**Total**	**13.24**
煤炭开采和洗选业	Mining and Washing of Coal	
石油和天然气开采业	Extraction of Petroleum and Natural Gas	
黑色金属矿采选业	Mining of Ferrous Metal Ores	
有色金属矿采选业	Mining of Non-ferrous Metal Ores	
非金属矿采选业	Mining and Processing of Nonmetal Ores	12.66
开采辅助活动	Auxiliary Activities of Mining	
其他采矿业	Mining of Other Ores	
农副食品加工业	Processing of Food from Agricultural Products	15.06
食品制造业	Manufacture of Foods	27.87
酒、饮料和精制茶制造业	Manufacture of Liquor, Beverage and Refind Tea	36.69
烟草制品业	Manufacture of Tobacco	
纺织业	Manufacture of Textile	
纺织服装、服饰业	Manufacture of Textile Wearing Apparel	0.92
皮革、毛皮、羽毛及其制品和制鞋业	Manufacture of Leather, Fur, Feather & Its Products Footwear	11.09
木材加工和木、竹、藤、棕、草制品业	Processing of Timbers, Manufacture of Wood, Bamboo, Rattan, Palm, and Straw Products	
家具制造业	Manufacture of Furniture	
造纸和纸制品业	Manufacture of Paper and Paper Products	6.93
印刷和记录媒介复制业	Printing, Reproduction of Recording Media	5.57
文教、工美、体育和娱乐用品制造业	Manufacture of Articles for Culture, Arts & Crafts, Sports and Entertainment	
石油加工、炼焦和核燃料加工业	Processing of Petroleum, Coking, Processing of Nucleus Fuel	57.97
化学原料和化学制品制造业	Manufacture of Chemical Raw Material and Chemical Products	5.23
医药制造业	Manufacture of Medicines	20.63
化学纤维制造业	Manufacture of Chemical Fiber	
橡胶和塑料制品业	Manufacture of Rubber and Plastic	3.65
非金属矿物制品业	Manufacture of Non-metallic Mineral Products	9.63
黑色金属冶炼和压延加工业	Smelting and Pressing of Ferrous Metals	3.35
有色金属冶炼和压延加工业	Smelting and Pressing of Non-ferrous Metals	3.68
金属制品业	Manufacture of Metal Products	1.32
通用设备制造业	Manufacture of General Purpose Machinery	2.77
专用设备制造业	Manufacture of Special Purpose Machinery	-1.00
汽车制造业	Manufacture of Vehicle	9.17
铁路、船舶、航空航天和其他运输设备制造业	Manufacture of Transport Equipment for Railway, Shipping, Aerospace and other uses	8.31
电气机械和器材制造业	Manufacture of Electrical Machinery & Equipment	5.29
计算机、通信和其他电子设备制造业	Manufacture of Computer, Communication Equipment and Other Electronic Equipment	12.44
仪器仪表制造业	Manufacture of Measuring Instrument	27.27
其他制造业	Manufacture of Other Products	4.59
废弃资源综合利用业	Recycling and Disposal of Waste Resources	
金属制品、机械和设备修理业	Maintenance of Metal Products, Machinery and Equipment	
电力、热力生产和供应业	Production and Supply of Electric Power and Heat Power	9.71
燃气生产和供应业	Production and Supply of Gas	
水的生产和供应业	Production and Supply of Water	0.21

资产负债率 (%) Assets-Liability Ratio(%)	流动资产周转次数(次/年) Number of Times of Annual of Turnover Current Assets(time/year)	工业成本费用利润率(%) Ratio of Profits to Industrial Costs(%)	产品销售率 (%) Ratio of Sales to Output(%)
65.04	**1.98**	**3.61**	**100.18**
84.17	1.46	2.53	87.78
26.37	23.60	2.43	98.15
28.12	1.90	13.93	100
61.53	2.52	19.38	97.42
			100.75
100.95	2.71	-2.63	94.67
52.62	1.50	6.39	106.18
63.97	3.52	1.04	96
8.54	1.64	2.36	89.85
83.65	8.67	-0.90	99.14
56.56	1.35	4.11	99.72
44.55	1.76	17.51	98.51
50.53	1.33	1.30	98.83
76.92	1.19	7.30	103.52
80.51	2.47	0.34	99.68
53.55	1.93	6.51	100.01
66.66	0.36	2.21	100
63.81	1.61	0.77	96.33
74.60	0.84	-9.69	89.77
56.90	0.96	8.33	100.13
68.40	1.28	6.62	97.81
58.19	1.72	1.85	101.46
52.21	2.19	5.04	108.76
18.69	1.46	10.18	86.58
71.27	0.89	2.10	100
64.08	2.72	6.99	99.24
63.81	0.70	-6.05	99.62

12－12 按行业分规模以上外商及港澳台商投资工业企业主要经济效益指标(2014 年)

MAIN INDICATORS ON ECONOMIC BENEFIT OF FOREIGN FUNDED ENTERPRISES AND ENTERPRISES WITH FUNDS FROM HONG KONG, MACAO AND TAIWAN ABOVE DESIGNATED SIZE BY INDUSTRIAL SECTOR(2014)

行　业	Sector	总资产贡献率(%) Ratio of Total Assets to Industrial Output Value(%)
总　计	**Total**	**11.87**
煤炭开采和洗选业	Mining and Washing of Coal	
石油和天然气开采业	Extraction of Petroleum and Natural Gas	
黑色金属矿采选业	Mining of Ferrous Metal Ores	86.32
有色金属矿采选业	Mining of Non-ferrous Metal Ores	
非金属矿采选业	Mining and Processing of Nonmetal Ores	
开采辅助活动	Auxiliary Activities of Mining	
其他采矿业	Mining of Other Ores	
农副食品加工业	Processing of Food from Agricultural Products	13.65
食品制造业	Manufacture of Foods	20.05
酒、饮料和精制茶制造业	Manufacture of Liquor, Beverage and Refind Tea	15.89
烟草制品业	Manufacture of Tobacco	
纺织业	Manufacture of Textile	16.89
纺织服装、服饰业	Manufacture of Textile Wearing Apparel	19.66
皮革、毛皮、羽毛及其制品和制鞋业	Manufacture of Leather, Fur, Feather & Its Products Footwear	25.80
木材加工和木、竹、藤、棕、草制品业	Processing of Timbers, Manufacture of Wood, Bamboo, Rattan, Palm, and Straw Products	18.29
家具制造业	Manufacture of Furniture	28.20
造纸和纸制品业	Manufacture of Paper and Paper Products	12.73
印刷和记录媒介复制业	Printing, Reproduction of Recording Media	12.73
文教、工美、体育和娱乐用品制造业	Manufacture of Articles for Culture, Arts & Crafts, Sports and Entertainment	30.63
石油加工、炼焦和核燃料加工业	Processing of Petroleum, Coking, Processing of Nucleus Fuel	29.38
化学原料和化学制品制造业	Manufacture of Chemical Raw Material and Chemical Products	29.38
医药制造业	Manufacture of Medicines	41.31
化学纤维制造业	Manufacture of Chemical Fiber	-0.42
橡胶和塑料制品业	Manufacture of Rubber and Plastic	15.11
非金属矿物制品业	Manufacture of Non-metallic Mineral Products	14.22
黑色金属冶炼和压延加工业	Smelting and Pressing of Ferrous Metals	4.43
有色金属冶炼和压延加工业	Smelting and Pressing of Non-ferrous Metals	30.42
金属制品业	Manufacture of Metal Products	22.14
通用设备制造业	Manufacture of General Purpose Machinery	13.59
专用设备制造业	Manufacture of Special Purpose Machinery	1.66
汽车制造业	Manufacture of Vehicle	12.07
铁路、船舶、航空航天和其他运输设备制造业	Manufacture of Transport Equipment for Railway, Shipping, Aerospace and other uses	10.72
电气机械和器材制造业	Manufacture of Electrical Machinery & Equipment	11.53
计算机、通信和其他电子设备制造业	Manufacture of Computer, Communication Equipment and Other Electronic E-quipment	7.97
仪器仪表制造业	Manufacture of Measuring Instrument	23.10
其他制造业	Manufacture of Other Products	3.83
废弃资源综合利用业	Recycling and Disposal of Waste Resources	18.56
金属制品、机械和设备修理业	Maintenance of Metal Products, Machinery and Equipment	15.74
电力、热力生产和供应业	Production and Supply of Electric Power and Heat Power	12.58
燃气生产和供应业	Production and Supply of Gas	15.83
水的生产和供应业	Production and Supply of Water	16.49

资产负债率 (%) Assets-Liability Ratio(%)	流动资产周转次数(次/年) Number of Times of Annual of Turnover Current Assets(time/year)	工业成本费用利润率(%) Ratio of Profits to Industrial Costs(%)	产品销售率 (%) Ratio of Sales to Output(%)
46.48	**2.16**	**5.88**	**99.34**
7.24	86.89	9.89	100
52.32	3.40	4.23	96.33
43.73	2.44	9.03	99.19
31.37	4.60	8.89	153.58
53.56	4.08	5.19	100.33
42.42	3.51	6.25	99.23
49.88	4.95	4.63	97.46
38.24	19.65	8.92	98.75
54.86	4.82	5.95	98.7
40.90	1.99	3.74	98.77
46.39	4.35	5.84	99.84
41.19	5.22	6.97	98.39
37.38	3.32	13.37	99.22
63.90	2.13	-1.25	95.38
37.11	5.68	7.48	93.18
66.04	1.14	-3.68	106.8
46.82	3.06	6.29	98.43
37.90	2.79	5.47	98.91
27.44	1.56	2.47	98.16
43.22	4.76	6.67	101.24
47.17	4.74	4.80	96.71
42.26	2.67	5.43	98.73
36.79	0.34	6.76	93.38
54.73	0.86	12.93	99.36
66.80	0.77	15.36	99.19
33.49	2.94	4.35	98.21
51.41	3.04	3.44	97.33
27.85	1.62	15.38	99.47
78.25	1.79	1.12	92.29
24.68	4.44	13.08	99.41
43.55	1.92	6.66	87.4
31.62	12.00	12.87	100
59.30	3.88	5.67	99.98
39.58	3.52	19.52	100

12－13 按行业分大中型工业企业主要经济效益指标（2014 年）

MAIN INDICATORS ON ECONOMIC BENEFIT OF LARGE AND MEDIUM-SIZED INDUSTRIAL ENTERPRISES BY INDUSTRIAL SECTOR(2014)

行　业	Sector	总资产贡献率(%) Ratio of Total Assets to Industrial Output Value(%)
总　计	**Total**	**11.44**
煤炭开采和洗选业	Mining and Washing of Coal	
石油和天然气开采业	Extraction of Petroleum and Natural Gas	
黑色金属矿采选业	Mining of Ferrous Metal Ores	
有色金属矿采选业	Mining of Non-ferrous Metal Ores	
非金属矿采选业	Mining and Processing of Nonmetal Ores	49.01
开采辅助活动	Auxiliary Activities of Mining	
其他采矿业	Mining of Other Ores	
农副食品加工业	Processing of Food from Agricultural Products	10.76
食品制造业	Manufacture of Foods	20.20
酒、饮料和精制茶制造业	Manufacture of Liquor, Beverage and Refind Tea	18.17
烟草制品业	Manufacture of Tobacco	
纺织业	Manufacture of Textile	30.27
纺织服装、服饰业	Manufacture of Textile Wearing Apparel	16.67
皮革、毛皮、羽毛及其制品和制鞋业	Manufacture of Leather, Fur, Feather & Its Products Footwear	29.89
木材加工和木、竹、藤、棕、草制品业	Processing of Timbers, Manufacture of Wood, Bamboo, Rattan, Palm, and Straw Products	28.24
家具制造业	Manufacture of Furniture	16.82
造纸和纸制品业	Manufacture of Paper and Paper Products	6.19
印刷和记录媒介复制业	Printing, Reproduction of Recording Media	17.86
文教、工美、体育和娱乐用品制造业	Manufacture of Articles for Culture, Arts & Crafts, Sports and Entertainment	27.31
石油加工、炼焦和核燃料加工业	Processing of Petroleum, Coking, Processing of Nucleus Fuel	58.38
化学原料和化学制品制造业	Manufacture of Chemical Raw Material and Chemical Products	0.72
医药制造业	Manufacture of Medicines	13.03
化学纤维制造业	Manufacture of Chemical Fiber	-1.96
橡胶和塑料制品业	Manufacture of Rubber and Plastic	8.70
非金属矿物制品业	Manufacture of Non-metallic Mineral Products	7.63
黑色金属冶炼和压延加工业	Smelting and Pressing of Ferrous Metals	3.48
有色金属冶炼和压延加工业	Smelting and Pressing of Non-ferrous Metals	4.01
金属制品业	Manufacture of Metal Products	14.24
通用设备制造业	Manufacture of General Purpose Machinery	12.68
专用设备制造业	Manufacture of Special Purpose Machinery	13.03
汽车制造业	Manufacture of Vehicle	8.40
铁路、船舶、航空航天和其他运输设备制造业	Manufacture of Transport Equipment for Railway, Shipping, Aerospace and other uses	7.84
电气机械和器材制造业	Manufacture of Electrical Machinery & Equipment	7.69
计算机、通信和其他电子设备制造业	Manufacture of Computer, Communication Equipment and Other Electronic E-quipment	10.88
仪器仪表制造业	Manufacture of Measuring Instrument	8.82
其他制造业	Manufacture of Other Products	4.35
废弃资源综合利用业	Recycling and Disposal of Waste Resources	
金属制品、机械和设备修理业	Maintenance of Metal Products, Machinery and Equipment	
电力、热力生产和供应业	Production and Supply of Electric Power and Heat Power	9.91
燃气生产和供应业	Production and Supply of Gas	-1.81
水的生产和供应业	Production and Supply of Water	-1.17

资产负债率 (%) Assets-Liability Ratio(%)	流动资产周转次数(次/年) Number of Times of Annual of Turnover Current Assets(time/year)	工业成本费用利润率(%) Ratio of Profits to Industrial Costs(%)	产品销售率 (%) Ratio of Sales to Output(%)
63.95	**1.92**	**4.76**	**99.66**
3.44	21.80	9.39	99.2
55.39	4.30	3.07	97.25
51.76	2.28	10.63	99.65
33.25	4.75	10.39	144.96
47.45	5.61	6.96	98.94
48.43	2.82	6.54	99.31
54.38	4.63	7.45	98.11
17.72	8.56	10.55	98.4
72.27	4.62	3.26	95.33
68.31	2.57	0.47	97.11
42.20	2.73	7.17	98.83
38.91	4.79	7.57	97.46
84.88	8.60	-0.69	99.73
67.45	1.91	-2.69	92.81
40.03	0.97	21.30	98.97
62.43	0.89	-6.67	101.97
56.94	3.14	3.42	98.89
65.41	1.26	6.60	97.27
78.43	2.45	0.31	99.66
54.45	2.73	0.36	96.86
47.95	3.30	4.98	96.8
56.00	2.68	4.33	97.58
54.95	1.56	7.28	96.25
59.65	1.05	7.07	99.71
69.52	1.18	6.70	98.24
75.70	1.09	6.50	99.35
52.78	2.44	4.52	103.73
69.66	1.00	6.68	98.13
79.16	1.80	1.44	91.67
63.08	2.79	6.61	98.46
73.07	2.93	-8.87	100
54.48	1.01	-8.38	99.29

12－14 主要年份主要工业产品产量

MAJOR YEAR'S PRODUCTS OUTPUT OF INDUSTRY ABOVE DESIGNATED SIZE

年份 Year	原盐（万吨）Salt (10000 tons)	发电量（亿千瓦小时）Electricity (100 million kW·h)	饮料酒（万吨）Beverage Liquor (10000 tons)	#啤酒 Beer	卷烟（万箱）Cigarettes (10000 cases)	罐头（吨）Canned Food (ton)	化学纤维（吨）Chemical Fiber (ton)	纱（吨）Yarn (ton)
1949	15.16	1.21	0.18	0.12	2.36			27 447
1952	35.08	2.11	0.37	0.18	12.27			59 674
1957	44.34	2.92	0.96	0.58	23.41			50 699
1962	38.60	3.86	1.58	0.79	16.59		28	17 939
1965	41.34	6.80	2.04	1.34	31.34		205	68 082
1970	29.96	10.57	3.39	2.55	42.16		621	85 591
1975	34.52	10.98	5.30	2.98	36.00		357	79 516
1978	60.68	13.63	6.25	3.75	44.00	4 743	1 413	85 233
1980	41.19	12.50	8.49	4.84	48.79	3 521	2 116	83 389
1985	47.34	26.97	13.76	10.05	51.81	6 400	1 747	91 839
1987	50.64	28.97	23.40	13.85	55.84	16 000	3 442	108 003
1988	53.28	29.35	26.61	15.58	57.01	27 200	3 393	107 720
1989	55.37	29.87	24.57	15.40	58.64	13 200	3 700	118 379
1990	35.70	40.22	29.18	19.61	61.94		2 900	100 381
1991	31.39	54.60	36.75	27.38	56.19	130 510	5 200	96 271
1992	46.24	58.63	44.59	37.01	59.37	3 200	6 000	99 043
1993	48.88	59.39	54.74	45.92	63.46	1 900	27 100	91 351
1994	53.02	59.62	60.00	50.92	69.20	2 300	21 400	86 744
1995	50.84	64.69	60.85	54.16	70.96	4 609	20 973	79 492
1996	41.39	83.02	61.79	54.40	73.04	1 719	22 945	66 832
1997	34.11	95.12	66.64	56.06	88.32	554	26 300	70 402
1998	19.08	79.65	47.33	42.79	77.10		23 858	66 504
1999	30.30	82.00	126.21	120.10	149.00	379	29 967	56 431
2000	41.83	90.84	211.47	206.50	148.10	225	65 362	69 561
2001	31.40	85.73	279.37	274.28	142.95	99	89 989	72 933
2002	42.50	89.70	323.20	320.60	138.10	11 690	91 394	70 888
2003	36.85	87.69	353.90	351.80	148.00		101 752	65 919
2004	34.36	89.01	393.30	390.60	147.10	10 889	115 187	71 931
2005	10.00	98.63	439.70	435.20	150.70	10 097	95 887	72 140
2006	15.30	124.54	101.60(本地)	95.60(本地)	95.16(本地)	1 668	72 381	56 128
2007	19.23	155.30	118.10(本地)	112.50(本地)	100.08(本地)	1 850	68 746	47 850
2008	15.90	164.58	132.07(本地)	124.75(本地)	100.02(本地)	1 510	51 751	43 102
2009	5.90	172.66	137.21(本地)	127.12(本地)	100.08(本地)	4 706	59 852	38 566
2010	11.25	181.93	144.66(本地)	141.65(本地)	102.55(本地)	1 092	68 654	35 278
2011		173.69	164.04(本地)	156.50(本地)	104.51(本地)	41 204	38 640	18 556
2012		174.72	174.03(本地)	163.95(本地)	106.03(本地)	35 026	32 371	19 404
2013	1.28	180.11	194.22(本地)	185.17(本地)	108.36(本地)	30 204	23 647	33 687
2014		178.29	169.85(本地)	164.59(本地)	112.06(本地)	23 970	22 053	32 336

注:1998 年以前为乡及乡以上工业。

Note: Before 1998, the data refer to those at and above county level.

12－14 续表 1
continued

年 份 Year	布(万米) Cloth (10000 m)	印染布 (万米) Printed Fabric (10000 m)	机制纸及纸板(万吨) Machine-made Paper and Paperboards (10000 tons)	硫 酸 (万吨) Sulfuric Acid (10000 tons)	烧 碱 (万吨) Caustic Soda (10000 tons)	纯 碱 (万吨) Soda Ash (10000 tons)
1949	10 608	2 947	0.98		0.01	
1952	30 069	13 658	0.44		0.17	
1957	27 806	16 053	1.54		0.74	
1962	7 444	7 375	1.45	0.06	0.89	
1965	29 538	13 670	2.22		1.66	5.32
1970	33 660	21 994	3.14	0.04	2.14	12.01
1975	31 242	22 828	3.10	0.53	2.36	9.15
1978	36 877	25 797	4.55	1.32	3.61	14.04
1980	34 937	22 900	5.25	4.11	4.33	18.18
1985	34 998	17 679	6.20	3.34	5.52	26.03
1987	38 155	21 833	6.52	4.40	6.15	29.53
1988	35 890	21 213	7.42	4.88	6.62	31.12
1989	36 188	19 842	6.20	4.30	6.95	32.25
1990	34 066	21 446	6.02	4.86	6.73	30.48
1991	34 076	19 999	5.99	5.62	5.99	29.50
1992	33 682	21 534	5.95	6.70	5.62	34.60
1993	35 912	16 606	8.84	6.96	6.07	40.43
1994	43 241	16 387	12.36	8.33	6.48	43.36
1995	41 170	17 864	11.06	9.69	7.90	43.20
1996	39 023	16 881	11.31	10.12	7.30	46.91
1997	43 615	15 722	7.78	10.16	8.45	50.55
1998	40 440	9 864	6.91	10.33	9.25	52.80
1999	39 576	4 340	7.77	12.56	8.96	53.70
2000	41 783	3 526	10.96	12.96	10.24	56.20
2001	40 640	3 402	23.05	13.03	11.44	58.47
2002	47 609	5 592	29.92	5.00	13.80	60.70
2003	35 922	10 131	31.76	4.50	13.53	62.50
2004	50 111	7 718	36.38	14.70	14.86	60.80
2005	51 307	16 027	31.95	14.80	16.10	62.50
2006	55 093	20 867	15.50	7.00	15.90	63.95
2007	44 251	18 708	24.04	9.22	14.91	71.02
2008	48 399	58 907	22.41	13.02	12.78	72.03
2009	31 048	27 998	34.59	1.40	12.24	68.21
2010	17 457	29 631	35.43	4.07	13.87	69.35
2011	49 617	28 449	32.28	5.06	13.20	70.07
2012	48 987	32 478	22.27	7.22	13.71	63.35
2013	51 646	34 381	17.95	4.32	11.06	61.66
2014	44 593	33 653	18.26			67.85

12－14 续表 2
continued

年 份 Year	合成氨 (万吨) Synthetic Ammonia (10000 tons)	化学肥料 (万吨) Chemical Fertilizer (10000 tons)	化学农药 (吨) Chemical Pesticides (ton)	油 漆 (吨) Paint (ton)	染 料 (吨) Dye (ton)
1949				30	599
1952				480	2 855
1957			1 226	1 247	4 307
1962		0.45	213	910	3 560
1965		1.42	2	4 727	8 667
1970	0.98	5.89	2 313	6 380	9 347
1975	3.46	12.46	4 439	7 016	5 967
1978	7.17	23.66	9 714	8 786	5 877
1980	7.24	7.82	8 333	14 556	2 159
1985	6.31	5.16	2 000	26 055	4 448
1987	8.20	8.32	2 200	28 323	5 316
1988	8.72	9.41	2 400	28 943	5 527
1989	8.47	8.84	2 500	27 713	5 784
1990	7.56	7.55	2 500	29 075	5 119
1991	8.52	8.04	2 800	33 548	5 263
1992	10.45	7.85	3 400	35 058	4 821
1993	10.70	8.02	3 600	33 054	4 550
1994	13.04	12.39	3 600	29 437	5 097
1995	14.98	12.62	4 934	37 772	7 185
1996	18.67	12.62	4 976	26 762	7 668
1997	16.94	12.52	4 600	19 743	11 189
1998	22.36	15.30	6 755	17 594	8 274
1999	26.09	20.19	4 480	3 730	7 866
2000	24.64	20.04	3 758	693	9 306
2001	35.53	28.07	3 915	1 349	9 757
2002	20.30	9.80	4 020	1 701	9 826
2003	21.55	9.70	2 039	2 106	10 734
2004	30.30	19.60	5 061	1 955	3 961
2005	33.80	22.10	6 524	1 687	13 979
2006	33.30	21.30	12 544		26 544
2007	28.22	25.70	16 433	2 957	28 269
2008	17.93	21.51	12 848	12 105	18 263
2009	17.71	21.23	49 684		24 893
2010	16.84	14.10	16 450		41 383
2011	10.78	9.26	23 286		
2012	7.71	6.98	28 801		
2013	6.48	5.10	27 715		
2014			27 160		

说明：根据市安全生产的有关要求，液氨企业整治，相关产品停产。

Note: According to the relevant requirements of work safety, ammonia manufacturers were under rectification, and the production of related products was suspended.

12－14 续表3
continued

年 份 Year	化学原料药 (吨) Chemical Medicines(ton)	水 泥 (万吨) Cement (10000 tons)	平板玻璃 (万重量箱) Plate Glass (10000 weight cases)	耐火材料 (万吨) Refractory Material (10000 tons)	粗钢 (万吨) Crude Steel (10000 tons)	钢 材 (万吨) Rolled-steel (10000 tons)
1949						0.06
1952				0.78	0.36	0.41
1957				3.39	1.77	4.30
1962		2.09		2.41	4.59	2.94
1965		6.59		2.91	11.72	8.43
1970		7.35	16.31	3.23	19.38	14.56
1975	55	20.93	19.44	4.88	21.25	20.01
1978	185	35.40	8.86	5.93	31.06	27.61
1980	123	44.66	70.13	5.38	37.14	32.82
1984	7 228	70.27	91.25	7.98	37.81	32.43
1985	4 222	82.70	77.00	4.35	37.51	32.68
1987	7 457	117.20	87.00	4.90	46.51	38.09
1988	7 655	141.00	108.81	4.56	50.17	38.26
1989	8 348	135.00	96.49	3.68	54.64	39.38
1990	6 913	139.48	83.13	3.91	54.55	38.04
1991	4 754	165.66	96.90	3.71	56.96	39.02
1992	5 743	191.50	120.00	3.86	63.75	50.09
1993	6 566	221.30	148.71	3.55	61.75	44.88
1994	4 238	246.50	145.12	3.06	60.82	46.95
1995	1 993	213.82	426.40	3.88	67.27	49.60
1996	5 505	181.45	423.60	3.54	72.02	50.60
1997	1 693	208.04	570.85	2.45	75.71	51.06
1998	910	131.51	509.38	0.99	84.02	64.93
1999	1 691	149.41	576.50	0.59	108.10	86.58
2000	2 131	137.52	556.58	0.62	101.17	93.35
2001	2 534	148.67	421.51	0.51	124.45	119.77
2002	2 712	140.30	405.40	0.45	145.90	142.20
2003	3 288	154.90	361.40	0.47	204.80	204.30
2004	4 394	181.19	163.30	0.69	225.70	230.97
2005	4 430	210.80	297.50	1.04	309.70	330.30
2006	32 232	232.72	418.74	1.21	325.82	375.52
2007	14 139	425.53	397.79	2.38	327.00	365.55
2008	17 910	363.57	599.87	3.65	300.19	350.14
2009	19 086	397.66	681.02	18.46	307.89	349.63
2010	26 170	442.66	662.04	8.17	300.04	333.46
2011	29 337	588.08	510.05	20.02	318.27	325.89
2012	49 290	556.57	494.54	33.44	252.78	274.67
2013	49 081	575.66	610.21	42.34	235.53	230.39
2014	50 713	597.35	612.40	39.37	214.43	212.79

12－14 续表4
continued

年 份 Year	金属切削机床 (台) Metal-cutting Machine Tools(unit)	锻压机械 (台) Metal Forming Machinery(unit)	汽 车 (辆) Motor Vehicles (set)	交流电动机 (万千瓦) AC Motors (10000 kW)
1949				0.02
1952	105			0.50
1957	76			3.61
1962	167	77		3.85
1965	526	111	13	6.48
1970	2 353	531	120	14.53
1975	3 213	788	490	15.56
1978	2 558	379	22	21.72
1980	595	444	1 644	20.11
1985	900	607	4 575	26.08
1987	1 175	887	2 304	27.02
1988	1 336	737	3 722	39.60
1989	1 107	1 010	3 404	38.60
1990	1 049	440	2 317	34.28
1991	869	764	1 514	44.17
1992	1 018	982	3 287	61.08
1993	1 532	919	4 828	64.13
1994	1 505	860	2 793	37.71
1995	972	2 563	5 210	39.18
1996	1 084	584	12 247	22.65
1997	449	416	13 020	20.74
1998	280		15 475	6.43
1999	251		20 038	11.10
2000	384		30 053	38.70
2001	472	2 477	40 658	42.72
2002	588		70 079	68.25
2003	990		65 612	95.63
2004	1 287		62 572	96.13
2005	1 347		31 055	63.50
2006	3 636		50 278	702.02
2007	3 392	1 869	61 016	119.23
2008	8 381	1 230	70 161	96.89
2009	668		458 900	728.03
2010	1 120		566 211	101.10
2011	1 194		488 330	74.08
2012	1 014		574 729	104.48
2013	2 689		708 966	126.82
2014	2 563		770 245	114.46

12 -14 续表 5
continued

年 份 Year	钢芯铝绞线(吨) Steel-cored Aluminum Stranded Wire(ton)	家用电冰箱(万台) Home Refrigerators (10000 sets)	家用洗衣机(万台) Home Washing Machines (10000 sets)	彩色电视机(万部) Color TV Sets (10000 sets)
1949				
1952				
1957				
1962				
1965	250			
1970	34			
1975	188			
1978	684			
1980	1 232			
1985	2 327	1.66	0.48	6.60
1987	2 849	9.08	22.08	14.20
1988	1 571	15.22	42.38	17.00
1989	2 805	21.65	35.02	18.11
1990	1 880	27.41	45.86	18.50
1991	2 463	31.51	45.70	22.27
1992	2 248	54.84	46.31	28.07
1993	1 144	50.48	56.59	36.08
1994	287	62.50	71.34	60.15
1995	1 659	107.91	64.34	60.53
1996	2 265	193.80	100.94	56.68
1997	2 616	257.10	171.95	124.86
1998	1 725	219.23	183.67	96.83
1999	2 805	259.60	256.30	285.20
2000	4 202	311.10	318.50	379.40
2001	4 498	396.30	367.89	455.40
2002	5 825	518.20	408.60	593.20
2003	4 940	598.30	471.50	671.70
2004	6 608	815.03	575.06	957.90
2005	116 592	908.80	614.90	1 324.30
2006	46 974	1 290.00	649.40	1 205.60
2007	22 564	1 421.40	769.40	1 243.10
2008	29 507	723.19	407.54	836.66
2009		827.21	488.72	1 064.70
2010		801.22	580.87	1 111.19
2011		718.54	604.55	1 154.20
2012		575.01	583.60	1 439.98
2013		524.35	606.65	1 512.05
2014		610.07	590.95	1 714.93

12－15 规模以上工业主要产品产量

OUTPUT OF MAJOR INDUSTRIAL PRODUCTS OF INDUSTRY ABOVE DESIGNATED SIZE

产品名称	Name	计量单位	Unit	2014	2013	2014年比2013年(±%) 2014/2013(±%)
冶金工业产品	**Products of Metallurgical Industry**					
粗钢	Crude Steel	万吨	10000 tons	214.43	235.53	-8.96
钢材	Rolled-steel	万吨	10000 tons	212.79	234.14	-9.12
耐火材料制品	Refractory Material	万吨	10000 tons	39.37	41.88	-6.01
电力工业产品	**Products of Electricity Industry**					
发电量	Electricity	亿千瓦小时	100 million kW · h	178.29	180.11	-3.49
化学工业产品	**Products of Chemical Industry**					
原油加工量	Processing Amount of Crude Oil	万吨	10000 tons	1 544.57	1 511.98	-1.97
汽油	Petrol	万吨	10000 tons	447.51	402.18	11.27
柴油	Diesel Oil	万吨	10000 tons	465.68	522.48	-10.87
燃料油	Fuel Oil	万吨	10000 tons	30.84	35.52	-13.18
硫酸	Sulfuric Acid	万吨	10000 tons		4.32	
纯碱	Soda Ash	万吨	10000 tons	67.85	61.66	10.03
烧碱	Caustic Soda	万吨	10000 tons		11.06	
农用化肥(100%)	Ag-fertilizer(100%)	万吨	10000 tons		5.09	
合成氨	Synthetic Ammonia	万吨	10000 tons		6.48	
化学农药	Chemical Pesticides	万吨	10000 tons	2.72	2.49	9.11
塑料制品	Plastic	万吨	10000 tons	34.43	33.27	3.47
化学药品(原料)	Chemical Medicines(Raw Materials)	万吨	10000 tons	5.07	4.91	3.32

12 -15 续表 1
continued

产品名称	Name	计量单位	Unit	2014	2013	2014 年比 2013 年 (±%) 2014/2013 (±%)
橡胶轮胎外胎	Tires	万条	10000 tires	5 199.10	4 813.49	8.01
机械工业产品	**Products of Machinery Industry**					
工业锅炉	Industrial Boiler	蒸发量吨	ton(evaporation amount)	24 414.82	29 494.22	-17.22
交流电动机	AC Motors	万千瓦	10000 kW	114.46	126.82	-9.75
金属切削机床	Metal-cutting Machine	台	set	2 563	2 689	-4.69
汽车	Motor Vehicles	辆	set	770 245	708 966	8.64
改装汽车	Refitted Motor Vehicles	辆	set	14 222	15 079	-5.68
民用钢质船舶	Civil Steel Ships	载重吨	syn-ton	737 467	492 502	49.74
电子产品	**Electronic Products**					
彩电电视机	Color TV Sets	万台	10000 sets	1 714.93	1 592.09	7.72
电子元件	Electronics	万只	10000 units	488 062.9	481 416.03	1.38
建材工业产品	**Products of Construction Industry**					
水泥	Cement	万吨	10000 tons	597.35	620.37	-3.71
平板玻璃	Plate Glass	万重量箱	10000 weight cases	612.4	610.21	0.36
砖(折标准砖)	Bricks	万块	10000 pieces	148 339	151 848	-2.31

12 -15 续表 2
continued

产品名称	Name	计量单位	Unit	2014	2013	2014 年比 2013 年 (±%) 2014/2013 (±%)
纺织工业产品	**Products of Textile Industry**					
纱	Yarn	吨	ton	32 336.26	38 367	-15.72
布	Cloth	万米	10000 m	44 593.23	52 356.12	-14.83
印染布	Printed Fabric	万米	10000 m	33 652.58	31 982.80	5.22
化学纤维	Chemical Fibers	万吨	10000 tons	2.21	2.50	-11.78
轻工产品	**Products of Light Industry**					
机制纸及纸板	Machine-made Paper and Paperboards	万吨	10000 tons	18.26	18.57	-1.66
家用洗衣机	Home Washing Machines	万台	10000 sets	590.95	606.65	-2.59
糖果	Sugar	吨	ton	12 100.00	10 848.90	11.53
卷烟	Cigarette	万箱	10000 cases	112.06	108.36	3.42
食用植物油	Vegetable Oil	万吨	10000 tons	43.00	57.01	-24.58
饮料酒	Beverage Liquor	万吨	10000 tons	169.85	182.68	-7.03
#白酒	Wine	万吨	10000 tons	1.79	1.62	10.58
#啤酒	Beer	万吨	10000 tons	164.59	177.6	-7.33
塑料制品	Plastic Products	万吨	10000 tons	34.43	33.27	3.47
家具	Furniture	万件	10000 units	813.97	845.43	-3.72
家用电冰箱	Home Refrigerators	万台	10000 sets	610.07	524.35	16.35
皮革鞋靴	Leather Shoes	万双	10000 pairs	6 138.78	6991.71	-12.20
服装	Clothing	万件	10000 articles	74 532.33	85 887.88	-13.22

12－16 规模以上工业主要产品生产能力
PRODUCTION CAPACITY OF MAJOR PRODUCTS OF INDUSTRY ABOVE DESIGNATED SIZE

产品名称	Name	计算单位	Unit	2014 生产能力 Production Capacity of 2014	2013 生产能力 Production Capacity of 2013
发电设备容量总计/发电量	Total Capacity of Generation Equipment	万千瓦/万千瓦小时	10000 kW/10000 kW·h	326	351
卷烟	Cigarettes	万支	10000 pieces	6 885 000	7 020 000
化学纤维	Chemical Fiber	吨	ton	35 637	36 637
棉纺锭/纺纱量	Knitting Spindle	锭/吨	spindle/ton	179 654	181 076
棉布织机/布	Cotton Cloth Loom	台/万米	set/10000 m	22 675	32 839
焦炭	Coke	吨	ton	600 000	600 000
农用氮、磷、钾化学肥料总计(折纯)	Chemical Fertilizer	吨	ton	39 400	83 520
水泥	Cement	吨	ton	8 716 060	7 794 000
平板玻璃	Plate Glass	重量箱	weight cases	7 150 000	7 150 000
生铁	Pig Iron	吨	ton	4 000 000	4 000 000
粗钢	Crude Steel	吨	ton	4 000 000	4 000 000
钢材	Rolled-steel	吨	ton	4 240 000	3 700 000
金属切削机床	Metal-cutting Machine	台	set	1 718	1 852
汽车	Motor Vehicles	辆	set	680 000	650 000
家用电冰箱	Home Refrigerators	台	set	7 500 000	6 310 000
房间空气调节器	Air Conditioner	台	set	9 660 000	9 400 000
移动通信手持机(手机)	Cell Phone	台	set	33 500 000	34 100 000
彩色电视机	Color TV Sets	台	set	17 570 000	16 170 000

说明:2014 年报汽车生产能力为载货汽车的生产能力。

Note:In 2014,the statistical scope of production capcity of motor vehicles is the production capcity of trucks.

主要统计指标解释

工业总产值　是以货币表现的工业企业在一定时期内生产的已出售或可供出售工业产品总量,它是反映一定时间内工业生产的总规模和总水平。

工业销售产值　是以货币表现的工业企业在一定时期内销售的本企业生产的工业产品产量。包括已销售的成品、半成品价值,以及对外提供的工业性作业价值和对本单位基本建设部门、生活福利部门等提供的产品和工业性作业及自制设备的价值。

工业增加值　指工业企业在报告期内以货币表现的工业生产活动的最终成果。是企业全部生产活动的总成果扣除了在生产过程中消耗或转移的物质产品和劳务价值后的余额,是企业生产过程中新增加的价值。

资产总计　指企业拥有或控制的能以货币计量的经济资源,包括各种财产、债权和其他权利。资产按其流动性(即资产的变现能力和支付能力)划分为:流动资产、长期投资、固定资产、无形资产、递延资产和其他资产。

负债合计　指企业所承担的能以货币计量,将以资产或劳务偿付的债务,偿还形式包括货币、资产或提供劳务。负债一般按偿还期长短分为流动负债和长期负债。

利润总额　指企业生产经营活动的最终成果,是企业在一定时期内实现的盈亏相抵后的利润总额(亏损以"-"号表示),它等于营业利润加上补贴收入加上投资收益加上营业外净收入再加上以前年度损益调整。

Explanatory Notes on Main Statistical Indicators

Gross Industrial Output Value　is the total volume of final industrial products produced and industrial services provided during a given period. It reflects the total achievements and overall scale of industrial production during a given period.

Sales Output Value of Industry　refers to total sales of products produced by industrial enterprises during a given period, including sales of fished goods, value of semi-products, value of industrial services provided to other units, value of products, industrial services provided for capital construction sector, welfare and self produced equipments within enterprise.

Value-added of Industry　refers to the final results of industrial production of industrial enterprises in money terms during the reference period.

Total Assets　refer to all economic resources, in monetary terms, that is owned or controlled by enterprises, including properties, creditors equity and other economic rights of all forms. Classified by the degree of equitability, total assets include circulating assets, long-term investment, fixed assets, intangible assets and deferred assets, and other assets.

Total Liabilities　refer to payable liabilities of enterprises that have to repay in terms of money, assets or labour services. In terms of payment, it can be divided into liquid liabilities and long-term liabilities.

Total Profits　refer to the final achievements of production and operation of the enterprises, represented by the total profits after deducting losses (loss is expressed by the negative figure). It is the sum of profits from operation, income from subsidies, investment earnings, net income from activities other than operation, and adjustment of profits and losses of previous years.

13 建筑业

CONSTRUCTION

简要说明

一、本篇资料的主要内容

本篇资料主要反映了全市建筑业基本情况，主要包括建筑业总产值、增加值、建筑企业生产指标、财务指标、重点建筑企业名单等方面的内容。

二、本篇资料的来源

本篇资料来源于建筑业统计年报，由市统计局固定资产投资统计处整理提供。

Brief Introduction

I. Main Content

Data in this chapter show the basic conditions of construction of the whole city, mainly including the gross output value of construction, value added, major production and financial indicators and list of key enterprises of construction, etc.

II. Source of Data

Data in this chapter are based on the annual report of construction industry, and complied by the Division of Investment and Construction Statistics of Qingdao Municipal Bureau of Statistics.

13－1 建筑业企业生产情况(2014 年)
PRODUCTION SITUATION OF CONSTRUCTION ENTERPRISES(2014)

项　目	Item	单位	Unit	合计 Total	#中央 of which: Central Enterprises	国有企业 State-owned Enterprises	集体企业 Collective-owned Enterprises	其他所有制企业 Other Ownership Enterprises
施工企业单位数	Number of Construction Enterprises	个	unit	556	8	22	22	512
建筑业总产值	Gross Output Value of Construction	万元	10000 yuan	12 650 274	2 337 990	510 237	48 226	12 091 811
#建筑工程	of which: Construction	万元	10000 yuan	11 548 915	2 054 683	272 688	30 152	11 246 075
安装工程	Installation	万元	10000 yuan	868 093	260 507	225 230	17 675	625 188
建筑业增加值	Value Added of Construction	万元	10000 yuan	4 625 900				
全年竣工产值	Output Value of Buildings Completed in the Year	万元	10000 yuan	5 108 437	618 255	508 290	9 206	4 590 941
施工房屋面积	Floor Space of Buildings under Construction	万平方米	10000 sq. m	10 992	1 132	21	10	10 961
#新开工	of which: Newly Operating	万平方米	10000 sq. m	2 904	280	9	3	2 892
投标承包	Bidding and Contracting	万平方米	10000 sq. m	8 450	1 132	20	7	8 423
竣工房屋面积	Floor Space of Buildings Completed	万平方米	10000 sq. m	2 006	92	2	3	2 001
#住宅	of which: Residential Buildings	万平方米	10000 sq. m	1 260	82	1	2	1 257
计算建筑业劳动生产率平均人数	Average Number of Persons for Calculating the Labor Productivity	人	person	372 582	61 758	14 611	3 395	354 576

13 -2 建筑业企业财务状况(2014 年)
FINANCIAL SITUATION OF CONSTRUCTION ENTERPRISES(2014)

项 目	Item	单位	Unit	合计 Total
流动资产	Circulating Funds	万元	10000 yuan	1 1535 880
#存货	of which: Inventory	万元	10000 yuan	2 979 272
年末固定资产原价	Original Value of Fixed Assets(year-end)	万元	10000 yuan	1 476 181
本年固定资产折旧	Depreciation of Fixed Assets in the Year	万元	10000 yuan	104 550
年末固定资产净值	Net Value of Fixed Assets(year-end)	万元	10000 yuan	795 936
年末资产合计	Total Assets(year-end)	万元	10000 yuan	14 028 044
年末负债合计	Total Liabilities(year-end)	万元	10000 yuan	10 528 963
所有者权益合计	Total Owners' Equity	万元	10000 yuan	3 499 081
#实收资本	Paid-in Capitals	万元	10000 yuan	2 191 443
主营业务收入	Revenue from Principal Business	万元	10000 yuan	13 263 735
主营业务成本	Cost of Principal Business	万元	10000 yuan	11 930 141
主营业务税金及附加	Taxes and Extra Charges on Principal Business	万元	10000 yuan	325 151
管理费用	Management Expenses	万元	10000 yuan	406 306
利润总额	Total Profits	万元	10000 yuan	415 080
利税总额	Total Pre-tax Profits	万元	10000 yuan	760 166
年末应收工程款	Account Receivable(year-end)	万元	10000 yuan	3 497 800

#中央 of which: Central Enterprises	国有企业 State-owned Enterprises	集体企业 Collective-owned Enterprises	其他所有制企业 Other Ownership Enterprises
2 522 470	1 482 332	36 280	10 017 268
716 619	451 014	7 376	2 520 882
530 312	227 436	10 242	1 238 503
43 564	14 284	874	89 392
240 647	129 742	4 661	661 533
3 078 812	1 742 162	48 457	12 237 425
2 616 567	1 442 912	34 771	9 051 253
462 245	299 250	13 685	3 186 146
263 669	141 826	12 494	2 037 123
3 666 060	1 919 979	80 211	11 263 545
3 375 344	1 766 876	73 650	10 089 615
69 032	13 108	2 523	309 520
119 124	61 379	2 245	342 682
86 226	47 684	1 835	365 561
157 362	62 307	4 632	693 227
863 767	363 524	9 842	3 124 434

13 -3 建筑业企业主要经济效益指标(2014 年)
MAIN INDICATORS ON ECONOMIC BENEFIT OF CONSTRUCTION ENTERPRISES(2014)

项 目	Item	单位	Unit	合计 Total	#中央 of which: Central Enterprises	国有企业 State-owned Enterprises	集体企业 Collective-owned Enterprises	其他所有制企业 Other Ownership Enterprises
建筑业劳动生产率	Labor Productivity of Construction							
按总产值计算	In Terms of Gross Output Value	元/人	yuan/person	339 529	378 572	349 214	142 050	341 021
竣工率	Rate of Buildings Completed							
按产值计算	In Terms of Gross Output Value	%	%	40.1	26.4	99.6	19.1	38.0
产值工资率	Ratio of Wages to Gross Output Value	%	%	12.2	12.3	30.8	30.5	11.3
资金利润率	Ratio of Profit to Funds	%	%	3.4	3.1	2.9	2.3	3.5
产值利润率	Ratio of Profit to Gross Output Value	%	%	3.3	3.7	9.4	3.8	3.1
流动比率	Current Ratio	%	%	121.3	111.2	126.9	187.3	120.3
资产负债率	Assets-Liability Ratio	%	%	75.1	84.8	82.8	71.7	74.0

13 -4 建筑业增加值(2014 年)

VALUE ADDED OF CONSTRUCTION(2014)

单位:亿元(100 million yuan)

市、区名称	Region	增加值 Value Added
全　市	Whole Municipal	462.59
市南区	Shinan District	40.71
市北区	Shibei District	52.74
李沧区	Licang District	10.10
崂山区	Laoshan District	56.01
黄岛区	Huangdao District	122.03
城阳区	Chengyang District	12.01
即墨市	Jimo	51.65
胶州市	Jiaozhou	54.98
平度市	Pingdu	27.10
莱西市	Laixi	33.70
红岛经济区	Qingdao National High-tech Industrial Development Zone	1.57

13－5 重点建筑企业一览表(2014 年)
LIST OF KEY CONSTRUCTION ENTERPRISES(2014)

序号 Precedence	企业单位名称	Name	所在地区 Location	资质等级 Qualification Criteria
1	青建集团股份公司	Qingjian Group Co. ,Ltd.	市北区 Shibei District	A001
2	中交一航局第二工程有限公司	China Communications 1nd Navigational Bureau 2nd Engineering Co. , Ltd.	市南区 Shinan	A104
3	中铁二十局集团第四工程有限公司	China Railway 20th Bureau Group 4th Engineering Co. ,Ltd.	崂山区 Laoshan	A103
4	青岛建安建设集团有限公司	Shandong Laigang Gonstruction Co. ,Ltd.	市南区 Shinan	A101
5	青岛海尔家居集成股份有限公司	Qingdao Haier Home Corp.	崂山区 Laoshan	B103
6	中启胶建集团有限公司	Zhongqi Jiaozhou Construction Group Co. , Ltd.	胶州市 Jiaozhou	A001
7	青岛博海建设集团有限公司	Qingdao Bohai Construction Group Co. , Ltd.	市南区 Shinan	A101
8	中建八局第四建设有限公司	China Construction 8th Devision Corp. Ltd. (Qingdao Branch)	市南区 Shinan	A101
9	青岛海川建设集团有限公司	Qingdao Haichuan Construction Group Co. , Ltd.	市北区 Shibei District	A101
10	山东莱钢建设有限公司	Shandong Laigang Gonstruction Co. ,Ltd.	市南区 Shinan	A108
11	中建筑港集团有限公司	China State Construction Port Engineering Group Co. ,Ltd.	市北区 Shibei District	A104
12	青岛一建集团有限公司	Qingdao Yijian Group Co. ,Ltd.	市北区 Shibei District	A101
13	青岛东亚建筑装饰有限公司	Qingdao Feiyu Construction and Decoration Co. ,Ltd.	市南区 Shinan	B103
14	莱西市建筑总公司	Laixi Construction Corp.	莱西市 Laixi	A001
15	山东兴华建设集团有限公司	Shandong Xinghua Construction Co. ,Ltd.	黄岛区 Huangdao District	A101
16	山东电力建设第三工程公司	Shandong Power Construction No. 3 Engineering Co. ,Ltd.	崂山区 Laoshan	A106
17	青岛温泉建设集团有限公司	Qingdao Hot Spring Construction Group Co. ,Ltd.	即墨市 Jimo	A101
18	青岛滨海建设集团有限公司	Qingdao Binhai Construction Group Co. , Ltd.	黄岛区 Huangdao District	A101
19	青岛公路建设集团有限公司	Qingdao Highway Construction Group Co. , Ltd.	崂山区 Laoshan	A102
20	中铁建工集团青岛工程有限公司	China Railway Construction Engineering Group Qingdao Engineering Co. , Ltd.	崂山区 Laoshan	A001
21	通广建工集团有限公司	Qingdao Tongguang Construction Engineering Co. ,Ltd.	即墨市 Jimo	A101
22	青岛城建集团有限公司	Qingdao City Construction Co. ,Ltd.	市北区 Shibei District	A110
23	青岛胶城建设集团有限公司	Qingdao Jiaocheng Construction Co. ,Ltd.	胶州市 Jiaozhou	A101
24	青岛土木建工集团有限公司	Qingdao Yinghai Construction Co. ,Ltd.	黄岛区 Huangdao District	A101
25	青岛建工集团有限公司	Qingdao Jiangong Group Co. ,Ltd.	崂山区 Laoshan	A102
26	中国石油天然气第七建设公司	China Petroluem 7th Construction Company	崂山区 Laoshan	A109
27	青岛亿联集团股份有限公司	Qingdao Yilian Group Co. ,Ltd.	黄岛区 Huangdao District	A101
28	青岛第一市政工程有限公司	Qingdao No. 1 Municipal Construction Engineering Co. ,Ltd.	市北区 Shibei District	A110
29	青岛瑞源工程集团有限公司	Qingdao Ruiyuan Engineering Group Co. , Ltd.	黄岛区 Huangdao District	A105
30	青岛平建建筑安装股份有限公司	Qingdao Pingjian Construction and Installation Co. ,Ltd.	平度市 Pingdu	A101
31	青岛福瀛建设集团有限公司	Qingdao Fuying Construction Group Co. , Ltd.	黄岛区 Huangdao District	A101
32	青岛安装建设股份有限公司	Qingdao Installation and Construction Co. , Ltd.	市北区 Shibei District	A112
33	青岛德泰建设工程有限公司	Qingdao Detai Construction Engineering Co. ,Ltd.	黄岛区 Huangdao District	A101

13－5 续表 1
continued

序号 Precedence	企业单位名称	Name	所在地区 Location	资质等级 Qualification Criteria
34	德才装饰股份有限公司	Decai Decoration Co. ,Ltd.	崂山区 Laoshan	B103
35	青岛港务局港务工程公司	Qingdao Port Engineering Co. ,Ltd.	黄岛区 Huangdao District	A204
36	青岛新华友建工集团股份有限公司	Qingdao Xinhuayou Construction Engineering Group Co. ,Ltd.	市北区 Shibei District	A101
37	青岛建祥建设集团有限公司	Qingdao Jianxiang Construction Group Co. , Ltd.	胶州市 Jiaozhou	A201
38	青岛海德路桥工程股份有限公司	Qingdao Haide Highway & Bridge Engineering Co. ,Ltd.	市南区 Shinan	A210
39	山东电建铁军电力工程有限公司	Shandong Tiejun Electric Power Engineering Co. ,Ltd.	崂山区 Laoshan	B148
40	青岛星火建筑工程有限公司	Qingdao Xinghuo Construction Engineering Co. ,Ltd.	黄岛区 Huangdao District	A101
41	青岛市市政工程集团有限公司	Qingdao Municipal Engineering Co. ,Ltd.	市南区 Shinan	A110
42	青岛金沙滩建设集团有限公司	Qingdao Jinsha Beach Construction Co. , Ltd.	黄岛区 Huangdao District	A101
43	青岛环海工程贸易发展有限公司	Qingdao Huanhai Engineering Trade Development Co. ,Ltd.	市北区 Shibei District	A201
44	青岛和瑞城市建设集团有限公司	Qingdao Herui City Construction Group Co. ,Ltd.	崂山区 Laoshan	A101
45	青岛恒生源集团建设有限公司	Qingdao Hengshengyuan Construction Engineering Co. ,Ltd.	即墨市 Jimo	A101
46	青岛地矿岩土工程有限公司	Qingdao Mine Engineering Co. ,Ltd.	市南区 Shinan	B101
47	青岛胶州湾建设集团有限公司	Qingdao Jiaozhouwan Construction Group Co. ,Ltd.	胶州市 Jiaozhou	A101
48	青岛望城三宝建设有限公司	Qingdao Wangcheng Sanbao Construction Co. ,Ltd.	莱西市 Laixi	A101
49	青岛九龙建设集团有限公司	Qingdao Jiulong Construction Co. ,Ltd.	胶州市 Jiaozhou	A201
50	青岛市黄岛区园林绿化工程有限公司	Qingdao Huangdao Green Enginnering Co. , Ltd.	黄岛区 Huangdao District	B101
51	青岛阳光东辉建设集团有限公司	Qingdao Yangguang Donghui Construction Group Co. ,Ltd.	胶州市 Jiaozhou	A201
52	山东巴龙建设集团有限公司	Shandong Ballon Construction Group Co. , Ltd.	市南区 Shinan	A201
53	青岛即建建设集团有限公司	Qingdao Jijian Construction Group Co. , Ltd.	即墨市 Jimo	A101
54	山东红建建安集团公司	Shandong Hongjian Construction and Installation Co. ,Ltd.	黄岛区 Huangdao District	A201
55	青岛营上建设集团有限公司	Qingdao Yingshang Construction Co. ,Ltd.	即墨市 Jimo	A101
56	青岛环城建工集团有限公司	Qingdao Huancheng Construction Engineering Group Co. ,Ltd.	黄岛区 Huangdao District	A201
57	青岛三林建筑工程有限公司	Qingdao Sanlin Construction Engineering Co. ,Ltd.	黄岛区 Huangdao District	A201
58	青岛通力建设集团有限公司	Qingdao Tongli Construction Group Co. , Ltd.	市南区 Shinan	A101
59	青岛多元建设集团有限公司	Qingdao Duoyuan Construction Group Co. , Ltd.	黄岛区 Huangdao District	A210
60	青岛爱华工程有限公司	Qingdao Aihua Engineering Co. ,Ltd.	市北区 Shibei District	A201
61	青岛福海洋建设集团有限公司	Qingdao Fuhaiyuang Construction Co. ,ltd.	胶州市 Jiaozhou	A201
62	青岛新世纪路桥工程有限公司	Qingdao New Century Highway & Bridge Engineering Co. ,Ltd.	即墨市 Jimo	A202
63	青岛颐金建筑装饰工程有限公司	Qingdao Yijin Construction and Installation Co. , Ltd.	市南区 Shinan	B103
64	青岛高新建筑安装工程有限公司	Qingdao Gaoxin Construction and Installation Co. ,Ltd.	崂山区 Laoshan	A101
65	青岛营海建设集团有限公司	Qingdao Civil Engineering Group Co. ,Ltd.	胶州市 Jiaozhou	A101
66	青岛恒源送变电工程有限公司	Qingdao Hengyuan Transmission and Distribution Project Co. ,Ltd.	城阳区 Chengyang	A201

13 -5 续表2
continued

序号 Precedence	企业单位名称	Name	所在地区 Location	资质等级 Qualification Criteria
67	青岛胶东建设集团有限公司	Qingdao Jiaodong Construction Co. ,Ltd.	胶州市 Jiaozhou	A101
68	青岛施运机械施工有限责任公司	Qingdao Shiyun Mechanized Construction Co. ,Ltd.	市北区 Shibei District	B101
69	青岛田横建筑工程有限公司	Qingdao Tianheng Construction Project Co. ,Ltd.	即墨市 Jimo	A201
70	青岛青房建安集团有限公司	Qingdao Qingfang Construction and Installation Co. ,Ltd.	市南区 Shinan	A101
71	青岛新城发展建筑工程有限公司	Qingdao New City Development Construction Engineering Co. ,Ltd.	市北区 Shibei District	A201
72	平度市金泰建筑有限公司	Pingdu Jintai Construction Engineering Co. ,Ltd.	平度市 Pingdu	A201
73	青岛建设集团建兴工程有限公司	Qingdao Construction Group Jianxing Engineering Co. ,Ltd.	市南区 Shinan	A201
74	胶南市建筑工程公司	Jiaonan Construction Engineering Co. ,Ltd.	黄岛区 Huangdao District	A101
75	山东国建工程集团有限公司	Shandong Guojian Construction Project Co. ,Ltd.	崂山区 Laoshan	B201
76	青岛润佳建筑工程有限公司	Qingdao Runjia Construction Project Co. , Ltd.	即墨市 Jimo	A201
77	青岛市神州建筑工程有限公司	Qingdao Shenzhou Construction Engineering Co. ,Ltd.	胶州市 Jiaozhou	A201
78	青岛经济技术开发区建筑安装工程总公司	Qingdao Development Zone Construction and Installation Co. ,Ltd.	黄岛区 Huangdao District	A201
79	青岛沙建建设集团有限公司	Qingdao Shajian Construction Group Co. , Ltd.	崂山区 Laoshan	A201
80	青岛市一宅建筑集团股份有限公司	Qingdao Yizhai Construction Co. ,Ltd.	市北区 Shibei District	A101
81	青岛铁路工程建筑有限公司	Qingdao Railway Engineering Co. ,Ltd.	市南区 Shinan	A203
82	青岛东捷建设工程有限公司	Qingdao Dongjie Construction Engineering Co. ,Ltd.	市北区 Shibei District	A101
83	青岛华山广泰建筑工程有限公司	Qingdao Huanshan Guangtai Construction Engineering Co. ,Ltd.	即墨市 Jimo	A301
84	青岛腾达建筑工程有限公司	Qingdao Tengda Construction Engineering Co. ,Ltd.	即墨市 Jimo	A201
85	青岛建国工程集团有限公司	Qingdao Jianguo Engineering Co. ,Ltd.	黄岛区 Huangdao District	A201
86	青岛市益水工程股份有限公司	Qingdao Yishui Engineering Co. ,Ltd.	市南区 Shinan	A210
87	青岛城阳兴源建筑工程有限公司	Qingdao Chengyang Xingyuan Construction Engineering Co. Ltd.	城阳区 Chengyang	A301
88	青岛亿佰建工集团有限公司	Qingdao Yibai Construction Engineering Co. ,Ltd.	黄岛区 Huangdao District	A201
89	山东省路通工程集团有限公司	Shandong Lutong Engineering Group Co. , Ltd.	崂山区 Laoshan	A102
90	青岛昶德建设集团有限公司	Qingdao Changde Construction Co. ,Ltd.	胶州市 Jiaozhou	A101
91	青岛市华鲁公路工程有限公司	Qingdao Hualu Highway Engineering Co. , Ltd.	黄岛区 Huangdao District	A202
92	青岛天一建设集团有限公司	Qingdao Tianyi Construction Group Co. , Ltd.	黄岛区 Huangdao District	A201
93	青岛金星科技工程有限公司	Qingdao Jinxing Science and Technology Enginnering Co. ,Ltd.	市南区 Shinan	B111
94	山东省即墨市第二建筑工程公司	Shandong Jimo Second Construction Engineering Company	即墨市 Jimo	A201
95	青岛高科技工业园市政有限公司	Qingdao High-tech Industrial Park Municipal Co. ,Ltd.	崂山区 Laoshan	A210
96	青岛胶州南关建安股份有限公司	Qingdao Jiaonan Nanguan Construction and Installation Co. ,Ltd.	胶州市 Jiaozhou	A201
97	青岛铁路红宇建设集团有限公司	Qingdao Railway Hongyu Construction Group Co. ,Ltd.	市南区 Shinan	A301
98	青岛华天建设集团有限公司	Qingdao Huatian Construction Group Co. , Ltd.	胶州市 Jiaozhou	A201
99	青岛隆昌达建筑安装有限公司	Qingdao Longchangda Construction and Installation Co. ,Ltd.	胶州市 Jiaozhou	A101

13 -5 续表 3
continued

序号 Precedence	企业单位名称	Name	所在地区 Location	资质等级 Qualification Criteria
100	青岛方圆达建设集团有限公司	Qingdao Fangyuanda Construction Group Co. ,Ltd.	李沧区 Licang	A201
101	青岛圣达电力服务中心	Qingdao Shengda Electrical Engineering Co. ,Ltd.	平度市 Pingdu	A306
102	胶州市众兴建筑安装有限公司	Jiaozhou Zhongxing Construction and Installation Co. Ltd.	胶州市 Jiaozhou	A301
103	青岛洋河建设集团有限公司	Qingdao Yanghe Construction Group Co. , Ltd.	胶州市 Jiaozhou	A201
104	青岛鸿润建设集团有限公司	Qingdao Hongrun Construction Group Co. , Ltd.	黄岛区 Huangdao District	A201
105	青岛胶南万德建筑工程有限公司	Qingdao Jiaonan Wande Construction Engineering Co. ,Ltd.	黄岛区 Huangdao District	A301
106	青岛市胶州水利工程有限公司	Qingdao Jiaozhou Water Engineering Co. , Ltd.	胶州市 Jiaozhou	A205
107	青岛枫和建设工程有限公司	Qingdao Fenghe Construction Engineering Co. ,Ltd.	市南区 Shinan	A310
108	青岛泰能工程股份有限公司	Qingdao Taineng Engineering Co. ,Ltd.	市北区 Shibei District	A210
109	青岛市自来水物资工程公司	Qingdao Tap Water Project Co. ,Ltd.	市北区 Shibei District	A310
110	青岛伟信建设工程有限公司	Qingdao Weixin Construction Engineering Co. ,Ltd.	平度市 Pingdu	A201
111	青岛康太源建设集团有限公司	Qingdao Kangtaiyuan Construction Group Co. ,Ltd.	李沧区 Licang	A101
112	青岛万福建筑工程有限公司	Qingdao Wanfu Construction Engineering Co. Ltd.	莱西市 Laixi	A301
113	青岛金坤建筑有限公司	Qingdao Jinkun Construction Co. ,Ltd.	平度市 Pingdu	A201
114	青岛市崂山区古建建筑工程有限公司	Qingdao Laoshan Gujian Construction Engineering Co. ,Ltd.	崂山区 Laoshan	A201
115	青岛平度市市政工程有限公司	Qingdao Pingdu Municipal Enginnering Co. ,Ltd.	平度市 Pingdu	A210
116	青岛和众建筑有限公司	Qingdao Hezhong Construction Co. Ltd.	即墨市 Jimo	A301
117	青岛宏远建筑工程有限公司	Qingdao Hongyuan Construction Engineering Co. ,Ltd.	莱西市 Laixi	A201
118	青岛岳海建设集团有限公司	Qingdao Yuehai Construction Group Co. , Ltd.	市南区 Shinan	A101
119	青岛嘉和建造有限公司	Qingdao Jiahe Construcion Co. ,Ltd.	即墨市 Jimo	A201
120	青岛汉河电气工程有限公司	Qingdao Hanhe Electrical Engineering Co. , Ltd.	崂山区 Laoshan	B349
121	青岛石化检修安装工程有限责任公司	Qingdao Petrochemical Repair and Installation Co. ,Ltd.	李沧区 Licang	A209
122	青岛飞宇建设集团有限公司	Qingdao Feiyu Construction Engineering Co. ,Ltd.	黄岛区 Huangdao District	A301
123	青岛天润工程有限公司	Qingdao Tianrun Enginnering Co. ,Ltd.	莱西市 Laixi	A305
124	青岛琅琊建筑有限公司	Qingdao Langyatai Construction Engineering Co. ,Ltd.	黄岛区 Huangdao District	A201
125	青岛吉安工程有限公司	Qingdao Jian Engineering Co. ,Ltd.	莱西市 Laixi	A205
126	青岛政益达实业有限公司	Qingdao Zhengyida Industrial Co. ,Ltd.	市北区 Shibei District	A210
127	青岛兴水实业有限公司	Qingdao Xingshui Industry Co. ,Ltd.	市北区 Shibei District	A210
128	青岛中奥体育专用地板有限公司	Qingdao Zhongao Sport Wooden Floor Co. , Ltd.	平度市 Pingdu	B159
129	青岛永威建筑集团有限公司	Qingdao Yongwei Construction Group Co. Ltd.	胶州市 Jiaozhou	A301
130	青岛一建集团建设有限公司	Yonghe Enginnering Company of Qingdao Yijian Group Co. ,Ltd.	李沧区 Licang	A201
131	青岛利民建筑安装有限公司	Qingdao Limin Construction and Installation Co. Ltd.	李沧区 Licang	A301
132	即墨市地质基础工程公司	Jimo Geological Foundation Engineering Corporation	即墨市 Jimo	A205

13-5 续表4
continued

序号 Precedence	企业单位名称	Name	所在地区 Location		资质等级 Qualification Criteria
133	青岛龙泰建设集团有限公司	Qingdao Longtai Construction Engineering Co., Ltd.	胶州市	Jiaozhou	A201
134	青岛四机建筑安装有限公司	Qingdao Siji Construction and Installation Co., Ltd.	市北区	Shibei District	B201
135	青岛市城阳区建设工程有限公司	Qingdao Chengyang Construction Engineering Co. Ltd.	城阳区	Chengyang	A301
136	青岛正东建设集团有限公司	Qingdao Zhengdong Construction Group Co. Ltd.	黄岛区	Huangdao District	A204
137	山东森泰源建设工程有限公司	Shandong Sentaiyuan Construction Engineering Co., Ltd.	黄岛区	Huangdao District	A210
138	青岛莱西九联建筑工程有限公司	Qingdao Laixi Jiulian Construction Project Co., Ltd.	莱西市	Laixi	A201
139	青岛万怡东方建设集团有限公司	Qingdao Wanyi Dongfang Construction Group Co., Ltd.	黄岛区	Huangdao District	A101
140	青岛城阳城建集团有限公司	Qingdao Chengyang Urban Construction Group Co., Ltd.	城阳区	Chengyang	A201
141	青岛市城阳区上马建筑工程有限公司	Qingdao Chengyang Shangma Construction Co., Ltd.	城阳区	Chengyang	A201
142	青岛九鼎峰建设集团有限公司	Qingdao Jiudingfeng Construction Co., Ltd.	黄岛区	Huangdao District	A201
143	青岛东部电气工程有限公司	Qingdao Eastern Electrical Engineering Co., Ltd.	崂山区	Laoshan	B349
144	青岛金楷装饰工程有限公司	Qingdao Jinkai Decoration Engineering Co. Ltd.	市北区	Shibei District	B202
145	青岛华恒建设工程有限公司	Qingdao Huaheng Construction Engineering Co. Ltd.	黄岛区	Huangdao District	B201
146	青岛市城阳区朝阳建筑工程有限公司	Qingdao Chengyang Chaoyang Construction Engineering Co., Ltd.	城阳区	Chengyang	A301
147	青岛福盛建设集团有限公司	Qingdao Fusheng Construction Group Co., Ltd.	城阳区	Chengyang	A101
148	青岛光大集团工程有限公司	Qingdao Guangda Group Co., Ltd.	黄岛区	Huangdao District	A201
149	青岛市红岛建筑工程有限公司	Qingdao Hongdao Construction Engineering Co., Ltd.	红岛经济区	Qingdao National High-tech Industrial Development Zone	A201
150	青岛北城建设工程有限公司	Qingdao Beicheng Construction Engineering Co., Ltd.	黄岛区	Huangdao District	A201
151	青岛江河水利工程有限公司	Qingdao Jianghe Water Project Co., Ltd.	平度市	Pingdu	A205
152	青岛红塔建筑工程有限公司	Qingdao Hongta Construction Engineering Co., Ltd.	黄岛区	Huangdao District	A201
153	青岛宝利建设有限公司	Qingdao Baoli Construction Co., Ltd.	莱西市	Laixi	A201
154	即墨市水利建筑安装工程公司	Jimo Water Construction and Installation Engineering Corp.	即墨市	Jimo	A205
155	青岛凯顺建设集团有限公司	Qingdao Kaishun Construction Group Co., Ltd.	胶州市	Jiaozhou	A201
156	平度市东苑建筑工程有限公司	Pingdu Dongyuan Construction Engineering Co., Ltd.	平度市	Pingdu	A201
157	青岛柳源鑫瑞市政园林建设集团有限公司	Qingdao Liuyuan Xinrui Municipal Green Construction Co., Ltd.	黄岛区	Huangdao District	A210
158	青岛胜利兄弟建筑有限公司	Qingdao Shangli Brothers Construction Co., Ltd.	胶州市	Jiaozhou	B114
159	山东远程建筑安装工程有限公司	Shandong Yuancheng Construction and Installation Engineering Co., Ltd.	城阳区	Chengyang	A201
160	胶南市张家楼建筑公司	Jiaonan Zhangjialou Construction Company	黄岛区	Huangdao District	A301
161	青岛新奥燃气设施开发有限公司	Qingdao ENN Gas Facilities Development Co., Ltd.	黄岛区	Huangdao District	B225
162	青岛城阳建筑有限责任公司	Qingdao Chengyang Construction Co. Ltd.	城阳区	Chengyang	A201
163	青岛平运路桥工程有限公司	Qingdao Pingyun Road & Bridge Project Co., Ltd.	平度市	Pingdu	A202
164	青岛坤源建筑工程有限公司	Qingdao Kunyuan Construction Engineering Co. Ltd.	即墨市	Jimo	A301
165	青岛市李沧区东李建筑工程有限公司	Qingdao Licang Dongli Construction Project Co., Ltd.	李沧区	Licang	A201

13 –5 续表 5
continued

序号 Precedence	企业单位名称	Name	所在地区 Location	资质等级 Qualification Criteria
166	青岛阳光电器工程有限公司	Qingdao Sunshine Electro-engineering Co. , Ltd.	市南区 Shinan	B111
167	青岛新凯达市政工程有限公司	Qingdao Xinkaida Municipal Engineering Co. Ltd.	市北区 Shibei District	A210
168	青岛水建集团有限公司	Qingdao Shuijian Group Co. ,Ltd.	胶州市 Jiaozhou	A205
169	青岛市房产工程公司	Qingdao Real Estate Enginnering Co. ,Ltd.	市南区 Shinan	B303
170	青岛鑫鸿泰建设工程有限公司	Qingdao Hongxintai Construction Engineering Co. ,Ltd.	胶州市 Jiaozhou	A201
171	青岛泰佳建筑工程有限公司	Qingdao Taijia Construction Engineering Co. Ltd.	胶州市 Jiaozhou	A201
172	青岛鲁赫建筑装饰有限公司	Qingdao Luhe Construction Decoration Co. Ltd.	市南区 Shinan	B203
173	青岛静力工程有限公司	Qingdao Static Project Co. ,Ltd.	市南区 Shinan	B301
174	青岛易通建安有限公司	Qingdao Yitong Construction and Installation Co. ,Ltd.	黄岛区 Huangdao District	A201
175	青岛大昌建筑工程有限公司	Qingdao Dachang Construction Engineering Co. Ltd.	胶州市 Jiaozhou	A201
176	青岛德惠建筑工程有限公司	Qingdao Dehui Construction Engineering Co. Ltd.	即墨市 Jimo	A201
177	青岛泓鑫源建筑安装工程有限公司	Qingdao Hongxinyuan Construction and Installion Project Co. ,Ltd.	胶州市 Jiaozhou	A201
178	青岛润达建设工程有限公司	Qingdao Runda Construction Engineering Co. ,Ltd.	黄岛区 Huangdao District	A210
179	青岛佳源建筑工程有限公司	Qingdao Jiayuan Construction Engineering Co. ,Ltd.	市北区 Shibei District	A201
180	青岛增春建设工程有限公司	Qingdao Zengchun Construction Engineering Co. Ltd.	黄岛区 Huangdao District	A201
181	青岛岩土基础工程公司	Qingdao Geotechnical Foundation Engineering Company	市南区 Shinan	B201
182	青岛泰华集团有限公司	Qingdao Taihua Group Co. ,Ltd.	黄岛区 Huangdao District	A201
183	青岛经济技术开发区天龙建筑安装工程有限公司	Qingdao Development Zone Tianlong Construction and Installion Co. ,Ltd.	黄岛区 Huangdao District	A201
184	青岛一建集团永和工程有限公司	Qingdao Yijian Group Co. ,Ltd.	即墨市 Jimo	A201
185	青岛市沙子口第二建筑工程有限公司	Qingdao Shazikou 2nd Construction Engineering Co. ,Ltd.	崂山区 Laoshan	A301
186	青岛金茂建设工程有限公司	Qingdao Jinmao Construction Engineering Co. ,Ltd.	黄岛区 Huangdao District	A301
187	青岛莱西市锦冠建筑安装工程有限公司	Qingdao Laixi Jinguan Construction & Installation Engineering Co. Ltd.	莱西市 Laixi	A301
188	青岛崂峰市政工程有限公司	Qingdao Laofeng Municipal Engineering Co. ,Ltd.	崂山区 Laoshan	A210
189	青岛捷通市政工程有限公司	Qingdao Jietong Municipal Engineering Co. Ltd.	市南区 Shinan	A310
190	平度市鲁兴建筑工程有限公司	Pingdu Luxing Construction Engineering Co. Ltd.	平度市 Pingdu	A201
191	青岛城阳恒升建筑安装工程有限公司	Qingdao Chengyang Hengsheng Construction and Installation Co. , Ltd.	红岛经济区 Qingdao National High-tech Industrial Development Zone	A201
192	山东省引黄济青青岛建筑安装有限公司	Qingdao Diverting the Yellow River Water to Qingdao Construction and Installion Co. ,Ltd.	胶州市 Jiaozhou	B201
193	青岛暖万家市政工程有限公司	Qingdao Nuanwanjia Municipal Engineering Co. , Ltd.	黄岛区 Huangdao District	A210
194	青岛金原建筑工程有限公司	Qingdao Jinyuan Construction Co. ,Ltd.	黄岛区 Huangdao District	A201
195	青岛市李沧建筑安装工程有限公司	Qingdao Licang Construction and Decoration Engineering Co. ,Ltd.	李沧区 Licang	A201
196	青岛华联装饰工程有限公司	Qingdao Hualian Decoration Engineering Co. , Ltd.	市北区 Shibei District	B203
197	青岛平度江北建筑工程有限公司	Qingdao Pingdu Jiangbei Construction Engineering Co. ,Ltd.	平度市 Pingdu	A201
198	青岛晶城设计装饰工程有限公司	Qingdao Jingcheng Design and Decoration Enginnering Co. ,Ltd.	市南区 Shinan	B103
199	平度市兴业建筑有限公司	Pingdu Xingye Construction Co. Ltd.	平度市 Pingdu	A301
200	青岛新业建筑工程有限公司	Qingdao Xinye Construction Engineering Co. ,Ltd.	李沧区 Licang	A301

主要统计指标解释

建筑业统计单位 指从事房屋、构筑物建造和设备安装活动的法人企业。建筑业法人企业应具有建筑业资质并能够独立核算,同时其应具备以下条件:①依法成立,有自己的名称、组织机构和场所,能够承担民事责任;②独立拥有和使用资产,承担负债,有权与其他单位签订合同;③独立核算盈亏,能够编制资产负债表。

建筑业总产值 是以货币形式表现的建筑业企业在一定时期内生产的建筑业产品和提供的服务的总和。建筑业总产值包括:

(1)建筑工程产值:指列入建筑工程预算内的各种工程价值。

(2)安装工程产值:指设备安装工程价值,不包括被安装设备本身的价值。

(3)其他产值:建筑业总产值中除建筑工程、安装工程以外的产值。包括房屋构筑物修理产值、非标准设备制造产值、总包企业向分包企业收取的管理费以及不能明确划分的施工活动所完成的产值。

建筑业增加值 指建筑业企业在报告期内以货币形式表现的建筑业生产经营活动的最终成果。建筑业增加值 = 劳动者报酬 + 生产税净额 + 本年折旧 + 营业盈余

Explanatory Notes on Main Statistical Indicators

Statistical Unit in Construction refers to corporate enterprise engaged in the construction of buildings and structures and in the installation of equipment. A corporate construction enterprise should have qualification certificates with independent accounting system, and should meet the following 3 requirements: a) being set up in line with relevant legal basis, having its full name, organization and location, and capable of taking civil liabilities; b) independently possessing and using its assets and assuming its liabilities, and entitled to sign contracts with other institutions; and c) making independent accounts of its profits and losses, and capable of compiling its own balance sheet.

Gross Output Value of Construction refers to total of construction products and services, expressed in money terms, produced or rendered by construction and installation enterprises during a given period of time. It includes:

(1) Output value of construction projects, that is the value of projects covered by the project budgets;

(2) Output value of installation projects, that is the value of the installation of equipment, (excluding the value of the equipment to be installed);

(3) Output value of others, that is the output value of construction industry excluding that of construction projects and installation projects. It includes: output value of repair of buildings and structures; output value of non-standard equipment manufacturing; overhead expenses received by contracted enterprises to the sub-contracted enterprises and the completed output value of construction activities that have no clear definition.

Value-added of Construction refers to the final result of the activities of production and management of construction industry in monetary terms in the reference period.

Value-added of construction = Compensation of Employees + Net Taxes on Production + Depreciation of Fixed Assets + Operating Surplus

14

运输、邮电
TRANSPORT, POSTAL AND TELECOMMUNICATION SERVICES

简要说明

一、本篇资料的主要内容

本篇资料主要反映了全市交通运输业和邮电业通讯业发展的基本情况，主要包括客货运输及港口吞吐量、民用汽车拥有量、独立核算运输邮电单位主要财务指标、邮电通讯基本情况等方面的内容。

二、本篇资料的来源

1、本篇资料中交通运输资料来源于全市交通运输业统计年报。

2、邮电通讯业资料来源于邮电通讯基本情况统计年报。

3、民用汽车拥有量资料来源于青岛市公安局交警支队车辆管理所。

本篇资料由市统计局服务业处整理提供。

Brief Introduction

I. Main Content

Data in this chapter show the basic conditions of the development of transport, post and telecommunications in Shandong Province, mainly including the freight traffic and passenger traffic, cargo handled at port, possession of civil motor vehicles, major financial indices and basic conditions of transport, postal and telecommunication services.

II. Source of Data

(1)Data on transport are based on the annual report of transport.

(2)Data on postal and telecommunication are based on the annual report of postal and telecommunication.

(3)Data on possession of civil motor vehicles are provided by Traffic Police Office of Vehicle Management of Qingdao Municipal Bureau of Public Security.

Data in this chapter are prepared and provide by the Division of Service Statistics of Qingdao Municipal Bureau of Statistics.

14－1 主要年份客货运输及港口吞吐量

MAJOR YEAR'S PASSENGER & FREIGHT TRAFFIC AND HANDLING CAPACITY OF THE PORTS

年份 Year	客运量(万人) Passenger Traffic(10000 persons)				货运量(万吨) Freight Traffic(10000 tons)				港口吞吐量(万吨) Cargo Handled at Ports (10000 tons)	集装箱吞吐量(万标箱) Containers (10000 TEU)
	铁路 Railways	公路 Highways	海运 Waterways	航空 Civil Aviation	铁路 Railways	公路 Highways	海运 Waterways	航空 Civil Aviation		
1949	327	14	9		386	162	22		73	
1952	571	49	13		447	399	44		181	
1957	1 054	149	13		747	548	118		269	
1962	3 100	141	39		909	524	97		391	
1965	1 424	230	19		1 257	690	158		524	
1970	1 329	373	20		1 856	736	232		695	
1975	1 803	159	30		2 325	817	282		1 542	
1978	1 986	274	49		2 917	1 561	528		2 081	
1980	1 896	713	73		2 596	1 642	941		1 779	
1985	2 063	1 894	86	1.0	3 009	2 303	919	0.03	2 610	
1987	2 019	2 133	159	7.0	3 288	4 948	1 085	0.04	3 070	
1988	2 083	3 300	234	8.8	3 418	6 486	1 160	0.04	3 153	
1989	1 802	3 441	308	11.3	3 717	8 926	1 450	0.10	3 145	
1990	1 488	3 639	316	14.1	3 741	6 433	1 556	0.20	3 068	
1991	1 453	4 144	366	19.0	3 774	6 896	1 789	0.31	3 194	
1992	1 488	4 965	437	27.0	3 899	6 822	1 981	0.45	3 240	
1993	1 499	6 436	499	35.3	4 044	7 685	1 910	0.64	3 650	
1994	1 564	6 787		47.0	4 112	8 336	1 804		4 331	
1995	1 480	9 785		66.6	4 205	11 788	2 185		5 165	
1996	1 230	10 738		79.9	4 415	10 749	474		6 056	81.1
1997	1 308	11 855			4 466	11 232	544		6 944	103.3
1998	1 549	11 754			4 028	14 311	1 792	1.44	7 044	121.3
1999	1 674	12 103			3 919	14 550	1 926	1.96	7 282	154.3
2000	1 780	12 145		124.1	4 256	17 234	2 998	2.30	8 661	212.0
2001	1 678	13 686		143.0	4 778	20 906	3 432	2.40	10 423	264.0
2002	1 530	14 516	777	163.7	5 079	24 480	2 530	3.00	12 252	341.0
2003	1 366	13 132	786	174.7	4 929	27 241	2 773	3.60	14 135	424.0
2004	1 496	16 420	862	241.9	5 119	29 937	3 503	5.30	16 303	514.0
2005	552	17 212	972	280.9	2 299	31 009	4 471	4.60	18 727	630.7
2006	810	17 752	999	320.2	2 790	32 047	4 768	5.10	22 438	770.0
2007	1 101	18 800	1 080	733.8	2 781	33 336	4 019	5.90	26 507	946.6
2008	1 278	19 909	1 055	755.8	3 225	34 172	5 080	7.20	30 029	1 037.7
2009	1 425	19 612	1 145	881.8	3 772	16 297	4 332	7.19	31 668	1 027.6
2010	1 537	20 460	1 302	1 010.9	5 031	17 525	4 407	8.44	35 012	1 201.0
2011	1 693	21 560	791	1 074.8	5 697	19 208	4 220	8.93	37 971	1 302.0
2012	1 881	22 724	414	1 173.1	6 126	21 312	1 791	9.06	41 465	1 450.0
2013	2 056	23 588	333	1 572.4	6 266	23 270	1 313	9.31	45 782	1 552.0
2014	2 301	5 588	324	1 641.2	5 564	19 043	1 434	10.22	47 701	1 658.0

注:2014 年交通部调整公路客、货运统计口径,数据不可直接比。

Note: In 2014, the Ministry of Transportation made an adjustment to the statistical gauge for highway passenger and freight transportation and the data are not comparable directly.

14-2 民用车辆拥有量(2014年底)
POSSESSION OF CIVIL MOTOR VEHICLES(END OF 2014)

单位:辆(unit)

项 目	Item	合计 Total 辆数 Number	#个人 of which: Private Vehicles 辆数 Number
一、汽车	**Automobile**	**1 722 889**	**1 448 160**
1. 载客汽车	Passenger Vehicles	1 531 492	1 352 794
其中:轿车	of which:Sedan	983 234	891 715
2. 载货汽车	Trucks	177 931	87 383
3. 其他汽车	Other Automobile	13 466	7 983
二、电车	**Tram**	**63**	
三、摩托车	**Motorcycle**	**292 329**	**290 331**
四、农用运输车	**Agricultural Camion**		
五、挂车	**Trailer Trucks**	**18 469**	**412**
六、其他类型车	**Other Vehicles**	**215**	**14**

补充资料:机动车驾驶员(人)Motor drivers(person) 2 565 952

其中:汽车驾驶员(人)of which:Automobile drivers(person) 2 491 567

14－3 客货运输及港口吞吐量(2014 年)

PASSENGER & FREIGHT TRAFFIC AND HANDLING CAPACITY OF THE PORTS(2014)

项　目	Item	货运量(万吨) Freight Traffic (10000 tons)	货物周转量(亿吨公里) Freight Ton-kilometers(100 million tons·km)	客运量(万人) Passenger Traffic (10000 persons)	旅客周转量(亿人公里) Passenger-Kilometers(100 million person-km)	旅客吞吐量(万人) Volume of Passenger Handled (10000 persons)	货物吞吐量(万吨) Volume of Freight Handled (10000 tons)	集装箱(万标箱) Containers (10000 TEU)
总　计	**Total**	**26 040.74**	**1 037.85**	**8 213.11**	**145.48**	**1 653.50**	**47 721.92**	**1 658**
铁路	Railways	5 564.2	169.15	2301.2	70.19			
公路	Highways	19 043	441.7	5 588	74.95			
水运	Waterways	1 433.54	427	323.91	0.34			
机场	Civil Aviation					1 641.18	20.44	
港口	Ports					12.32	47 701.48	1 658

14－4 独立核算运输邮电单位主要财务指标(2014 年)

MAIN FINANCIAL INDICATORS OF INDEPENDENT ACCOUNTING UNITS OF TRANSPORT, POSTAL AND TELECOMMUNICATION SERVICES(2014)

单位:万元(10 000 yuan)

项目	Item	主营业务收入 Revenue from principal Business	主营业务成本 Cost of principal Business	营业利润 Operating Profits	营业税金及附加 Operating Taxes and Extra Charges	利润总额 Total Profits
总　计	**Total**	**4 786 185.7**	**3 585 780.5**	**607 849.8**	**58 471.5**	**821 989**
铁路	Railways					
公路	Highways	972 975.4	954 863.6	-171 594.6	9 522.3	-39 080.5
水运	Waterways	319 263.1	234 742.3	69 749.1	11 395	91 254.1
航空	Civil Aviation	111 778.5	79 815.8	25 669.3	2 639.5	24 809.9
港口	Ports	2 305 452.3	1 799 621.9	366 818	16 950	429 340
邮政	Postal Services	87 840.5	79 135.1	1 543.7	705.2	1 647.1
电信	Telecommunication Services	988 875.9	437 601.8	315 664.3	17 259.5	314 018.4

14 -5 邮电通讯基本情况(2014 年)
BASIC CONDITIONS OF POSTAL AND TELECOMMUNICATION SERVICES(2014)

市、区名称	Region	邮电局(处) Post Office (unit)	#提供邮政全功能服务的 of which:Providing Omni-directional Services	邮路总长度(公里) Length of Postal Routes(km)	邮运汽车(辆) Vehicles for Postal Services(unit)	信筒、信箱(个) Post Boxes (unit)
总 计	**Total**	**645**	**217**	**5 153**	**294**	**755**
#市内三区	The Three Districts of Qingdao City	131	33	2 605	127	286
崂山区	Laoshan District	34	8	127	21	56
黄岛区	Huangdao District	109	31	668	40	92
即墨市	Jimo	96	34	522	31	75
胶州市	Jiaozhou	70	29	295	27	63
平度市	Pingdu	124	50	636	26	127
莱西市	Laixi	70	25	300	22	56

14 -5 续表 1
continued

市、区名称	Region	固定电话市话交换机容量(门) Capacity of Urban Fixed Telephone Exchanges(line)	固定电话市话用户数(户) Urban Fixed Telephone Subscribers (subscriber)	固定电话农村交换机容量(门) Capacity of Rural Fixed Telephone Exchanges(line)	固定电话农村用户数(户) Rural Fixed Telephone Subscribers (subscriber)	移动电话交换机容量(户) Capacity of Mobile Telephone Exchanges (subscriber)	年末移动电话用户(户) Mobile Telephone Subscribersat Year-end (subscriber)
总　计	**Total**	**3 086 269**	**1 383 822**	**875 736**	**640 262**	**26 160 000**	**13 010 845**
#市内三区	The Three Districts of Qingdao City	160 863	884 391		210 306	9 890 000	5 691 178
崂山区	Laoshan District	3 917	119 787	1 112	29 895	1 360 000	839 230
黄岛区	Huangdao District	52 630	151 641	14 934	77 773	3 840 000	1 821 941
即墨市	Jimo	19 958	72 097	5 663	111 092	2 400 000	1 446 056
胶州市	Jiaozhou	22 615	70 158	1 640	50 480	170 000	1 038 615
平度市	Pingdu	10 215	39 532	937	86 325	1 610 000	1 126 472
莱西市	Laixi	13 689	28 827	886	36 391	1 060 000	682 953

14 –5 续表 2
continued

市、区名称	Region	函件(出口)(万件) Number of Letters (10000 pcs)	邮政储蓄期末余额(万元) Balance of Postal Savings at Term-end (10000 yuan)	特快专递(万件) Express Mail Services (10000 pcs)	邮电业务总量(万元 2010 年价) Business Volume of Postal and Telecommunication Services(10000 yuan at 2010 price)	报纸期发份数(万份) Issue of Newspapers (10000 copies)	杂志期发份数(万份) Issue of Magazines (10000 copies)
总　计	**Total**	**7 363.54**	**2 571 227.14**	**60.34**	**2 614 874.81**	**55.64**	**36.76**
#市内三区	The Three Districts of Qingdao City	2 041.56	257 388.22	18.75		17.72	18.53
崂山区	Laoshan District	609.5	108 766.19	7.44		4.63	2.86
黄岛区	Huangdao District	1 410.25	394 275.12	12.1		9.33	3.39
即墨市	Jimo	833.41	558 566.44	6.16		5.95	2.04
胶州市	Jiaozhou	1 121.98	416 529.39	5.95		6.7	2.49
平度市	Pingdu	858.79	618 982.65	5.87		6.96	6.34
莱西市	Laixi	488.05	216 719.13	4.07		4.35	1.11

主要统计指标解释

货(客)运量　指在一定时期内,各运输部门实际运送的货物(旅客)数量。是反映运输业为国民经济和人民生活服务的数量指标,也是制定和检查运输生产计划,研究运输发展规模和速度的重要指标。货运按吨计算,客运按人计算。货物不论运输距离长短,货物类别,均按实际重量统计;旅客不论行程远近或票价多少,均按一人一次作为客运量统计。半价票、小孩票也按一人统计。

货物(旅客)周转量　指在一定时期内,由各种运输工具运送的货物(旅客)数量与其相应运输距离的乘积之总和,是反映运输业生产总成果的重要指标,也是编制和检查运输生产计划,计算运输效益、劳动生产率以及核算运输单位成本的主要基础资料。通常以吨公里和人公里为计算单位。计算货物周转量通常按发出站与到达站之间的最短距离,也就是计费距离计算。

港口货物吞吐量　指经水运进出沿海主要港区范围,并经过装卸的货物数量,包括邮件及办理托运手续的行李、包裹以及补给运输船舶的燃、物料和淡水。货物吞吐量按货物流向分为进口、出口吞吐量,按货物交流性质分为外贸货物吞吐量和国内贸易货物吞吐量。货物吞吐量的货类构成及其流向,是衡量港口生产能力大小的重要指标。

邮电业务总量　指以货币表现的邮电部门用于传递信息和提供其他邮电服务的总数量。它综合反映了一定时期邮电工作的总成果,是研究邮电业务量构成和发展趋势的重要指标。根据邮电管理体制不同,分为中央国营业务总量和地方国营业务总量。它用各种邮电分类业务量,如函件件数、电报份数、长话张数、市内电话和农村电话的年均户数、订销报刊累计份数等,分别乘以相应的平均单位(不变价),加总后再加上出租电路和设备的收入、代用户维护电话交换机和线路等设备的收入、其他业务收入求得。

Explanatory Notes on Main Statistical Indicators

Freight (Passenger) Traffic　refers to the volume of freight (passenger) transported with various means. Freight transport is calculated in tons and passenger traffic is calculated in the number of persons. Despite the type of freight and traveling distance, the freight transport is calculated in the actual weight of the goods; and despite the traveling distance and ticket price, the passenger traffic is calculated by the principle that one person can be counted only once in one travel. The passengers who travel with a half price ticket or a child ticket is also calculated as one person. The freight (passenger) traffic provides a quantitative measure to show how the transport industry serves the national economy and people, and is also an important indicator for planning the transport industry and for studying the development scale and speed of the transport industry.

Freight Ton-kilometers (Passenger-kilometers)　refer to the sum of the products of the volume of transported cargo (passengers) multiplying by the transport distance. It is an important indicator to reflect the achievement of transportation industry. Normally, the shortest distance between the departure station and the destination station (i. e., the payable distance) is the basis to calculate the freight ton-kilometers. This is an important indicator to show the total results of the transport industry, to prepare and examine the transport plan and to measure the efficiency, the labour productivity and the unit cost of transport.

Volume of Freight Handled in Ports　refers to the volume of cargo passing in and out the harbor area of the major coastal ports and having been loaded and unloaded. The volume includes that of the postal matters, registered luggage and fuels, materials and fresh water as supplies of the ships. The volume of freight handled may be classified by direction of flow as freight for import and freight for export, or by nature of cargo as freight for domestic trade and freight for foreign trade. As an important indicator, the volume of freight handled by type of cargo and by main flow direction reflects the production capacity of ports.

Businesss Volume of Postal and Telecommunication Services　refers to the total amount of the information delivered and other post and telecommunication services provided by the post and telecommunication departments for the customers. It is arrived by first multiplying the business volume of different types, such as number of letters, telegrams, long distance calls, city and rural telephone (fixed price) and then adding these products together, plus the income from maintenance of telephone switchboards and lines, and the income from other business operations. The service revenue of posts and telecommunications reflects the total achievements by the post and telecommunication departments during a given period of time in a comprehensive way, and is an important indicator to study the composition and development of the post and telecommunication business.

15 批发和零售业 WHOLESALE AND RETAIL TRADES

简要说明

一、本篇资料的主要内容

本篇资料主要反映了全市批发和零售业经营情况和效益情况，主要包括批发和零售业商品流转及财务情况、批发和零售业网点及从业人员、亿元以上商品交易市场、社会消费品零售总额等内容。

二、本篇资料的来源

本篇资料来源于批发和零售业统计年报和定期报表统计资料；网点资料依据第三次经济普查资料和市工商局提供的个体私营经济注册登记资料测算。由市统计局外经贸易统计处整理提供。

Brief Introduction

I. Main Content

Data in this chapter show the development of wholesale and retail trade of the whole city, mainly including the circulation and financial indices of commodities in the wholesale and retail trade, outlets and employment of wholesale and retail trade, commodity exchange markets over 100 million yuan, Total retail sales of consumer goods, etc.

II. Source of Data

Data in this chapter are based on annual report and regular reports of wholesale and retail trade. Outlet data are based on the information of the third economic census and the individual and private businesses' registration information provided by Qingdao Administration for Industry and Commerce. Data in this chapter are prepared and compiled by the Division of Trade and External Economic Relations Statistics of Qingdao Municipal Bureau of Statistics.

15-1 社会消费品零售总额(1985-2014年)

TOTAL RETAIL SALES OF CONSUMER GOODS(1985-2014)

单位:万元(10 000 yuan)

年份 Year	消费品零售总额 Total Retail Sales of Consumer Goods	批发零售业 Wholesale and Retail Trades	住宿餐饮业 Hotels and Catering Services	其他行业 Others
1985	307 222	231 477	16 996	18 753
1986	364 091	269 418	21 384	27 118
1987	432 569	310 658	23 319	32 617
1988	590 538	434 572	32 304	45 449
1989	619 941	450 812	34 083	56 303
1990	658 264	484 770	35 568	67 863
1991	760 562	566 767	43 320	56 812
1992	888 411	666 911	53 045	67 392
1993	1 384 533	1 031 794	80 077	96 759
1994	1 880 654	1 352 073	127 313	202 937
1995	2 376 776	1 637 349	186 028	305 947
1996	2 708 527	1 873 008	220 322	321 325
1997	3 008 981	2 105 728	241 928	361 248
1998	3 368 736	2 322 209	277 696	411 210
1999	3 762 754	2 715 635	315 307	391 388
2000	4 282 871	3 116 990	387 944	403 854
2001	4 911 735	3 561 731	507 012	433 851
2002	5 574 364	4 162 676	638 358	402 654
2003	6 455 113	5 283 584	849 032	322 497
2004	7 475 022	6 266 750	1 017 193	191 079
2005	8 701 057	7 304 660	1 176 539	219 858
2006	10 163 457	8 458 226	1 443 120	262 111
2007	12 162 246	9 995 772	1 837 754	328 720
2008	14 922 153	12 995 842	1 554 086	372 225
2009	17 302 231	14 232 954	2 549 203	520 074
2010	19 611 331	17 151 504	2 459 827	
2011	23 023 703	20 153 079	2 870 624	
2012	26 356 180	23 043 005	3 313 175	
2013	29 868 133	26 142 405	3 725 728	
2014	33 617 217	29 435 856	4 181 361	

注:1. 自2003年开始消费品零售总额不再包括制造业零售额和农民对非农居民的销售额分组。
2. 自2005年起, 住宿业从其它行业调整到住宿餐饮业中。
3. 根据第二次经济普查结果,对2005年以来的历史数据进行了调整。

Note:1. Since 2003, retail sales of manufacturing and retail sales of rural residents to urban residents are excluded in total retail sales of consumer goods.
2. Since 2005, hotels is adjusted to hotels and catering services from the others.
3. Historical data since 2005 have been adjusted according to results of the Second China Economic Census.

15－2 分市、区社会消费品零售总额(2014 年)
TOTAL RETAIL SALES OF CONSUMER GOODS BY REGION(2014)

单位:万元(10 000 yuan)

市、区名称	Region	消费品零售总额 Total Retail Sales of Consumer Goods	按行业分 Grouped By Sector	
			批发零售业 Wholesale and Retail Trades	住宿餐饮业 Hotels and Catering Services
全　市	**Whole Municipality**	**33 617 217**	**29 435 856**	**4 181 361**
市南区	Shinan District	4 634 692	3 856 840	777 852
市北区	Shibei District	5 996 645	5 374 915	621 730
李沧区	Licang District	2 975 548	2 669 962	305 586
崂山区	Laoshan District	1 747 540	1 609 127	138 413
黄岛区	Huangdao District	4 134 788	3 530 656	604 132
保税港区	Qingdao Free Trade Port Area of China	166 596	163 886	2 710
城阳区	Chengyang District	1 914 072	1 670 186	243 886
即墨市	Jimo	3 466 051	3 156 491	309 560
胶州市	Jiaozhou	2 938 331	2 474 056	464 275
平度市	Pingdu	3 148 288	2 787 952	360 336
莱西市	Laixi	2 388 466	2 052 557	335 909
红岛经济区	Qingdao National High-tech Industrial Development Zone	106 200	89 228	16 972

15－3 限额以上批发和零售业商品购销存总额(2014 年)

TOTAL PURCHASES,SALES AND STOCK OF ENTERPRISES ABOVE DESIGNATED SIZE OF WHOLESALE AND RETAIL TRADES(2014)

单位:万元(10 000 yuan)

项目	Item	商品销售总额 Total Sales Value	#批发总额 Wholesale Value	零售总额 Retail Value	库存总额 Stock
总计	**Total**	**52 377 079**	**41 262 059**	**11 115 020**	**2 787 465**
国有企业	State-owned Enterprises	117 698	72 344	45 355	19 368
集体企业	Collective-owned Enterprises	521 400	490 849	30 551	2 335
其它企业	Other Enterprises	51 737 981	40 698 866	11 039 114	2 765 762
农、林、牧产品批发	Wholesale of Farm Produce and Livestock Products	1 442 534	1 423 550	18 984	53 525
食品、饮料及烟草制品批发	Wholesale of Food, Beverages and Tobaccos	2 964 564	2 892 230	72 334	234 580
纺织、服装及家庭用品批发	Retail of Textiles, Garments and Daily Consumer Articles	7 966 923	7 747 441	219 482	361 717
文化、体育用品及器材批发	Wholesale of Culture, Sports Appliances and Equipments	148 300	141 781	6 519	9 725
医药及医疗器材批发	Wholesale of Medicines and Medical Appliances	1 151 668	1 114 635	37 034	67 333
矿产品、建材及化工产品批发	Wholesale of Mineral Products, Building Materials and Chemical Products	22 298 696	22 153 873	144 823	733 075
机械设备、五金产品及电子产品批发	Wholesale of Machinery, Hardware and Electronic Equipment	2 927 970	2 901 759	26 211	123 664
贸易经纪与代理	Trade Broker and Agency	34 219	34 185	34	784
其它批发业	Other Wholesale not Classified Elsewhere	2 131 757	1 977 181	154 575	83 664
综合零售	Integrated Retail Trade	3 689 879	257 931	3 431 948	253 733
食品、饮料及烟草制品专门零售	Retail of Food, Beverages and Tobaccos	118 204	45 430	72 774	10 385
纺织、服装及日用品专门零售	Retail of Textiles, Garments and Daily Consumer Articles	674 946	127 631	547 314	181 275
文化、体育用品及器材专门零售	Retail of Culture, Sports Appliances and Equipments	176 229	50 639	125 590	52 222
医药及医疗器材专门零售	Retail of Medicines and Medical Appliances	334 297	55 368	278 929	53 088
汽车、摩托车、燃料及零配件专门零售	Retail of Motor Vehicles, Motorcycles, Fuel and Parts	4 877 902	181 342	4 696 559	450 253
家用电器及电子产品专门零售	Retail of Household Electric Appliances and Electronic Products	1 137 019	130 278	1 006 741	102 037
五金、家具及室内装饰材料专门零售	Retail of Hardware, Furniture and Decoration Materials	113 390	23 436	89 954	10 075
货摊、无店铺及其他零售业	Non-shop and Other Retails	188 582	3 369	185 215	6 330

15 -4 限额以上批发和零售业商品分类销售额(2014 年)

SALES VALUE OF ENTERPRISES ABOVE DESIGNATED SIZE OF WHOLESALE AND RETAIL TRADES BY CATEGORY OF COMMODITIES(2014)

单位:万元(10 000 yuan)

项目	Item	销售总额 Total Sales Value	#批发总额 Wholesale Value	零售总额 Retail Value
销售总额	**Total Sales Value**	**55 728 142**	**44 059 020**	**11 669 122**
一、粮油、食品、饮料、烟酒类	Grain & Oil,Food, Beverages, Tobacco and Liquor	4 634 529	3 183 111	1 451 418
#粮油、食品类	Grain & Oil and Food	2 637 383	1 564 317	1 073 066
粮油类	Grain and Oil	660 977	524 838	136 139
肉禽蛋类	Meat, Poultry and Eggs	385 379	171 475	213 904
水产品类	Aquatic Products	131 325	87 838	43 487
蔬果类	Vegetable and Fruit	104 418	61 352	43 066
干鲜果品类	Dried and Fresh Fruit	128 498	64 147	64 352
饮料类	Beverages	216 868	86 160	130 708
烟酒类	Tobacco and Liquor	1 780 279	1 532 634	247 645
二、服装鞋帽、针、纺织品类	Clothing, Shoes, Hats and Textiles	2 889 198	1 463 461	1 425 736
#服装类	Clothing	1 595 585	688 977	906 608
鞋帽类	Shoes and Hats	554 331	113 917	440 414
针、纺织品类	Knitwear and Textiles	739 282	660 567	78 714
三、化妆品类	Cosmetics	286 632	75 360	211 272
四、金银珠宝类	Gold, Silver and Jewellery	362 450	28 644	333 806
五、日用品类	Articles for Daily Use	635 924	286 558	349 366
#洗涤用品类	Washing Articles	94 709	31 125	63 584
儿童玩具类	Children Toys	15 875	138	15 738
六、五金、电料类	Hardware and Electrical Materials	409 551	278 761	130 790
七、体育、娱乐用品类	Sports and Recreation Articles	82 299	24 936	57 363
八、书报杂志类	Newspapers and Magazines	106 890	40 581	66 309
九、电子出版物及音像制品类	E-journals and Video Products	9 125	2 882	6 243
十、家用电器和音像器材类	Household Appliances and Video Appliances	3 838 008	2 689 634	1 148 373
十一、中西药品类	Traditional Chinese and Western Medicines	1 340 577	1 027 111	313 467
#西药类	Western Medicines	1 187 482	924 323	263 159
中草药及中成药类	Traditional Chinese Medicines	126 446	85 894	40 552
十二、文化办公用品类	Cultural and Offices Appliances	425 049	187 451	237 598
十三、家具类	Furniture	49 903	13 747	36 156
十四、通讯器材类	Communication Appliances	356 347	184 925	171 422
十五、煤炭及制品类	Coal and Related Products	4 559 130	4 513 968	45 163
十六、木材及制品类	Wood and Wooden Products	252 984	252 984	
十七、石油及制品类	Petroleum and Related Products	5 103 481	3 346 262	1 757 219
十八、化工材料及制品类	Chemical Materials and Related Products	2 853 214	2 853 214	
#化肥类	Fertilizers	422 520	422 520	
十九、金属材料类	Metal Materials	15 329 794	15 329 794	
二十、建筑及装潢材料类	Building and Decoration Materials	713 836	649 111	64 725
二十一、机电产品及设备类	Mechanical and Electrical Products	2 095 877	2 086 244	9 633
#农机类	Agricultural Machineries	60 519	60 519	
二十二、汽车类	Automobiles	4 446 673	785 453	3 661 219
二十三、种子饲料类	Seeds and Feedstuff	641 501	641 501	
二十四、棉麻类	Cotton, Hemp	255 953	255 953	
二十五、其他类	Others	4 049 217	3 857 374	191 844

注:此表为定期报表数据。

Note:The data are from regular reports.

15-5 限额以上批发业财务状况(2014年)

FINANCIAL POSITION OF ENTERPRISES ABOVE DESIGNATED SIZE OF WHOLESALE TRADE(2014)

单位:万元(10 000 yuan)

指标	Indicator	合计 Total	国有经济 State-owned Enterprises	集体经济 Collective-owned Enterprises	外商及港澳台经济 Foreign Funded Enterprises and Enterprises with Funds from Hong Kong, Macao and Taiwan	其它 Other Enterprises
单位数	**Number of Enterprises**	**1 040**	**6**	**3**	**61**	**970**
年末资产负债	**Year-end Assets-Liability**					
资产总计	Total Assets	17 175 031	64 038	492 369	782 862	15 835 762
流动资产总计	Sub-total of Current Assets	14 713 375	45 455	478 920	560 737	13 628 263
负债合计	Total Liabilities	14 286 812	43 774	486 278	451 507	13 305 253
所有者权益合计	Total Owners' Equities	2 888 219	20 264	6 092	331 355	2 530 509
损益及分配	**Loss, Profits and Distribution**					
主营业务收入	Revenue from Principal Business	37 088 660	73 692	416 386	1 187 321	35 411 261
主营业务成本	Cost of Principal Business	35 175 390	70 386	394 022	1 114 550	33 596 433
主营业务税金及附加	Taxes and Extra Charges on Principal Business	136 701	240	134	1 548	134 778
营业利润	Profits from Principal Business	694 330	-1 413	3 871	10 891	680 981
其他业务利润	Profits from other Business	114 961	1 496		56	113 409
销售费用	Operating Costs	656 497	2 139	210	33 407	620 740
管理费用	Management Expenses	381 075	2 916	15 447	22 203	340 509
财务费用	Financial Expenses	147 491	935	5 575	6 142	134 838
利润总额	Total Profits	531 840	645	3 868	10 941	516 387
经济效益	**Economic Benefit**					
商品经营费用率%	Ratio of Operating Costs to Revenue from Principal Business	1.77	2.90	0.05	2.81	1.75
商品销售利润率%	Ratio of Profit to Sales Revenue	1.43	0.87	0.93	0.92	1.46

15－6 限额以上零售业财务状况(2014 年)

FINANCIAL POSITION OF ENTERPRISES ABOVE DESIGNATED SIZE OF RETAIL TRADE(2014)

单位:万元(10 000 yuan)

指标	Indicator	合计 Total	国有经济 State-owned Enterprises	集体经济 Collective-owned Enterprises	外商及港澳台经济 Foreign Funded Enterprises and Enterprises with Funds from Hong Kong,Macao and Taiwan	其它 Other Enterprises
单位数	**Number of Enterprises**	**639**	**6**	**3**	**37**	**593**
年末资产负债	**Year-end Assets-Liability**					
资产合计	Total Assets	6 018 615	39 782	18 262	791 773	5 168 798
流动资产合计	Sub-total of Current Assets	3 338 612	32 692	16 457	566 553	2 722 910
负债合计	Total Liabilities	3 970 043	32 378	17 672	584 761	3 335 232
所有者权益合计	Total Owners' Equities	2 048 658	7 404	590	207 012	1 833 651
损益及分配	**Loss,Profits and Distribution**					
主营业务收入	Revenue from Principal Business	9 877 945	40 878	31 736	1 365 532	8 439 799
主营业务成本	Cost of Principal Business	8 825 943	36 886	29 213	1 123 139	7 636 705
主营业务税金及附加	Taxes and Extra Charges on Principal Business	39 825	67	26	6 639	33 093
营业利润	Profits from Principal Business	169 781	204	78	9 408	160 091
其他业务利润	Profits from other Business	130 758	315	100	36 710	93 634
销售费用	Operating Costs	539 296	759	755	145 477	392 306
管理费用	Management Expenses	361 147	3 125	1 535	105 920	250 567
财务费用	Financial Expenses	77 539	142	229	6 865	70 303
利润总额	Total Profits	208 019	216	78	12 489	195 236
经济效益	**Economic Benefit**					
商品经营费用率%	Ratio of Operating Costs to Revenue from Principal Business	5.46	1.86	2.38	10.65	4.65
商品销售利润率%	Ratio of Profit to Sales Revenue	2.11	0.53	0.24	0.91	2.31

15－7 分市、区城乡亿元商品交易市场分布情况(2014 年)
BASIC STATISTICS ON COMMODITY EXCHANGE MARKETS OF TRANSACTION VALUE OVER 100 MILLION YUAN BY REGION(2014)

市、区名称	Region	亿元商品交易市场数量(个) Number of Commodity Exchange Markets of Transaction Value over 100 Million Yuan(unit)			亿元商品交易市场成交额(亿元) Turnover of Commodity Exchange Markets of Transaction Value over 100 Million Yuan (100 million yuan)		
		合计 Total	#综合市场 Integrated Markets	#专业市场 Special Markets	合计 Total	#综合市场 Integrated Markets	#专业市场 Special Markets
全市	**Whole Municipality**	**63**	**9**	**54**	**1 215.3**	**234.1**	**981.2**
市南区	Shinan Area						
市北区	Shibei District	13	1	12	120.7	38.0	82.7
李沧区	Licang District	5	1	4	74.0	14.9	59.1
崂山区	Laoshan District	2		2	2.9		2.9
黄岛区	Huangdao District	7	1	6	54.0	5.9	48.1
保税港区	Qingdao Free Trade Port Area of China						
城阳区	Chenyang District	4		4	228.5		228.5
即墨市	Jimo	11	1	10	507.6	113.8	393.8
胶州市	Jiaozhou	8	2	6	127.0	44.4	82.6
平度市	Pingdu	12	3	9	96.6	17.1	79.5
莱西市	Laixi	1		1	4.0		4.0
红岛经济区	Qingdao National High-tech Industrial Development Zone						

15－8 批发和零售业企业网点数(2014 年底)
ENTERPRISES OUTLETS OF WHOLESALE AND RETAIL TRADES(END OF 2014)

单位:个(unit)

市、区名称	Region	合 计 Total	批发业 Wholesale Trade	零售业 Retail Trade
全市	**Whole Municipality**	**87 543**	**72 436**	**15 107**
市南区	Shinan Area	11 439	9 471	1 968
市北区	Shibei District	39 789	36 409	3 380
李沧区	Licang District	4 363	3 347	1 016
崂山区	Laoshan District	3 082	2 165	917
黄岛区	Huangdao District	9 368	6 568	2 800
保税港区	Qingdao Free Trade Port Area of China	10	8	2
城阳区	Chenyang District	5 668	4 598	1 070
即墨市	Jimo	4 568	3 430	1 138
胶州市	Jiaozhou	4 427	3 251	1 176
平度市	Pingdu	2 429	1 627	802
莱西市	Laixi	2 314	1 514	800
红岛经济区	Qingdao National High-tech Industrial Development Zone	86	48	38

15 -9 批发和零售业企业从业人员(2014 年底)

ENTERPRISES EMPLOYMENT OF WHOLESALE AND RETAIL TRADES(END OF 2014)

单位:人(person)

市、区名称	Region	合计 Total	批发业 Wholesale Trade	零售业 Retail Trade
全市	**Whole Municipality**	**651 270**	**555 228**	**96 042**
市南区	Shinan Area	63 033	53 610	9 423
市北区	Shibei District	227 402	212 978	14 424
李沧区	Licang District	30 516	23 373	7 143
崂山区	Laoshan District	18 599	14 718	3 881
黄岛区	Huangdao District	100 396	79 258	21 138
保税港区	Qingdao Free Trade Port Area of China	653	636	17
城阳区	Chenyang District	39 473	34 546	4 927
即墨市	Jimo	55 371	44 230	11 141
胶州市	Jiaozhou	67 403	54 065	13 338
平度市	Pingdu	21 617	16 487	5 130
莱西市	Laixi	26 525	21 123	5 402
红岛经济区	Qingdao National High-tech Industrial Development Zone	282	204	78

15－10 批发和零售业个体网点数(2014 年底)

INDIVIDUAL OUTLETS OF WHOLESALE AND RETAIL TRADES(END OF 2014)

单位:个(unit)

市、区名称	Region	合　计 Total	批发业 Wholesale Trade	零售业 Retail Trade
全市	**Whole Municipality**	**380 885**	**69 724**	**311 161**
市南区	Shinan Area	15 494	567	14 927
市北区	Shibei District	45 954	7 541	38 413
李沧区	Licang District	15 797	1 454	14 343
崂山区	Laoshan District	9 318	757	8 561
黄岛区	Huangdao District	81 042	5 859	75 183
保税港区	Qingdao Free Trade Port Area of China	201	11	190
城阳区	Chenyang District	32 081	4 187	27 894
即墨市	Jimo	55 542	22 378	33 164
胶州市	Jiaozhou	53 223	8 740	44 483
平度市	Pingdu	40 946	10 900	30 046
莱西市	Laixi	30 001	7 280	22 721
红岛经济区	Qingdao National High-tech Industrial Development Zone	1 286	50	1 236

15－11 批发和零售业个体从业人员(2014 年底)

INDIVIDUAL EMPLOYMENT OF WHOLESALE AND RETAIL TRADES(END OF 2014)

单位:人(person)

市、区名称	Region	合计 Total	批发业 Wholesale Trade	零售业 Retail Trade
全市	**Whole Municipality**	**1 191 686**	**244 447**	**947 239**
市南区	Shinan Area	39 103	1 308	37 795
市北区	Shibei District	125 334	22 949	102 385
李沧区	Licang District	51 418	5 161	46 257
崂山区	Laoshan District	20 289	1 887	18 402
黄岛区	Huangdao District	223 470	18 324	205 146
保税港区	Qingdao Free Trade Port Area of China	425	31	394
城阳区	Chenyang District	138 731	19 033	119 698
即墨市	Jimo	206 875	88 577	118 298
胶州市	Jiaozhou	192 159	34 166	157 993
平度市	Pingdu	108 952	30 547	78 405
莱西市	Laixi	82 048	22 285	59 763
红岛经济区	Qingdao National High-tech Industrial Development Zone	2 882	179	2 703

主要统计指标解释

社会消费品零售总额 指各种经济类型的批发和零售业、住宿和餐饮业以及其他行业对城乡居民和社会集团的消费品零售额总和。该指标从2003年开始不再包括制造业零售额和农民对非农居民的零售额。

商品购进总额 指从本企业(单位)以外的单位和个人购进(包括从国外直接进口)作为转卖或加工后转卖的商品。这个指标反映批发零售贸易业从国内、国外市场上购进商品的总量。商品购进总额包括:(1)从工农业生产者购进的商品;(2)从出版社、报社的出版发行部门购进的图书、杂志和报纸;(3)从各种类型的批发零售贸易企业(单位)购进的商品;(4)从其他单位购进的商品,如从机关、团体、企业、单位购进的剩余物资,从餐饮业、服务业购进的商品,从海关、市场管理部门购进的缉私和没收的商品,向居民收购的废旧商品等;(5)从国(境)外直接进口的商品,但不包括企业(单位)为自身经营用和未通过买卖行为而收入的商品以及销售退回、商品损益等。

商品销售总额 指对本企业(单位)以外的单位和个人出售(包括对国(境)外直接出口)的商品。这个指标反映批发零售贸易业在国内市场上销售商品以及出口商品的总量。商品销售总额包括:(1)售给城乡居民和社会集团消费用的商品;(2)售给工业、农业、建筑业、运输邮电业、批发零售贸易业、餐饮业、服务业等作为生产、经营使用的商品;(3)售给批发零售贸易业作为转卖或加工后转卖的商品;(4)对国(境)外直接出口的商品。不包括:出售本企业(单位)自用的废旧包装用品,未通过买卖行为付出的商品,经本单位介绍,由买卖双方直接结算,本单位只收取手续费的业务,购货退出的商品以及商品损耗和损失等。

Explanatory Notes on Main Statistical Indicators

Total Retail Sales of Consumer Goods refers to the sum of retail sales of consumer goods sold by all sectors of the national economy to urban and rural residents and social groups. Sectors of the national economy include wholesale and retail trade, accommodation and catering trade and others. Since 2003, retail sales of manufacture and retail sales of rural residents to urban residents are excluded in total retail sales.

Total Purchases of Commodities refer to the total value of purchases of commodities by the enterprises (establishments) from other establishments or individuals (including direct import from abroad) for the purpose of re-selling, either with or without further processing of the commodities purchased. This indicator is used to show the total value of purchases of commodities by wholesale and retail establishments from domestic and overseas markets. The total purchases include: (1) agricultural and industrial products purchased from producers; (2) books, magazines and newspapers purchased from distribution departments of the publishers; (3) commodities purchased from wholesale and retail establishments of different status of registration; (4) commodities purchased from other units, such as surplus materials purchased from government agencies, enterprises or institutions, commodities purchased from catering and service establishments, confiscated goods purchased from customs authorities or market management agencies, second-hand goods and wastes purchased from residents; and (5) commodities directly imported from abroad. Excluded are commodities purchased by enterprises (establishments) for use in their own business operation, commodities obtained without buying or selling procedures, rejected commodities, etc.

Total Sales of Commodities refer to value of commodities sold by the establishments to other establishments and individuals (including direct export). This indicator is used to show the total value of sales of commodities at domestic markets and export. The total sales include: (1) commodities sold to urban and rural residents and social groups for their consumption; (2) commodities sold to establishments in industry, agriculture, construction, transportation, post and telecommunications, wholesale and retail trades, hotels and catering services, and public utility for their production and operation; (3) commodities sold to wholesale and retail establishments for re-selling, with or without further processing; and (4) commodities for direct export to other countries. Excluded are selling of waste packaging materials used by the establishments (units) themselves, commodities transferred without buying or selling procedures, commission income from brokerage in transactions for which settlement is directly handled by buyers and sellers, rejected commodities in the purchase, loss in commodities, etc.

16 住宿、餐饮业和旅游

HOTELS, CATERING SERVICES AND TOURISM

简要说明

一、本篇资料的主要内容

本篇资料主要反映了全市住宿和餐饮业的经营情况和效益情况以及旅游的基本情况，主要包括住宿和餐饮业经营情况和财务情况、网点及从业人员、涉外以及国内旅游基本情况等方面的内容。

二、本篇资料的来源

本篇资料中住宿和餐饮业经营情况和财务情况资料来源于住宿和餐饮业统计年报和定期报表统计资料；网点资料依据第三次经济普查资料和市工商局提供的个体私营经济注册登记资料测算。旅游资料来源于市旅游局。由市统计局外经贸易统计处整理提供。

Brief Introduction

I. Main Content

Data in this chapter show the development of wholesale and retail trade and tourism of the whole city, mainly including the circulation and financial indices of hotels and catering services, outlets and employment, international and domestic tourism, etc.

II. Source of Data

Data on hotels and catering services are based on annual report and regular reports of hotels and catering services. Outlet data are based on the information of the third economic census and the individual and private businesses' registration information provided by Qingdao Administration for Industry and Commerce. Data on international tourism are provided by Qingdao Tourism Bureau. The above data are prepared and compiled by the Division of Trade and External Economic Relations Statistics of Qingdao Municipal Bureau of Statistics.

16－1 限额以上住宿和餐饮业法人企业经营情况(2014 年)

BUSINESS CONDITIONS OF ENTERPRISES OF HOTELS AND CATERING SERVICES ABOVE DESIGNATED SIZE(2014)

单位:万元(10 000 yuan)

项目	Item	营业额 Turnover	#客房收入 Income from Guest Rooms	餐费收入 Catering Income	商品销售收入 Income from Commodity Sales	其他收入 Other Income
总　计	**Total**	**868 212**	**215 622**	**582 655**	**30 379**	**39 556**
一、住宿业	**Hotels**	**396 287**	**197 194**	**149 276**	**14 686**	**35 131**
国有企业	State-owned Enterprises	82 699	33 033	34 967	1 646	13 053
集体企业	Collective-owned Enterprises	796	330	462	4	
其他企业	Other Enterprises	312 792	163 831	113 847	13 036	22 078
独立门店	Freestanding Stores	373 397	183 957	142 107	13 712	33 620
连锁总店	General Chain Stores	408	355	11	5	37
连锁门店	Chain Stores	9 133	8 290	710	59	75
其他门店	Other Stores	13 349	4 592	6 448	910	1 399
五星	Five Star Class	119 724	61 022	47 414	938	10 351
四星	Four Star Class	109 107	49 301	49 684	3 468	6 654
三星	Three Star Class	54 508	26 776	21 944	2 047	3 742
二星	Two Star Class	3 724	1 474	1 709	122	419
一星	One Star Class					
其他	Others	109 224	58 621	28 525	8 111	13 965
二、餐饮业	**Catering Services**	**471 926**	**18 428**	**433 379**	**15 693**	**4 425**
国有企业	State-owned Enterprises	3 381	1 656	1 653		72
集体企业	Collective-owned Enterprises	1 949	478	1 466		5
其他企业	Other Enterprises	466 596	16 294	430 260	15 693	4 348
独立门店	Freestanding Stores	165 996	17 244	135 932	10 282	2 538
连锁总店	General Chain Stores	276 389	679	274 245	1 465	
连锁门店	Chain Stores	1 221		1 221		
其他门店	Other Stores	28 320	505	21 981	3 946	1 887

16－2 限额以上住宿业财务状况(2014 年)
FINANCIAL SITUATION OF HOTELS ABOVE DESIGNATED SIZE(2014)

单位:万元(10 000 yuan)

指标	Indicator	合　计 Total	国有经济 State-owned Enterprises	集体经济 Collective-owned Enterprises	外商及港澳台经济 Foreign Funded Enterprises and Enterprises with Funds from Hong Kong, Macao and Taiwan	其它 Other Enterprises
单位数	**Number of Enterprises**	**155**	**23**	**1**	**10**	**121**
年末资产负债	**Year-end Assets-Liability**					
资产合计	Total Assets	1 043 988	449 642	17 152	97 196	479 998
流动资产合计	Sub-total of Current Assets	437 569	69 847	786	66 906	300 030
负债合计	Total Liabilities	765 692	70 805	2 779	254 920	437 188
所有者权益合计	Total Owners' Equities	278 296	70 569	－1 148	20 242	188 633
损益及分配	**Loss Profits and Distribution**					
主营业务收入	Revenue from Principal Business	379 439	77 998	809	70 727	229 905
主营业务成本	Cost of Principal Business	117 691	23 110	210	16 115	78 255
主营业务税金及附加	Taxes and Extra Charges on Principal Business	21 355	3 956	44	4 243	13 111
营业利润	Profits from Principal Business	－12 170	－2 237	－37	－8 282	－1 614
其他业务利润	Profits from other Business	16 614	5 531		3 839	7 244
销售费用	Operating Costs	110 573	32 481	248	17 713	60 131
管理费用	Management Expenses	129 217	23 909	339	36 516	68 453
财务费用	Financial Expenses	17 560	1 026	5	5 665	10 865
利润总额	Total Profits	－12 310	－523	－61	－8 920	－2 806
其他	**Others**					
应付职工薪酬	Total Wages Payable in This Year	85 524	22 084	276	12 040	51 125
主营业务利润率	Profitability of Principal Business	－3.24	－0.67	－7.54	－12.61	－1.22

16－3 限额以上餐饮业财务状况(2014 年)

FINANCIAL SITUATION OF CATERING SERVICES ABOVE DESIGNATED SIZE(2014)

单位:万元(10 000 yuan)

指标	Indicator	合计 Total	国有经济 State-owned Enterprises	集体经济 Collective-owned Enterprises	外商及港澳台经济 Foreign Funded Enterprises and Enterprises with Funds from Hong Kong, Macao and Taiwan	其它 Other Enterprises
单位数	**Number of Enterprises**	**174**	**4**	**3**	**17**	**150**
年末资产负债	**Year-end Assets-Liability**					
资产合计	Total Assets	485 313	7 614	676	164 400	312 623
流动资产合计	Sub-total of Current Assets	220 448	2 258	283	50 191	167 716
负债合计	Total Liabilities	405 284	3 947	704	141 044	259 590
所有者权益合计	Total Owners' Equities	80 029	3 667	-28	29 713	46 677
损益及分配	**Loss Profits and Distribution**					
主营业务收入	Revenue from Principal Business	464 802	3 381	1 949	239 195	220 278
主营业务成本	Cost of Principal Business	235 838	1 878	1 460	119 881	112 619
主营业务税金及附加	Taxes and Extra Charges on Principal Business	25 053	194	122	13 034	11 703
营业利润	Profits from Principal Business	2 235	-42	-1	7 856	-5 579
其他业务利润	Profits from other Business	3 386	247		91	3 049
销售费用	Operating Costs	135 039	877	306	67 229	66 628
管理费用	Management Expenses	57 917	703	38	26 059	31 116
财务费用	Financial Expenses	11 550	17	24	5 204	6 305
利润总额	Total Profits	82	-108	0	9 764	-9 574
其他	**Others**					
应付职工薪酬	Total Wages Payable in This Year	96 286	1 722	359	44 253	49 952
主营业务利润率	Profitability of Principal Business	0.02	-3.20	-0.01	4.08	-4.35

16 -4 住宿和餐饮业企业网点数(2014 年底)
ENTERPRISES OUTLETS OF HOTELS AND CATERING SERVICES(END OF 2014)

单位:个(unit)

市、区名称	Region	合　计 Total	住宿业 Hotels	餐饮业 Catering Services
全市	**Whole Municipality**	**2 305**	**860**	**1 445**
市南区	Shinan District	679	317	362
市北区	Shibei District	372	161	211
李沧区	Licang District	159	44	115
崂山区	Laoshan District	185	71	114
黄岛区	Huangdao District	446	120	326
保税港区	Qingdao Free Trade Port Area of China			
城阳区	Chengyang District	199	49	150
即墨市	Jimo	119	45	74
胶州市	Jiaozhou	74	31	43
平度市	Pingdu	42	16	26
莱西市	Laixi	27	5	22
红岛经济区	Qingdao National High-tech Industrial Development Zone	3	1	2

16－5 住宿和餐饮业企业从业人员(2014 年底)

ENTERPRISES EMPLOYMENT OF HOTELS AND CATERING SERVICES(END OF 2014)

单位：人(person)

市、区名称	Region	合 计 Total	住宿业 Hotels	餐饮业 Catering Services
全市	**Whole Municipality**	**21 415**	**8 695**	**12 720**
市南区	Shinan District	6 636	3 685	2 951
市北区	Shibei District	2 856	1 288	1 568
李沧区	Licang District	1 202	543	659
崂山区	Laoshan District	1 879	703	1 176
黄岛区	Huangdao District	4 129	1 077	3 052
保税港区	Qingdao Free Trade Port Area of China			
城阳区	Chengyang District	1 535	408	1 127
即墨市	Jimo	1 595	437	1 158
胶州市	Jiaozhou	928	360	568
平度市	Pingdu	385	125	260
莱西市	Laixi	228	57	171
红岛经济区	Qingdao National High-tech Industrial Development Zone	42	12	30

16-6 住宿和餐饮业个体网点数(2014年底)

INDIVIDUAL OUTLETS OF HOTELS AND CATERING SERVICES(END OF 2014)

单位:个(unit)

市、区名称	Region	合计 Total	住宿业 Hotels	餐饮业 Catering Services
全市	**Whole Municipality**	**46 238**	**7 707**	**38 531**
市南区	Shinan District	4 015	847	3 168
市北区	Shibei District	5 549	1 267	4 282
李沧区	Licang District	2 543	366	2 177
崂山区	Laoshan District	2 441	319	2 122
黄岛区	Huangdao District	10 085	1 877	8 208
保税港区	Qingdao Free Trade Port Area of China	11	1	10
城阳区	Chengyang District	6 148	816	5 332
即墨市	Jimo	4 019	550	3 469
胶州市	Jiaozhou	5 974	978	4 996
平度市	Pingdu	3 242	507	2 735
莱西市	Laixi	1 959	143	1 816
红岛经济区	Qingdao National High-tech Industrial Development Zone	252	36	216

16－7 住宿和餐饮业个体从业人员(2014 年底)

INDIVIDUAL EMPLOYMENT OF HOTELS AND CATERING SERVICES(END OF 2014)

单位：人(person)

市、区名称	Region	合　计 Total	住宿业 Hotels	餐饮业 Catering Services
全市	**Whole Municipality**	**193 122**	**27 084**	**166 038**
市南区	Shinan District	20 470	3 231	17 239
市北区	Shibei District	20 117	3 678	16 439
李沧区	Licang District	14 221	1 045	13 176
崂山区	Laoshan District	9 508	831	8 677
黄岛区	Huangdao District	37 848	6 059	31 789
保税港区	Qingdao Free Trade Port Area of China	24	3	21
城阳区	Chengyang District	30 103	3 981	26 122
即墨市	Jimo	17 310	2 294	15 016
胶州市	Jiaozhou	24 016	3 870	20 146
平度市	Pingdu	11 253	1 553	9 700
莱西市	Laixi	7 493	460	7 033
红岛经济区	Qingdao National High-tech Industrial Development Zone	759	79	680

16-8 入境旅游人数(2000-2014 年)
NUMBER OF OVERSEA VISITOR ARRIVALS (2000-2014)

项目	Item	2000	2005	2006	2007
总　计	**Total**	**260 592**	**684 407**	**854 462**	**1 081 476**
一、外国人	**Foreigner**	**177 098**	**596 177**	**751 403**	**925 384**
#韩国	Korea	69 878	295 111	373 712	509 369
日本	Japan	67 215	177 121	221 542	242 500
美国	United States	10 384	23 284	32 256	37 509
俄罗斯	Russia	4 820	12 062	17 457	10 949
德国	Germany	3 820	10 646	14 440	14 560
新加坡	Singapore	6 321	6 060	8 332	10 918
英国	United Kingdom	2 798	5 744	10 047	12 175
加拿大	Canada	1 865	4 397	5 727	7 095
法国	France	2 491	5 166	7 377	8 452
意大利	Italy	1 555	3 963	4 022	6 062
澳大利亚	Australia	1 817	4 257	7 106	8 505
菲律宾	Philippines	7 947	3 459	1 812	2 461
泰国	Thailand	780	3 261	2 464	2 682
印尼	Indonesia	1 241	2 349	2 301	3 127
新西兰	New Zealand	442	710	980	1 106
二、港澳和台湾同胞	**Chinese Compatriots from Hong Kong, Macao and Taiwan**	**60 367**	**88 230**	**103 059**	**156 092**

16-9 入境旅游收入(2000-2014 年)
EARNINGS FROM INTERNATIONAL TOURISM (2000-2014)

项目	Item	2000	2005	2006	2007
总　计	**Total**	**118 164**	**340 899**	**434 100**	**502 926**
旅游购物	Shopping	20 742	67 047	78 882	95 705
住宿费	Accommodation	17 443	37 277	44 011	53 662
餐饮费	Dining	11 223	33 557	39 611	48 182
交通费	Transportation	35 252	128 112	140 831	183 425
邮电费	Postal and Telecommunication Services	5 502	18 394	21 654	26 111
文化娱乐费	Culture and Entertainment	6 894	20 240	23 900	29 180
游览	Sightseeing				26 502
其他	Other Services		36 272	85 210	40 158

单位:人次(person-time)

2008	2009	2010	2011	2012	2013	2014
800 455	**1 000 670**	**1 080 511**	**1 156 391**	**1 270 113**	**1 282 814**	**1 280 526**
697 391	**801 424**	**826 628**	**809 043**	**877 593**	**905 415**	**951 732**
340 648	363 181	382 225	298 096	338 383	338 191	366 584
210 090	261 553	242 082	216 755	185 613	146 080	135 179
28 998	28 745	35 539	45 842	48 431	54 178	57 907
3 774	9 525	15 793	15 750	26 432	26 519	25 356
11 261	14 735	21 626	26 178	26 311	19 014	21 723
10 683	17 453	13 444	16 626	16 316	16 305	19 975
10 657	9 103	17 639	23 955	28 385	19 496	22 817
5 467	7 741	9 279	12 007	11 678	9 727	9 483
6 067	7 030	11 766	12 019	15 595	21 422	17 828
3 871	3 747	3 867	7 028	5 622	5 679	7 705
7 940	6 641	8 223	15 465	16 644	11 149	15 339
2 075	7 800	14 140	14 259	7 546	18 630	6 668
2 236	3 685	2 572	3 271	2 369	3 692	4 803
1 589	4 221	7 863	8 128	4 571	10 011	6 568
1 161	2 029	1 597	6 265	6 448	1 452	2 549
103 064	**199 246**	**253 883**	**347 348**	**392 520**	**377 399**	**328 794**

单位:万元(10 000 yuan)

2008	2009	2010	2011	2012	2013	2014
347 645	**377 000**	**399 688**	**441 171**	**519 495**	**511 158**	**503 900**
66 053	70 763	74 104	80 823	93 872	94 055	109 246
37 198	41 093	43 933	59 823	59 378	58 577	62 232
33 374	36 569	38 747	40 191	51 378	51 065	44 041
9 039	9 877	145 551	134 425	170 238	180 945	160 492
17 382	18 812	19 081	16 720	23 014	22 950	19 400
20 163	22 394	24 032	36 132	32 832	32 103	33 409
18 773	21 037	22 978	51 705	32 832	32 152	44 192
145 663	29 745	31 262	21 353	55 951	39 311	30 888

16 -10 国内旅游人数及收入(2014 年)
NUMBER OF DOMESTIC TOURISM INCOME(2014)

指　标	Indicator	单位	Unit	2014
国内旅游人数	**Number of Domestic Tourists**	**万人次**	**10000 person-times**	**6 716**
1. 过夜旅游者人数	Number of Overnight Tourists	万人次	10000 person-times	4 028
(1)旅游住宿设施国内旅游人数	Domestic Tourists Staying Overnight at Hotels	万人次	10000 person-times	2 592
(2)住亲友家去景点的国内旅游人数	Domestic Tourists Staying Overnight at Relatives and Friends's Home	万人次	10000 person-times	1 436
2. 不过夜旅游者(一日游人数)	Number of Same-day (One-day Sightseeing) Tourists	万人次	10000 person-times	2 688
旅游景点接待一日游人数	One-day Sightseeing Tourists Received by Tour Scenes	万人次	10000 person-times	2 688
(1)本地一日游人数	Number of Local One-day Sightseeing Tourists	万人次	10000 person-times	1 743
(2)外地一日游人数	Number of One-day Sightseeing Tourists from Outside Areas	万人次	10000 person-times	945
国内旅游人均花费	**Per Capita Expenditure of Domestic Tourist**	**元**	**yuan**	**1 505**
国内旅游收入	**Earings from Domestic Tourism**	**亿元**	**100 million yuan**	**1 011**
1. 接待过夜旅游者收入	Earings from Overnight Tourists	万元	10000 yuan	8 354 443
2. 接待不过夜旅游者(一日游)收入	Earings from Same-day(One-day Sightseeing) Tourists	万元	10000 yuan	1 755 557

主要统计指标解释

住宿餐饮业营业额 指住宿和餐饮业法人企业、产业活动单位在经营活动中因提供服务或销售商品等取得的收入，包括客房收入、餐费收入、商品销售收入和其他收入。客房收入指住宿和餐饮业法人企业、产业活动单位在经营活动中因提供住宿服务取得的客房收入。餐费收入指住宿和餐饮业法人企业、产业活动单位因为顾客提供就餐服务取得的收入，包括经烹饪、调制加工后出售的各种食品，如主食、炒菜、凉拌菜等的收入。商品销售收入指住宿和餐饮业法人企业、产业活动单位伴随服务而出售商品所取得的收入。其他收入指营业收入中除客房收入、餐费收入、商品销售收入以外的其他收入，包括娱乐、健身和商务服务等。

国内旅游者 是指不以谋求职业、获取报酬为目的，离开惯常居住环境，到国内其它地方从事参观、游览、度假等旅游活动（包括外出探亲、疗养、考察、参加会议和从事商务、科技、文化、教育、宗教活动过程中的旅游活动），出行距离超过10公里，出游时间超过6小时，但不超过12个月的我国大陆居民。

入境旅游者 指来我国参观、访问、旅行、探亲、访友、休养、考察、参加会议和从事经济、科技、文化、教育、体育、宗教等活动的外国人、华侨、港澳和台湾同胞的人数。不包括外国在我国的常驻机构，如领事馆、通讯社、企业办事处的工作人员；来我国常住的外国专家、留学生以及在岸逗留不过夜人员。

Explanatory Notes on Main Statistical Indicators

Business Revenue of Hotels and Catering Services refer to revenue received from providing services or selling commodities by corporate enterprises and establishments engaged in hotel and catering services, including income from hotel rooms, from catering services, from selling of commodities and from other services. Income from hotel rooms refers to income of corporate enterprises and establishments by providing lodging services. Income from catering services refers to income of corporate enterprises and establishments by providing catering services, including selling of cooked or prepared foods such as stable food, cooked dishes or cold dishes. Income from selling of commodities refers to income of corporate enterprises and establishments by selling commodities that accompany the services they provide. Income from other activities refers to income received other than income from hotel rooms, catering services or selling of commodities, such as income from providing recreation, fitness or business services.

Domestic Tourists refers to residents in mainland China who are not for the purpose of seeking employment, remuneration, and leaving the usual living environment, elsewhere to engage in domestic visitors, sightseeing, vacation travel (including to go out to visit relatives, infirmary, observing, participate in the meeting and engage in business, science and technology, culture, education, religious activities in the course of tourism activities), trip distance of more than 10 km, trips longer than six hours, but not more than 12 months.

Entrance Tourists refers to foreigners, overseas Chinese, Chinese compatriots from Hong Kong, Macao and Taiwan coming to China for sight-seeing, visits, tours, family reunions, vacations, study tours, conferences and other activities of a business, scientific and technological, cultural, educational and religious nature. It does not include representatives and employees of resident institutions of foreign countries in China such as embassies, consulates, news agencies and offices of foreign companies and organizations, nor does it include long-term foreign experts or students residing in China, or persons in transition without spending a night in China.

17 教育、科技和文化

EDUCATION SCIENCE & TECHNOLOY AND CULTURE

简 要 说 明

一、本篇资料的主要内容

本篇资料主要反映了全市教育、科技和文化事业基本情况。教育部分主要包括高等教育、中等教育、初等教育、成人教育、职业教育、幼儿园等方面的基本情况。科技部分主要包括科研机构、科学技术奖励、大中型工业企业技术开发情况。文化部分主要包括文化、文物、广播、电视、报纸杂志出版、图书出版等方面的发展状况。

二、本篇资料的来源

1、教育部分，技工学校的资料来源于市人力资源和社会保障局，其他资料来源于市教育局。

2、科技部分，科研机构及科技奖励资料来源于市科技局，大中型工业企业科技活动资料来源于市统计局统计调查年报。

3、文化部分，图书、杂志、报纸出版有关资料来源于青岛出版集团、海大出版社，其他资料来源于市文化广电新闻出版局。

本篇资料由市统计局人口和社会科技统计处整理提供。

Brief Introduction

I. Main Content

Data in this chapter show the basic conditions of education, science & technology and culture. Data on education show the development of higher education, secondary education, primary education, adult education, vocational education and kindergartens. Data on science & technology show the basic conditions of science research institutions, scientific and technological achievements and prizes, scientific & technological activities of large and medium-size industrial enterprises. Data on culture show the basic conditions of arts, cultural relics, broadcasting, television and publication of newspapers, magazines and books.

II. Source of Data

(1)In education component, data on the basic conditions of technical schools are provided by Qingdao Municipal Bureau of Human Resources and Social Security, and the other data on education are provided by Qingdao Municipal Bureau of Education.

(2)In science & technology component, data on science research institutions and scientific & technological achievements and prizes are provided by Qingdao Municipal Bureau of Science and Technology. Data on scientific and technological activities are from the annual report of scientific and technological activities, which is provided by Qingdao Municipal Bureau of Statistics.

(3)In culture component, data on publication of books, magazines and newspapers are provided by Qingdao Publishing Group and Ocean University Press. The other data are provided by Qingdao Municipal Bureau of Cluture, Broadcasting, Television, Press and Publication.

Data in this chapter are provided and compiled by the Division of Population and Science & Technology of Qingdao Municipal Bureau of Statistics.

17 -1 各级各类学校基本情况(2014 年)
BASIC STATISTICS ON SCHOOLS BY LEVEL AND TYPE OF SCHOOL(2014)

项目	Item	学校数(所) Schools (unit)	毕业生数(人) Graduates (person)	招生数(人) New Students Enrollment(person)	在校学生数(人) Students Enrollment(person)	教职工数(人) Teachers and Staff(person)	#专任教师 of which: Full-time Teachers
研究生	Postgraduates			9 165	10 441	29 622	6 581
普通高等学校	Regular Institutions of Higher Education	22	77 503	90 127	313 486	28 944	18 587
中等专业学校	Specialized Secondary Schools	6	8 444	10 133	28 751	929	636
技工学校	Technical Schools	23	6 941	9 629	29 740	2 097	1 837
职业学校	Vocational Schools	50	22 482	21 461	58 170	7 238	5 629
普通中学	Regular Secondary Schools	295	117 595	115 788	362 599	37 407	31 999
初中	Junior Secondary Schools	235	74 659	78 242	242 386	24 184	21 594
高中	Senior Secondary Schools	60	42 936	37 546	120 213	13 223	10 405
小学	Primary Schools	794	78 863	96 661	516 529	33 831	32 181
特殊教育学校	Special Education Schools	12	344	342	1 584	595	487
幼儿园	Kindergartens	2 340	77 565	77 083	224 363	24 357	16 080
成人高等学校	Adult Institutions of Higher Education	1	31 714	38 002	107 095	108	64
成人中等学校	Adult Secondary Education Schools	4	4 189	1 629	10 571	146	103
成人初等学校	Adult Primary Education Schools						

注:1. 研究生栏中专任教师指的是指导教师。
2. 成人中等学校仅包括成人中学和成人中专。

Note:1. Full-time teachers of postgraduates refer to instructors.
2. Adult secondary education schools refer to adult secondary schools and adult specialized secondary schools.

17 -2 主要年份各级各类学校在校学生数

MAJOR YEAR'S STUDENTS ENROLLMENT OF SCHOOLS BY LEVEL AND TYPE OF SCHOOL

单位:人(person)

年份 Year	普通高等学校 Regular Institutions of Higher Education	中等学校 Secondary Schools	中等专业学校 Specialized Secondary Schools	普通中学 Regular Secondary Schools	职业中学 Vocational Schools	技工学校 Technical Schools	小学 Primary Schools
1949	1 007	13 804	1 600	12 204			213 470
1952	2 761	27 951	3 770	24 181			413 286
1957	3 133	56 689	4 985	51 604	100		482 397
1962	4 381	62 646	2 791	58 639	243	973	522 921
1965	2 987	99 605	9 405	88 187	1 490	523	788 485
1970	320	222 521	105	220 262	2 154		728 433
1975	1 151	350 309	3 144	346 403		762	928 153
1978	3 465	464 584	4 269	457 460	2 000	865	634 905
1980	6 783	325 935	5 195	318 193	1 344	1 203	816 970
1985	10 631	327 446	11 475	279 915	33 945	2 111	691 341
1988	14 408	352 576	11 819	306 943	28 933	4 881	629 212
1989	15 183	348 367	14 401	296 318	32 283	5 365	634 794
1990	15 433	351 365	15 118	296 163	34 568	5 516	632 314
1991	15 491	353 410	14 618	298 568	34 421	5 803	612 772
1992	16 470	367 480	14 763	307 903	38 242	6 572	585 381
1993	23 858	383 043	16 877	318 179	40 743	7 244	583 585
1994	25 018	420 077	20 582	347 667	43 734	8 094	593 419
1995	24 908	450 212	23 744	372 335	46 044	8 089	595 891
1996	26 076	468 561	26 951	382 760	50 131	8 719	607 284
1997	27 434	463 619	28 543	362 305	61 640	11 131	626 749
1998	29 507	442 525	28 757	336 918	65 989	10 861	625 308
1999	33 681	459 520	26 955	352 238	70 236	10 091	583 594
2000	46 131	497 391	25 192	398 458	63 894	9 847	534 922
2001	60 728	542 400	25 358	443 693	62 003	11 346	499 147
2002	82 539	575 599	27 421	467 628	67 085	13 465	478 634
2003	168 439	586 704	28 948	461 435	75 221	21 100	467 560
2004	201 739	598 804	30 881	436 117	101 553	30 253	476 897
2005	239 761	569 230	33 522	391 148	106 400	38 160	479 781
2006	260 339	554 308	32 051	365 192	116 487	40 578	483 892
2007	264 917	558 527	28 011	360 410	130 156	39 950	484 775
2008	269 314	582 932	25 330	373 884	143 126	40 592	477 230
2009	275 157	56 4476	22 739	377 427	127 792	36 518	465 031
2010	284 788	535 079	24 014	380 025	98 560	32 480	462 722
2011	291 453	505 051	25 905	373 226	74 892	31 028	479 513
2012	296 645	489 103	27 005	369 580	65 419	27 099	484 985
2013	300 246	484 025	28 389	365 110	61 594	28 932	496 343
2014	313 486	479 260	28 751	362 599	58 170	29 740	516 529

17-3 主要年份普通高等学校基本情况

MAJOR YEAR'S BASIC STATISTICS ON REGULAR INSTITUTIONS OF HIGHER EDUCATION

单位:人(person)

年份 Year	学校数(所) Schools (unit)	毕业生数 Graduates	招生数 New Students Enrollment	在校学生数 Students Enrollment	教职工数 Teachers and Staff	#专任教师 of which: Full-time Teachers
1949	1		250	1 007	779	226
1952	2	262	565	2 761	12 530	308
1957	2	356	755	3 133	1 308	622
1962	5	647	653	4 381	1 866	749
1965	3	741	529	2 987	1 539	623
1970	2	684		320	1 178	486
1975	2	460	473	1 151	1 353	582
1978	4	739	1 782	3 465	2 829	1 176
1980	6	431	1 717	6 783	4 182	1 606
1985	7	1 828	3 823	10 631	5 561	2 181
1988	7	3 496	4 687	14 408	6 875	2 499
1989	7	3 891	4 567	15 183	7 174	2 554
1990	7	4 495	4 745	15 433	7 305	2 624
1991	7	4 880	4 954	15 491	7 282	2 489
1992	7	4 458	5 428	16 470	7 344	2 523
1993	7	3 140	9 449	23 858	7 366	2 520
1994	4	7 059	8 042	25 018	7 466	2 650
1995	4	7 828	7 978	24 908	7 545	2 682
1996	4	6 691	7 956	26 076	7 606	2 745
1997	4	7 091	8 503	27 434	7 790	2 813
1998	4	6 912	8 849	29 507	7 662	2 907
1999	4	7 202	11 584	33 681	7 662	2 928
2000	6	7 128	18 427	46 131	8 030	3 278
2001	6	8 991	22 787	60 728	8 706	4 058
2002	7	13 053	29 731	82 539	9 517	4 723
2003	25	25 747	61 975	168 439	18 911	10 293
2004	25	34 860	70 022	201 739	21 437	12 347
2005	25	46 114	79 725	239 761	23 078	13 894
2006	25	55 931	79 094	260 339	24 881	15 195
2007	25	68 354	78 728	264 917	25 956	16 005
2008	25	75 198	86 878	269 314	26 654	16 805
2009	25	69 475	81 025	275 157	26 983	16 870
2010	25	70 450	82 220	284 788	28 145	16 996
2011	22	79 466	84 434	291 453	28 151	17 120
2012	22	79 791	87 981	296 645	29 445	18 183
2013	22	78 974	85 707	300 246	28 958	18 396
2014	22	77 503	90 127	313 486	28 944	18 587

17 -4 各类成人教育基本情况(2014 年)
BASIC STATISTICS ON ADULT EDUCATION(2014)

单位:人(person)

各类学校	Schools by Type of School	学校数(所) Schools (unit)	毕业生数 Graduates	招生数 New Students Enrollment	在校学生数 Students Enrollment	教职工数 Teachers and Staff	#专任教师 of which: Full-time Teachers
总　计	**Total**	**5**	**35 903**	**39 631**	**117 666**	**254**	**167**
成人高等教育	Adult Higher Education	1	31 714	38 002	107 095	108	64
广播电视大学	Broadcasting and TV Universities	1	94	301	506	108	64
职工、农民大学	Universities of Vocational and Agricultural Education						
函授、夜大学	Correspondence and Evening College Education		31 620	37 701	106 589		
管理干部学校	Cadre Management Schools						
成人中等教育	Adult Secondary Education	4	4 189	1 629	10 571	146	103
成人中等专业学校	Adult Specialized Secondary Schools	4	4 189	1 629	10 571	146	103

注:本年度成人高等自学考试毕业 2 714 人;参加成人高等单科班、进修班、短训班、专业证书班学习毕业(结业)32 890 人。

Note:2 714 persons have been graduated from adult higher tech-oneself tests in the year, 32 890 persons have been graduated from adult higher single subject courses, training courses, short-term training course and specialized diploma courses.

17－5 分市、区普通中学情况(2014 年)

BASIC STATISTICS ON REGULAR SECONDARY SCHOOLS BY REGION(2014)

单位:人(person)

市、区名称	Region	普通高中 Regular Senior Secondary Schools				普通初中 Regular Junior Secondary Schools			
		学校数(所) Schools (unit)	毕业生数 Graduates	招生数 New Students Enrollment	在校生数 Students Enrollment	学校数(所) Schools (unit)	毕业生数 Graduates	招生数 New Students Enrollment	在校生数 Students Enrollment
全　市	**Whole Municipality**	**60**	**42 936**	**37 546**	**120 213**	**235**	**74 659**	**78 242**	**242 386**
市　直	Municipal Level	16	7 342	7 191	22 513	3	1 984	1 863	5 760
市南区	Shinan District	1	100	155	389	10	3 766	3 779	11 667
市北区	Shibei District					22	6 040	6 763	19 967
李沧区	Licang District					11	3 204	3 522	10 585
崂山区	Laoshan District	7	1 713	1 755	5 334	10	1 959	2 294	6 604
黄岛区	Huangdao District	11	7 319	6 133	20 348	35	11 984	12 787	38 727
城阳区	Chengyang District	5	2 781	2 656	7 999	15	4 665	5 543	16 021
即墨市	Jimo	7	6 215	5 404	18 054	30	11 148	12 784	36 774
胶州市	Jiaozhou	6	4 894	4 333	14 470	22	8 501	9 020	27 207
平度市	Pingdu	5	8 225	6 919	20 777	44	14 454	12 796	40 356
莱西市	Laixi	2	4 347	3 000	10 329	31	6 244	6 415	26 552
红岛经济区	Qingdao National High-tech Industrial Development Zone					2	710	676	2 166

17－6 分市、区职业中学、小学情况(2014年)
BASIC STATISTICS ON VOCATIONAL SECONDARY SCHOOLS AND PRIMARY SCHOOLS BY REGION(2014)

单位:人(person)

市、区名称	Region	职业中学 Vocational Secondary Schools				小 学 Primary Schools			
		学校数(所) Schools (unit)	毕业生数 Graduates	招生数 New Students Enrollment	在校生数 Students Enrollment	学校数(所) Schools (unit)	毕业生数 Graduates	招生数 New Students Enrollment	在校生数 Students Enrollment
全 市	**Whole Municipality**	**50**	**22 482**	**21 461**	**58 170**	**794**	**78 863**	**96 661**	**516 529**
市 直	Municipal Level	19	4 691	4 570	10 938				
市南区	Shinan District					28	4 929	5 412	28 138
市北区	Shibei District					64	7 119	9 944	48 225
李沧区	Licang District					31	3 850	5 514	26 622
崂山区	Laoshan District	1	1 447	665	1 885	26	2 452	4 173	18 141
黄岛区	Huangdao District	19	6 822	8 700	20 752	90	12 823	16 194	88 909
城阳区	Chengyang District	3	353	265	1 326	46	5 731	9 017	43 443
即墨市	Jimo	3	1 811	2 014	5 859	172	12 887	14 766	82 066
胶州市	Jiaozhou	1	2 743	2 183	7 215	81	9 000	10 998	63 497
平度市	Pingdu	1	2 812	1 652	5 329	154	12 962	12 318	76 138
莱西市	Laixi	3	1 803	1 412	4 866	96	6 423	7 567	37 186
红岛经济区	Qingdao National High-tech Industrial Development Zone					6	687	758	4 164

17 -7 分市、区中小学教职工情况(2014 年)

BASIC STATISTICS ON TEACHERS AND STAFF IN SECONDARY AND PRIMARY SCHOOLS BY REGION(2014)

单位:人(person)

市、区名称	Region	普通中学 Regular Secondary Schools		职业中学 Vocational Secondary Schools		小学 Primary Schools	
		教职工数 Teachers and Staff	#专任教师 of which: Full-time Teachers	教职工数 Teachers and Staff	#专任教师 of which: Full-time Teachers	教职工数 Teachers and Staff	#专任教师 of which: Full-time Teachers
全　市	**Whole Municipality**	**37 407**	**31 999**	**7 238**	**5 629**	**33 831**	**32 181**
市　直	Municipal Level	3 065	2 347	2 196	1 513		
市南区	Shinan District	1 218	993			1 955	1 871
市北区	Shibei District	2 051	1 573			3 368	3 093
李沧区	Licang District	1 004	826			1 606	1 518
崂山区	Laoshan District	1 512	1 113	229	168	1 270	1 209
黄岛区	Huangdao District	5 932	5 270	1 461	1 238	5 774	5 436
城阳区	Chengyang District	2 449	2 102	721	573	2 329	2 242
即墨市	Jimo	5 741	4 907	691	598	5 295	5 152
胶州市	Jiaozhou	3 975	3 445	672	460	3 914	3 790
平度市	Pingdu	6 429	5 768	687	618	5 171	4 898
莱西市	Laixi	3 797	3 428	581	461	2 860	2 685
红岛经济区	Qingdao National High-tech Industrial Development Zone	234	227			289	287

17 -8 分市、区幼儿园基本情况(2014 年)
BASIC STATISTICS ON KINDERGARTENS BY REGION(2014)

单位:人(person)

市、区名称	Region	幼儿园(所) Kindergartens(unit)	幼儿数 Children	教职工数 Teachers and Staff	#专任教师 of which: Full-time teachers
全 市	**Whole Municipality**	**2 340**	**224 363**	**24 357**	**16 080**
市南区	Shinan District	57	12 577	1 959	989
市北区	Shibei District	97	23 306	2 733	1 518
李沧区	Licang District	41	12 969	1 787	848
崂山区	Laoshan District	103	9 879	1 580	882
黄岛区	Huangdao District	365	37 804	4 626	3 249
城阳区	Chengyang District	131	20 939	2 521	1 835
即墨市	Jimo	422	33 233	2 777	1 994
胶州市	Jiaozhou	446	25 157	2 696	1 912
平度市	Pingdu	478	32 099	2 250	1 729
莱西市	Laixi	176	14 402	1 166	890
红岛经济区	Qingdao National High-tech Industrial Development Zone	24	1 998	262	234

17 -9 科研机构基本情况(1978 -2014 年)
BASIC STATISTICS ON SCIENTIFIC RESEARCH INSTITUTIONS(1978 -2014)

年份 Year	独立自然科研机构(个) Independent Institutions of Natural Scientific Research(unit)	独立自然科研机构中科技人员(人) Personnel of Independent Institutions of Natural Scientific Research(person)	完成科研项目(项) Number of Scientific Research Projects Completed(item)	取得科技成果(项) Number of Achievements in S&T(item)
1978	31	2701	306	306
1980			481	297
1982	41	2 345	451	451
1983	48	3 182	530	530
1984	53	3 312	507	507
1985	52	3 673	552	552
1986	63	3 998	577	577
1987	76	4 629	579	579
1988	101	5 199	544	510
1989	111	5 885	544	688
1990	141	6 046	414	931
1991	72	5 665	753	753
1992	71	5 726	659	659
1993	69	5 545	546	546
1994	69	5 540	467	467
1995	59	5 286	441	441
1996	58	4 738	613	613
1997	54	4 577	418	418
1998	52	4 142	517	517
1999	58	3 771	606	606
2000	54	3 637	621	621
2001	50	3 191	457	457
2002	52	3 248	406	406
2003	53	3 246	589	589
2004	50	3 226	506	506
2005	50	3 234	438	438
2006	50	3 291	548	548
2007	50	3 432	506	506
2008	42	3 709	416	416
2009	43	3 727	572	572
2010	44	4 088	472	472
2011	47	4 548	345	345
2012	48	4 967	304	304
2013	48	6 057	433	433
2014	50	5 438	415	415

注:1991 年以后不包括民办科研机构。

Note:Since 1991,private institutions of scientific research are not included.

17－10 独立科学研究机构情况(2014 年)
BASIC STATISTICS ON INDEPENDENT INSTITUTIONS OF SCIENTIFIC RESEARCH(2014)

项　目	Item	计量单位	Unit	总　计 Total	中央属 Central	地方属 Local
机构数	Number of Institutions	个	unit	50	18	32
职工人数	Staff and Workers	人	person	7 249	5 057	2 192
科技人员	Personnel Engaged in S&T	人	person	5 438	3 841	1 597
经费收入	Funding for S&T	万元	10 000 yuan	356 012	312 040	43 972
经费支出	Expenditures for S&T	万元	10 000 yuan	313 713	268 925	44 788

17－11 科学技术奖励情况(2014 年)
AWARD STATISTICS ON SCIENCE AND TECHNOLOGY(2014)

项　目	Item	单位	Unit	自然科学奖 Natural Science Prizes Awarded	技术发明奖 Invention Prizes Awarded	科技进步奖 Scientific And Technological Progress Prizes Awarded	科学技术功勋奖 Scientific And Technological Credit Prizes Awarded	国际科技合作奖 International S&T Cooperation Prizes Award	最高奖 Highest Prizes Award
国家级	**National Level**	**项**	**item**	**2**	**1**	**4**			
#一等	First Prize	项	item						
二等	Second Prize	项	item	2	1	4			
省级	**Provincial Level**	**项**	**item**	**9**	**6**	**41**			**1**
#一等	First Prize	项	item		2	6			
二等	Second Prize	项	item	6	3	26			
三等	Third Prize	项	item	3	1	9			
市级	**Municipal Level**	**项**	**item**	**11**	**18**	**119**		**2**	**1**
#一等	First Prize	项	item		4	8			
二等	Second Prize	项	item	5	7	50			
三等	Third Prize	项	item	6	7	61			

注：国际科技合作奖、最高奖不分等级。

Note:There is no grade in international scientific and technological cooperation prizes award and highest prizes award.

17-12 大中型工业企业技术开发主要相对指标(1995-2014年)

MAJOR INDICATORS OF TECHNOLOGY DEVELOPMENT OF LARGE AND MEDIUM-SIZE INDUSTRIAL ENTERPRISES(1995-2014)

项目	Item	单位	Unit	1995	2000	2005	2006	2007	2008	2009	2010	2011	2012	2013	2014
企业技术开发人员占全部职工比重	Percentage of Technology Development Personnel to Staff and Workers	%	%	2.6	5.7	4.4	4.9	5.9	5.6	5.8	6.7	7.7	7.4	8.3	8.5
科学家工程师占技术开发人员比重	Percentage of Scientists and Engineers to Technology Development Personnel	%	%	39.0	62.3	66.1	63.1	62.4	63.0						
设有开发机构的企业占企业总数比重	Percentage of Enterprises Having Development Institutions to Total Number of Enterprises	%	%	59.3	29.7	20.8	21.8	26.1	24.6	24.0	26.2	28.1	26.7	25.1	25.8
科学家工程师占开发机构人员比重	Percentage of Scientists and Engineers to Personnel of Development Institutions	%	%	48.1	77.6										
平均每个企业技术开发经费筹集额	Average Funding for Technology Development of Each Enterprise	万元	10 000 yuan	118.2	873.0	1 535.8	1 577.0	1 805.0	1 815.6						
平均每个企业技术开发经费支出额	Average Expenditures for Technology Development of Each Enterprise	万元	10 000 yuan	114.5	812.0	1 626.0	1 716.0	1 931.0	1 894.9						
开发新产品用款占经费支出比重	Percentage of Expenditures on New Product Development to Total Expenditures	%	%	50.8	52.6	55.9	58.4	63.3	66.2						
技术开发经费支出占产品销售收入比重	Percentage of Expenditures on Technology Development to Revenue from Product Sales	%	%	1.0	3.1	2.7	2.7	2.6	2.3						
新产品产值比重	Percentage of Output Value of New Products	%	%		35.5	31.3	32.7	28.4	26.8	27.4	28.4	28.8	26.0	25.3	28.1
新产品销售额比重	Percentage of Sales Volume of New Products	%	%	12.2	32.7	32.5	32.4	30.5	28.7	28.8	28.9	29.3	27.0	27.2	28.0
新产品利税额比重	Percentage of Profits and Taxes of New Products	%	%	18.7	30.6										

17－13 主要年份文化机构数
MAJOR YEAR'S INSTITUTIONS OF CULTURE

单位:个(unit)

年份 Year	合计 Total	#影剧院 Cinemas	文化馆 Cultural Centers	艺术表演团体 Art Performance Troupes
1949	24	9	3	3
1952	50	11	15	8
1957	99	16	11	15
1962	103	17	12	13
1965	117	18	13	13
1970	121	20	12	13
1975	249	21	12	16
1978	402	24	13	15
1980	661	24	12	17
1985	1 290	81	12	11
1988	1 473	84	12	11
1989	1 308	106	12	11
1990	1 323	106	12	11
1991	1 185	108	12	11
1992	1 167	108	12	11
1993	1 079	103	12	11
1994	964	78	12	11
1995	767	61	13	11
1996	761	61	13	11
1997	634	61	12	11
1998	491	51	12	11
1999	638	43	12	11
2000	637	45	12	11
2001	614	44	12	11
2002	590	44	11	11
2003	492	50	11	11
2004	476	29	12	11
2005	478	39	12	12
2006	446	40	12	12
2007	451	40	12	12
2008	456	40	12	12
2009	459	40	12	12
2010	465	40	12	12
2011	470	40	12	10
2012	475	36	12	8
2013	480	40	12	8
2014	488	43	13	9

17 –14 文化、文物事业机构、人员数(2014 年)
NUMBER OF INSTITUTIONS AND PERSONNEL IN CULTURE AND CULTURAL RELICS(2014)

项　目	Item	文化机构数(个) Number of Cultural Institutions(unit)		文化人员数(人) Number of Cultural Personnel(person)	
		2014	2013	2014	2014
总　计	**Total**	**262**	**250**	**3 759**	**3 159**
文化事业合计	**Culture**	**213**	**212**	**2 587**	**2 228**
一、艺术事业	Art	27	22	1 184	755
1. 艺术表演团体	Art Performance Troupes	9	8	889	646
2. 艺术表演场所	Art Centers	10	9	226	83
3. 艺术创作机构	Art Creation Institutions	5	3	39	8
4. 艺术研究机构	Art Research Institutions		2		18
5. 艺术展览机构	Art Exhibition Institutions				
6. 其他	Others	3		30	
二、图书馆事业	Libraries	13	13	276	274
公共图书馆	Public Libraries	13	13	276	274
#县(区)级图书馆	County Libraries	12	12	167	166
三、群众文化事业	Mass Culture	149	156	665	626
1. 群众艺术馆	Mass Art Centers		1		52
2. 文化馆	Cultural Palaces	13	12	204	164
3. 文化站	Cultural Centers	136	143	461	410
4. 其他	Others				
四、其他文化事业	Other Cultural Units	24	21	462	573
文物事业合计	**Cultural Relics**	**49**	**38**	**1 172**	**931**
一、文物机构	Cultural Relics Institutions	7	7	358	243
二、博物馆纪念馆	Museums and Memorial Halls	41	30	800	674
三、文物商店	Cultural Relics Shops				
四、文物科研机构	Scientific and Research Institutions of Cultural Relics	1	1	14	14

注:博物馆、纪念馆数量包含文物部门、其他部门及民办的博物馆数量。

Note:The number of museums and memorial halls in includes those operated by the cultural relics departments, other government departments and the private sector.

17 -15 分市、区艺术表演、电影发行及放映机构数(2014 年)

NUMBER OF INSTITUTIONS OF ART PERFORMANCE,FILMS DISTRIBUTION AND PROJECTION BY REGION(2014)

单位:个(unit)

市、区名称	Region	合计 Total	影剧院 Cinemas	电影发行机构 Institutions of Films Distribution	流动放映单位 Travelling Projection Units
全　市	**Whole Municipality**	**314**	**43**	**1**	**270**
市南区	Shinan District	7	6	1	
市北区	Shibei District	9	9		
李沧区	Licang District	6	4		2
崂山区	Laoshan District	5	2		3
黄岛区	Huangdao District	77	5		72
城阳区	Chengyang District	16	4		12
即墨市	Jimo	43	6		37
胶州市	Jiaozhou	38	3		35
平度市	Pingdu	66	3		63
莱西市	Laixi	45	1		44
红岛经济区	Qingdao National High-tech Industrial Development Zone	2			2

17 -16 艺术表演、电影放映情况(2014 年)

STATISTICS ON ART PERFORMANCE AND FILMS PROJECTION(2014)

项　目	Item	机构数(个) Number of Institutions (unit)	座位数(个) Number of Seats (unit)	演出场次(场) Number of Performances (show)	观众人数(万人次) Number of Spectators (10 000 person-times)	票款收入(万元) Income from Ticket Sales (10 000 yuan)
艺术表演总计	Art Performance	10	7 428	410	29.9	1 381.6
电影放映总计	Films Projection	313	36 471	525 202	1 456.7	27 141
#影剧院	Cinemas	43	36 471	454 558	776.7	27 141
流动放映单位	Travelling Projection Units	270		70 644	680	

17－17 文化部门艺术剧团情况(2014 年)
STATISTICS ON ART TROUPES OF CULTURAL DEPARTMENT(2014)

项目	Item	剧团数(个) Number of Troupes (unit)	职工人数(人) Staff and Workers (person)	演出场次(场) Number of Performances (show)	观众人数(万人次) Number of Spectators (10 000 person-times)	演出收入(万元) Income from Performance (10 000 yuan)	拨款经费(万元) Appropriation Funds (10 000 yuan)
总　计	**Total**	**9**	**889**	**1 914**	**128.8**	**1 145.5**	**8 194.5**
一、按隶属关系分	**Grouped by Administrative Relationship**						
国营剧团	State-run Troupes	9	889	1 914	128.8	1 145.5	8 194.5
集体经营剧团	Collective-owned Troupes						
二、按剧种分	**Grouped by Type of Drama**						
1.话剧团	Drama Troupes	1	110	174	8.7	171.2	89.7
2.歌舞团	Song and Dance Troupes	1	312	289	14.5	482.1	2 025.0
3.戏曲剧团	Local Opera Troupes	4	208	692	73.1	194.5	1 026.6
#京剧	of which:Beijing Opera	1	93	174	7.4	97.7	170.0
4.曲艺团	Recitation and Ballad Troupes						
5.文工团(艺术团)	Cultural and Performance Troupes	3	259	759	32.5	297.7	5 053.2

17－18 图书馆、博物馆、文化馆情况
STATISTICS ON LIBRARIES,MUSEUMS AND CULTURAL CENTERS

项目	Item	单位	Unit	2014		2013	
				全市合计 Total	#市区 Urban Area	全市合计 Total	#市区 Urban Area
公共图书馆	**Public Libraries**	个	**unit**	**13**	**9**	**13**	**9**
工作人员	Staff and Workers	人	person	276	213	274	210
藏书册数	Collection Books	千册	1 000 copies	5 829	4 807	5 457	4 450
阅览席位	Seating Capacity of Reading Rooms	张	seat	5 261	4 363	5 083	4 125
读者人数	Readers	万人次	10 000 person-times	442.5	372.1	381.7	320.2
博物馆、纪念馆	**Museums and Memorial Halls**	个	**unit**	**41**	**31**	**30**	**24**
工作人员	Staff and Workers	人	person	800	651	674	589
藏品数量	Collections	万件	10 000 copies	44	35	43	34
参观人数	Visitors	万人次	10 000 person-times	553	517	563	246
文化馆	**Cultural Centers**	个	**unit**	**13**	**9**	**12**	**7**

注:博物馆、纪念馆数量包含文物部门、其他部门及民办的博物馆数量。

Note:The number of museums and memorial halls in includes those operated by the cultural relics departments, other government departments and the private sector.

17－19 图书、杂志、报纸出版情况(1995－2014 年)
PUBLICATION OF BOOKS, MAGAZINES AND NEWSPAPERS(1995－2014)

项　目	Item	单位	Unit	1995	2000	2005
图书出版	**Publication of Books**					
种数	Number of Publication	种	kind	530	572	896
总印数	Total Printed Copies	万册	10 000 copies	2 109	1 542	2 873
总印张数	Total Printed Sheets	千印张	1 000 sheets	75 242	71 826	191 671
杂志出版	**Publication of Magazines**					
种数	Number of Publication	种	kind	34	35	44
每期平均印数	Average Printed Copies per Issue	万册(份)	10 000 copies	37.42	75.41	76.95
总印数	Total Printed Copies	万册	10 000 copies	409	1 249	1 755
总印张数	Total Printed Sheets	千印张	1 000 sheets	5 630	31 946	69 635
报纸出版	**Publication of Newspapers**					
种数	Number of Publication	种	kind	8	14	12
每期平均印数	Average Printed Copies per Issue	万份	10 000 copies	81.51	84.74	174.16
总印数	Total Printed Copies	万份	10 000 copies	16 318	21 309	53 947
总印张数	Total Printed Sheets	千印张	1 000 sheets	231 642	555 503	4 188 151

注:自 2008 年图书出版种数改按种次统计,总印数,总印张数均按此口径进行统计。

Note: Number of book publication in 2008 are according to the type and times of statistical. The total printed copies and total printed sheets are the same calibre.

2006	2007	2008	2009	2010	2011	2012	2013	2014
926	788	3 609	3 642	2 562	4 102	4 555	5 428	6 051
1 697	1 376	6 055	6 124	6 443	6 713	7 891.3	10 181.4	8 995.9
194 584	112 337	376 404	396 753	413 917	412 686	459 639	618 984	582 326
44	44	45	49	50	47	48	48	48
85.41	72.26	106.5	99.97	100.93	96.3	100	100.02	56.36
1 779	1 936	2 587	2 616	2 650	2 766	2 788	2 866	1 725
56 913	63 235	83 748	86 064	98 136	80 345	80 348	90 265	67 028
12	12	13	14	15	15	14	15	16
183.26	202.82	231.20	257.89	291.54	297.48	298.6	272.3	255.62
57 135	63 800	74 143	78 239	93 255	107 615	107 656	84 479	81 428
3 944 883	4 773 915	5 624 658	5 877 377	7 130 931	12 346 098	12 347 198	12 263 541	6 022 930

17－20 广播电视业基本情况(2000－2014 年)

BASIC STATISTICS ON RADIO AND TELEVISION STATIONS(2000－2014)

项 目	Item	单位	Unit	2000	2005	2006
一、广播基本情况	**Basic Statistics on Radio**					
电台个数	Number of Radio Stations	座	set	1	1	1
发射台个数	Number of Transmission Stations	座	set	9	11	10
节目套数	Number of Programs	套	set	10	12	12
平均日播音时间	Broadcasting Hours per Day	时:分	hour: minute	119:15	174:01	190:43
#自办节目	of which: Self-programs	时:分	hour: minute	107:50	111:12	139:25
#本年自制广播节目时间	Hours of Programs Making in the Year	小时	hour		36 964	48 604
广播人口覆盖率	Radio Coverage of Population	%	%	96.02	97.90	98.00
二、电视基本情况	**Basic Statistics on Television**					
电视台个数	Number of Television Stations	座	set	1	1	1
发射台个数	Number of Transmission Stations	座	set	29	11	10
节目套数	Number of Programs	套	set	9	15	15
平均每周播出时间	Broadcasting Hour per Week	时:分	hour: minute	489:20	1 522:38	1 653:25
#自办节目	of which: Self-programs	时:分	hour: minute	410:54	597:55	827:06
#本年自制广播节目时间	Hours of Programs Making in the Year	小时	hour		11 977	12 774
电视人口覆盖率	TV Coverage of Population	%	%	95.04	97.70	97.80
三、有线电视基本情况	**Basic Statistics on CATV**					
总用户数	Number of Users of CATV	万户	10 000 households		176.60	201.60
有线电视入户率	CATV Coverage of Household	%	%		75.05	84.96
网络总长	Length of the Network	公里	km		44 827	46 479
广播电视卫星收转系统	Satellite Relaying Systems of Radio and Television	座	set		1 062	168

2007	2008	2009	2010	2011	2012	2013	2014
1	1	1	1	1	1	1	8
10	10	10	10	10	10	10	9
12	12	12	12	12	12	12	11
195:23	221:09	220:39	237:23	237:12	238:30	253:06	221:14
137:48	163:49	174:44	183:40	182:48	182:18	194:35	183:10
50 853	60 892	61 642	64 146	66 075	65 767	70 360	64 417
98.10	98.20	98.30	98.40	98.50	98.60	98.70	98.74
1	1	1	1	1	1	1	9
10	10	10	10	10	10	10	10
15	15	15	15	15	15	15	12
1 659:37	1 618:56	1 640:32	1 771:36	1 712:36	1 766:27	1 948:44	1 687:31
717:47	652:41	660:52	760:18	727:01	734:11	853:34	712:33
13 089	11 874	9 713	15 406	12 974	16 702	19 894	17 888
97.90	98.00	98.10	98.20	98.30	98.41	98.52	98.55
218.48	218.57	241.55	253.83	268.20			225.32
91.29	90.48	93.79	103.72				101.58
49 303	50 871	51 297	52 617				52 782
178	162	121	113				

主要统计指标解释

普通高等学校 指按照国家规定的设置标准和审批程序批准举办,通过国家统一招生考试,招收高中毕业生为主要培养对象,实施高等教育的全日制大学、独立设置的学院和高等专科学校、短期职业大学。

成人高等学校 指按照国家有关规定审批,招收通过全国成人高教统一招生考试的具有高中毕业或同等学历的在职从业人员,利用脱产、半脱产、业余或函授等多种形式对其实施高等学历教育,培养高等教育专科或本科毕业水平的专门人才,修业年限、课程设置和总学时数均按高等学历教育要求付诸实施的学校。包括广播电视大学、职工高等学校、农民高等学校、管理干部学院;教育学院、独立设置的函授学院等。

科技活动人员 指直接从事科技活动、以及专门从事科技活动管理和为科技活动提供直接服务,累计的实际工作时间占全年制度工作时间 10% 及以上的人员。

文化事业机构 指从事专业文化工作和为专业文化工作服务的独立建制的单独核算的单位。不包括这些单位另外举办独立核算的其他机构和各部门的业余文化组织。

Explanatory Notes on Main Statistical Indicators

Regular Institutions of Higher Education refer to educational establishments set up according to the government evaluation and approval procedures, enrolling graduates from senior secondary schools and providing higher education courses and training for senior professionals. They include full-time universities, colleges, high professional schools, high professional vocational schools and others.

Adult Institutions of Higher Education refer to educational establishments, set up in line with relevant rules approved by the government, enrolling staff and workers with senior secondary school or equivalent education, and providing higher education courses in many forms of correspondence, spare time, or full time for adults. Professionals thus trained receive a qualification equivalent to graduates studying regular courses at regular universities, colleges and professional colleges. Institutions of higher learning for adults include schools of high education for staff and workers, schools of high education for peasants, colleges for management cadres, pedagogical colleges, independent correspondence colleges, Radio and TV universities and other educational establishments.

Personnel Engaged in S&T Activities refer to personnel directly engaged in S&T activities, in the management of S&T activities, and in providing direct service to S&T activities, who spend over 10% of the total working hours in a year in S&T activities.

Cultural Institutions refer to units, which have their own organizational system and independent accounting system and specialize in or serve cultural development. They exclude other establishments run by these cultural institutions and amateur cultural groups established by various departments.

18 体育、卫生和民政、司法

SPORTS,PUBLIC HEALTH AND CIVIL AFFAIRS,JUDICIAL AFFAIRS

简要说明

一、本篇资料的主要内容

本篇资料反映了全市体育、卫生、民政、司法等社会事业的基本情况。体育部分主要包括主要年份运动员、教练员、裁判员发展人数、体育运动破纪录、获奖情况。卫生部分主要包括各类卫生机构及其人员、床位数。民政部分主要包括婚姻登记、社会救济、社会福利事业基本情况、殡葬服务情况。司法部分主要包括律师、公证、调解、社会治安基本情况。

二、本篇资料的来源

1、体育部分来源于市体育局。

2、卫生部分来源于市卫生局。

3、民政部分来源于市民政局。

4、司法部分，社会治安资料来源于市公安局，其他资料来源于市司法局。

本篇资料由市统计局人口和社会科技统计处整理提供。

Brief Introduction

I. Main Content

Data in this chapter show the basic conditions of sports, public health, civil affairs and judicial affairs. Data on sports are mainly including the number of athletes, coaches and referees, conditions of record and awards. Data on public health are mainly including the number of health institutions, personnel and beds. Data on civil affairs are mainly including the conditions of marriage registration, social relief, social welfare and funeral services. Data on judicial affairs are mainly including the conditions of lawyers, notarization, mediation and social order.

II. Source of Data

(1)Data on sports are provided by Qingdao Municipal Bureau of Physical.

(2)Data on public health are provided by Qingdao Municipal Bureau of Health.

(3)Data on civil affairs are provided by Qingdao Municipal Bureau of Civil Affairs.

(4)In judicial affairs component, data on social order are provided by Qingdao Municipal Bureau of Public Security and the other data are provided by Qingdao Municipal Bureau of Justice.

Data in this chapter are provided and compiled by the Division of Population and Science & Technology of Qingdao Municipal Bureau of Statistics.

18－1 体育事业情况(2000－2014 年)

STATISTICS ON SPORTS(2000－2014)

单位:人(person)

项目	Item	2000	2005	2006	2007	2008	2009	2010	2011	2012	2013	2014
体育部门职工人数	**Staff and Workers in Sports Commissions**	**849**	**834**	**848**	**772**	**1 210**	**910**	**1 015**				
#运动员	Athletes	90	87	81	55	452	512	287				
教练员	Coaches	174	235	221	211	173	106	170	136			
重点体校	Key Sports Schools	126	117	166	249	109	97	115	129			
业余体校	Sparetime Sports Schools	142	223	220	145		160					
体育专业队	Professional Sports Teams	135	132	154	121		144	192	87	84	42	38
优秀运动员	Excellent Athletes	90	87	81	55	71	72	146	57			
优秀运动队专职教练员	Full-time Coaches of Excellent Sports Teams	18	23	48	47	106	92	97	54			
等级裁判员发展人数	**Certified Referees**	**1 114**	**275**	**1 068**	**781**	**205**	**292**	**212**	**510**	**558**	**512**	**514**
#二级	Second Grades	451	275	1 068	781	181	252	169	510	484	463	514
三级	Third Grades	616										
等级运动员发展人数	**Certified Athletes**	**343**	**260**	**267**	**108**	**310**	**512**	**229**	**436**	**362**	**362**	**283**
#二级	Second Grades	209	260	267	108	281	448	229	436	256	362	283
三级	Third Grades	46										
少年级	Juvenile88											

18 -1 续表
continued

项目	Item	单位	Unit	2000	2005	2006	2007	2008	2009	2010	2011	2012	2013	2014
全年获得奖牌数	**Number of Medals Won in the Year**	**枚**	**unit**	**347.5**	**669**	**829**	**481**	**494**	**602**	**754**	**829**	**746**	**659**	**576.5**
#国家级金牌	Golden Medals at National Level	枚	unit	45	62	71	61	26	30	14	105	88	90	48
国家级银牌	Silver Medal at National Level	枚	unit	28	48	54	38	21	23	7	49	100	44	21
省级金牌	Golden Medals at Provincial Level	枚	unit	116.5	187	363	116	168	207	459	225	193	174.5	202.5
省级银牌	Silver Medals at Provincial Level	枚	unit	62	174	144	93	122	149	116	155	110	111.5	121.5
体育运动破全国记录	**Records Broken the National Records**													
项目	Number of Events	项	item		2		1		1	1	2	1		
人数	Number of Persons	人	person		2		1		1	1	2	1		
次数	Number of Times	人次	person-time		4		1		1	1	2	1		
体育运动破全省记录	**Records Broken the Provincial Records**													
项目	Number of Events	项	item	7	3	5		2		1				
人数	Number of Persons	人	person	7	1	3		2		1				
次数	Number of Times	人次	person-time	7	3	5		2		1				

18 -2 主要年份卫生事业基本情况
MAJOR YEAR'S BASIC STATISTICS ON PUBLIC HEALTH

年份 Year	卫生机构数（个）Health Institutions (unit)	#医院 of which: Hospitals	医疗床位数（张）Beds in Health Institutions (bed)	#医院 of which: Hospitals	卫生技术人员（人）Medical and Technical Personnel(person)	#医生 of which: Doctors	每千人口拥有医生数(人) Number of Doctors per 1000 Population(person)	每千人口拥有床位数(张) Number of Hospital Beds per 1000 Population(bed)
1949	80	26	1 079	970	2 637	1 292	0.32	0.27
1952	260	34	2 943	1 691	3 748	1 559	0.37	0.70
1957	624	45	5 163	2 656	6 941	2 578	0.53	1.07
1962	849	149	7 167	4 526	8 279	2 972	0.64	1.55
1965	912	162	8 428	5 003	9 051	3 586	0.73	1.72
1970	712	170	8 613	6 603	9 591	3 761	0.70	1.60
1975	959	181	10 902	9 078	13 558	4 566	0.80	1.90
1978	1 192	212	13 084	10 709	16 921	5 893	1.01	2.24
1980	1 253	212	14 170	11 345	19 265	6 781	1.14	2.38
1985	1 517	219	18 469	13 214	23 413	9 694	1.55	2.95
1987	1 553	228	21 667	15 463	26 669	11 738	1.81	3.34
1989	1 566	232	22 668	15 670	27 195	13 555	2.06	3.46
1990	1 563	235	23 541	16 586	27 932	13 761	2.08	3.56
1991	1 579	235	23 727	16 796	27 772	13 227	1.98	3.54
1992	1 562	236	24 765	17 269	28 305	13 157	1.95	3.67
1993	1 540	237	24 885	17 469	28 705	13 312	1.97	3.68
1994	1 335	242	24 732	17 882	28 938	13 535	1.99	3.64
1995	1 347	228	25 282	18 126	29 816	13 840	2.02	3.69
1996	2 216	228	24 334	18 344	30 048	13 790	2.00	3.53
1997	2 193	239	25 201	19 046	31 121	14 400	2.07	3.62
1998	2 190	237	24 887	19 083	31 623	14 327	2.05	3.56
1999	2 185	235	25 481	19 798	31 965	14 453	2.06	3.62
2000	2 911	231	24 392	20 057	32 160	14 860	2.10	3.45
2001	3 199	217	24 755	20 313	32 765	15 772	2.22	3.48
2002	3 050	213	21 370	20 662	31 469	13 371	1.87	2.99
2003	3 111	213	23 980	21 605	32 337	13 452	1.87	3.33
2004	2 923	219	25 432	23 465	32 937	13 953	1.91	3.48
2005	2 609	235	30 627	28 564	33 942	15 008	2.03	4.13
2006	2 834	232	28 724	26 653	34 360	15 451	2.06	3.83
2007	2 116	251	30 062	28 107	33 807	15 018	1.98	3.97
2008	1 985	249	32 350	29 874	36 574	16 260	2.14	4.25
2009	2 017	252	32 803	30 527	40 217	16 734	2.19	4.30
2010	2 147	254	36 066	33 383	43 285	17 696	2.32	4.72
2011	2 549	280	39 980	35 600	4 7347	18 310	2.39	5.22
2012	2 607	288	47 254	41 186	54 488	21 593	2.81	6.14
2013	2 936	285	44 876	39 725	59 961	24 113	3.12	5.80
2014	3 126	297	47 081	42 961	62 738	24 946	3.20	6.03

18－3 各类卫生机构、床位、人员数(2014 年底)

NUMBER OF HEALTH INSTITUTIONS, BEDS AND EMPLOYED PERSONS(END OF 2014)

项　　目	Item	机构数(个) Health Institutions (unit)	床位数(张) Beds in Health Institutions (bed)	人员数(人) Personnel (person)
总　　计		**3 126**	**47 081**	**74 383**
一、医院合计	**Sub-total of Hospitals**	**297**	**42 961**	**54 841**
1. 医院	Hospitals	190	35 114	47 000
#综合医院	General Hospitals	114	24 684	33 623
中医医院	Hospitals Specialized in Traditional Chinese Medicine	16	3 565	4 842
中西医结合医院	Hospitals of Combination of Chinese and Western Medicine	3	557	552
专科医院	Specialized Hospitals	56	6 258	7 965
#口腔医院	Stomatological Hospitals	2	8	205
眼科医院	Ophthalmology Hospitals	3	177	341
肿瘤医院	Tumor Hospitals	2	432	582
心血管病医院	Cardiovascular Diseases Hospitals	5	797	1 151
精神病医院	Mental Hospitals	6	1 600	867
传染病医院	Infectious Disease Hospitals	2	640	482
皮肤病医院	The Skin Disease Hospital	1	20	23
骨科医院	Orthopaedics Hospitals	4	251	179
其它专科医院	Other Specialized Hospitals	16	1 400	2 461
2. 卫生院	Sanitation Stations	107	7 847	7 841
二、社区卫生服务中心	**Neighborhood Service Centers**	**60**	**751**	**2 342**
三、门诊部	**Outpatient Service Stations**	**88**	**84**	**1 622**
四、诊所	**Clinics**	**1 952**	**0**	**6 872**
五、卫生所、医务室、护理站	**Medical Houses Nursing Station**	**302**	**190**	**1 001**
六、社区卫生服务站	**Neighborhood Service Stations**	**207**	**605**	**2 674**
七、急救中心	**First Aid Centers**	**3**	**0**	**162**
八、采供血机构	**Institutions of Blood Collection and Supply**	**1**	**0**	**232**
九、妇幼保健院(所、站)	**Maternity and Child Care Centers**	**13**	**404**	**1 117**
十、专科疾病防治院(所、站)	**Specialized Disease Prevention & Treatment Institutions**	**9**	**537**	**425**
十一、疾病预防控制中心(防疫站)	**Centers for Disease Control and Prevention (Epidemic Prevention Stations)**	**27**	**0**	**953**
十二、卫生监督所	**Sanitation Control Stations**	**12**	**0**	**348**
十三、卫生监督检验所(站)	**Sanitation Control and Test Stations**			
十四、计划生育技术服务机构	**Family Planning Service Institutions**	**105**	**0**	**569**
十五、临床检验中心(所、站)	**Clinical Laboratory Center**	**1**	**0**	**76**
十六、健康教育所(站、中心)	**Health Education Stations**	**1**	**0**	**4**
十七、其它卫生机构	**Other Health Institutions**	**38**	**0**	**293**
十八、疗养院	**Sanatoriums**	**10**	**1 549**	**852**

#卫生技术人员 Medical and Technical Personnel	#医生 Doctors	注册护士 Registered Nurses	药剂人员 Pharmacists	检验人员 Laboratory Technicians
62 738	**24 946**	**27 125**	**3 247**	**2 124**
45 924	**16 264**	**21 617**	**2 629**	**1 612**
38 831	13 402	19 166	2 088	1 334
28 191	9 668	14 174	1 444	908
4 009	1 460	1 871	265	121
430	178	167	51	26
6 186	2 090	2 948	327	279
167	100	60	1	1
221	81	105	10	9
480	150	266	30	22
885	275	397	43	45
695	190	422	29	18
391	139	185	26	30
18	6	6	2	1
148	56	49	11	5
2 056	706	955	119	93
7 093	2 862	2 451	541	278
1 943	**796**	**627**	**178**	**73**
1 323	**679**	**454**	**67**	**61**
6 842	**4 203**	**2 390**	**69**	**12**
961	**528**	**319**	**16**	**6**
2 231	**1 068**	**834**	**179**	**60**
84	**32**	**48**	**2**	**1**
159	**50**	**53**	**1**	**48**
896	**382**	**328**	**40**	**65**
347	**148**	**130**	**27**	**17**
729	**333**	**60**	**11**	**140**
293	**0**	**0**	**0**	**0**
329	**171**	**72**	**4**	**3**
27	**5**	**2**	**0**	**10**
4	**3**	**0**	**1**	**0**
211	**115**	**45**	**3**	**2**
435	**169**	**146**	**20**	**14**

18－4 分市、区各类卫生机构、床位、人员数(2014 年底)

NUMBER OF HEALTH INSTITUTIONS, BEDS AND EMPLOYED PERSONS BY REGION(END OF 2014)

市、区名称	Region	机构数(个) Institutions (unit)	医院小计 Sub-total of Hospitals	#医院 Hospitals	卫生院 Sanitation Stations	社区卫生服务中心 Neighborhood Service Centers
全　市	**Whole Municipality**	**3 126**	**297**	**190**	**107**	**60**
市南区	Shinan District	385	27	27		10
市北区	Shibei District	662	39	39		23
李沧区	Licang District	433	14	14		11
崂山区	Laoshan District	215	12	10	2	2
黄岛区	Huangdao District	469	40	21	19	5
城阳区	Chengyang District	171	18	13	5	3
即墨市	Jimo	237	40	18	22	
胶州市	Jiaozhou	232	31	17	14	4
平度市	Pingdu	219	46	17	29	
莱西市	Laixi	103	30	14	16	2

18－4 续表 1

continued

市、区名称	Region	采供血机构 Institutions of Blood Collection and Supply	妇幼保健院(所、站) Maternity and Child Care Centers	专科疾病防治院(所、站) Specialized Disease Prevention & Treatment Institutions
全　市	**Whole Municipality**	**1**	**13**	**9**
市南区	Shinan District	1	1	1
市北区	Shibei District		3	
李沧区	Licang District		1	
崂山区	Laoshan District		1	
黄岛区	Huangdao District		2	2
城阳区	Chengyang District		1	
即墨市	Jimo		1	1
胶州市	Jiaozhou		1	
平度市	Pingdu		1	3
莱西市	Laixi		1	2

社区卫生服务站 Neighborhood Service Stations	门诊部 Outpatient Service Stations	诊所、卫生所、医务室 Clinics Medical Houses	急救中心 First Aid Centers
207	**88**	**2 254**	**3**
35	21	273	
49		543	1
41	10	352	
24	19	150	
4	19	357	1
		129	
43	2	100	
	5	174	1
	11	138	
11	1	38	

疾病预防控制中心(防疫站) Centers for Disease Control and Prevention (Epidemic Prevention Stations)	卫生监督所 Sanitation Control Stations	卫生监督检疫所(站) Sanitation Control and Test stations	计划生育技术服务机构 Family Planning Service Institutions
27	**12**		**105**
1	1		
2	2		
1	1		1
1	1		4
8	2		27
9	1		10
1	1		22
1	1		12
1	1		17
2	1		12

18 -4 续表2
continued

市、区名称	Region	健康教育所（站、中心） Health Education Station	临床检验中心（所、站） Clinical Laboratory Center	其他卫生机构 Other Health Institutions	疗养院 Sanatoriums	床位数(张) Beds in Health Institutions(bed)
全　市	**Whole Municipality**	**1**	**1**	**38**	**10**	**47 081**
市南区	Shinan District			5	9	6 878
市北区	Shibei District					10 502
李沧区	Licang District			1		2 424
崂山区	Laoshan District		1			926
黄岛区	Huangdao District			2		5 681
城阳区	Chengyang District					2 668
即墨市	Jimo	1		24	1	4 950
胶州市	Jiaozhou			2		4 575
平度市	Pingdu			1		4 582
莱西市	Laixi			3		3 895

18 -4 续表3
continued

市、区名称	Region	专科疾病防治院(所、站) Specialized Disease Centers	人员数(人) Personnel (person)	卫生技术人员 Medical and Technical Personnel
全　市	**Whole Municipality**	**537**	**74 383**	**62 738**
市南区	Shinan District		11 693	9 203
市北区	Shibei District		18 780	15 590
李沧区	Licang District		6 603	5 759
崂山区	Laoshan District		2 555	1 942
黄岛区	Huangdao District	165	9 257	8 192
城阳区	Chengyang District		4 361	3 678
即墨市	Jimo		6 063	5 218
胶州市	Jiaozhou		5 537	4 790
平度市	Pingdu	302	5 183	4 613
莱西市	Laixi	70	4 351	3 753

医院小计 Sub-total of Hospitals	#医院 Hospitals	卫生院 Sanitation Stations	门诊部 Outpatient Service Stations	妇幼保健院(所、站) Maternity and Child Care Centers
42 961	**35 114**	**7 847**	**84**	**404**
5 517	5 517		2	
9 775	9 775			
2 138	2 138			
807	755	52	33	
5 146	3 591	1 555	22	100
2 579	2 343	236		
4 660	2 986	1 674		100
4 427	3 356	1 071		68
4 157	2 227	1 930	27	96
3 755	2 426	1 329		40

执业(助理)医师 Certified(Assistant) Doctors	注册护士 Registered Nurses	药剂人员 Pharmacists	检验人员 Laboratory Technicians	其他人员 Other Personnel
24 946	**27 125**	**3 247**	**2 124**	**4 417**
3 764	3 971	463	392	492
6 236	7 068	872	583	647
2 448	2 359	251	153	481
849	757	113	70	127
3 156	3 640	371	233	682
1 372	1 585	198	131	326
2 020	2 087	323	147	568
1 771	2 132	209	137	456
1 926	1 940	245	156	261
1 404	1 586	202	122	377

18－5 收养性社会福利单位情况(2014 年)
BASIC STATICTICS ON SOCIAL WELFARE INSTITUTIONS(2014)

市、区名称	Region	单位数(个) Number of Institutions (unit)	年末职工人数(人) Number of Staff and Workers at Year-end (person)	年末床位数(张) Number of Beds at Year-end (bed)
全　市	**Whole Municipality**	**267**	**3 923**	**49 636**
市本级	Municipal Level	15	734	7 958
市南区	Shinan District	13	339	2 498
市北区	Shibei District	65	1 273	10 025
李沧区	Licang District	23	283	2 669
崂山区	Laoshan District	9	58	1 840
黄岛区	Huangdao District	36	194	4 077
城阳区	Chengyang District	17	212	3 772
即墨市	Jimo	30	292	6 838
胶州市	Jiaozhou	20	181	3 511
平度市	Pingdu	17	98	2 496
莱西市	Laixi	22	259	3 952

注:年末在院人数仅包括老年人与残疾人服务机构。

Note:At the end of the year, the number of people in hospitals includes the elderly and disabled service organizations only.

18－6 社会救济情况(2014 年)
BASIC STATISTICS ON SOCIAL RELIEF(2014)

市、区名称	Region	城镇居民最低生活保障人数(人) Number of Persons Receiving Minimum Living Allowance in Urban Area(person)	城镇居民最低生活保障家庭数(户) Number of Households Receiving Minimum Living Allowance in Urban Area(household)	城镇低保资金计划支出(万元) Planned Expense of Funds for Minimum Living Allowance in Urban Area (10 000 yuan)
全　市	**Whole Municipality**	**44 182**	**23 310**	**16 736.1**
市南区	Shinan District	8 027	4 313	5 224.9
市北区	Shibei District	20 179	10 973	768.6
李沧区	Licang District	9 232	4 092	6 705.8
崂山区	Laoshan District	516	281	313.2
黄岛区	Huangdao District	2 138	1 156	1 234.1
城阳区	Chengyang District	517	300	392.9
即墨市	Jimo	1 364	880	812.8
胶州市	Jiaozhou	934	513	533.4
平度市	Pingdu	704	458	413.8
莱西市	Laixi	571	344	336.6

年末在院人数(人) Residences at Year-end (person)	优抚对象 Disabled Military Servicemen and Family Members of War Heroes and Military Servicemen	"三无"对象 Senior Citizen, Disabled Persons, Minors Non-ability to Work, Non-source of income and Non-supports the human or the provider	自费人员 Self-supporting Persons
24 133	**1 075**	**4 034**	**13 442**
5 904		294	419
960		19	941
5 795	40		5 755
2 194			2 194
373	1	85	288
1 929	293	816	698
1 080	15	109	956
1 627	34	396	1 144
1 681	15	1 074	456
1 135	644	434	
1 455	33	807	591

农村居民最低生活保障人数(人) Number of Persons Receiving Minimum Living Allowance in Rural Area (person)	农村居民最低生活保障家庭数(户) Number of Households Receiving Minimum Living Allowance in Rural Area (household)	农村低保资金计划支出(万元) Planned Expense of Funds for Minimum Living Allowance in Rural Area (10 000 yuan)
111 952	**68 472**	**38 854.1**
4 136	1 970	1 384.8
20 930	11 937	9 328.3
7 417	3 773	2 955.8
25 304	17 061	6 751.6
18 253	10 724	7 048.8
20 221	12 941	6 790.6
15 691	10 066	4 594.2

18－7 分市、区婚姻登记情况(2014 年)
BASIC STATISTICS ON MARRIAGE REGISTRATION BY REGION(2014)

市、区名称	Region	准予登记结婚 Registered Marriages					准予登记离婚(对) Registered Divorces (couple)	涉外婚姻登记(对) Registered Marriages with Foreigner(couple)
		合计(对) Total(couple)	初婚(人) First Marriages (person)	恢复结婚(对) Resumed Marriages (couple)	再婚(人) Remarriages(person)			
					男 Male	女 Female		
全 市	**Whole Municipality**	**71 104**	**109 862**	**729**	**17 395**	**14 951**	**20 980**	**296**
市本级	Municipal Level	296	384	1	121	87	39	296
市南区	Shinan District	7 835	12 663	2	1 609	1 398	2 289	
市北区	Shibei District	9 157	13 449		2 571	2 294	3 470	
李沧区	Licang District	3 042	4 563		792	729	1 075	
崂山区	Laoshan District	3 209	5 433		517	468	594	
黄岛区	Huangdao District	11 515	16 511		4 974	1 545	3 359	
城阳区	Chengyang District	4 358	7 089		841	786	917	
即墨市	Jimo	8 511	12 885		2 054	2 083	2 440	
胶州市	Jiaozhou	6 857	10 530		1 583	1 601	2 290	
平度市	Pingdu	10 841	16 754	726	2 333	2 595	2 862	
莱西市	Laixi	5 483	9 601		0	1 365	1 645	

18－8 律师、公证、调解、社会治安基本情况(2000－2014 年)
BASIC STATISTICS ON LAWYERS,NOTARIZATION,MEDIATION AND SOCIAL ORDER (1995－2014)

项 目	Item	单位	Unit	2000	2005	2006	2007	2008	2009
一、律师工作	**Lawyers**								
律师事务所	Law Offices	个	unit	76	116	122	140	159	203
律师工作者	Lawyers	人	person	1 439	1 941	2 218	2 594	2 915	3 144
专职	Full-time Lawyers	人	person	971	1 542	1 616	1 738	1 855	1 934
兼职(含特邀)	Part-time Lawyers	人	person	150	73	75	79	90	86
聘请常年法律顾问单位	Units with Permanent Legal Advisors	个	unit	2 508	3 564	4 032	4 075	4 086	4 457
全年办理民事代理	Agent of Civil Cases	件	case	5 571	11 104	10 556	19 460	20 547	29 025
刑事辩护	Defender of Criminal Cases	件	case	1 755	3 003	2 917	3 311	3 655	3 758
非诉讼事件	Agent of Non-litigious Legal Affairs	件	case	5 251	6 501	10 049	7 710	5 467	5 897
解答法律询问	Agent of Legal Advisory Services	件	case	58 385	27 880	26 518	27 393	31 571	30 123
代写法律事务文书	Agent of Legal Documents Written on Behalf of Clients	件	case	9 335	8 595	8 171	8 012	9 077	6 015
二、公证工作	**Notarization**								
公证处	Notary Offices	个	unit	15	15	15	13	13	13
公证人员	Notarial Personnel	人	person	152	196	209	208	214	214
公证员	Notaries	人	person	106	112	117	116	117	118
办理公证文书	Notarized Documents	件	case	120 849	105 787	100 513	95 704	101 766	97 019
三、人民调解	**People's Mediation**								
人民调解委员会	People's Mediation Committees	个	unit	9 750	11 480	10 897	11 216	11 223	9 643
调解人员	Mediators	人	person	34 714	46 735	34 487	35 553	33 875	32 675
调解民间纠纷	Civil Disputes Mediated	件	case	18 501	13 658	14 094	16 586	12 803	14 660
四、社会治安	**Social Order**								
交通事故发生次数	Traffic Accidents	次	time	15 601	7 051	5 559	4 465	3 025	2 570
死亡人数	Deaths	人	person	1 371	776	689	556	489	402
受伤人数	Injuries	人	person	8 620	6 639	5 685	4 603	3 273	2 943
经济损失	Losses	万元	10 000 yuan	4 815.70	2 208.20	1 514.00	1 291.40	991.50	854.80
火灾发生次数	Fire Accidents	次	time	3 088	1 948	1 400	962	840	773
死亡人数	Deaths	人	person	10	3	8	9	16	5
受伤人数	Injuries	人	person	43	3	5		13	
经济损失	Losses	万元	10 000 yuan	1 531.06	550.40	544.00	929.60	979.70	865.50

18 -8 续表
continued

项 目	Item	单位	Unit	2010	2011	2012	2013	2014
一、律师工作	**Lawyers**							
律师事务所	Law Offices	个	unit	222	247	266	285	322
律师工作者	Lawyers	人	person	2 487	2 801	3 130	3 143	3 637
专职	Full-time Lawyers	人	person	2 377	2 643	2 944	2 980	3 443
兼职(含特邀)	Part-time Lawyers	人	person	94	105	107	93	110
聘请常年法律顾问单位	Units with Permanent Legal Advisors	个	unit	4 779	5 180	5 228	5 374	5 647
全年办理民事代理	Agent of Civil Cases	件	case	26 935	27 702	30 586	31 147	36 317
刑事辩护	Defender of Criminal Cases	件	case	3 964	4 535	4 935	4 858	5 370
非诉讼事件	Agent of Non-litigious Legal Affairs	件	case	4 274	3 576	4 251	4 133	4 833
解答法律询问	Agent of Legal Advisory Services	件	case	21 102	42 428	45 388	53 775	33 717
代写法律事务文书	Agent of Legal Documents Written on Behalf of Clients	件	case	6 210	6 762	6 388	7 376	5 961
二、公证工作	**Notarization**							
公证处	Notary Offices	个	unit	13	13	13	13	13
公证人员	Notarial Personnel	人	person	214	221	225	244	249
公证员	Notaries	人	person	117	119	118	113	119
办理公证文书	Notarized Documents	件	case	94 077	88 506	87 703	99 852	100 553
三、人民调解	**People's Mediation**							
人民调解委员会	People's Mediation Committees	个	unit	8 014	8 486	8 426	8 448	8 027
调解人员	Mediators	人	person	27 820	28 094	27 421	27 035	25 646
调解民间纠纷	Civil Disputes Mediated	件	case	20 550	22 882	23 999	19 525	23 737
四、社会治安	**Social Order**							
交通事故发生次数	Traffic Accidents	次	time	2 313	2 164	1 951	1 896	1 857
死亡人数	Deaths	人	person	393	374	343	333	321
受伤人数	Injuries	人	person	2 504	2 240	1 913	1 840	1 796
经济损失	Losses	万元	10 000 yuan	811.27	861.05	652.10	609.80	561.80
火灾发生次数	Fire Accidents	次	time	683	369	366	742	1 170
死亡人数	Deaths	人	person	9	1	6	7	12
受伤人数	Injuries	人	person	4	2	2	11	9
经济损失	Losses	万元	10 000 yuan	5 566.11	598.20	601.90	2 348.10	1 725.50

18－9 分区、市殡葬服务情况(2014 年)
BASIC STATISTICS ON FUNERAL SERVICES(2014)

市、区名称	Region	单位数(个) Number of Institutions (unit)	年末职工人数(人) Number of Staff and Workers at Year-end (person)	火化炉数(台) Number of Cremators (unit)	处理遗体数(具) Number of Remains Cremated (body)
全 市	**Whole Municipality**	**10**	**216**	**48**	**59 400**
市本级	Municipal Level	1	51	12	11 959
市南区	Shinan District				
市北区	Shibei District				
李沧区	Licang District				
崂山区	Laoshan District				
黄岛区	Huangdao District	2	23	7	8 518
城阳区	Chengyang District	1	19	5	6 239
即墨市	Jimo	1	14	7	8 933
胶州市	Jiaozhou	1	10	4	6 506
平度市	Pingdu	2	31	7	11 068
莱西市	Laixi	2	68	6	6 177

18-9 续表
continued

市、区名称	Region	穴位数(个) Number of Graves (unit)	本年销售穴位数 Number of Graves Saled in the Year	安葬数(具) Number of Remains Buried(body)	本年安葬数 Number of Remains Buried in the Year
全 市	**Whole Municipality**	**23 506**	**325**	**4 768**	**661**
市本级	Municipal Level	19 730	184	1 994	511
市南区	Shinan District				
市北区	Shibei District				
李沧区	Licang District				
崂山区	Laoshan District				
黄岛区	Huangdao District				
城阳区	Chengyang District				
即墨市	Jimo				
胶州市	Jiaozhou				
平度市	Pingdu	1 353	59	1 358	78
莱西市	Laixi	2 423	82	1 416	72

主要统计指标解释

卫生机构 包括医疗机构、疾病预防控制中心(防疫站)、采供血机构、卫生监督及监测(检验)机构、医学科研和在职培训机构、健康教育所等。

医疗机构 包括医院、社区卫生服务中心(站)、疗养院、卫生院、门诊部、诊所(卫生所、医务室)、妇幼保健院(所、站)、专科疾病防治院(所、站)、急救中心(站)和临床检验中心。医疗机构分为非赢利性医疗机构和赢利性医疗机构。

医院 包括综合医院、中医医院、中西医结合医院、民族医院、各类专科医院和护理院。

医生 指在医疗、预防保健机构工作且取得《执业医师证书》的执业医师和执业助理医师。

卫生技术人员 指卫生事业机构中现任职务为卫生技术工作的人员。包括中医师、西医师、中西医结合高级医师、护师、中药师、西药师、检验师、其他技师、中医士、西医士、护士、助产士、中药剂士、西药剂士、检验士、其他技士、其他中医、护理员、中药剂员、西药剂员、检验员、其他初级卫生技术人员。

社会福利事业单位 指集中收养社会孤老、残、幼的机构,包括由民政部门管理的社会福利院、儿童福利院、精神病人福利院和城镇集体举办的福利院及农村集体举办的敬老院以及优抚医院和具有收养能力的社区服务中心等。

Explanatory Notes on Main Statistical Indicators

Health Care Institutions include: medical institutions, disease prevention and control centers (epidemic prevention stations), blood gathering and supplying institutions, health supervision and inspection (check up) institutions, medicinal scientific research and on-job training institutions, health education and so on.

Medical Organizations include: hospitals, health service centers (stations) of communities, nursing homes, health centers, clinics, clinics (health stations and infirmaries), maternity and child care agencies (centers and stations), special disease prevention and curing agencies (centers and stations), first aid centers (stations) and clinical inspection centers. Medical organizations are grouped by two types: profit-making and non-profit-making medical organizations.

Hospitals include: polyclinics, traditional Chinese medical hospitals, hospitals integrated with traditional Chinese therapeutics and western therapeutics, ethical hospitals, various specialties hospitals and nursing hospitals.

Doctors refer to certified physicians and certified assistant physicians with certifications working in medical and health care and prevention agencies.

Medical Technical Personnel refers to those medical workers employed institutions, including doctors of Chinese and Western medicine, senior doctors of integrated Chinese-Western medicine, head nurses, pharmacists of Chinese and Western medicine, laboratory specialists, other specialists, junior doctors of Chinese and Western medicine, nurses, midwives, druggists of Chinese and Western medicine, laboratory technicians, other technicians, other practitioners of Chinese medicine, nursing attendants, pharmacological workers of Chinese and Western medicine, laboratory workers, and other primary medical personnel.

Social Welfare Institutions refer to institutions taking care of old people without children, handicapped people and orphans. They include social welfare institutions run by civil affairs departments, children welfare institutions, social welfare institutions for mental patients, collective-owned old people's homes in rural areas, convalescent homes and community service centers with the capacity of receiving those people.

附　录
APPENDIX

2014年省内各市主要经济指标对比情况

MAJOR ECONOMIC INDICATORS ON CITIES OF THE PROVINCE(2014)

主要指标 Indicator	单位 Unit	全省	青岛市 Qingdao	济南市 Jinan	淄博市 Zibo	枣庄市 Zaozhuang	东营市 Dongying
全市生产总值(GDP)	亿元 (100 million yuan)	59 426.60	8 692.10	5 770.60	4 029.77	1 980.13	3 430.49
比上年增长 YOY Growth	%	8.7	8.0	8.8	7.4	9.0	10.0
第一产业 Primary Industry	亿元 (100 million yuan)	4 798.4	362.6	299.1	143.8	156.1	124.0
比上年增长 YOY Growth	%	3.8	3.9	4.2	4.0	3.6	4.0
第二产业 Secondary Industry	亿元 (100 million yuan)	28 788.1	3 882.4	2 215.2	2 251.5	1 099.8	2 345.1
比上年增长 YOY Growth	%	9.2	8.4	8.8	8.4	9.2	10.5
第三产业 Tertiary Industry	亿元 (100 million yuan)	25 840.10	4 447.13	3 256.33	1 634.46	724.28	961.42
比上年增长 YOY Growth	%	8.9	7.9	9.1	5.8	9.7	9.2
三产占比	%	43.5	51.2	56.4	40.6	36.6	28.0
规模以上工业增加值比上年增长 YOY Growth of Industrial Added Value above Designated Size	%	9.62	9.40	10.05	8.60	10.45	11.36
固定资产投资额 Investmentin Fixed Assets	亿元 (100 million yuan)	41 599.13	5 766.03	3 063.44	2 404.59	1 430.01	2 708.20
比上年增长 YOY Growth	%	15.8	16.1	16.1	15.7	15.5	16.1
进出口总额 Imports and Exports	亿美元 (100 million USD)	2 771.15	798.88	105.00	89.39	14.40	132.56
比上年增长 YOY Growth	%	4.0	2.5	9.7	-0.6	15.1	4.1
#出口 #Exports	亿美元 (100 million USD)	1 447.45	457.77	60.61	55.98	11.54	60.95
比上年增长 YOY Growth	%	7.9	9.1	10.5	6.9	21.9	5.1
社会消费品零售总额 Total Retail Sales of Consumer Goods	亿元 (100 million yuan)	24 492.04	3 268.79	2 964.43	1 739.49	706.60	659.06
比上年增长 YOY Growth	%	12.6	12.6	12.6	12.4	12.7	12.6
一般公共预算收入 General Public Budget Revenue	亿元 (100 million yuan)	5 026.71	895.25	543.13	292.55	137.88	206.24
比上年增长 YOY Growth	%	10.2	13.5	12.7	7.1	5.5	12.2
城市居民人均可支配收入 Per Capita Disposable Income of Urban Households	元 (yuan)	29 222	38 294	38 763	33 534	27 596	36 940
比上年增长 YOY Growth	%	8.7	8.7	8.7	8.6	9.3	8.7
农民人均纯收入 Per Capital Net Income of Rural Households	元 (yuan)	11 882	17 461	14 726	15 531	12 145	14 456
比上年增长 YOY Growth	%	11.2	11.0	11.2	11.5	11.6	11.2

注:本表进出口数据均为省局反馈;山东省居民收支数据为新口径数据,分城乡收支数据为常住居民新口径数据;17地市城市居民人均可支配收入和农村居民人均纯收入为老口径数据。

Note:The import and export data in this table are feedback of the provincial bureau. The income and expenditure data of residents in Shandong province are the data counted by the new gauge, the residents are permanent residents in rural and urban areas. The per capita disposable income of urban residents in the 17 prefecture-level cities and the per capita net income of rural residents are the data counted by the old gauge.

烟台市 Yantai	潍坊市 Weifang	济宁市 Jining	泰安市 Taian	威海市 Weihai	日照市 Rizhao	莱芜市 Laiwu	临沂市 Linyi	德州市 Dezhou	聊城市 Liaocheng	滨州市 Binzhou	菏泽市 Heze
6 002.08	4 786.74	3 800.06	3 002.19	2 790.34	1 611.87	687.60	3 569.80	2 596.08	2 516.40	2 276.71	2 222.19
9.1	9.1	9.6	9.4	9.8	10.0	8.8	10.1	10.0	9.4	7.6	10.2
441.3	456.2	443.3	271.4	214.5	139.3	53.2	340.8	289.0	310.8	221.4	265.0
3.9	4.0	4.3	3.9	4.2	4.2	3.6	3.9	4.2	4.2	4.2	3.0
3 212.4	2 432.0	1 912.6	1 447.5	1 410.1	811.9	374.8	1 648.9	1 338.3	1 296.2	1 145.4	1 190.8
8.8	9.7	10.4	10.5	10.0	9.6	9.7	10.7	10.8	9.9	8.3	11.0
2 348.46	1 898.54	1 444.15	1 283.27	1 165.77	660.64	259.67	1 580.04	968.75	909.38	909.90	766.35
10.4	9.3	9.8	9.1	10.6	12.0	8.1	10.8	10.4	10.3	7.2	11.7
39.1	39.7	38.0	42.7	41.8	41.0	37.8	44.3	37.3	36.1	40.0	34.5
9.62	10.45	11.72	11.36	11.77	10.86	11.65	14.52	14.02	11.51	9.55	15.05
4 101.06	3 969.08	2 538.18	2 298.96	2 229.37	1 234.75	545.43	2 825.99	1 961.34	1 833.13	1 748.86	940.70
15.9	15.7	16.0	16.0	15.9	15.5	15.4	16.2	16.3	16.0	15.3	16.0
527.52	177.86	52.32	29.74	165.87	347.69	22.19	107.91	35.07	57.53	71.99	35.22
7.6	10.1	0.0	19.5	-3.3	5.2	-11.4	14.4	-3.1	-6.9	-12.9	19.0
294.04	123.29	32.69	17.31	113.72	47.89	9.21	56.94	22.27	23.86	37.82	21.58
0.8	6.3	-2.0	26.7	6.3	23.5	22.6	22.9	9.9	19.1	6.8	23.3
2 377.65	1 979.50	1 664.10	1 188.10	1 181.87	535.98	290.36	2 008.40	1 116.79	924.66	738.50	1 147.88
12.7	12.6	12.8	12.8	12.9	12.6	12.7	12.8	12.8	12.7	12.2	13.0
490.16	430.18	334.20	187.39	220.79	111.07	49.60	251.01	171.26	156.19	187.15	161.97
12.1	12.1	10.6	11.0	13.1	11.0	6.1	16.2	14.2	15.2	10.0	1.7
35 791	30 973	30 428	30 715	34 254	27 540	31 728	33 026	27 180	28 382	30 870	23 344
8.6	9.1	8.8	8.9	8.9	9.8	8.7	8.9	9.5	8.8	8.8	9.9
16 656	14 776	12 650	12 913	17 296	12 635	13 540	11 629	12 135	11 232	12 691	10 436
11.4	11.3	11.5	11.8	11.0	11.8	11.3	11.9	11.6	11.4	11.7	12.1

2014 年十五个副省级城市主要经济指标对比情况

MAJOR ECONOMIC INDICATORS ON CITIES UNDER PROVINCIAL LEVELS(2014)

指标名称 Indicator	单位 Unit	青岛 Qingdao	沈阳 Shenyang	大连 Dalian	长春 Changchun	哈尔滨 Harbin
全市生产总值(GDP)	亿元 (100 million yuan)	8 692.10	—	7 655.58	5 382.00	5 332.70
比上年增长 YOY Growth	%	8.0	6.0	5.8	6.6	6.9
第一产业 Primary Industry	亿元 (100 million yuan)	362.56	—	441.83	340.10	639.80
比上年增长 YOY Growth	%	3.9	—	2.9	4.7	7.0
第二产业 Secondary Industry	亿元 (100 million yuan)	3 882.41	—	3 696.51	2 862.80	1 785.30
比上年增长 YOY Growth	%	8.4	—	5.0	6.9	5.1
第三产业 Tertiary Industry	亿元 (100 million yuan)	4 447.13	—	3 517.24	2 179.10	2 907.60
比上年增长 YOY Growth	%	7.9	—	7.0	6.6	8.2
三产占比	%	51.2	—	45.9	40.5	54.5
规模以上工业增加值 YOY Growth of Industrial Added Value above Designated Size	%	9.4	4.9	4.3	6.7	7.7
固定资产投资额 Investment in Fixed Assets	亿元 (100 million yuan)	5 766.00	6 564.10	6 773.63	3 924.50	—
比上年增长 YOY Growth	%	16.1	2.8	4.6	15.1	12.2
社会消费品零售总额 Total Retail Sales of Consumer Goods	亿元 (100 million yuan)	3 268.79	3 570.10	2 828.42	2 217.50	3 070.90
比上年增长 YOY Growth	%	12.6	12.1	12.0	12.6	12.6
进出口总额 Imports and Exports	亿美元 (100 million USD)	798.88	158.0	657.7	207.2	68.1
比上年增长 YOY Growth	%	2.5	10.6	-4.4	1.6	4.1
#出口 Exports	亿美元 (100 million USD)	457.77	71.4	302.3	24.7	34.4
比上年增长 YOY Growth	%	9.1	2.1	-19.3	-25.1	18.8
实际使用外资金额 Foreign Investment Actually Utilized	亿美元 (100 million USD)	60.81	34.93	26.10	2.98	4.73
比上年增长 YOY Growth	%	10.2	-2.4	-10.9	-32.5	-13.6
一般公共预算收入 General Public Budget Revenue	亿元 (100 million yuan)	895.20	785.50	780.80	397.30	423.50
比上年增长 YOY Growth	%	13.5	-1.9	-8.2	4.1	5.3
城市居民人均可支配收入 Per Capita Disposable Income of Urban Households	元 (yuan)	38 294	31 720	33 591	—	—
比上年增长 YOY Growth	%	8.7	9.1	8.7	—	—
农民人均纯收入 Per Capital Net Income of Rural Households	元 (yuan)	17 461	15 945	13 547	—	—
比上年增长 YOY Growth	%	11.0	10.2	9.7	—	—
居民消费价格指数 Consumer Price Index	%	102.6	102.2	102.0	102.2	102.0

注:因居民收入统计制度改革,部分城市暂无同口径居民收入数据;暂无沈阳 GDP 数据。

Note: Because of the reform of the statistical system for residents′ incomes, some cities do not have the data counted by the same gauge for residents′ incomes for the time being; the GDP numbers for Shenyang are not available by now.

南京 Nanjing	杭州 Hangzhou	宁波 Ningbo	厦门 Xiamen	济南 Jinan	武汉 Wuhan	广州 Guangzhou	深圳 Shenzhen	成都 Chengdu	西安 Xi'an
8 820.75	9 201.16	7 602.51	3 273.54	5 770.60	10 069.48	16 706.87	16 001.98	10 056.60	5 474.77
10.1	8.2	7.6	9.2	8.8	9.7	8.6	8.8	8.9	9.9
223.96	274.36	275.18	23.74	299.11	350.06	237.52	5.29	370.80	214.55
3.5	1.8	1.9	2.5	4.2	5.0	1.8	-19.4	3.6	5.1
3 671.45	3 858.90	3 935.57	1 499.27	2 215.16	4 785.66	5 606.41	6 823.05	4 561.10	2 205.37
8.8	8.1	7.9	9.7	8.8	10.2	7.4	7.7	9.8	11.3
4 925.34	5 067.90	3 391.76	1 750.53	3 256.33	4 933.76	10 862.94	9 173.64	5 124.70	3 054.85
11.5	8.5	7.6	8.7	9.1	9.5	9.4	9.8	8.6	9.0
55.8	55.1	44.6	53.5	56.4	49.0	65.0	57.3	51.0	55.8
9.5	8.9	7.4	10.5	10.1	10.9	8.1	8.4	12.2	11.1
5 430.77	4 952.70	3 989.46	1 572.95	3 063.40	7 002.85	4 889.50	2 717.42	6 620.40	5 903.98
6.6	16.2	16.6	16.7	16.1	16.7	14.5	13.6	1.8	15.0
3 957.97	3 838.73	2 992.03	1 072.94	2 964.40	4 369.32	7 697.85	4 844.00	4 202.40	2 872.90
13.0	8.7	13.5	10.0	12.6	12.7	12.5	9.3	12.0	12.8
572.2	680.0	1047.0	835.5	105.0	264.3	1306.0	4877.7	558.5	249.8
2.6	4.5	4.4	-0.6	9.7	21.4	9.8	-9.2	10.4	38.9
326.3	491.7	731.1	531.7	60.6	137.9	727.2	2844.0	338.2	119.6
1.1	9.8	11.3	1.6	10.5	15.5	15.8	-7.0	6.1	41.1
29.06	26.25	29.18	21.49	14.35	15.50	52.62	56.94	27.19	12.71
-8.2	-33.5	-33.4	12.8	8.7	-35.7	12.5	-13.1	-17.4	-59.8
903.49	1 027.32	860.61	543.80	543.10	1 101.02	1 241.53	2 082.44	1 025.20	583.76
8.7	8.7	8.6	10.8	12.7	15.6	8.7	20.3	14.1	16.3
42 568	44 632	44 155	39 625	38 763	33 270	—	—	32 665	—
8.8	9.1	9.2	8.2	8.7	9.9	—	—	9.0	—
17 660.9	23 555	24 283	16 220	14 726	16 160	—	—	14 478	—
10.3	11.1	11.0	10.6	11.2	12.3	—	—	11.5	—
102.6	102.0	101.9	102.2	102.2	101.9	102.3	102.0	101.3	101.4

2014 年副省级城市之外部分城市主要经济指标情况
THE MAIN ECONOMIC INDICATORS OF SOME OTHER CITIES THAN THE SUB-PROVINCIAL CITY FOR(2014)

主要指标 Indicator	单位 Unit	北京 Beijing	天津 Tianjin	上海 Shanghai	重庆 Chongqing	苏州 Suzhou	无锡 Wuxi
全市生产总值(GDP)	亿元 (100 million yuan)	21 330.83	15 722.47	23 560.94	14 265.40	13 760.89	8 205.31
比上年增长 YOY Growth	%	7.3	10	7	10.9	8.3	8.2
#第一产业 Primary Industry	亿元 (100 million yuan)	159	201.53	124.26	1061.03	227.91	156.96
比上年增长 YOY Growth	%	-0.1	2.8	0.1	4.4	3.3	3.2
第二产业 Secondary Industry	亿元 (100 million yuan)	4 545.51	7 765.91	8 164.79	6 531.86	7 034.10	4 186.34
比上年增长 YOY Growth	%	6.9	9.9	4.3	12.7	6.2	6.6
第三产业 Tertiary Industry	亿元 (100 million yuan)	16 626.32	7 755.03	15 271.89	6 672.51	6 498.88	3 862.01
比上年增长 YOY Growth	%	7.5	10.2	8.8	10	11.1	10.3
第三产业增加值占 GDP 比重	%	77.9	49.3	64.8	46.8	47.2	47.1
规模以上工业增加值同比增长 YOY Growth of Industrial Added Value above Designated Size	%	6	10	4.3	12.3	—	6.6
固定资产投资额 Investmentin Fixed Assets	亿元 (100 million yuan)	7 562.27	11 654.09	6 016.43	13 223.75	6 054.00	4 634.21
比上年增长 YOY Growth	%	7.5	15.1	6.5	18	4	16
社会消费品零售总额 Total Retail Sales of Consumer Goods	亿元 (100 million yuan)	9 098.09	4 738.65	8 718.65	5 096.20	4 061.11	3 054.75
比上年增长 YOY Growth	%	8.6	6	8.7	13	12	11.5
进出口总额(含中央省公司) Imports and Exports	亿美元 (100 million USD)	4 156.52	1 339.12	4 666.22	954.50	3 113.06	741.70
比上年增长 YOY Growth	%	-3.3	4.2	5.6	39	0.6	5.4
#出口总额 Exports	亿美元 (100 million USD)	623.45	525.97	2 102.77	634.10	1 811.78	442.31
比上年增长 YOY Growth	%	-1.2	7.3	3	35.5	3.1	7.5
实际使用外资金额 Foreign Investment Actually Utilized	亿美元 (100 million USD)	90.41	188.67	181.66	42.33	81.2	31.16
比上年增长 YOY Growth	%	6.1	12.1	8.3	2.2	-6.6	-6.7
一般公共预算收入 General Public Budget Revenue	亿元 (100 million yuan)	4 027.16	2 390.02	4 585.55	1 921.88	1 443.82	768.01
比上年增长 YOY Growth	%	10	15	11.6	13.9	8.5	8
城市居民人均可支配收入 Per Capita Disposable Income of Urban Households	元 (yuan)	43 910	31 506	47 710	25 147	46 677	41 731
比上年增长 YOY Growth	%	8.9	8.7	8.8	9.1	8.6	8.6
农民人均纯收入 Per Capital Net Income of Rural Households	元 (yuan)	20 226	17 014	—	9 490	23 560	22 266
比上年增长 YOY Growth	%	10.3	10.8	—	11.7	10.0	10.1
居民消费价格指数 Consumer Price Index	%	101.6	101.9	102.7	101.8	102.1	102.2

中国统计出版社最新图书简目

（仅供参考，以实际出版为准）

统计资料

中国统计年鉴　中国统计摘要　中国发展报告
中国经济普查年鉴2013　国际统计年鉴　金砖国家联合统计手册
中国-东盟国家统计手册　中国区域经济统计年鉴　中国县域统计年鉴
中国城市统计年鉴　中国农村统计年鉴　中国地区经济监测报告
中国贸易外经统计年鉴　中国对外直接投资统计公报　中国商品交易市场统计年鉴
大中型批发零售和住宿餐饮企业统计年鉴　中国零售和餐饮连锁企业统计年鉴　中国住户调查年鉴
中国价格统计年鉴　中国农产品价格调查年鉴　全国农产品成本收益资料汇编
中国环境统计年鉴　中国能源统计年鉴　国外资源、能源和环境统计资料汇编
中国工业统计年鉴　中国建筑业统计年鉴　中国房地产统计年鉴
中国城市建设统计年鉴　中国城乡建设统计年鉴　中国第三产业统计年鉴
中国证券期货统计年鉴　中国科技统计年鉴　中国高技术产业统计年鉴
工业企业科技活动资料　中国劳动统计年鉴　中国人口和就业统计年鉴
中国人才资源统计报告　中国社会统计年鉴　中国文化及相关产业统计年鉴
文化及相关产业统计概览　中国教育经费统计年鉴　中国民政统计年鉴
中国民族统计年鉴　中国工会统计年鉴　中国残疾人事业统计年鉴
中国妇女儿童状况统计资料（英）　中国乡镇街道行政区域简册

省级综合统计年鉴系列

北京 天津 河北 山西 内蒙古 辽宁 吉林 黑龙江 上海 江苏 浙江 安徽 福建 江西 山东 河南 湖北 湖南
广东 广西 海南 重庆 四川 贵州 云南 西藏 陕西 甘肃 青海 宁夏 新疆 新疆生产建设兵团

市(县)级综合统计年鉴系列

天津滨海新区 石家庄 唐山 邯郸 保定 沧州 邢台 廊坊 承德 衡水 秦皇岛 张家口 太原 大同 阳泉 长治 晋城
朔州 晋中 运城 忻州 临汾 呼和浩特 呼和浩特新城区 鄂尔多斯 包头 沈阳 大连 长春 四平 哈尔滨 齐齐哈尔
黑龙江垦区 上海浦东新区 南京 无锡 徐州 常州 苏州 南通 连云港 淮安 盐城 扬州 镇江 泰州 宿迁 江阴
丹阳 杭州 宁波 温州 嘉兴 绍兴 金华 衢州 舟山 台州 丽水 合肥 安庆 马鞍山 福州 厦门 宁德 南昌 九江
上饶 新余 抚州 济南 青岛 枣庄 滕州 郑州 洛阳 平顶山 三门峡 南阳 商丘 济源 武汉 十堰 荆州 宜昌 荆门
咸宁 长沙 广州 深圳 惠州 东莞 南宁 柳州 桂林 来宾 海口 三亚 成都 贵阳 昆明 西安 兰州 庆阳 银川
乌鲁木齐 兵团一师 兵团十师

调查年鉴系列

天津 山西 内蒙古 辽宁 吉林 上海　福建 河南 湖北 湖南 广西 重庆　四川 云南 甘肃 宁夏 新疆

“十二五”规划教材

统计学（经济管理类专业本科适用，单薇 等）　抽样调查理论与方法（冯士雍 等）
贝叶斯统计（茆诗松 等）　统计学（黄良文 等）　试验设计（茆诗松 等）
统计学：从数据到结论（吴喜之）　医学统计学（于浩）　统计学（经济、管理类专业基础教材，张小斐）
概率论与数理统计三十三讲（魏振军）　概率论与数理统计三十三：学习指导与习题解答（魏振军）
非参数统计（吴喜之 等）　统计学：经济与管理中的数据分析（李慧云 等）
卫生管理统计学（新编医学院校基础课教材，尚磊）　医院统计学（新编医学院校基础课教材，徐天和 等）
社会统计学（蒋萍 等）　现代金融投资统计分析（李腊生 等）
国民经济核算初级教程（经济类、统计类、管理类专业适用，蒋萍 等）

重点图书

图解中国经济2015　新编英汉汉英统计大词典　中华医学统计百科全书
挑大学选专业2016—考研择校指南　挑大学选专业2015—高考志愿填报指南